ARROGANT ARMIES

✦

Great Military Disasters and the Generals Behind Them

JAMES M. PERRY

John Wiley & Sons, Inc.
New York / Chichester / Brisbane / Toronto / Singapore

For (in order of seniority)
Brendan John Lynch, James Moorhead Kelly,
and Lindsay Knight Lynch

This text is printed on acid-free paper.

Copyright © 1996 by James M. Perry
Published by John Wiley & Sons, Inc.

Library of Congress Cataloging-in-Publication Data
Perry, James M. (James Moorhead)
    Arrogant armies : great military disasters and the generals behind
them / James M. Perry.
        p. cm.
    Includes bibliographical references and index.
    ISBN 0-471-11976-8 (cloth)
    1. Military history, Modern. 2. Disasters. 3. Command of troops.
I. Title.
D214.P49   1996
904'.7—dc20   95-38345

Printed in the United States of America

10 9 8 7 6 5 4 3 2 1

Contents

Preface

The only campaigns I have ever covered are political ones. I am, by background, a political writer, and I have been writing about American politics since 1962. Some knowledge of history, I have been telling colleagues for years, is a handy thing for journalists. I once worked with a young reporter covering the Pentagon who asked me if the United States Marines had served in World War II. I assured him they had. An editor, a little weak in both history and geography, wanted to know if Wales was in Scotland. I said I didn't think so. My stepfather, William Hollingsworth Whyte, was an accomplished amateur historian, specializing in the American Revolution. With his encouragement, I began reading books about history, lots of them about military history, at a reasonably tender age, and I have been reading them ever since. Covering political campaigns requires long, boring rides on planes and buses, and nothing is so curiously comforting, it has sometimes seemed, while traveling with Barry Goldwater or George McGovern or Michael Dukakis, as a book about a really awful military disaster.

If this book encourages young people (or anyone else, for that matter) to spend more time reading, and thinking about, history, and if it convinces them that history can be exciting, the effort will have been worthwhile.

I have been supported, even tolerated, in writing this book by my wife, Peggy. My agent, David Black, made me do it. My employer, the *Wall Street Journal*, allowed me to take a leave of absence to finish it. And anyone who believes book publishers no longer employ tough editors should meet mine, Hana Umlauf Lane, at John Wiley & Sons.

Most of the research was done at the Library of Congress, one of the seven wonders of the world. On those rare occasions when books and jour-

v

nals failed to turn up there, I have used my own neighborhood library, Lloyd House, in Alexandria, Virginia, a few blocks from Carlyle House, to track down copies elsewhere. It was at Carlyle House that the arrogant British general, Edward Braddock, met the colonial governors from New York, Massachusetts, Pennsylvania, Maryland, and Virginia, on April 15, 1755, to make final plans for his expedition against the French and the Indians.

Introduction

Nothing defines the dark side of the human race more precisely than its deadly preoccupation with war. For centuries, young men have been called to their nation's service, fitted out in distinctive uniforms—red, blue, green, brown—and sent off to kill other young men, called upon to defend *their* colors, and dressed in their own distinctive uniforms.

France against Russia. The United States against Japan. These are big wars, and most of us know a good deal about them. But I am not dealing with big wars here. This book is about a special kind of war—military expeditions dispatched by imperial governments to crush native tribes or "inferior" cultures in the raw pursuit of power, trade, land, or world status.

These are small wars, what Kipling called the "savage wars of peace." And while this kind of war goes back almost to the dawn of recorded history—and reached a considerable level of sophistication with the likes of Alexander the Great and Julius Caesar—this book will explore eleven different military expeditions launched by a variety of world powers in the imperial age—the eighteenth, nineteenth, and early twentieth centuries.

Each of these eleven expeditions stands alone as a separate snapshot of history. But they all have one thing in common: every one of these arrogant armies meets its match in strange and distant corners of the earth fighting tribesmen and dirty, rumpled soldiers representing those "inferior" cultures.

The fate of these arrogant imperial armies—the awful defeats they suffered—is a powerful commentary on human folly. Nothing goes wrong quite so dramatically as a disastrous military expedition. Consider just one

1

example in this book: A British expeditionary army and its camp followers, 16,500 people in all, are forced to retreat from Kabul to Jalalabad, in
Afghanistan, and only one man, Dr. William Brydon, manages to complete
the march.

Some of these generals are breathtakingly ignorant. The politicians who
sent them on their way are often criminally incompetent. Armies are
forced to fight in cruel, inaccessible places, often without enough food or
ammunition. Sometimes the soldiers are so hungry they sell their rifles for
vegetables. Their officers can't read maps, and they lose their way. Soldiers
are forced to wear scarlet jackets, and when they come together in the forest they form a perfect red bull's-eye for their sharpshooting enemies.

The pattern is repeated endlessly, in astonishing variations. Hardly any
colonial power escaped participation in an overseas disaster. The British,
simply because they built the largest empire of all, become involved in
more little wars than anyone else. During Victoria's reign, from 1837 until
1901, the British army was fighting someone, somewhere, every year. "It
was the price of empire, of world leadership, and of national pride," Byron
Farwell, a specialist in Victoria's colonial wars, has written. And no one said
it was wrong.

Yet anyone who has visited the small parish churches dotting the British
countryside can see what was wrong with it. Almost every one of them contains a memorial to their local young men, from Norfolk, or Shropshire, or
the Scottish highlands, who died in some distant, long-forgotten campaign
in the service of the British Empire.

What Britain started, others soon followed. There is a moving photo-
graph in this book (see page 214) showing a group of Italian officers on the
eve of the battle at Adowa, when their army was destroyed by Ethiopian
tribesmen. They are arm in arm, shamelessly mugging for the camera. The
photographer has numbered those who died in the battle. Almost all of
these smiling young men have numbers; almost all of them died.

The American intervention in the civil war in Vietnam began as an expedition, but as more and more American soldiers were poured into combat, it became a full-scale war; as such, it does not fit the guidelines for this
book. Even so, it had many of the characteristics of disastrous expeditions—bad intelligence, arrogant assumptions, political incompetence. It
had the same tragic result, too—fifty thousand dead Americans, so terrible
a toll it led to a society wracked by dissent, with its echoes haunting the
United States almost a quarter-century later.

And still it goes on. With the cold war at an end, expeditions now tend to parade lofty goals—getting food to starving people, keeping battling armies from killing each other, attempting to restore democracy in countries torn by factions. But soldiers die all the same, and those who survive ask the age-old questions: Why me? What was the reason for this?

ONE

General Edward Braddock and the French and Indian War (1754–1763)

George Washington, seated on the veranda of his newly acquired estate, Mount Vernon, watched in wonder early in March of 1755 as a flotilla of seventeen merchant vessels worked its way up the Potomac River to Alexandria, Virginia.

First came *Anna*, then *Terrible*, followed by *Osgood, Concord, Industry, Fishburn, Halifax, Fame, London, Prince Frederick, Isabel* and *Mary, Molly,* and *Severn*, one after another, firing their pop guns in salute as they passed the big riverside plantations. Bringing up the rear, in lonely, explosive isolation, were the three ordnance storeships, *Whiting, Newall*, and *Nelly*.

Aboard these ships, the twenty-three-year-old Washington knew, were two regiments of British regulars come to America from Cork, in Ireland, under orders from William Augustus, Duke of Cumberland, George II's second son and captain general of the British army. The regiments were sent to destroy French power in North America. Washington knew something about that, too; a year earlier, he had led his own Virginia regiment into the wilderness, a reconnaissance expedition to determine how far the French had encroached on British colonial territory, which culminated in a humiliating surrender to these same Frenchmen, along with their Indian allies, at Fort Necessity.

But that was amateur warfare; this would be professional. "The ponderous Cannon o'er the surges sleep, the flaming muskets swim the raging deep," proclaimed the *Pennsylvania Gazette* in a burst of giddy doggerel to welcome the army from across the sea.

In fact, though, these were two of the worst regiments in the British army—Sir Peter Halkett's Forty-eighth Foot, which had been routed by the Scots at Prestonpans, and Colonel Thomas Dunbar's Forty-fourth, which had been nearly annihilated in the assault on Cartagena, in Colombia. Both regiments had been raised as recently as 1741; both were undermanned and scattered all over Ireland at the time they were summoned for duty in America. They were partly filled out by drafts from other regiments serving in Ireland and England; canny commanders, acting in time-honored tradition, had unloaded every regimental troublemaker in their ranks on the American expedition. But when the regiments set out, they were still undermanned. The numbers would finally be filled up with colonial troops, of whom the haughty British commanders thought even less.

Cumberland had turned to an obscure major general named Edward Braddock to lead these misfits into the forests. Braddock at the time was sixty years old, stout in build, slightly dense in mental capacity, and extremely rude in social intercourse. Born into a military family, he had followed in his father's footsteps, working his way up slowly, ploddingly, as an officer in the elite Coldstream Guards. Despite forty years in service, at a time when the British army was busily fighting in Europe and putting down Jacobin rebellions at home, Braddock had never heard a gun fired in earnest.

Hardly anyone in London knew who he was. He "had not done anything to earn himself a place in the chronicles of the times," wrote Winthrop Sargent in his 1855 history of the colonial expedition. "He was prone to the debaucheries of his day and class, the bottle and the gaming-table; he was imperious, arrogant and self-opinionated." Better known was his ill-starred sister, Fanny. Having run up heavy debts at the gambling tables in Bath, she hanged herself with her own girdle. "Poor Fanny," said her brother. "I always thought she would play till she would be forced to tuck herself up!" Even the poet Oliver Goldsmith wrote about her tragic end.

Braddock may have sensed his own impending disaster. During his last night in London, he called on his old friend—his "pet"—the twenty-year-old George Anne Bellamy, an actress with a dubious reputation. He unfurled a map and showed her where he and his redcoats were headed. "Pop," he said, using the young woman's nickname, "we are sent like lambs to the altar"—meaning, no doubt, slaughter. He wrote his will, too, leaving almost everything he had to his Gibraltar mistress, Mary Yorke, wife of an artillery lieutenant.

Cumberland was no fool, but he had blundered badly in a kind of triple whammy—choosing the wrong troops, giving the wrong man the command, and setting off on the wrong line of march.

General Edward Braddock. (Library of Congress collections)

Why?

He had turned to the Forty-fourth and Forty-eighth regiments as a bookkeeping dodge. Because they were based in Ireland, their expenses could be laid off on the sister kingdom's budget. For this and most other British armies, the bottom line frequently directed the front line. No doubt he had other reasons. Why, he may have asked, send the best troops in the kingdom to fight an outnumbered enemy in such a dreary corner of the world? Discipline, even with poor material, should carry the day. Braddock was chosen as a kind of eighteenth-century bow to the old boys' network. Cumberland, too, had served in the Coldstreams. Alexandria was chosen because it was in Virginia, and Cumberland wanted to reward the colony's lieutenant governor, Robert Dinwiddie, a wealthy Glasgow merchant, who was popular in London. Cosmopolitan Philadelphia, with good roads heading west, would have been a more appropriate jumping-off point; but Pennsylvania, still a little Quakerish about going to war, maintained no militia.

And so it was that the first real army with the first real general that

George Washington and the rest of his Virginia militiamen had ever seen came tumbling ashore at tiny Alexandria, so small it didn't even have a decent wharf. The thirsty, randy soldiers were aghast: there was only one miserable tavern and no whorehouses at all. The town, with Washington's help, had been laid out in 1749, and the biggest excitement up until Braddock's arrival was watching "Bobtail Bowie" exercise his considerable skills at the public whipping post in the town square.

Braddock's duty was clear. It had all been spelled out for him in his formal letters of instruction. "His Majesty's intentions in sending the forces to North America," these instructions began, "being to recover the Territories belonging to His Colonies there & to His subject and allies the Indians, which the French have (most unjustly & contrary to Solemn Treaties subsisting between the two Crowns of Great Britain & France) invaded, & possessed themselves . . . " Win them back—the territories and the Indians, now allied with the French—he was told, and "secure for the future His Majesty's subjects & allies in the just possession of their respective Lands & Territories."

In pursuit of this plan, Braddock was ordered to move his troops from Alexandria up the Potomac River to Wills Creek, the present-day Cumberland, Maryland, where his deputy quartermaster general, Sir John St. Clair, would already have erected a fort. They would then begin their march west through the wilderness to Fort Duquesne, situated on the east side of the Monongahela River, on a tongue of land that forms what is now Pittsburgh's Golden Triangle, where the Monongahela and the Allegheny meet to form the Ohio.

Braddock had sailed to America aboard the fifty-gun warship *Norwich*. His immediate military family was a small one—Thomas Bishop, his batman, and Francis Delboux, his cook, along with Captain Robert Orme, his chief military aide, and William Shirley Jr., son of the able governor of Massachusetts, his private secretary. They took over Major John Carlyle's handsome new home, backing up to the Potomac River, as their Alexandria headquarters; there, they dazzled the townsfolk by mounting a guard—a lieutenant and thirty redcoats—at the doorway. On April 15, the governors of New York, Pennsylvania, Massachusetts, Maryland, and Virginia sat down with General Braddock and his naval commander, Commodore Augustus Keppel, in Major Carlyle's "Blue Room" to review final details for the campaign.

Braddock, grumpy by nature—"a very Iroquois in disposition," Horace Walpole, author and politician, called him—liked hardly anything about the little town or the New World of which it was a part, and he didn't like anything about the kind of cooperation he was getting from the five governors. He needed colonial soldiers, colonial cash, colonial horses and wagons, and so far he hadn't seen any of it. After the Blue Room council was over, he wrote an angry letter to London: "I have been greatly disappointed by the neglect and supineness of the Assemblies of those Provinces with which I am concerned; they promised great matters and have done nothing, whereby instead of forwarding they have obstructed the service. When I get to Wills Creek, I will send you . . . what other information or intelligence I shall get there, it being impracticable to get any here, the people of this part of the country laying it down for a maxim, never to speak truth upon any account."

Washington was something of an exception; Braddock was impressed by his personal appearance—Washington always looked like a soldier— and by the fact he already had commanded troops in battle. But even though Washington had just returned from an exhausting unsuccessful campaign in these same woods, against the same enemy, Braddock and the rest of the British professional officers found it difficult to ask him for advice. Only one serious discussion about tactical considerations seems to have taken place, in which Washington confirmed Braddock's thinking. For Washington, a proud (and ambitious) man even at this early stage of his career, lecturing a British major general uninvited would have been out of character. Washington could have told Braddock that it would make more sense to cross the mountains with packhorses than with wagons and carriages. But, of course, he wasn't asked.

Serving in a place of honor as one of Braddock's personal family was the only circumstance in which Washington was willing to accept a role in the expedition, given the King's order on November 12, 1754, "denying all precedence of rank to the colonial military in comparison with the bearers of commissions signed by himself or his American generalissimo, Braddock." The colonials—Washington most of all—deeply resented the second-class citizenship implicit in the order.

Braddock also warmed up to one other colonial—Benjamin Franklin, already forty-nine years old and perhaps the wisest man in the New World. Franklin was the deputy postmaster general for the North American colonies and a kind of special emissary for the colonial government in Philadelphia. In an early conversation with Braddock, Franklin caught the drift of a major problem troubling the unhappy general. "I happened to say," he wrote in his autobiography years later, "I thought it was a pity they had not landed rather in Pennsylvania, as in that country almost every farmer had his own wagon." Braddock, Franklin said, leaped at the bait, handing over £800 on the spot to begin acquiring the wagons he thought were crucial to the outcome of the campaign. A few days later, Franklin printed circulars to be distributed to the Pennsylvania-German farmers in Lancaster, York, and Cumberland counties. If the farmers didn't cooperate, he warned, in a brilliant public relations ploy, Sir John St. Clair, *the hussar*, with a body of troops would fall on the colony and seize the wagons by force. These Pennsylvania Dutchmen knew all about hussars; they had watched these Hungarian-style light cavalrymen in rapacious action in Europe, and they feared them. The wagons—150 in all—began rolling.

Franklin had some parting advice for the general. Watch out, he said, for "ambuscades of Indians, who by constant practice are dexterous in laying and executing them." Braddock's "slender line, near four miles long," he said, would be a likely target for an Indian attack. It could come "in its flanks" and the line could "be cut like a thread into several pieces . . . "

Braddock was no doubt amused. At any rate, according to Franklin, he replied: "These savages may indeed be a formidable enemy to your raw American militia, but upon the King's regulars and disciplined troops, sir, it is impossible they should make any impression."

The old general was set on marching into the forests, his troops in bright scarlet, his musicians blaring away on drums and fifes, with every movement dictated by his personal bible, Major General Humphrey Bland's manual, *Treatise on Discipline.*

In another slap at the colonials—Braddock had already discriminated against colonial officers—he noted that "the two regiments now employed have servd under the command of His Royal Highness [the Duke of Cumberland] and are well acquainted with military discipline. His Excellency [meaning himself] expects their conduct will be so conformable to order as to set the most soldier-like example to the new Service of this country. . . ." He assigned downy-cheeked ensigns from the two regular regiments to drill the colonials, European style. "To avoid confusion if the regiment should be ordered to wheel or fire by platoons," he said, "every officer commanding a company is to tell it off in two divisions and to post the second commissioned officer and non commissioned officer's, and when the Regiment decamps or are to form, the commanding officer of the company is to instruct his mens arms, compleat the Files, Post the Officers and see his men loaded that they may wheel up and ye Battalion be instantly formed."

Reading that absurd military jargon, the colonial officers must have smiled themselves. Wheel and fire by platoons? In the woods? Against Indians? But when the fighting began, that's exactly what they were told to do.

In Braddock's defense, he did issue at least one sensible order. Because supplies would be short, including forage for the horses, he urged all his officers "to take no more baggage than they find absolute occasion for." He also warned his troops not to be alarmed by "stragling Fires from the Indians in the woods, they being of no consequence. . . ." He told the enlisted men they wouldn't need their swords, and should take into the field "one spare shirt, one spare pair of stockings, one spare pair of shoes and [for the regulars] one pair of Brown Gaters."

But who were these British ordinary soldiers, taught to wheel and fire and wear Brown Gaters? The names crop up only in dry descriptions of their disciplinary proceedings. James Anderson, for example, a private soldier from Colonel Dunbar's regiment, was sentenced to one thousand lashes with a "Cat and Nine Tails," apparently for drunkenness. Thomas Conelly, James Fitzgerald, and James Hughes were caught stealing a keg of beer worth thirty-three shillings, in Maryland currency. Conelly was given nine hundred lashes; the other two, six hundred each. John Nugent, a private soldier in the Forty-fourth Regiment, found guilty of stealing an unspecified amount of money, was given one thousand lashes and "drum'd out of the Reg't through the line with a halter about his neck."

The little army eventually was formed into two brigades. The First Brigade, commanded by Sir Peter Halkett, consisted of his regiment, the Forty-fourth, 700 men in all, along with two companies from New York, two ranger companies from Virginia, and one ranger company from Maryland. The Second Brigade, commanded by Colonel Thomas Dunbar, consisted of his regiment, the Forty-eighth (650 men), along with three companies of Virginia rangers and single companies from South and North Carolina. The colonial contingent also included two companies of carpenters (engineers), about 100 men in all. To serve the British officers, Braddock hired "numbers of Mulattoes and free Negroes of whom I shall make batmen, whom the province are to furnish with pay and Frocks. . . ."

And to help haul fourteen heavy pieces of artillery over the mountains, Commodore Keppel agreed to hand over thirty sailors from his warships, including Lieutenant Charles Spendlowe, presumed to be the author of one of the rare surviving journals of the campaign. Braddock had been promised a fair number of friendly Catawba and Cherokee Indians to act as scouts for the expedition, with the possibility of larger numbers of Indians from the Six Nations joining up later. (When the veteran Indian fighter George Croghan, from Pennsylvania, showed up at the camp at Wills Creek with a handful of Indians, Braddock tried to deal with them, but failed to understand their customs. Worse, he allowed his officers to dally with their women. One young Indian woman, Bright Lightning, became so popular that Braddock was forced to issue orders curtailing such paramilitary activity. The Indian warriors were so outraged by the treatment of their women that they sent messages to their friends in other tribes, urging them to stay home.)

Braddock was frantic to get under way. "I am impatient to begin my march over the mountains," he wrote London.

The army began moving out of Alexandria early in April, setting out in two directions. Halkett and his brigade headed to the west for Winchester on April 8 and 9. Dunbar's brigade set out to the north for Frederick on April 18. Braddock followed along in his personal chariot, a gilded wagon loaned to him by the governor of Maryland. With his light-horse bodyguard, he caught up with Halkett on the tenth. "The troops saluted, the drums rolled out the Grenadier's March, and the cortege passed by," according to one account. The colonials stared in disbelief; they had never seen men go to war like this.

Major Carlyle, in Alexandria, was delighted to see the last of the British. Braddock and the other English officers, Carlyle said, "seemed to be afraid of nothing but that the French and Indians would not give them a meeting and try their courage. We who knew [the strength of the French and the Indians] endeavored to set them right [but without success]. They used us like an enemy country; took everything they wanted, and paid nothing or very little for it. When complaints were made to the commanding officers, they cursed the country and [its] inhabitants, calling us the spawn of convicts, the sweeping of the gaols, etc., which made their company very disagreeable."

Carlyle said that the general, who lodged with him, "took everything he wanted, abused my home and furniture, and made me little or no satisfaction . . . " Braddock, Carlyle concluded, was "opinionated and very indolent, [a] slave to his passions, women and wine, as great an epicure (a glutton) as could be in his eating. . . ."

It wasn't until May 20 that both divisions of the army—2,150 men in fighting trim —were finally assembled at St. Clair's newly built Fort Cumberland, on Wills Creek. They were accompanied by the usual train of non-combatants—washerwomen who sometimes provided other services to the troops, wagonmasters, and the small band of Indians. "The most desolate place I ever saw," wrote Mrs. Charlotte Browne, a widow traveling with her brother, a commissary officer.

The general, reported Captain Robert Orme in his journal, the best surviving account of the expedition, now had "frequent opportunities of seeing and hearing of the appearance and disposition of the Virginia Recruits and companies. Mr. Allen [the ensign in charge of their training] had taken the greatest pains with them, and they performed their evolutions and firings as well as could be expected, but their languid, spiritless, and unsoldierlike appearance considered with the lowness and ignorance of most of their Officers, gave little hopes of their future good behavior."

There wasn't enough flour to bake bread, and most of the beef "had no pickle" to preserve it, so it was condemned. Horses wandered off, never to be seen again, while most of those harnessed to the wagons were small by British standards and too weak to put in a full day's work. The soldiers were bitten by fierce chiggers and alarmed by poisonous rattlesnakes. Sometimes, to balance their diet, the soldiers ate rattlesnake.

On May 30, St. Clair and six hundred men moved out of camp to begin clearing a road to Little Meadows on the Youghiogheny River, twenty-four miles to the west. It took them ten days to get there. Clearing the way was ghastly, difficult work. "Roads were to be cut through the forests and over the steep mountains; streams were to be bridged, and morasses made passable," wrote Sargent in his campaign history. Braddock was apoplectic. "This part of the country is absolutely unknown to the Inhabitants of the lower parts of Virginia and Maryland, their Account of the Roads and provisions utterly false," he wrote London. Returning once again to a familiar theme, he said it would take too much time to discuss the "want of Honesty and Inclination to forward the Service in all Orders of people in these Colonies, which have occasion'd the great delays in getting hither. . . ." Braddock came to realize, too late, that he should have marched from Philadelphia to the crossing of the Youghiogheny, for the road was "as good as from Harwich to London."

St. Clair, who performed valiant work in cutting a path one hundred miles through the mountains from Fort Cumberland west to the Monongahela, was just as taken aback by the terrain. "It is certain," he wrote, "that the ground is not easy to be reconoitered for one may go twenty Miles without seeing before him ten yards." The trails, he said, "are either Rocky or full of Boggs; we are obliged to blow the Rocks and lay the

Bridges every day; What an happiness it is to have wood at hand for the latter!"

Aware now of the difficulties, Braddock called a council of war of all his field officers in his tent at Fort Cumberland. He had privately consulted Washington earlier—a rare tribute to colonial intelligence—and sought his approval of a plan to push a light division forward, leaving the heavy troops and the artillery to follow. Washington said he thought it was a good idea. The council of war adopted a line of march, in which the various companies would march two men deep, on each side of St. Clair's twelve-foot-wide road. Baggage would be transported in the middle of the column, and there would be flankers on both sides and forward and rear guards. Halkett was chosen to lead the light division, while Dunbar—who would later show himself to be a shirker—was put in charge of the heavy column.

The initial object of the expedition was Fort Duquesne, one hundred miles away. The fort was a parallelogram—the longest sides, fifty yards, the shortest, forty yards. It was built of large squared logs, twelve feet high. A shallow ditch surrounded the fort, protected by a second stockade fence, seven feet high. Inside the fortification were the magazine and the kitchen, along with substantial log houses, storehouses, and barracks. The fort was defended by eight cannon, four of them three-pounders, the rest four-pounders. Braddock intended to drag his artillery to the top of a nearby hill and fire hot shot down onto the roofs of the wooden structures, "and so subdue the post." This was the reason the sailors had been enlisted—to drag, with block and tackle, four 3,200-pound naval guns, capable of firing twelve-pound shot, across the mountains.

But what about the enemy? Who occupied the fort? How many Frenchmen? How many French-speaking colonial militiamen? How many Indians? Braddock, blinded because he had almost no Indian scouts of his own, had no idea. In fact, the post was commanded by the man who had built it, Pierre Claude Pecaudy, Sieur de Contrecoeur. He had named it for his governor, the Marquis of Duquesne. But he was finishing up his frontier service, and the man sent to replace him was already on hand. His name, a tongue stretcher, was Captain Daniel Hyacinth Mary Lienard de Beaujeu, the forty-four-year-old son of the old mayor of Quebec, and he would save the day. French records of the campaign are scanty, so there is no exact reckoning of how many men were available to Contrecoeur and Beaujeu. A good guess would put the number at something less than three hundred regulars and Canadian militiamen, paltry opposition for Braddock's well-equipped army. Outside the fort, living in bark wigwams, were eight hundred Indians—some of them "French-praying" Indians from Canada, the ones the missionaries had reached, the rest a motley assortment from the surrounding territory. Not one was thought to be reliable.

The French commanders had three options: defend the fort; abandon it and burn it down and live to fight another day; or—a more interesting possibility—move out of the fort and attack Braddock on the march. Captain Jean Dumas, one of the regulars, originated the idea of pushing for a battle in the forest.

Braddock knew none of this. His job was to advance on the stockaded outpost, blast it apart with his big guns, and then march on to Fort Niagara at the western end of Lake Ontario, a key link in the line of French fortifications. This first assault was just one part of a three-pronged movement. A second army, also under Braddock's overall command, had been ordered to occupy Oswego, on the southern shore of Lake Ontario, and to restore and garrison the fort there. A third army, under the command of William Johnson, the Indian agent, was under orders to capture the French fort at Crown Point, at the southern end of Lake Champlain, from where the enemy threatened the entire Hudson valley. Also contemplated was a separate attack on Nova Scotia.

It was certainly ambitious. Young Shirley, Braddock's private secretary, watched the campaign unfold and found his concerns rising. In a letter to Governor Robert Hunter Morris of Pennsylvania, he said: "We have a G—— most judiciously chosen for being disqualified for the service he is employed in, in almost every respect. He may be brave for ought I know and he is honest in pecuniary affairs. . . ." But, quoting King George in a different context, he went on to say that "a little more ability and a little less honesty upon the present occasion might serve our turn better."

The army set out from Fort Cumberland for Little Meadows, twenty-four miles away, on June 7 and 8, in three divisions. Sir Peter Halkett, a baronet from Fifeshire married to the second daughter of the earl of Moray, was in the lead; Colonel Dunbar, an unenthusiastic professional soldier who constantly complained about his health, brought up the rear. Lieutenant Colonel Thomas Gage commanded the middle division.

Men who would one day become part of even more dramatic events keep popping up as bit players in Braddock's campaign. Gage, for example, would go on to command British forces in Boston and launch a frontal assault up Breed's (not Bunker) Hill, during the opening stages of the American Revolution. Commodore Keppel, safely anchored in Hampton in the old *Centurion*, one of the most famous warships in Royal Navy history, would become a viscount and First Lord of the Admiralty. Late in joining the expedition was Captain Horatio Gates, in command of an independent company from New York; the godson of Horace Walpole, he would one day accept the surrender of Gentleman Johnny Burgoyne's entire British army at Saratoga. And a twenty-one-year-old Daniel Boone joined the army as a wagonmaster; later when he saw how the fighting was going, he moved out—fast. He wasn't alone. Another wagoner who took the same precipitous action was Daniel Morgan, who would eventually command the finest regiment of riflemen in the American Revolution. Washington, of course, saw it all, and Franklin had come through with the wagons.

The march had barely begun when it came to a halt, at the bottom of Wills Mountain, where St. Clair's road was too precipitous for the wagons. Navy lieutenant Spendlowe saved the day by finding a better route around the bottom of the mountain, and the train, sometimes four miles long, with twenty drums from each regiment beating the march—this was a very noisy army—pushed on. Camped at night, the train was still half a mile long. It wasn't until June 16 that the first brigade arrived at Little Meadows, where St. Clair had built a small fortification. The rest of the army completed the march two days later. It had been hard going. "The horses grew every day fainter, and many died," Captain Orme wrote in his journal. Many of the soldiers contracted "a general sickness," and even Washington's hardy constitution succumbed. He dropped out to give himself time to recover.

The army was now in deep wilderness. "We marched about nine miles to Bear Camp over a chain of very rocky mountains and difficult passes," Orme wrote. "We could not reach our ground 'till about 7 of the clock [on June 19], which was three hours later than common, as there was no water, nor even earth enough to fix a tent. . . ." Braddock ordered that "upon every halt, though ever so small, the men are to form two deep, face outwards, and stand shouldered." He told them, too, to listen to the drums—coming to a halt when they heard the beat of the long roll and to start marching again when they heard another distinct beat, the long march. They were now aware that Indians lurked in these deep woods—scouts discovered the remains of a just-abandoned Indian camp on the twenty-fourth—and fear began to creep into the long, thin line. The next day, at daybreak, three soldiers were shot and scalped. On the twenty-fifth, Braddock ordered that every soldier or friendly Indian taking an enemy Indian scalp should be rewarded with the payment of five pounds. The next day, after making only four miles through the forest, they found still another Indian camp, "their fires being yet burning," according to Orme. They encountered, too, an eighteenth-century version of graffiti: "They [the enemy] had marked in triumph upon trees, the scalps they had taken two days before, and a great many French had also written on them their names and many insolent expressions."

What impression these ominous proceedings must have had on the ordinary British soldiers, uneducated lads for the most part, can only be imagined. Beyond the Great Savage Mountain—even the names held terror in them—were "dark forests of enormous white pines," wrote Sargent. "The loneliness and perfect monotony of such a scene are not readily to be described; it more resembles the utter stillness of the desert than anything beside. No bird chirps among the foliage, or finds its food in these inhospitable boughs; no wild creature has its lair beneath its leafy gloom. . . . At every step the traveler half looks to find a bloody corse [corpse], or the blanched skeleton of some long murdered man. . . ." The woods, Sargent pointed out, were called the "Shades of Death."

Not surprisingly, the soldiers began seeing shadows in the woods, and shooting at them. Braddock ordered that "if any officer, of whatever rank, shall suffer the men to fire their pieces, he shall be put under arrest."

To make matters worse, the field officers were feuding. The dyspeptic Dunbar said that both Braddock and his personal favorite, Captain Orme, were slighting him, and maybe they were. Braddock already suspected that he had a shirker on his hands in Dunbar, who drove everyone to distraction by boasting of the great generals he had served under. During one such monologue, Orme heard more than he could take. "Stuff," he interrupted, "you might as well talk of your grandmother."

"Sir," said Dunbar, "if she was alive, she would have more sense, more good manners, and know as much of military matters as you do."

"Gentlemen," interrupted Braddock, "you are both too warm."

Washington, still recovering from a serious case of dysentery, was just as unimpressed as Shirley, Braddock's aide, with the progress the army was making. "Instead of pushing on with vigor, without regarding a little rough road," he wrote to his brother Jack, "they were halting to level every mole hill and to erect bridges over every brook, by which we were four days getting twelve miles."

The army had crossed from Maryland into Pennsylvania on June 21, moving slowly across what Sargent called "the high and watery glades of Somerset county and the precipitous region of Fayette [county], whose mountain tops attain an altitude of 2,500 feet above the sea, with valleys scooped between, 1,000 feet below their summits." They reached Stewart's Crossing on the Youghiogheny, only about thirty-five miles east of their destination, on June 30. By now, Indian scouts were lurking on their flanks day and night. Eighteen-year-old James Smith, a road builder, was captured by the Indians on July 3 and taken back to Fort Duquesne. There he was beaten, temporarily blinded with sand, and made to run the gauntlet. Despite his agonies, Smith asked a Delaware warrior who spoke a little English how Braddock's army was progressing. The Indian said he and the other scouts "saw him [Braddock] every day from the mountains—that he was advancing in close columns through the woods"—this he indicated by placing a number of red sticks parallel to each other and pressed closely together. He boasted to the American prisoner that the Indians "would shoot 'um down all one pigeon."

Indian warriors liked nothing better than seeing the redcoats—or American bluecoats, for that matter— closely bunched. The closer they got, the easier it was to kill them. They became, in one observer's vivid phrase, a "huge red bull's eye."

Braddock did make a faint effort to reconnoiter the enemy position. He sent one small Indian scouting party ahead, and followed that up by sending his personal scout, Christopher Gist, the frontiersman, to take a peek. The Indians got close enough to the French fort to meet one of the officers hunting in the woods. They shot him, took his scalp, and claimed their five-pound reward when they returned to camp. Gist was attacked by an Indian scouting party and barely made it back to camp alive.

The army actually marched past what remained of Washington's little outpost, Fort Necessity, now overgrown with weeds. Braddock contemptuously criticized it, for its structure (too spindly) and its location (surrounded by hills). Some of the Americans who had been with Washington the previous year took the occasion to emphasize to their British colleagues that all the drills in wheeling and platoon firing wouldn't be much help against the Indians. One of the Americans, Captain Thomas Waggener, in command of a company of Virginia rangers, said that when the time came the Indians would scatter in the woods, taking cover behind trees and elevated ground, where they would pick off the tightly packed redcoats one by one. The redcoat officers scoffed.

But the Virginia rangers were far from infallible themselves. Eager to track down the enemy Indians who had killed and scalped the three army stragglers, they opened fire upon an Indian scouting party, believing them to be the ones responsible for the killings. But these were the army's own Indian scouts, and the rangers, blind to signals of friendship, fired upon them. Killed in this early example of friendly fire was the son of the army's most responsible Indian scout, Scarouady. Braddock expressed his condolences and the young warrior was given a full military funeral, including a volley over his grave.

Braddock, though grumpy as ever, never wavered in his belief that he would capture Fort Duquesne, if he could just get there. He apparently was so unconcerned about the fighting that was now just hours away that he began making arrangements for reorganizing his little army after the battle was won. He planned to incorporate the colonials into a new royal regiment, to be commanded by Lieutenant Colonel Burton of the Forty-eighth. Orme would have taken Burton's place, and perhaps, historians speculate, there might even have been a royal commission for Washington. There was nothing in the world he wanted more.

"We are now," as Sargent said in his account, "approaching the last dread scene of our tragic story, and events crowd thick and rapidly upon us."

Braddock called a council of war on July 3 at Salt Lick Creek, with Gage, Burton, St. Clair, Orme, and Major Sparks in attendance. St. Clair proposed that the army halt and that all the horses be sent to the rear to bring up Dunbar and his detachment. But Dunbar was more than a day's march away, and so the council agreed that no advantage would be gained by waiting so long for him to lumber into position. Besides, the horses were now so weak it was doubtful they would be of much help, and supplies were running low. Any delay, they worried, would give the French, Sargent later wrote, "time to receive their reinforcements and provisions, and to entrench themselves, or strengthen the fort, or to avail themselves of the strongest passes to interrupt our march.

"Under all these considerations, the council were unanimously of opinion not to halt there for Colonel Dunbar, but to proceed the next morning."

Harry Gordon, the army's chief engineer and a favorite of the Duke of Cumberland, wrote a friend (still unidentified by historians) after the battle was over; his letter offers the best description of the descent on the enemy outpost. "On the 8th," he said, "we cross'd the Long Run which was a small rivulet that runs to the Monongahela about 12 miles from the F. [French] fort. We were oblig'd to cross it many times in the Space of two Miles, in which Distance we came along a Narrow Valley at the widest a

Quarter of a Mile, very much commanded on both sides by Steep Hills." Gordon said that Braddock had ordered the steep hills secured and the grenadiers to "shut up the valley in our front."

The last orders to the troops were issued that night, at a camp near the Monongahela. The password, for recognizing friend from foe, was Burntwood. The field officer for July 9 was Lieutenant Colonel Burton. The Forty-fourth Regiment was told to mount the general's guard. The troops were to receive, immediately, "two days meat & two days flower which compleats them with provisions to the Tenth Inclusive. All the men but those who mount the Picquet this night to draw their pieces And to Load with frish Cartridges tomorrow at Genl Beating." The grenadiers—the tallest, most professional-looking troops—from the two regiments were ordered to parade at 2 A.M. the next day "at the head of their Respective Collours," and from there to move out and join the advance party under Lieutenant Colonel Gage. The troops "are to be Compleated with 24 rounds of powder and ball And Are to take their napsacks & Haversacks but leave their tents behind." The main body was told to begin the march to the battle in the woods at 5 A.M.

The still-sickly Washington, confined to a wagon and in pain, had arrived at Braddock's camp the night before the battle. He was warmly greeted and took note of the debate taking place on which route to follow in making the final approach on Fort Duquesne, now only a few miles away. The one the commanders settled on would take the army across the Monongahela at what Harry Gordon called "the nearer end of the Narrows," and then move it toward the enemy fort along the south side of the river. The army would make its final crossing of the river at another shallow, pebbly ford, "below where Turtle Creek runs in."

By now, almost everyone, from Braddock down to the Virginia carpenters, was feeling slightly euphoric. Some of the British officers, one of the colonial officers wrote, "were of the opinion that we should hear the explosion of the French fort blown up and destroyed before we approached it." Only Halkett seemed concerned. He urged Braddock the night before the battle to examine more carefully the land between his camp and the fort, "beating the forest as hunters in the Highlands would drive their game." The idea was rejected. Halkett, perhaps the best soldier in the army, had twelve hours to live.

With Gage and his advance party of 350 crack men and two brass sixpounder cannons in the lead, followed by St. Clair with 250 carpenters and wagons, the van moved out about 4 A.M. on the ninth, already running late.

It wasn't until 8 A.M. that Braddock and the main force, with its huge naval twelve-pounders and its four eight-inch howitzers, reached the first ford. Colonel Gage sent back a message that his party had crossed the second ford with only a single glimpse of the enemy—20 Indian scouts who fled upon his approach.

Braddock and the main body made the final crossing about 2 P.M. Washington said years later he had never seen such a beautiful sight. The redcoats, every man in his best uniform, crossed the shallow river as though they were on parade, drums furiously beating and fifes blaring away at Braddock's favorite tune, the "Grenadier's March." Halkett's Forty-fourth went first, followed by the sailors, then the artillery teams, and finally the rangers with the wagons and the cattle. The Forty-eighth brought up the rear. Gordon wrote that "everyone . . . hugged themselves with joy at our Good Luck in having surmounted our greatest Difficultys, & too hastily concluded the Enemy never wou'd dare to Oppose us."

Braddock could hardly be blamed for thinking the enemy wasn't going to make a stand. He and his army were now within a few miles of their fort, safely through the most dangerous terrain for an ambush, and still nothing was happening. It was because the French commander, Contrecoeur, was torn about what action to take. He considered mounting a single cannon and firing off one shot in defiance, then surrendering the whole outpost to his vastly superior enemy. Beaujeu, in a delicate position because he had yet to take command of the fort, wanted to make a fight by taking a small force of regulars and Indians to dispute the crossing at the second ford. Contrecoeur agreed, reluctantly. But to make it work, Beaujeu needed the Indians—the Delawares, Shawnees, Ojibwas and Potawatomis, Ottawas and Hurons. He had called them to a council under the fort's palisades on the eighth, as the British army closed in. The Indians were recalcitrant. According to Sargent, one of them asked, "How, my father, are you so bent upon death that you would also sacrifice us? With our eight hundred men do you ask us to attack four thousand English? Truly, this is not the saying of a wise man." They drifted away. Beaujeu called them back, now desperate for a commitment, the next morning. As he was speaking, a scout burst into the assembly and, in Sargent's words, "heralded the advent of the foe." Beaujeu seized the day. "I am determined to go out against the enemy," he said. "I am certain of victory. What! will you suffer your father to depart alone?" It worked. The Indians, in a frenzy, began preparing for battle. Barrels of powder and bullets were broken open, and rolled out to the gates. The best estimate of the column that now streamed away from the fort is that it numbered 72 French regulars, 146 Canadian militiamen, and about 640 Indians. Beaujeu was almost as naked as the Indians, wearing only a hat, a breechclout and a silver gorget (a decorative military necklace). He was supported by Captains Dumas and DeLegneris, from the regular army, and four lieutenants, six ensigns, and twenty cadets.

Meanwhile, his army having crossed the river at the second ford, "the general again halted," wrote Orme, "till they formed according to the annexed plan. It was now nearly two o'clock and the advanced party under Lieutenant Colonel Gage and the working party under Sir John St. Clair were ordered to march on till three. No sooner were the pickets upon their respective flanks, and the word given to march, but we heard an excessive quick and heavy firing in the front." The initial fighting occurred where the trail curved around the charred ruins of a cabin built by John Fraser, a trader and gunsmith. Washington knew the place well; he'd stopped there seven months earlier, in bitter cold. Now it was warm and sunny, too warm for the British regulars in their finest, and heaviest, red swallowtail jackets, buff pantaloons, and brown gaters.

Engineer Gordon was right in the middle of it. "Gage's party march'd by files four deep, our front had not got above half a mile from the Banks of the River, when the Guides which were all the scouts we had, & who were before [out front] only about 200 yards came back, & told a Considerable Body of the Enemy, mostly Indians, were at hand.

"I was just then rode up in Search of these Guides, had got before [out front of] the Grenadiers, and had an opportunity of viewing the Enemy, and was Confirm'd by the Guides and what I saw myself that their whole numbers did not exceed 300." Gordon, wounded twice in the impending battle, was one of only a handful of combatants on the British side who managed to get a good look at the enemy.

Because of the time-consuming negotiations with his Indians, Beaujeu was late reaching the field. But he quickly summed up the situation, waved his hat right and left over his head in a preconcerted signal, and watched as his warriors divided to flank the British column. The bone-chilling Indian war whoop echoed through the woods, terrifying redcoats who had never heard it before.

The guides took off for the rear, but the grenadiers, the best troops in Braddock's army, turned smartly to face the shadowy enemy. First, they formed a line of battle across the woodland trail, and fixed bayonets. Then, in perfect European order—the front line kneeling, the back line standing—they slammed a musket volley into the bushes. "God save the King!"

one of them shouted. "Huzza!" shouted a few more. They fired a second volley, and then a third. It was the most effective action Braddock's army would take all day. Beaujeu was killed by the third volley, shot through the head. The Canadian militiamen, terrified by the disciplined musket fire (four Canadians and fifteen Indians may have died in the fusillade), began to run.

Most battles have a decisive moment; this was it for this battle. But instead of advancing to seize their opportunity, the British began to fall back. First it was some of Gage's command; they collapsed into St. Clair's carpenters and pioneers. Gage bellowed furiously at his men, as bullets clipped his hat and waistcoat. He was cool enough to realize the strategic importance of a small, crested hill on his right, already occupied by a handful of grenadiers. He ordered a platoon forward to secure it, but they were too frightened to move. Sir John St. Clair galloped forward to help, an easy target for the Indians who had now hunkered down in gulleys and taken cover behind trees. A bullet struck him in the body, but still he managed to make his way back, on foot, to the colonial carpenters and rangers, urging them to bring the two six-pounder cannons into action. They touched off a couple of rounds in the general direction of the bushes.

Suddenly, wrote Orme, "there was an alarum . . . that the Enemy were attacking the Baggage in the Rear, which Occasion'd a second retreat of the Advanc'd party. They had not Retir'd but a few paces when they were join'd by the rest of the troops, coming up in the greatest confusion, & Nothing afterwards was to be Seen Amongst the Men But Confusion and Panick." Gage's men took off to the east, sweeping St. Clair's pioneers with them. The two cannons were abandoned. And the grenadiers surrendered their position on that key hill on the army's right.

Into this confusion rode Braddock, with Washington, mounted on a horse with pillows to protect his aching bones, at his side. The redcoated British army began to huddle together in the middle of the road, slowly forming that awful red bull's-eye. The bull's-eye grew larger as Burton hurried forward with eight hundred men and the sailors' big twelve-pounders. But before he could move into position, what was left of Gage's grenadiers and St. Clair's pioneers came running down the trail. The forest path suddenly became clogged with redcoats and rangers, wagons and litters bearing the wounded.

At the first sound of gunfire, Braddock had galloped forward, followed by his men "without any form or order but that of a parcell of school boys coming out of school," according to an anonymous letter written after the battle. Braddock left Halkett behind in command of the baggage, which itself was attacked soon after as the Indians, in a kind of half-moon formation, moved down both flanks of Braddock's army. Braddock, critics contended after the battle was lost, should have posted guards around his wagons and then moved forward in a more disciplined way.

The key was still that hill on the right, now occupied by the enemy and the source of most of the deadliest fire. St. Clair wrote after the battle that he too had run "to the front to see what the matter was, when I received a shot through the body. I then return'd to my own people, posted Capt. Polsons company of Artificers and Capt. Periwees Company of Rangers to cover my two cannon. I then went up to General Braddock who was then at the head of his own Guns and beg'd of him for God-Sake to gain the rising ground on our Right to prevent our being totally surrounded. I know no further of this unlucky affair . . . being afterward insensible." He had fainted.

Braddock responded to St. Clair's plea by ordering Burton to take 150 men and seize the hill. Burton tried to sort soldiers from the Forty-fourth from those of the Forty-eighth, rangers from carpenters. It helped a little when the huge battle colors of the Forty-fourth were marched off in one direction, the colors of the Forty-eighth marched off in another. European soldiers instinctively rallied around their regimental colors. Burton, on horseback, collected 100 men from the Forty-eighth and began the attack on the hill. Predictably, he was one of the first to be shot. The men straggled part way up the hill, and then turned tail and ran back down. Captain Thomas Waggener, the Virginia ranger, rallied his men and made a second attempt to climb the hill. But the confused British regulars mistook his bluecoated troops for Frenchmen, and opened fire. An angry Waggener withdrew, with the loss of 30 of his 50 men. Washington pleaded with Braddock to allow colonial troops to make a third try. Braddock simply shook his head.

A diary, presumably written by Lieutenant Spendlowe, noted that the soldiers were "intimidated," having seen so many of "their comrades scalp'd in their sight and such numbers falling . . . as they advanc'd up towards the hill, and their Officers being pict' off, which was generally the case [and so] they turned . . . about and Retired down the hill." Captain Robert Cholmley's batman—name unknown—left an unsigned diary, too, noting that his master was killed within ten minutes of the commencement of the action. "We was drawn up in large Bodies together, a ready mark," he noted. "But if we saw of them five or six at one time [it] was a great sight and they [concealed themselves] either on their Bellies or Behind trees or running from one tree to another. . . ."

In another journal, an unidentified soldier who was almost surely a British officer noted that "the men from what storys they had heard of the Indians in regard to their scalping and Mahawking were so pannick struck that their Officers had little or no command over them." This unknown officer speculated that a large percentage of the British casualties were caused by friendly fire.

Washington, having watched the failed attempts on the strategic hill, came up with another suggestion. He sought Braddock's permission to deploy three hundred or more of the colonial troops in the woods and fight the enemy Indian-style. Bill Brown, Burton's black servant, thought he heard Braddock curse Washington's suggestion, saying: "I've a mind to run you through the body. We'll sup today in Fort Duquesne or else in hell." It sounds much too contrived to be true.

A little more likely is the story that when Braddock urged to his aides that the big twelve-pounders be used to clear away the underbrush so the soldiers could get a clear shot at the enemy, Washington responded, "General, be assured, even if you cut away the bushes, your enemy can make enough of them artificially to answer the purpose of shelter and concealment." Braddock is said to have replied, "What do you think of this from a young hand, from a beardless boy?"

No contemporary account of the battle cast doubt on Braddock's courage. Confused he may have been; but cowardly, no. He rode up and down the tumbled masses of his shattered army, cursing and swinging his saber at skulkers. Four horses were shot out from under him. Though two horses were shot from under him, Washington escaped injury—he always did—with bullets nipping his hat and coat. He stood out, Orme wrote, for "the greatest courage and resolution."

Braddock's officers were taking terrible casualties. Halkett, commanding the convoy at the rear of the army, galloped to the front with his son, James, to see what was happening. He tried to rally his own men, urging that they would be better off if they took cover like the enemy. But he was killed, a bullet through his body, before he could do anything. His servant died tending his wound; his son died riding to his side. Lieutenant Spendlowe was dead too, and Orme and Gordon wounded. Poor Shirley, who had raised doubts about Braddock's competence, paid the price for being right. He, too, fell to the curious, almost silent, pop-pop-pop of the enemy fire.

By four o'clock, almost half of Braddock's officers were dead or wounded. Now it was Braddock's turn. As he attempted to climb aboard his fifth horse, a bullet struck his right arm and kept on going into his lungs. Thomas Bishop, his faithful batman and an old Coldstreamer himself, unwrapped the general's great scarlet sash from around his ample waist and turned it into a stretcher. With the help of Bishop, Gage, and Captain Robert Stewart, a Virginian, he was carried down the trail to the rear and the convoy of wagons. He was conscious, but in great pain. He had told "Pop," his actress friend, that he might die in these deep woods, and now he was doing just that.

It was about this time, noted the anonymous British officer in his journal, that "the Wagoners, who imagined things would turn out badly, had taken the Gears from their Horses & galloped quite away so that if Fortune had turned our way we had not one horse left to draw the Train (of artillery) forwards." Daniel Boone and Daniel Morgan were among those galloping away to make history later, on more suitable ground.

Even before he was shot, Braddock had concluded that his only choice was to fall back on his wagon convoy and attempt to regroup there. He ordered the movement, and the drums began to beat the retreat. But the battlefield was so chaotic that many officers didn't get the orders and couldn't hear the drums. Small groups fought on, in one or two instances beating off Indian attacks. In time, though, panic became universal. "When the men had fired away all their ammunition," Orme wrote, "and the general and most of the officers were wounded, they by one common consent left the field, running off with the greatest precipitation."

"Everyone was trying [to be] the first," wrote the unknown British officer. "The Enemy," he added, "pursued us butchering as they came as far as the other side of the river; during our crossing they shot in the water both men and women, & dyed the stream with their blood, scalping and cutting them in a most barbarous manner. . . . Melancholy situation!"

Washington was appalled. "Despite of all the efforts of the officers to the contrary," he later wrote, "they ran, as sheep pursued by dogs, and it was impossible to rally them." The very effort, he said, met with as much success "as if we had attempted to have stopped the wild boars of the mountains."

Harry Gordon reported that the surviving officers, many of them wounded, managed to keep two hundred soldiers in the field after the mass retreat was under way. But they refused to attack that deadly hill again, "or advance far enough to support the cannon, whose officers & men were mostly kill'd and wounded. The Cannon silenc'd, & the Indian's shouts upon the Right advancing, the whole Body gave way. . . ."

Gordon, who had seen the opening of the engagement, also saw its

General Edward Braddock's retreat, from a painting by Chappel, 1858. (Library of Congress collections)

horrific conclusion: "Before I had got 40 yards in the River, I turn'd about on hearing the Indians Yell, & saw them tomahawk some of our women and wounded people, others of them fir'd very Briskly on those that were then crossing, at which time I receiv'd another Shot thro' the Right Shoulder."

Colonel Burton, Gordon said, tried to rally the survivors on the far side of the river, after they had made the perilous crossing. He "made a speech to them to Beg them to get into some Order, but Nothing would Do, and we found that every man would Desert us; therefore we were obliged to go along, & never halted till we came to Guest's [Gist's], which was near 60 miles from the place of the Action."

Washington found a small cart with its team of horses, put Braddock in it, "and conveyed the hard-breathing commander over the ford." With Burton and Orme, both wounded, Washington tried to bring some order to the survivors now clustered on the Monongahela's left bank. The three officers chose high ground a quarter of a mile from the river and set up camp, hoping to remain there until Colonel Dunbar came up with the rest of the army. But the soldiers would have none of it. One by one, then in larger groups, they slipped away into the night, in a desperate effort to put more distance between themselves and the awful scenes they had witnessed at the battlefield and in the river itself. Braddock, in one of his last orders, commanded Washington to carry the news of the defeat to Dunbar, and to tell him to send hospital supplies and wagons for the wounded. Washington said years later that he would never forget that terrible ride in the dark of night: "The dead, the dying, the groans, lamentation and cries along the road of the wounded for help . . . were enough to pierce a heart of admanant." Late on the morning of the tenth, weary beyond description, he made his way into Dunbar's camp at a place called Rock Fort.

Fortunately for the army's survivors, no serious effort was made by the French to mount a pursuit. The Indians were content to roam the battlefield, scalping both the dead and the wounded. Young Smith, the Pennsylvania road builder who was being held prisoner, heard the scalping parties as they returned to the fort throughout the night. They came back wearing grenadier caps and scarlet jackets, as well as carrying English muskets. One party, Smith said, brought back about a dozen prisoners. One of them "was tied to a stake on the river bank opposite the fort. A fire was kindled at his feet. Indian tormentors kept poking at him with blazing sticks and red hot irons." Smith figured all of the prisoners must have died, for he never saw any of them again.

Braddock, in terrible pain, accompanied the retreating army, sometimes carried by his own officers. Orme tried to bribe soldiers to help, offering thirty, seventy, even eighty guineas. For a while, the old general was even forced to get back on a horse. Once, he asked, perhaps to himself, "Who would have thought it?" And again: "We shall know better how to deal with them another time."

He remained in command and somehow continued to issue orders. He concluded that the army couldn't remain at Rock Fort, and so he ordered everything destroyed that couldn't be carried away. "Nearly 150 wagons were burnt, the powder casks staved into a spring, the cohorns [small mortars] broke or buried and the shell bursted," according to an army report.

What was left of the proudest European army North America had ever seen set out for Fort Cumberland the morning of July 13. Braddock gave one final instruction to Orme, still at his side: to tell Commodore Keppel what happened, and to say to him that "nothing could equal the gallantry and good conduct of the officers nor the bad behavior of the men."

"All is over," he said, as the sun began to set. He died about 9 P.M.

Washington, one of the few officers still on his feet and no longer very much in awe of British professionals, took charge of the old general's burial on the morning of the fourteenth. He chose a spot in the middle of the road near the head of the column, where he ordered the digging of a short, deep trench. The idea was to hide the grave from the Indians, who might otherwise be tempted to dig the body up and make a trophy of it. Washington had the wagons roll over the spot to erase signs that the grave existed at all.

The command now fell upon the unfortunate Colonel Dunbar. De facto Governors Morris of Pennsylvania and Dinwiddie of Virginia said later that they had hoped he might rally the army and resume the campaign. Failing that, they expected he would remain at Fort Cumberland and protect the frontier. Dunbar had no such intentions. "I purpose leaving some of the Independants and provincial Troops to protect them [the wounded] and proceed with the remains of the two regiments to Philadelphia for winter quarters," he wrote Robert Napier, the army's adjutant general, in London, on July 24. He ended the letter with a personal complaint that gives some measure of the man: "This Climate by no means Agrees with My time of Life and bad Constitution . . . therefore beg Your Interest to gett Me leave to go home; was I able as I am willing I assure You I would gladly stay."

"I must confess," Dinwiddie told Maryland governor Horatio Sharpe, "the whole conduct of Col. Dunbar appears monstrous to me."

As word of the defeat spread, the finger-pointing began. Scarouady, the last loyal Indian scout, said, "It was the pride and ignorance of that General that came from England. He looked upon us as dogs, and would never hear anything what was said to him."

"We have been most scandalously beaten by a trifling body of men," Washington complained. "Braddock's defeat still remains in the situation of the longest battle that ever was fought with nobody," Horace Walpole wrote.

Franklin, as usual, was more thoughtful. "The general was, I think, a brave man," he wrote in his autobiography, "and might probably have made a figure as a good officer in some European war. But he had too much self-confidence, too high an opinion of the validity of regular troops, and too mean a one of both Americans and Indians." Exactly.

Word of the disaster reached London on August 26 and made its way soon after to George Ann Bellamy's country house outside London. "Bad news from America," she is supposed to have cried to Jack Calcraft, her current lover and a war office clerk. "My fears are too prophetic, and I have lost a second father."

The nation, of course, had lost an army. Of 69 grenadiers in the company from Halkett's regiment, less than a dozen survived. Every grenadier officer had been killed or wounded. Fifteen of the sailors were dead. Washington figured that only 30 Virginians survived. Of the 1,500 officers and men who had gone into action, about 1,000 had been killed and wounded. Three or four women were missing. All the artillery and wagons with the advance force, one hundred cattle, and between four hundred and five hundred horses had been left on the battlefield. In one of the wagons were all of Braddock's papers, including his no-longer-secret instructions. A rare French document listed the booty: "grande quantité de fusils, de Service et hors de Service . . . 19,740 cartouches chargées pour mousquets . . . 20 hommes ou femmes faits prisonniers par les sauvages . . . 4 canon de fonte aux armes d'Angleterre." The document stated that three French officers were killed, including Beaujeu, along with three Canadian officers, two Canadian soldiers, and "15 sauvages de différentes nations." It also reported that 16 men were wounded, including 12 "sauvages."

Back on his veranda at Mount Vernon, Washington contemplated his own unhappy military record. "I have been on the losing order ever since I entered the service," he said. But if he had lost a general, he had gained a batman. Thomas Bishop, Braddock's servant, came to work for him. He served at George Washington's side, faithfully, for twenty-five glorious years.

✦

Braddock's defeat on the Monongahela was the Pearl Harbor of the French and Indian War, an American affair that soon spread to Europe, where it is known as the Seven Years' War. British blundering survived Braddock: a new standard in stupidity may have been raised by a second British general, James Abercrombie, who charged an entrenched French army at Fort Ticonderoga and lost almost two thousand men. The luckless Forty-fourth Regiment took part in that disaster, as well.

The turnaround began in 1758, with William Pitt as the new prime minister. He chose Jeffrey Amherst as his commander in chief in North America, with James Wolfe in the field as his principal fighting general. The reinvigorated British army recaptured both Louisbourg and Duquesne (renaming it Fort Pitt), and in 1759 Wolfe won the greatest victory of all, defeating Montcalm on Quebec's Plains of Abraham. Both generals died on the field of battle. The whole of Canada was surrendered to Great Britain, ending France's role as a North American power.

Even so, almost 250 years later, French-speaking Quebec continued to fidget as a minority part of a dominant English-speaking culture, still talking about independence.

TWO

Brigadier General Josiah Harmar and Major General Arthur St. Clair and the Indian Wars on the Northwest Frontier (1790–1791)

On May 15, 1788, Major Ebenezer Denny reported in his journal that he and "some gentlemen of Pittsburgh accompanied the General in a barge, on a visit up the Monongahela to Braddock's Field. We viewed the battle ground. Saw several small heaps of bones which had been collected, with a little brushwood thrown over them."

The general on that day's lugubrious outing was Josiah Harmar, an undistinguished veteran of the American Revolution who would in two year's time command the first American federal army in President George Washington's first major military expedition. Harmar, a sophisticated Philadelphian with a fondness for the bottle, learned nothing by viewing those sad little piles of bones from Edward Braddock's army, for he was on the road to compounding the very same egregious errors Braddock had committed more than thirty years earlier. And, when Harmar was routed in his campaign to destroy recalcitrant Indian tribes in the Old Northwest, Washington appointed an even more incompetent general, white-haired, gout-ridden Arthur St. Clair (no relation to Braddock's Sir John St. Clair), to wage a second campaign, with even bloodier results. In tandem, Harmar and St. Clair led the American army into one of the most disastrous, and unnecessary, campaigns in its history.

It was, in the immortal words of Yogi Berra, déjà vu all over again. George Washington becomes the Duke of Cumberland, giving the command to the wrong man, twice, allowing both of them to go into battle with soldiers trained (to the extent they were trained at all) for the wrong war.

Harmar and St. Clair appear as Braddock, fighting by the book, against an enemy that didn't generally tend to read military manuals.

The problem, once again, was Indians.

Different Indians, this time. The Iroquois, long the dominant Indian federation (though they had taken no role in defeating Braddock), were now in decline, and as likely to turn their backs on their brothers and make deals with the new American government as anything else. The fight had gone out of them, in no small part due to a crushing expedition sent deep into their heartland in 1779 during the Revolution. John Sullivan, a faithful if not very brilliant Continental officer, had led forty-five hundred well-trained, well-disciplined, well-provisioned troops in a textbook wilderness campaign.

The new United States had first laid down the law to these confused Indians in a spurious, nonrepresentative conference at Fort Stanwix, near what is now Rome, New York, in October of 1784. "You are subdued people," the shocked Indians were told by the American commissioners. ". . . You now stand out alone against our whole force!" The Iroquois were informed they would no longer have any claims to land west of New York and Pennsylvania. And, the commissioners said, the Americans in the future might choose to seize any land in "Indian Country" they desired. The treaty was signed on October 22, 1784, by representatives of the assembled Senecas, Mohawks, Onondagas, Oneidas, Cayugas, and Tuscaroras— the Six Nations of the Iroquois. It split the Iroquois federation apart, and never again would they play a commanding role in Indian resistance to the march of the white man. Washington argued the way was now clear for a peaceful resolution of the new nation's Indian affairs. The Indians, he said, "will ever retreat as our settlements advance upon them."

With the Iroquois shattered, Indian power had moved west, and the most turbulent tribes were now the Miamis, led by the resourceful Little Turtle, and the Shawnees, led by Blue Jacket, a white man captured by Indians and adopted by that tribe. They formed a loose confederation that also included Ottawas, Chippewas, Sacs and Foxes, Potawatomies, Winnebagoes, Wyandots, Kickapoos, Piankeshaws, Weas, Delawares, a few Senecas and Mohawks, and even some mysterious, vagabond Mingoes. All together, according to some estimates, they could put ten thousand warriors in the field. William Henry Harrison called them the finest light troops in the world.

These were no ignorant "savages," living naked in the woods. Kekionga, the principal Miami village and a major British fur-trading post (Fort

Brigadier General Josiah Harmar (from "Winthrop Sargent's Diary," *Ohio Archaeological and Historical Quarterly* 33, 1924).

Wayne, Indiana, today), had regular streets and sidewalks, a council hall and a ballroom, and even a whorehouse. Little Turtle's house had glass panes in the windows, framed paintings on the walls, and, near the back door, a five-seat privy.

This was the old Northwest Territory, 250,000 square miles in all, which would eventually include the states of Ohio, Indiana, Illinois, Michigan, and Wisconsin. The Indians staked the Ohio River as the boundary between their land and the white man's land; everything northwest of the river, they said, was theirs—it had always been theirs—and they argued, with

Major General Arthur St. Clair (from St. Clair's *Narrative*, 1812).

considerable justification, that no one else had any right to buy it, sell it, or settle it.

But the historic Northwest Ordinance, passed by Congress on July 13, 1787, ignored these Indian claims. It provided for a territorial government until the huge landmass was ready to be divided into anywhere from three to five states. Slavery was specifically excluded from these lands, which were already beginning to be settled by white Americans, many of them veterans of the Revolution. They had come floating down the Ohio River, led by old Gen. Rufus Putnam, on a barge he called *Mayflower*, establishing a settlement, Marietta, at the mouth of the Muskingum River in 1788.

The French, defeated in the French and Indian War, were no longer the Indians' ally; this time, it was the British. Defeated themselves in the Revolution but still holding on to their frontier outposts—Detroit, Michilimackinac, Niagara, Oswego—supposedly ceded to the new United

States by the Treaty of Paris in 1783, they were encouraging the Indians, with the help of such vicious renegades as Simon Girty, to attack the Americans moving west to make homes in this extraordinarily fertile new land.

The British didn't care about colonizing the land; their interest was plainly economic, and at the root of that interest was the valuable fur trade. They believed that to keep it they needed to maintain their outposts and hold the loyalty of the Indians supplying them with the pelts. The Spaniards were part of the problem, too: Spain held vast tracts of the new American West, which it had picked up in 1763 from the French. They infuriated western settlers by closing the Mississippi River, at New Orleans, to American trade.

The new American government, in seeking to challenge both Britain and Spain, cow the Indians, protect American settlers, and discourage frontiersmen from taking the law into their own hands, had one weakness: no army. On June 2, 1784, the entire American army had consisted of fifty-five artillerymen at West Point and twenty-five more at Fort Pitt (once Fort Duquesne), with no officers above the rank of captain. On June 3, Congress had passed a resolution calling for a federal regiment of seven hundred men, to be furnished by Pennsylvania, New Jersey, New York, and Connecticut. It would become the First American Regiment, getting the same pay—$40 a month for its lieutenant colonel, in command, and $6.67 a month for a private—as the Continental army in the Revolution.

Because Pennsylvania, no longer so Quakerish, supplied the most men (260), it was allowed to choose the commanding officer. It chose thirty-one-year-old Josiah Harmar, an orphan reared by Quaker relatives. He had enlisted in the Continental army in 1775 and worked his way up to brevet lieutenant colonel, along the way forming an important political attachment to Thomas Mifflin, serving as his private secretary when Mifflin was president of the Continental Congress. Mifflin pushed him for the job. In 1786, Harmar and his handsome Philadelphia bride, Sarah Jenkins, took up residence on the frontier at the recently restored Fort McIntosh, thirty miles below Pittsburgh on Beaver Creek.

"I wish you were here to view the beauties of Fort M'Intosh," Harmar wrote a friend, Francis Johnson. "What think you of pike of 24 lbs., perch of 15 to 20 lbs., cat-fish of 40 lbs., bass, pickerel, sturgeon &c,&c. You would certainly enjoy yourself." Harmar was also taken with the strawberries: "The earth is most luxuriantly covered with them—we have them in such plenty that I am almost surfeited with them; the addition of fine rich cream is not lacking." To wash it down, Harmar ordered substantial quantities of Madeira wine, Lisbon wine, cognac, whiskey, rum, and lime juice from Philadelphia.

Later that year, Harmar was ordered to move his tiny detachment down the Ohio River and build a new fort on the west bank of the Ohio River, across from the present-day Marietta. That outpost, a two-story stockade fort, became, modestly, Fort Harmar. The general liked Fort Harmar, too. "Venison, two or three inches deep cut of fat," he wrote his sponsor, Thomas Mifflin, "turkeys at one pence per pound, buffalo in abundance, and cat fish of one hundred pounds weight"—more than double the size of those at Fort McIntosh—"are stories that are by no means exaggerated." He noted, too, that "cornfields, gardens &c, now appear in places which were lately the habitation of wild beasts. Such are the glories of industry."

"By 1789," wrote Wiley Sword in his wonderfully detailed book, *President Washington's Indian War: The Struggle for the Old Northwest, 1790–1795*, "such luxuries as two Windsor chairs and six Windsor side chairs were included among the (Harmar) furnishings, providing a curious contrast to their rough-hewn garrison abode." Harmar's "considerable urbanity," Sword concluded, straight-faced, "may have rendered him somewhat suspect as an Indian fighter." In fact, away from the dining table, he was another martinet in the Braddock mold, following by rote the manual introduced into the Continental Army by Major General Baron von Steuben during the American Revolution. Harmar carried a dog-eared copy of it everywhere he went, and even when his military service was over, and he had retired to his home near Philadelphia, appropriately known as Harmar's Retreat, he was still recommending it to anyone who would listen. In 1793, he would offer to print one thousand copies "on good paper, with well-executed plates," for the militia serving under Governor Richard Howell of New Jersey.

"Steuben's manual was aimed at combatting British and Hessian forces—not the backwoods guerrilla fighting of the highly skilled American Indian warriors the regiment would eventually fight," noted William H. Guthman, in his *March to Massacre: A History of the First Seven Years of the United States Army, 1784–1791*. "Shortsightedness on the part of the military was the reason that no preparatory training in guerrilla warfare was ever imposed on the Army . . . no federal unit under Harmar or St. Clair was ever instructed in the frontiersmen's method of warfare."

This was surely inexcusable. There was now no secret about fighting in the woods. Sullivan's expedition against the Iroquois had shown the way. Members of Daniel Morgan's celebrated rifle regiment had accompanied the expedition (though not Morgan himself), and they were in large part responsible for its success. More recently, Benjamin Logan, with his Kentucky militiamen, frustrated by the lack of federal support to control attacks on their settlements by Indian "banditti," had launched a counterstroke. He did some real damage with his mounted troops; they included a familiar figure, Braddock's old wagonmaster Daniel Boone, now a colonel and famous all over the frontier as an Indian fighter. Logan's ferocious frontiersmen swept down on unsuspecting Shawnees, killing women and plundering Indian huts. Before they were finished, they had destroyed eight principal Indian villages, losing only three men in the process. Major Denny, General Harmar's closest aide and the author of a superb military journal covering his service on the frontier, criticized the soldiers' conduct. "Logan" he wrote, "found none but old men, women and children in the towns; they made no resistance; the men were literally murdered." The raid probably did more harm than good, by arousing the Shawnees and their confederate tribesmen to an even higher pitch of outrage. But, cruel as it was, it did highlight a tactic that would be useful in fighting Indians. Experienced riflemen, moving swiftly on horseback, could surprise and overcome Indian resistance.

What the country needed was a small, well-trained, highly mobile army, led by experienced officers with a background in frontier combat. Washington must have known that, but there is no record to indicate he was willing to push hard for such a military organization. Instead, he permitted one of his old generals, the artilleryman Henry Knox, to become the first secretary of war, and he would make a mess of everything. Knox, a hero in the Revolution, was both a fool and a knave in directing the fighting on the old Northwest Frontier. He was a fool because he continued to reject the notion of a standing army, of any size at all. "An energetic nation and militia," he wrote, "is to be regarded as the Capital Security of a free republic, and not a standing army forming a distinct class in the community." He was a knave because he was up to his ears in land speculation, and some of his fellow speculators were odious even by modern-day standards.

So, to flesh out the paltry numbers represented by the regular establishment, Washington and Knox ordered the calling up of 1,500 militiamen. Even Harmar, no military genius, saw the danger in that shortcut personnel solution. "No person can hold a more contemptible opinion of the militia in general than I do," he said. Later, he pointed out, with considerable wisdom, "It is lamentable . . . that the government is so feeble as not to afford three or four regiments of national troops properly organized that would soon settle the business with these perfidious villains upon the Wabash."

Both Harmar and St. Clair, the territorial governor, worried about what would happen if raw militia colonels were allowed to take precedence over regular army majors. "If the ragamuffins of the militia were to take command," St. Clair said, "I have seen few in my life that would be fit for it."

But ragamuffins they would be, for Harmar would be forced to go into battle with an army in which eight of ten soldiers were militiamen. These were no ordinary militiamen; the troops being sent to Harmar were simply awful. Major Denny, a Revolutionary War veteran from western Pennsylvania who had served under Harmar in the Carolinas, called the Kentuckians "misfits and loiterers" who were "raw and unused to the gun or the woods; indeed, many are without guns." The Pennsylvania militia was, if anything, even worse. Harmar said they were "hardly able to bear arms—such as old, infirm men and young boys." One of their officers, Major James Paul, conceded most of them couldn't oil their gun locks because they didn't know how to remove them from their muskets.

These troops came from the streets and the gutters. No one else really wanted to serve, given the low pay and the dangers facing the volunteers on the frontier. Clothing for the troops was scavenged from old Revolutionary War warehouses; artillery hats were often issued to infantry soldiers, and infantry hats to artillerymen. Many of the raw recruits grabbed the clothing and headed home.

The proper uniform for the federal troops was a blue regimental coat with red lapels and cuffs. The infantry wore white vests with white buttons, the artillerymen white vests with yellow buttons. Revolutionary War veterans were authorized to wear a special badge recognizing their service. They all wore cocked hats. Harmar thought they ought to have a national marching song too, but no one seemed eager to compose one. They were all issued muskets left over from the War for Independence. Harmar wanted some riflemen for the expedition, but that didn't work either. Anyway, rifles were in short supply—there were only 6 of them at West Point, and another 104 at Fort Pitt.

On June 7, 1790, Knox ordered Harmar "to extirpate, utterly, if possible, the said [Indian] banditti." He made it clear that this was a "standing order." It was to be a two-pronged attack. Harmar would take his 1,300 ragamuffin militiamen and 353 regulars and march on the Miami heartland, the ultimate goal being Kekionga itself. Another column, consisting of 400 Kentucky militiamen and 100 regulars commanded by Major John Hamtramck, was supposed to provide a distraction by attacking Indian villages along the Wabash River. They began their march on September 30, found the Wea villages empty, and turned around and marched home, without firing a shot, three weeks later. Hamtramck, some said, lacked ardor.

That left it up to Harmar. But, right from the start, his militia officers began arguing about precedence. "Much difficulty in regulating and organizing the militia," Major Denny reported in his journal on September 25. "Colonels dispute about the command." Harmar, he noted, offered a compromise: The three battalions of Kentuckians would serve under Lieutenant Colonel James Trotter of Kentucky, the single battalion of Pennsylvanians under Lieutenant Colonel Christopher Truby, with all of the militia under the command of Colonel John Hardin, another Kentuckian. Harmar would retain overall command. But the compromise, adopted reluctantly by those involved, did nothing to hide the fact that Trotter and Hardin despised one another.

To make matters worse, Knox had committed a monumental blunder; he ordered Governor St. Clair to notify Major Patrick Murray, the British commander at Detroit, that this little Yankee army was coming, but not to worry, because it had nothing but a "pacific disposition" towards the British. "Its sole design," Major Murray was told, was the "humbling and chastising of the savage tribes, whose depradations have become intolerable. . . ." With a naïveté that almost passeth understanding, he even told St. Clair to ask Murray to keep these plans a secret from the Indians. Washington, hearing about the letter, said he thought it was "unseasonable," as, among other things, it surely was. The British, of course, sent out messages in all directions, notifying their Indian allies of the Harmar expedition. They also offered $50 for an American scalp and $100 for an American prisoner.

The American army headquarters was now based at Fort Washington, a new post located three hundred miles from Fort Harmar, near present-day Cincinnati. Maybe they couldn't fight, but this little army made a fine construction battalion; in seven years, from 1784 to 1791, it built nine new forts and restored two old ones, an astonishing feat of rude engineering.

Harmar's confidence wasn't exactly boosted when he received a secret letter from Knox saying that reports had reached him that "you are too apt to indulge yourself to excess in a convivial glass," to the extent that the general's "self-possession" came into question. If heavy drinking led to disaster, Knox warned, Harmar's reputation "would be blasted forever."

Heavy drinking probably wasn't much more of a problem for Harmar than it was for plenty of other officers of his time, who regularly consumed vast quantities of wine and spirits at the table. Food, Harmar's letters reveal, was really his passion. He talked about meat, fish, vegetables, and fruit all the time. Unquestionably, though, he was a genial, convivial man, ill-suited for the hardship that lay ahead.

On September 26, Major Denny reported in his journal, "the whole of the militia took the field under the direction of Colonel Hardin, an old continental officer, amounting to 1,133. They marched on the direct route to the Indian towns." The general and the regulars moved out of camp on the twenty-ninth and the thirtieth. The federal troops were formed into two small battalions, under the immediate command of Majors John Palsgrave Wyllys and John Doughty. Captain William Ferguson commanded a small company of artillerymen, with three light brass pieces. The regulars numbered 320. They were joined on October 5 by a small detachment—about 100 men—of mounted infantry commanded by Major John Fontaine.

The march formation was hardly different than Braddock's—two columns, one on either side of the trace, with a strong front and rear guard, the baggage in the center. Six scouts fanned out in front of the army, backed up by thirty men, who were in turn followed by twenty-four pioneers flanked on either side of the cavalry. Next came the militia, the general, with staff music (fifes and drums) and colors, then the main body and the rear guard. On the march, they averaged about ten miles a day. At the end of the day they formed a hollow square. Horses and cattle were herded into the center, but so many packhorses drifted away during the night, never to be seen again, that one of the federal officers concluded it was a plot by the drivers to get rid of their spindly charges and collect fat damages when the campaign was over.

If Harmar had learned nothing from the history of frontier fighting, the thirty-eight-year-old Little Turtle had learned quite a lot. The Iroquois committed a fatal mistake in the Revolution, making a stand at one of their main villages (present-day Elmira, New York) and paying the price. Little

Turtle concluded towns and villages were no place to make a stand against white armies. He planned to set his villages on fire and retire to the friendly woods.

A prisoner the army captured on October 13 told the Americans that Little Turtle already was burning his villages and "clearing out as fast as possible," according to Major Denny's journal. The fear, Denny wrote, was that "the towns would be evacuated before our arrival." And so, just like Braddock, Harmar created a light brigade—six hundred mounted militia from Kentucky under Colonel Hardin—and told them to move out of camp at daybreak on the fourteenth. For Harmar's men, it was a miserable morning, with driving cold rain; Hardin didn't get under way until 10:30, barely ahead of the rest of the army. His guides got lost in what Sword, the campaign historian, called "a country of sprawling lakes, meandering streams, and dense undergrowth." The result was that the advance party made camp at the end of the day barely four miles from the main body.

The morning of October 15 was clear and sunny, and Colonel Hardin's mounted Kentuckians made good time as they closed in on Kekionga, strategically located where the St. Marys and St. Joseph Rivers meet to form the Maumee, only twenty miles away. When they reached their destination in mid-afternoon, they found the capital of the Miamis empty, and on fire. The frenzied militiamen immediately set off on a search for booty and plunder, spreading beyond Kekionga to nearby towns and villages. "The militia picked up as much plunder as [they could carry home]," Denny wrote. "A great deal is found hidden and buried about, and many things left as if the enemy went off in a hurry."

Harmar and the rest of the army arrived at the still-smoking town the afternoon of October 17. The general, convinced that he had won a great victory without firing a shot, was so euphoric that he began talking about advancing on the Wabash and cleaning out those villages Hamtramck had failed to subdue. That night, though, he and his army got what should have been a serious reality check: Indians crept up on his camp and drove off as many as one hundred packhorses and several cavalry horses, a huge loss to the little army.

Even so, Harmar remained convinced the Indians were in disarray, running helter-skelter through the woods. He ordered Lieutenant Colonel Trotter to take three hundred militiamen (forty of them mounted) and regulars and run them down. They had gone hardly a mile when they encountered a solitary Indian on horseback riding down the trail. They killed him and on their way back to join the main detachment they encountered another. Sword described the pursuit as a kind of "sportive fox hunt," as the mounted Americans, sabers rattling, thundered off after him. They killed him, too, after which Trotter decided to set up an ambush for Indians he thought might come wandering down the trail to see what the excitement was all about. Instead, one of his own horsemen came galloping in to report he had seen at least fifty Indian warriors. Trotter, unnerved by the news, abandoned the feeble attempt at an ambush, wandered around the woods for a time, and then returned to camp.

Colonel Hardin, Trotter's archenemy, "showed displeasure at Trotter's return without executing the orders he had recived," Denny wrote, "and desired the General to give him the command of the detachment." The general agreed, and Hardin marched off in a northwest direction with 180 men, including 30 regulars under Captain John Armstrong, on the morning of October 19. By now, many of Harmar's troops were beginning to have second thoughts about participating in what had once seemed to them to be more a lark than a campaign. Indians were lurking, and they wanted none of that. "I saw that the men moved off with great reluctance," Denny said, "and am satisfied that when three miles from camp he [Hardin, an unpopular officer with the rank and file] had not more than two-thirds of his command; they dropped out of the ranks and returned to camp."

Hardin, eager to show up Trotter and make himself a hero, paused briefly at a point some five miles from the main camp. When he moved forward again, he inadvertently left a militia company under Captain William Faulkner behind. The only explanation is that in his rush for glory he forgot all about them. When the column halted a second time, someone asked about Faulkner and his men. Major John Fontaine and his cavalrymen were sent back to fetch them. The main column, stretched out now about half a mile in the woods, blundered on, with Armstrong and the regulars in the lead. Armstrong sent back warnings that he had encountered evidence that a significant number of Indian warriors were nearby; Hardin, a perfect fool, disregarded the messages.

The detachment emerged from the woods into a small meadow near the Eel River, sixteen miles from Kekionga. A fire was burning at one end and trinkets covered the ground. The militiamen quickly dispersed to begin collecting the plunder. This is just what Little Turtle, with the advice of both Blue Jacket and Simon Girty, astride a black horse and wearing a scarlet cape, had hoped for. Little Turtle, a great commander, closed the trap. "The Indians," wrote Denny, "commenced a fire at the distance of 150 yards, and advanced. The greatest number of militia"—including Hardin—"fled without firing a shot; the 30 regulars that were part of the detachment stood and were cut to pieces."

The rest of the militia infantrymen, still advancing on the field, refused to move forward, and then they too fled pell-mell. But the regulars, with perhaps nine militiamen, continued to stand firm, and fired a volley into the woods. Little Turtle ordered his Miamis, plus a few Shawnees and Potawatomis, to charge. They poured from the woods, armed only with tomahawks, and began their attack before the regulars could reload. The bluecoated soldiers fixed bayonets and fought hand to hand, the war cries of the Indians audible as much as a mile away. In just a few minutes, twenty-two of the thirty regulars, and almost all of the brave militiamen who had stood their ground, were killed.

"They fought and died hard," said Armstrong following the massacre. It was, Sword pointed out, "perhaps a rather humble beginning for the modern United States Army, yet a proud combat tradition was rapidly emerging."

Armstrong escaped the carnage by diving into a nearby swamp. He watched through the reeds as his own men were scalped and their bodies torn apart by Little Turtle's warriors.

As the survivors ran down the trail in terror, heading back to camp, they encountered Major Fontaine bringing up the lost militia company. "For God's sake," one of the survivors cried, "retreat! You will all be killed. There are Indians enough to eat you up!" It was all they needed to hear. The column straggled back into camp after dark and told their story to a stunned Harmar. He ordered a cannon fired at regular intervals to help survivors find their way home. Armstrong came in the next morning, furious at the "dastardly" conduct of the militia. He claimed that the detachment was attacked by fewer than one hundred Indians, some of whom were armed only with tomahawks. Armstrong vowed that never again would he go into battle with troops like these. Harmar issued orders that should such conduct occur again, he would shoot down the culprits with cannon fire.

If they couldn't fight the Indians, Harmar concluded, they could at least get on with the pillaging. On October 20, Denny reported, "The army all engaged burning and destroying everything that could be of use: corn, beans, pumpkins, stacks of hay, fencing and cabins, &c." In two days, he said, they burned five villages, not including Kekionga itself, and destroyed twenty thousand bushels of corn. They also killed an Indian, Big Shawnee Ben, and propped his body against a log fence, so that it could watch one of the fires. Harmar thought the whole business was a great success, predicting that the firing of the little villages would seriously damage the Indians' ability to carry on the fight.

Believing he had successfully completed his assignment, Harmar planned to begin his withdrawal to Fort Washington the morning of October 21, a decision widely welcomed by his nervous troops. They "encamped eight miles from the ruins" of Kekionga that night, Denny said. But the ineffable Hardin had an idea: why not send a detachment back to the Miami village and surprise the returning Indians digging up their buried possessions? Harmar foolishly agreed, and "ordered out four hundred choice men, to be under the command of Major Wyllys, to return to the towns, intending to surprise any parties that might be assembled there. . . ."

Wyllys, a ferocious veteran of the Continental army, had a premonition about the campaign. "We are about agoing forth to war in this part of the world," he wrote to a friend. "I expect to have not a very agreeable campaign. . . . Tis probable the Indians will fight us in earnest, the greater part of our force will consist of militia; therefore there is some reason to apprehend trouble."

He ordered his little column—consisting of 60 regulars and 340 militiamen—to assemble late on the twenty-first under clear skies and a full moon. Hardin was once again in nominal command of the militia, although he was officially a volunteer reporting to Wyllys. "The Major (Wyllys) marched about midnight in three divisions," Denny wrote, "at the distance of a few hundred yards apart, intending to cross the Omee [Maumee] as day broke, and come upon the principal ruins all at the same instant but at different quarters." Some of the soldiers, fearing the worst, burst into tears when they learned they would once again face the Indians.

Wyllys prepared a complicated plan of attack, ordering Major Horatio Hall and 150 Kentuckians to sweep across the St. Marys River and then circle back, striking the village from the rear. At the same time, Major James McMillan and the remaining Kentuckians would sweep in from the west. Wyllys's regulars and Major Fontaine's mounted infantrymen would make a frontal assault.

"The wings commanded by Hall and M'Millen came upon a few Indians immediately after crossing the Omee, put them to flight and, contrary to orders, pursued up the Saint Joseph for several miles," wrote Denny.

"The centre division, composed chiefly of the regular troops, were left un-supported." In putting these few Indians to flight, the militiamen had fired off several rounds, awakening any other Indians to the danger that was fast approaching. Wyllys, the most vulnerable, was understandably furious.

Waiting for Fontaine's cavalrymen and Wyllys's regulars at the Maumee River ford, barely a foot deep, was the main body of Indians, fully on alert. Commanding them, once again, was Little Turtle, joined this time by Jean Baptiste Richardville, son of a French trader and a Miami mother; he would one day become a celebrated Miami chief.

When Fontaine's horsemen reached midstream, the infantrymen strung out behind him, Little Turtle sprung his second trap. Private John Smith of Fontaine's Kentucky cavalry looked up, Sword reported in his campaign history, "to see the opposite riverbank erupt in sheets of flame. Horses and riders were struck down as if by some whirlwind force." The shallow water soon ran dark with American blood. Richardville said years later that the river was so full of American bodies that he could have walked across it dry-shod.

Brave Fontaine charged across the river and mounted the bank, thrusting himself among the two hundred warriors forming the ambuscade. "Stick to me!" he shouted to his men. Only one of them, George Adams, stuck, ultimately escaping with five wounds. Fontaine was badly wounded himself. McMillan came up to join Wyllys, and managed to ford the river without much opposition, flanking the enemy. The Indians simply gathered their possessions and departed, almost invisibly. The Americans thought they were beaten, and rushed after them, helter-skelter, past Kekionga all the way to the St. Joseph River. Wyllys pulled his regulars together and marched after the whooping militiamen. Little did he know the whole thing was a sham: the Indians weren't retreating, they were just drawing him into another trap. Little Turtle was a genius, and now he had the regulars just where he wanted them, exposed in an open cornfield. "Suddenly," said Sword, "a 'hideous yell' shattered the air. Out of the adjacent underbrush poured the largest body of Indians yet seen in the vicinity of the Miami Towns." As Wyllys feverishly tried to bring his troops into order to defend against the unexpected attack, a messenger rushed up to tell him that the troops on his right, commanded by Captain John Asheton, were also under attack.

But Wyllys had trouble enough of his own, and only minutes to live. His regulars fired off one volley, but ran out of time to fire another. They fixed bayonets and fought hand to hand with Indians armed with tomahawks and—this time—spears. Wyllys fell, his hand clasped to his breast. A prancing Indian was seen moments later wearing his huge cocked hat. The demoralized regulars—the handful that were left—joined the militia in a tumultuous retreat. Of the 60 regulars who had entered the fight, only 10 survived. McMillan and his Kentucky militiamen heard the gunfire and started to return to the bloody river ford, encountering some scattered Indian opposition along the way, putting the Indians to rout. Little Turtle had had enough for the day, and allowed the survivors to begin their retreat to Harmar's camp. Along with 50 regulars, the militia lost 68 men dead and missing. The Kentucky troops were so demoralized they left their dead and wounded on the battlefield.

Hardin was one of the first to make his way back to his general's tent, where he reported a great victory had been won, with the militia performing "charmingly." Others knew better; it had been a terrible defeat. The victory belonged to a great military commander, Little Turtle. Denny was disgusted. The plan had been a good one, he said, "provided due obedience had been observed on the part of the militia, but owing to their ungovernable disposition, an excellent laid plan has in some measure been defeated, and our loss is equal if not greater than the savages'. The General advised with his principal officers about returning to the towns. It was agreed not to return."

The Indians "advised," too, and considered attacking the retreating army—they now had seven hundred warriors for the job—but a lunar eclipse dispirited some of them; a bad omen, they said. And so the American army straggled back to Fort Washington, the militia "ungovernable" and close to mutiny. Harmar ordered the regulars to fix bayonets to keep them in line.

They reached Fort Washington on November 3. The militia was mustered out the next day, given a general discharge and sent home. Good riddance, said some.

When the bad news spread, Harmar was roundly criticized. People who had been miles from the battle noted that he had never taken part in any of the fighting himself. Others said he spent most of the time in his tent, drinking. When Washington heard what had happened, he wrote, "I expected little from the moment I heard he [Harmar] was a drunkard."

Harmar, in fact, became something of a scapegoat. Washington was just as culpable. He could have insisted on a more experienced, more able officer to lead the expedition. He didn't. He could have demanded the troops be trained in frontier fighting, for he, more than anyone else, knew all about that. He didn't. He could, in fact, have done his best to build a decent little army for a nasty little war. He didn't do that, either. And now he made an even bigger blunder: He named Arthur St. Clair, governor of the territory, as Harmar's replacement, with the rank of major general, and asked him to try again. Harmar was a calamity; St. Clair would be a catastrophe.

◆

Arthur St. Clair began his military career as a British officer. He served in the French and Indian War, switched sides, and rose to the rank of major general in the Continental army during the American Revolution—drawing criticism for abandoning Fort Ticonderoga in 1777. By 1785, he was a member of the Continental Congress, serving briefly as its president. Taking on the job of governor of the new Northwest Territory in 1788 "was the most imprudent act in my life," he said, for it meant he had to resign his post as auctioneer of the city of Philadelphia, "one of the best offices in Pennsylvania." Good pay, short hours. He complained the frontier post "was, in a great measure, forced upon me." He was in poor health, suffering painful seizures from gout. Yet, after Harmar's defeat, he was the man chosen on March 4, 1791, to command the frontier army, with orders to march back into Indian Country and build a fort at Kekionga. "Disciplined valor," Knox told St. Clair, "would triumph over the undisciplined Indians."

Washington summoned his new general to Philadelphia, where they discussed the campaign. He concluded by saying: "General St. Clair, in three words, beware of surprise. Trust not the Indian; leave not your arms for the moment; and when you halt for the night be sure to fortify your camp. Again and again, General, beware of surprise!"

That same month, the new government ordered the raising of a second regiment of regulars from the New England states, most of them slated for service in undermanned southern outposts. To bring the armed forces up to three thousand men, Knox ordered the enlistment of two thousand "levies"—troops serving under federal orders for six months—from New Jersey, Pennsylvania, and Maryland. And if that still wasn't enough, St. Clair could call up more militia.

General St. Clair, bubbling with confidence, set out from Philadelphia to take over his new command on March 28. Two days later, he said in his self-serving "narrative" of the expedition, "[I] was seized with the gout, [but] . . . I determined to persevere at all hazards; and, though with a degree of pain and difficulty that cannot be well imagined by those who have never felt the tortures of that disease, arrived at Lexington [Kentucky] in proper time." Feeling better, he pushed on to his headquarters, Fort Washington, arriving there on May 15.

"Present fit for duty," he wrote, were "85 privates. The distant garrisons of Fort Harmar, Fort Steuben, and Fort Knox were to form a part of the army," he said, but they couldn't supply more than 200 troops. But even these troops, all that was left of the First United States Regiment, seemed ragged. Some were former convicts, others were drunkards, Sword reported, and all of them "had been thrown together and sent West totally unfamiliar with army methods and frontier life." The six-month levies, commanded by Major General Richard Butler of Pennsylvania, were slow coming forward. That left St. Clair with a choice: he could call for 1,500 volunteer cavalrymen from Kentucky or call up the same number of typically ragamuffin militia infantrymen. The cavalry, he explained, would cost "two thirds of a dollar a day, to be under the command of their own officers, and to do pretty much what they pleased, and footmen were to receive but three dollars a month, and be subject to military law." He chose the footmen.

William Duer, a New York financier and a close friend of Knox, Washington, and Treasury Secretary Alexander Hamilton, was chosen as the army's contractor. He was a crook, and would die in prison in 1799. He took advances from the Treasury, supposedly to pay for supplies for the army, but used the money to speculate in land, instead. Once, he loaned $10,000 of the army's money to Knox. "The net result of these activities," Sword wrote, "was that Duer grossly neglected the army contract."

The army's quartermaster general, Samuel Hodgdon, another Knox crony, was so incompetent he might as well have been a crook. St. Clair, in his narrative, said, "I would have brought him to a court-martial the moment he set his foot on shore at Fort Washington, if I had a proper person to put in his place. . . ." Incompetence reached a kind of art form when Hodgdon ordered four-pound shot for the expedition's three-pound cannon.

Everything that could go wrong did go wrong. "The carriages of the guns which had been used in General Harmar's campaign were found to be unfit for service, and, of course, new carriages were to be made," wrote St. Clair in his narrative. "The whole [musket] ammunition for the campaign," he said, "was to be made up" on the spot in a "laboratory"— dangerous work, St. Clair agreed. The new gun carriages from Philadelphia "were unfit for service," too, and had to be remounted, he wrote. "The arms of the detachment were in bad order also, and had nearly all to be repaired." Army artificers were called upon to make axes, camp kettles, canteens, knapsacks, kegs for musket cartridges, and splints for the wounded.

There weren't any shoes for the troops, and when some were finally purchased from the crooked William Duer, they wore out in a week. Hodgdon, though ordered forward to Fort Washington, malingered at Fort Pitt; his representative was "constantly drunk." He wasn't alone; most of the troops were drunk, too. St. Clair sent some of them six miles north to Ludlow's Station, "to deprive them of the means of intoxication," an investigation by a House committee—the first of thousands to come—reported after the disaster was complete. Yet, St. Clair told Knox, "the troops seem to be in perfectly good disposition" for battle.

The young, English-speaking Tecumseh, a Shawnee who would one day become one of the greatest of all Indian warriors, knew better. At Little Turtle's behest, he had visited Fort Washington itself four times, according to his biographer, Allan W. Eckert. Dressed in "Shemanese" (white man's) clothing, a wide-brimmed hat hiding his Indian features, he paused from time to time to read notices, perhaps even the army's general orders. As the march began, Tecumseh tagged along, sending a rider to Little Turtle each day to report the army's progress.

Major Denny was there, too. He had consulted his old friend and patron, General Harmar, about joining the expedition. Harmar predicted a defeat. "You must go on the campaign—some will escape, and you may be among the number," Harmar said. With those ringing words of encouragement, Denny rode off into battle again.

To rattle the Indians, St. Clair permitted two Kentucky militia commanders, Charles Scott and the traitor James Wilkinson (he was in the pay of the Spanish government), to mount diversionary raids into Indian Country. "The principal effects of both these expeditions were an enormous public expense," Winthrop Sargent, St. Clair's adjutant general, a Harvard man and a veteran of the Revolutionary War, wrote in his diary. Sargent, celebrated as the best-dressed man in the Continental army, traveled through the wilderness with a kit of plated silverware made by Paul Re-vere. Many of the regular officers found him distant and haughty, the very stereotype of a Harvard man. Even St. Clair said he was "very obnoxious." Small world—Sargent was the grandfather of the Winthrop Sargent who wrote the history of the Braddock campaign.

From Ludlow's Station, the army moved north to the Great Miami River, where Captain William Ferguson, an artilleryman, built a new fort called Hamilton. The troops, Adjutant General Sargent wrote, were "generally wanting the essential stamina of soldiers. Picked up and recruited from the offscourgings of large towns and cities; enervated by idleness, debaucheries and every species of vice, it was impossible they could have been made competent to the arduous duties of Indian warfare. An extraordinary aversion to service was also conspicuous among them and demonstrated by the most repeated desertions, in many instances to the very foe we were to combat. The late period at which they had been brought into the field left no leisure or opportunity to discipline them. They were, moreover, badly clothed, badly paid and badly fed." St. Clair, Sargent added, "was worn down by the fatigues before the commencement of the campaign."

At this point—it was now September and already getting cold—Washington and Knox should have put a halt to the expedition, sent the six-month levies home, sought out a new, more energetic general, and begun training a real little army. Anyone with even a trace of good sense could see that this was a disaster in the making. And yet Washington persisted; he badgered St. Clair to advance with greater speed.

Predictably, in a campaign where everything went wrong, the commanding general and his second in command didn't get along. Butler, an old frontier fighter, didn't think much of St. Clair and doubted he knew very much about "managing Indians." St. Clair said he thought that Butler was "soured and disgusted." They fell out over the line of march. St. Clair wanted to cut two parallel roadways, separated by more than one hundred yards, through the forests. Using that method, the army moved little more than a mile a day. Butler countermanded St. Clair's orders and pushed ahead with a single roadway, twelve feet wide, following the Braddock example. But to hack their way through the wilderness, the army needed tools, and—surely no surprise—they had hardly any. "The provision of tools . . . has been scanty in the extreme," Sargent wrote in his diary. "Eighty axes only can be furnished by the quartermaster, and of these thirteen are borrowed from the troops, who are but ill supplied for this season of the year. Besides the axes, are one saw and one frow [a cleaving tool]. Of spades and mattocks [picks] we have sufficient." The light tents, made of coarse muslin, leaked. Knox had ordered them to save money. Food was in short supply, and St. Clair was forced to ration flour.

Major Denny joined St. Clair on October 1, taking up his duties as aide-de-camp. The general's "family" consisted of Sargent, Denny, and the Viscount de Malartie, "a young Frenchman . . . in character of volunteer aid." Hours before he joined, Denny discovered, "upward of one hundred horses have been stolen, supposed by the enemy, from the vicinity of Fort Washington, some of them cut from their fastenings under the walls of the fort." Days after joining, he reported "a number of the militia are reported to have deserted already." Two deserters, John Oneil and John Wade, "two Irishmen who professed former loyalty to the king," according to Sword, "made straight for Detroit after abandoning the American army, carrying with them important military information."

The army moved out of Fort Hamilton on the Great Miami River on October 4. "Fair and pleasant weather," wrote Sargent, as the troops— 2,500 of them—moved slowly but steadily north, towards Indian Country—and Little Turtle. "We passed an old Indian camp yesterday," Sargent wrote on the tenth, "and several today, and have observed some fresh tracks. . . . The country rich, level and well watered . . . the woods open and timber good . . . "

By October 21, the army was camped at another newly built stockade, called Fort Jefferson, near what is now Greenville, Ohio, a typical square structure with bastions at each corner. For the final move against Kekionga and Little Turtle, St. Clair ordered most of the horses and two pieces of artillery to be left behind, inside the fort, with its invalid garrison of ninety men. Butler dropped by to ask permission to take one thousand men, the pick of the army, and move quickly against the enemy camp before the weather—now cold, with ice beginning to form—got worse. St. Clair said "he had liked to have laughed in his face."

On the twenty-second, Denny reported, St. Clair cut the flour ration, for making bread, to half a pound a day. But he increased the allotment of beef to make up for it: "This, however, would not satify militia; twenty of them deserted last night, and some more this morning."

In desperation, St. Clair, once again in pain with attacks of gout, ordered the death penalty for two artillerymen caught trying to desert and for one of the levies for trying to shoot one of his comrades. They were hanged on the twenty-third in front of the entire army. "Examples (in terrorem) are necessary," Sargent said. "Consult the orderly book," St. Clair noted in his narrative, "[it] may be truly called a book of pains and penalties."

The army, including sixty camp followers—women and children—began its march to destruction at 9 A.M. on October 24. St. Clair was suffering badly in both his left arm and hand. "Calm and cloudy," wrote Sargent, with mild weather. During the day, the army for the first time came across significant evidence of the unseen Indian enemy. "Many new and old camps have been observed," said Sargent. "The ashes at some of them were warm upon our arrival, and we are probably now upon the last hunting grounds of the Indians." By the twenty-sixth, he wrote, "the commander-in-chief very ill."

By now, Indians were lurking all around the army, picking off stragglers as opportunities arose. "We had a soldier killed and scalped this morning three miles from camp," Sargent wrote on the twenty-eighth. One of the sentries, said Denny the same day, "imagined that he saw an Indian, and fired three times at some object." The regulars, Denny observed, "are tolerably well-disciplined" but the levies "take great liberties. This morning, there was a constant firing kept up round the camp, notwithstanding it is known there is a general order against it . . . In fact, at present they [the levies] are more troublesome and far inferior to the militia."

On the thirty-first, shortly after breakfasting with Lieutenant Colonel William Oldham, commanding the militia, St. Clair was told that as many as half the militiamen had deserted (about one hundred of them, in fact), "and that they had declared their intention to plunder the convoy" that was bringing food and supplies to the hungry army. He ordered the regulars from the First Regiment, under Major John Hamtramck, "to march immediately, with the double view of securing the provisions, which was of the utmost consequence. . . ." That meant, Sargent wrote, "that we are hereby deprived for a time of a corps of 300 effective men (effective from the experience of the officers and the opportunities they have had for discipline) which must be estimated at the best in the service."

All the troops that remained—regulars, levies, and militia, about fifteen hundred men—were increasingly restless, with many of the levies maintaining that their enlistments had expired and that they should be discharged and allowed to go home. "Our prospects are gloomy," wrote Sargent. "But the general is compelled to move on, as the only chance of continuing our little army."

Yet St. Clair still regarded the Indian threat to be insignificant. "The few Indians that have been seen were hunters only, who we fell upon by accident," he wrote to Knox. The extraordinary fact is that not once during the entire expedition did St. Clair send out scouts to measure his enemy's strength. As for "a knowledge of the collected force of the enemy, of this we were perfectly ignorant," Denny pointed out.

But Little Turtle and Blue Jacket knew all about their enemy's strength. Once again, they were making plans—and this time they would meet the Americans with more than one thousand warriors. At a council preceding the battle, Girty brought the warriors to their feet with a dramatic presentation. He pulled a white egg from his pocket, saying, "This represents the whites coming towards us, while my fingers encircling it represent our brotherhood of Indians here. What will be the outcome when they meet? See!" Then he crushed the shell and watched as the egg dripped on the ground. Girty said later that he had never seen Indians "in greater heart to meet their enemy."

St. Clair's condition continued to deteriorate. Lieutenant Colonel William Darke of the levies reported that he had to be moved on a litter, "like a corpse between two horses." The army didn't move at all on November 1, ostensibly to give St. Clair time to write dispatches. The real reason was St. Clair's discomfort.

The march was resumed the next day, following an old Indian path. "The first four miles very flat and wet," Denny wrote. Worse, it began snowing. Disaster was now not very far away. The army marched another nine miles on the third, and prepared to make camp on dry land in deep woods near a shallow stream. But Adjutant Denny and Quartermaster Hodgdon urged St. Clair to move on to a new camp two miles farther on, where the water was better. "It was later than usual when the army reached the ground this evening," Denny wrote, "and the men much fatigued prevented the General from having some works of defense immediately erected . . . the high ground barely sufficient to encamp the army; lines rather contracted." ("Be sure to fortify your camp," Washington had told St. Clair. Sound advice, events would soon prove.) So contracted, in fact, that the Kentucky militia was forced to make an advance camp on a bluff seventy yards west of the main camp and on the other side of the shallow Wabash River. The Indians instinctively understood what was happening: the fatigued Americans were drawing together in two great blue bull's-eyes. "So auspicious were the signs," reported Eckert, "that many of the warriors, especially the Sacs, Winnebagoes and Kickapoos, wished to leap to the attack immediately, but Michikiniqua [Little Turtle] and Blue

Jacket stayed them." Instead, under cover of night, they began encircling the sleeping American army: Wyandots on the right; Shawnees, Miamis, and Delawares in the center; Ottawas, Chippewas, and Potawatomis on the right.

Richard Butler, St. Clair's second in command, was unable to sleep. Pacing his tent, he told some comrades, "Let us eat, drink and be merry, as tomorrow we may die."

Little Turtle launched his attack just before dawn against the exposed militia camp. The Indians, whooping their war cries, fell on the unprepared Kentucky militiamen. One of them, Robert Bradshaw, managed to get off one shot with his rifle before the Indians were upon him. He and the rest of the militiamen fled in terror, seeking to gain safe ground with the rest of the army across the shallow waters of the Wabash River. In a matter of minutes, said Sword in his campaign history, the entire 270-man militia force had scattered.

Sargent said that "the firing of the enemy was preceded for about five minutes by the Indian yell, the first I had ever heard. Not terrible, as has been represented, but more resembling an infinitude of horse's bells suddenly opening to you than any other sound I could compare it to." It may not have scared Sargent, but it seems to have scared almost everyone else. "The resistance of the militia," Sargent said, "deserves not the name of defense, but should be branded as the most ignominious flight. . . . Dashing 'helter-skelter' into our camp they threw the battalions, not then quite formed, into some confusion. . . . During the whole action, their conduct was cowardly in the most shameful degree." Some of the militiamen took the opportunity the chaos supplied to loot officers' tents.

Poor St. Clair, out of uniform in a coarse coat and a huge three-cornered cocked hat, tried to rally his troops, but he had trouble mounting a horse to do the job. "The first I attempted to mount," he said in his narrative, "was a young horse, and the firing alarmed him so much, that I was not able to accomplish it, though there were three or four people assisting me . . . I had just moved to a place where I could have some advantage of the ground, when the beast was shot through the head, and the boy that was leading him up, through the arm." He tried to get on another horse, but it, too, along with one of Sargent's servants, was killed. "I could wait no longer," he said, "my pains were forgotten, and for a considerable time I could walk with a degree of ease and alertness that surprised everybody."

The little army's six cannon—three six-pounders and three three-pounders—were wheeled into line, and began firing at the Indian attackers. But the guns were aimed too high, and the round shot and canister simply whistled over the Indians' heads.

"The enemy from the front filed off to the right and left, and completely surrounded the camp," said Denny. They "killed and cut off nearly all the guards, and approached close to the lines. They advanced from one tree, log, or stump to another, under cover of the smoke of our fire. The artillery and musketry made a tremendous noise, but did little execution. The Indians seemed to brave everything, and when fairly fixed around us they made no noise other than their fire, which they kept up very constant and which seldom failed to tell, although scarcely heard."

Lieutenant Colonel George Gibson shouted to his levies, "Fight them! Fight them!" until a bullet severed his spine.

The left flank, said Denny, gave way first, "probably from the nature of the ground. The enemy got possession of that part of the encampment, but it being pretty clear ground, they were too much exposed and were soon repulsed."

Ten days before the battle, St. Clair had issued a general order saying that "savages if violently attacked will always break and give way—and when once broke, for the want of discipline, will never rally." Now he got his chance to prove his general order, one way or another. He ordered a bayonet charge. But the Viscount de Malartie, his chief aide, was shot, and failed to get through to deliver the order. Other officers, William Darke among them, took it upon themselves to charge the Indians, bayonets fixed. "The battalions in the rear charged several times," said Denny, "and forced the savages from their shelter, but they always turned with the battalions and fired upon them back; indeed they seemed not to fear anything we could do. They could skip out of the reach of the bayonet and return, as they pleased. The ground was literally covered with the dead. The wounded were taken to the center, where it was thought most safe, and . . . crowded together."

Darke, with three hundred men, many of them Second Regiment regulars, actually made it across the shallow river and, circling from the south, turned the Indian flank. That would have been something of a triumph in a battle with European-style troops. But the Indians simply spread out, and attacked the spot in the main camp's lines that Darke had opened up to make his charge. They swarmed over the American position, scalping the wounded and throwing them on the burning camp fires. Not far away, other Indians broke through to the center of the American position and attacked the camp followers. Women, a young officer said, lay scattered

General Arthur St. Clair's defeat, shown in an1842 lithograph. (Library of Congress collections)

about, "some of them cut in two, their boobies cut off, and burning with a number of our officers on our own fires."

Darke received a flesh wound and his son was shot in the face. Butler was badly wounded; propped up against a tree, he held off swarming Indians with his pistols as long as he could. His skull was crushed by a tomahawk; later, his heart was cut out and eaten by victorious Indians.

"As our lines were deserted the Indians contracted theirs," said Denny, "until their shot centred from all points, and now meeting with little opposition, took more deliberate aim and did great execution. Exposed to a cross fire, men and officers were seen falling in every direction. The distress too of the wounded made the scene such as scarcely can be conceived. Delay was death . . . there was no alternative."

The survivors began a retreat at about 9 A.M., perhaps three hours after the fighting had begun. "A few officers put themselves in front, the men followed, the enemy gave way, and perhaps not being aware of the design, we were for a few moments left undisturbed," Denny said.

"We pushed out from the left of the rear line," Sargent wrote, "sacrificing our artillery and baggage; and, with them, we were compelled to leave some of our wounded." St. Clair, piled aboard a packhorse, joined the retreat. Sargent had no doubt that the Indians "had it in their power to have cut us off, almost to a man." But they preferred to occupy the battlefield, where, said Sword, "tragic consequences" [were] enacted.

"Heads, body extremities and sexual organs were severed and mutilated. Persons still living were sometimes tossed on camp fires to burn in excruciating pain. At least one female captive was spread-eagled, and then stakes 'as thick as a person's arm' were driven through her body."

"The conduct of the army after quitting the ground was in a most supreme degree disgraceful," said Sargent, who was wounded in the action. "Arms, ammunition and accoutrements were almost all thrown away, and even the officers in some instances divested themselves of their fusees. . . ."

"The road for miles was covered with firelocks, cartridge boxes and regimentals," said Denny.

The remains of the shattered army reached Fort Jefferson, twenty-nine miles from the battlefield, by seven in the evening. "Here," said Sargent, "we met the First United States Regiment," the best troops in the army, still looking for the missing food convoy. They pushed on, still fearful of an Indian attack, and arrived at Fort Washington by noon on the eighth. The regulars from the First and Second regiments maintained some form of discipline, but, said Sargent, "the levies were lost forever."

When the Americans began counting their dead, wounded, and missing, they discovered, to their horror, that they had lost more than half of their army. It remains the worst defeat Indians ever inflicted on an American army, far worse than Custer's loss at the Little Bighorn. Denny figured that of the 1,400 men who took part in the action, only 500 escaped uninjured. More than 630 men were either dead or missing. Of the 124 commissioned officers involved in the brief battle, 69 were dead, wounded, or missing.

A Boston broadside made no excuses for the defeat:

> A Horrid Fight there hap'd of late,
> The Fourth Day of November,
> When a Vast Number Met their Fate.
> We all shall well remember,
> 'Twas over renown'd Ohio land,
> And fatal prov'd of old,

> Bad to relate! Our federal band,
> Were slain by Indians bold!

The Indians lost twenty-one killed and forty wounded. For Little Turtle and Blue Jacket, hard upon their defeat of General Harmar, it was one of the most lopsided battles in American history. And yet no one on the American side gave them any credit for what they had done. Knox, a fool to the very end, wrote St. Clair on December 23 and said, "Your misfortune, to be sure, has been great and unexpected but, sir, it was one of those incidents which sometimes happen in human affairs, which could not, under existing circumstances, have been prevented. . . . [B]oth your reputation, and the reputation of the troops under your command are unimpeached . . . "

But St. Clair's career was over; his reputation was destroyed, and it would take Anthony Wayne, a fighting general, to restore the army's reputation. St. Clair spent his declining years in genteel poverty, killed at the age of eighty-four when he was thrown from a pony wagon near his home at Laurel Hill in western Pennsylvania.

✦

President Washington finally got lucky in choosing a third commander to take on the surging tribes in the Old Northwest. The new man, Anthony Wayne, vigorous at forty-seven years of age, was the general he should have chosen in the first place. Wayne's critics argued he was too emotional, too cantankerous for the job. But Wayne was a fighter. Moreover, mired in debt, he needed the job.

He took command of the western army in 1792, only to find his total strength was forty recruits and a handful of dragoons. He increased the army's strength to twelve hundred by April of 1793, exercising fierce discipline (he executed five deserters in the fall of 1792 alone). He called his army the Legion of the United States and dressed them in fancy uniforms. But he also taught them how to maneuver and, best of all, how to shoot. He and his army occupied the site of St. Clair's defeat on Christmas Day, 1793, and finally met Little Turtle in the decisive battle—surely the most lastingly significant battle fought by Native Americans—at a place called Fallen Timbers on August 20, 1794. This time, the Indians lost, and were forced to give up much of their land in the Treaty of Greenville in 1795. On July 11, 1796, the American flag was finally raised over Detroit.

Plains Indians fought on into the middle of the nineteenth century, and those anticlimactic battles are better known to most Americans. But the sad fate of the American Indian had been decided years earlier, in the middle heartland of America.

THREE

British and French Generals and Their Disastrous Efforts to Restore Slavery to Haiti (1791–1804)

At the height of a lightning-filled tropical storm on August 22, 1791, thousands of black slaves led by the gigantic voodoo priest, Boukmann, a fugitive from Jamaica, rose in rebellion near Le Cap François, Haiti's largest city. The rebellion spread like wildfire, involving one hundred thousand slaves in the Northern Province alone. White planters were dragged from their homes and shot. Young children were impaled on the ends of bayonets, and carried at the heads of the ragged slave columns.

The smoke from the blazing plantations drifted so far out to sea that it could be seen in the Bermudas.

Between 1791, when history's only successful slave rebellion began, and 1804, when the black armies triumphed, Haiti, the world's richest colony, was destroyed. And so were tens of thousands of troops from Europe. First the British, at the urging of their prime minister, William Pitt (the Younger), and then the French, under orders from the great Napoléon himself, sent soldiers to win control of this chaotic place; together, they lost an astonishing 150,000 men, many (but nowhere near all) to the dreaded "black vomit"—yellow fever. It was worse for the Haitians themselves; by the time the fighting ended, more than 200,000 of them had died.

What happened two hundred years ago reverberates down through the years; Haiti is a poor, cruel, divided nation, and it was these bloody events that made it that way.

In 1790, Saint-Domingue, the French colony that became Haiti (the name we will use, for simplicity's sake), produced vast quantities of sugar

60

from plantations along the coast, coffee from newer plantations higher in the mountains, along with cotton and indigo dye. The French employed more than six hundred ships and fifteen thousand seamen to haul the stuff home to Bordeaux. Moreover, it was these oceanic seamen who provided the bulk of the sailors for the French navy in time of war. The trade flowing from this tiny French colony "was as great as that of the entire United States," according to Michael Duffy, the West Indies historian.

The British had their own prize colony, Jamaica. They used seven hundred ships (smaller, generally, than the French ships) and fourteen thousand seamen to bring their goods back to London, Liverpool, and Bristol.

When Britain and France went to war—and they were at war, off and on, most of the time during these years—the fighting inevitably switched to both Haiti and Jamaica and more than a dozen other islands; each side sought to gain advantage, so that newly captured islands could be used as bargaining chips when the peace talks began.

What made these islands so prosperous was the endless supply of cheap slave labor. Almost as many ships were used to haul slaves as were used to transport the product of their labor. In one year alone, 1787, British slavers transported thirty-eight thousand Negroes from Africa to the West Indies; the French, twenty thousand. These slaves made thousands of plantation owners and absentee landlords back home in France and Great Britain rich. Nothing frightened white planters more than the thought that the black slaves might rise up and throw off their yoke.

Why did the greatest of all slave rebellions begin in Haiti? Plantation life in Haiti was cruel, even by slave-economy standards. But Haiti's slaves had never shown very much in the way of aggressive behavior prior to 1791. The explanation for why they rose then almost surely lies in the highly symbolic importance of the French Revolution. The Bastille had fallen on July 14, 1789. The Declaration of the Rights of Man, promising "liberty, property security, and resistance to oppression," was promulgated on August 26.

Haiti was a racist society seething with discontent, where talk about "resistance to oppression" provided a real sting.

"Whites, mulattos, and blacks loathed each other," the historian Paul Fregosi wrote. "The poor whites couldn't stand the rich whites, the rich whites despised the poor whites, the middle-class whites were jealous of the aristocratic whites, the whites born in France looked down upon the locally-born whites, mulattos envied the whites, despised the blacks and were despised by the whites; free Negroes brutalized those who were still slaves, Haitian-born blacks regarded those from Africa as savages. Everyone—quite rightly—lived in terror of everyone else. . . . Haiti was hell, but Haiti was rich."

Word of what was happening in France had seeped slowly into the consciousness of the island's slaves. One of them, François-Dominique Toussaint, already forty-five years old, was in charge of the livestock at the prosperous Breda plantation, just a mile or two from Le Cap, where he had been taught to read. He knew Caesar's *Commentaries* and the Abbé Raynal's work on the East and West Indies. He could even reel off long stretches of scrambled Latin.

"They [the slaves] had heard of the revolution and had construed it in their own image: the white slaves in France had risen, and killed their masters, and were now enjoying the fruits of the earth," wrote the Marxist historian (and part-time cricket correspondent) C. L. R. James in the best-known (and sometimes the most impenetrable) of all the books dealing with the Haitian revolution, *The Black Jacobins.*

Toussaint—who was "small, ugly and ill-shaped," according to James—watched with interest as the surrounding plantations were set afire in 1791. Fearing for their safety, he led his kindly master, Bayou de Libertas, and his mistress to safety in Le Cap. And then he climbed on Bel-Argent, his horse—all his horses were called Bel-Argent—and rode off to war, in time changing his name to Toussaint-Louverture. This "gilded African," as Napoléon contemptuously called him, this absolutely extraordinary human being, would become the greatest black general in modern history.

More than forty thousand slaves, many of them naked, armed with sticks and spears, invested Le Cap, where ten thousand whites—*grands blancs* and *petits blancs*—huddled for safety. In Port-au-Prince, the colony's second city, more than four thousand mulattoes were poised to mount an assault.

The grands blancs fighting for their lives were the great landowners, a lazy and self-indulgent class. The petits blancs were the plantation overseers, the shopkeepers, the hangers-on. They hated almost everyone else, especially the mulattoes. By most accounts, by 1790 there were 24,000 whites in the colony, both grand and petit, 20,000 mulattoes and free slaves, and 450,000 slaves.

Within days of the August 22 uprising, two thousand whites had been killed, 180 sugar plantations and 900 coffee plantations destroyed, and two million francs' worth of damage inflicted. And then, in a three-week counterattack, the whites struck back, killing as many as fifteen thousand slaves and mulattoes. What followed was chaos, a kind of three-way civil war, in which whites, blacks, and mulattoes seemed to be all fighting each other.

Toussaint, though, was quietly building an army. Alone among all the black leaders, Toussaint early on saw the need for military discipline and organization. James said he developed "a method of attack based on their [the blacks'] overwhelming numerical superiority. They did not rush forward in mass formation like fanatics. They placed themselves in groups, choosing wooded spots in such a way as to envelop their enemy, seeking to crush him by weight of numbers. They carried out these preliminary maneuvers in dead silence, while their priests (the black ones) chanted the wanga, and the women and children danced in a frenzy. When these had reached the necessary height of excitement the fighters attacked. If they met with resistance they retired without exhausting themselves, but at the slightest hesitation in the defence they became extremely bold and, rushing up to the cannon, swarmed all over the opponents."

Prior to the Revolution in France, the colonial governors sent from Paris had always been partners with the rich planters. They ruled the colony with the backing of a small garrison of regular French soldiers and a small militia formed of white planters and overseers. Now, however, the rich whites on the island had to contend with Léger Félicité Sonthonax, the new man sent from Paris. He openly aligned himself with the rebellious slaves, even abolishing slavery in the Northern Province. Sonthonax, a true revolutionary, opposed his own wealthy countrymen, believing that they held royalist sympathies. Feeling themselves abandoned and fearing for their future, the French planters in Haiti appealed to British authorities in Jamaica, just a daylong sail across the Jamaica Channel, for help. They sensed, correctly, that the English colonial authorities, still closely allied with their white planters, with their three hundred thousand slaves, would be sympathetic to their plight and worried that the terror might begin island-hopping.

In London, William Pitt and his chief war minister, Henry Dundas, preparing for war with France—it would last, on and off, until Napoléon's final defeat at Waterloo in 1815—considered the opportunities. They already had six thousand troops in the Caribbean, and more were on the way. They figured they could make a couple of points. First, they could protect their own interests in Jamaica and elsewhere by cutting off the slave rebellion in Haiti. Second, and maybe even more important, they believed they could pluck off a number of ripe French possessions, Haiti chief among them, to serve as valuable bargaining chips at the peace conference table.

France declared war against Britain on February 1, 1793, a war that would be fought in Europe and around the world. As usual, the rich colonies in the West Indies would play a key role. Pitt and Dundas immediately set about preparing an expedition for the Caribbean that would "provide Britain's profit from the war," according to the historian Michael Duffy. "It was a fairly well established fact that the proper time to send an expedition to the West Indies was in late September, so as to arrive in the Caribbean in early November, at the end of the sickly season and with six clear months ahead for active campaigning."

That's what Dundas, the energetic Scot, now set out to do. But he only had two deputies, and he was also in charge of everything in Scotland, domestic affairs in England, policy matters in India, and finances for the Royal Navy (he was the treasurer). On top of that, he was Pitt's chief spokesman in the House of Commons. He admitted that taking on a war meant he was "rather overloaded." But he never doubted he was the man for the job.

"Yet," wrote Sir John Fortescue in his massive history of the British army, "so profoundly ignorant was Dundas of war that he was not even conscious of his own ignorance."

Undeterred, Dundas adopted an ambitious plan. The British government now heeded those voices from Jamaica, and agreed to consider taking Haiti under British protection. London told its commanders in Jamaica to get ready for war, and told the British garrison at Barbados to attack the French on Tobago, Saint Lucia, Guadeloupe, and Marie Galante.

Even before the expedition could get under way from England, the governor of Jamaica jumped the gun and sent a small squadron of frigates and six hundred men—the Thirteenth Foot, the flank companies of the Forty-ninth, a regiment of light dragoons and some artillerymen with three guns—to take possession of Haiti. They landed at Jérémie on September 20 and were greeted with cries of "Vivent les Anglais!" from the French planters and a twenty-one-gun salute. In his opening proclamation, the British commander, Lieutenant Colonel John Whitelocke, tried to convince the white colonists that "the small size of his army was deliberately designed to test their goodwill before he proceeded with a greater force to conquer the colony." It is not known how many of them bought the story. Whitelocke's first sortie wasn't encouraging; he attempted a landing at Tiburon on October 4 and was driven off, with two causalties, by spirited gunfire.

The British had achieved a greater success a few days earlier, on September 22, without firing a shot. The great naval base, Mole St. Nicolas, along with all of its guns, ammunition and stores, was handed over to Commodore John Ford by the city's white inhabitants. London was so excited when it heard the good news it fired off the cannon in the Tower of London.

But poor Whitelocke didn't have enough men to do the job. Typical was the day he sent 50 men to take control of Saint-Marc, below Gonaïves, and found 150 French troops in the town square, quite unprepared to put down their arms. They were finally led off to captivity at gunpoint, but it had been a tense moment.

With so few troops, the British had to use bluff, and sometimes try bribery. Commodore Ford sailed into Port-au-Prince twice, each time demanding Sonthonax's surrender. Twice, Sonthonax refused. Whitelocke offered Sonthonax's able general, Etienne Maynard-Bizefranc Laveaux, a bribe to give up Port-de-Paix, just east of the Mole on the north coast. Laveaux was so outraged he challenged Whitelocke to a duel.

The French colonists who had been so warm to welcome the British troops now began to despair. "They had capitulated upon condition that they should be protected," wrote Sir John, who never discussed a West Indian expedition in any condition other than apoplexy. "But this was impossible without more troops." The result, he said, was that these white colonists "began to suspect they had been deceived."

"A campaign without soldiers was not going to succeed," the historian David Geggus wrote.

But help was on the way. Dundas had finally offered command of the Caribbean expedition to Lieutenant General Charles Grey. He was a good choice; for Grey, unlike Braddock, was a fighting general, nicknamed "No-flint Grey" for ordering his men to remove the flints from their muskets in preparation for a bayonet charge against Americans in the War for Independence. Though sixty-four years old, he was still robust and well-qualified to command the expedition. The Admiralty gave the naval command to Vice Admiral Sir John Jervis, another good choice. He and Grey were old friends and would work together in harmony.

The original idea was that Grey would take fourteen complete regiments and parts—the flank companies—of fourteen more with him. He would also be reinforced by troops serving in the West Indies, though many of them already were dying from yellow fever and other diseases. But when the expedition finally sailed on November 26, 1793, it was eight weeks behind schedule and had not much more than half of its projected strength—seven thousand against thirteen thousand. It "was the result of discreditable oversight and want of decision," said Duffy. Eight of Grey's battalions had been taken away from him, and sent off on an unnecessary errand to Europe.

There was simply no excuse for being so late, fumed Sir John Fortescue, for tardiness flew in the face "of warnings and entreaties reiterated for a full century by governors, generals and admirals in the West Indies."

Because he was so late in getting started, Grey was given a choice—reinforce and secure Haiti or sail to windward and attack Martinique. Grey replied to Dundas that if he sent a detachment to Haiti, he would be too weak to attack Martinique, "and that if he sailed to St. Domingue with his whole force he could never in the teeth of the trade-wind beat back to Martinique." Dundas, Sir John wrote, never understood the role of the trade winds in the West Indies.

It is possible, some historians have insisted, that if Grey had taken his full force to Haiti as soon as he arrived in the Caribbean he might have been able to win control of the island and save its rich plantation economy. Others have said it was already too late, because, by 1793, the black insurgents had concluded they would never again accept servitude.

No one will ever know, for on February 4, 1794, Grey sailed from Barbados with seven thousand men to attack an easier target, Martinique. After fierce fighting, much of it with "no flints," Grey prevailed. The garrison surrendered on March 23. Grey then moved against nearby Saint Lucia, and won an easy success, without the loss of a man. He added Guadeloupe to his string of victories in May.

With the fighting in the Windwards completed, Grey ordered reinforcements sent to Whitelocke's beleaguered detachment in Haiti. They arrived at the naval base, the Mole, on May 19—sixteen hundred men in all under the command of Major General John Whyte.

It was a calamitous mistake to continue the operation in Haiti, Sir John Fortescue argued. Even in its peaceful days, he said, Haiti was "no small change to make over and to accept by a stroke of the pen." But now, in 1794, "the country was in a hideous state of anarchy, torn asunder by the most furious passions of caste, color, and political fanaticism. Of the white proprietors . . . not a few had perished by massacre, and fully half had fled across the sea." The only semblance of power and authority were in the hands of the French commissioner, Sonthonax, with his garrison of 6,000 regular troops from France (they had been there all along), plus about 14,000 white militia "and a band of desperate ruffians of all colors, making in all about 25,000 more or less disciplined and organized men."

But Sonthonax couldn't depend on all, or even most, of his regulars. Less than half of them stood by him; the rest favored the French planters and went over to join the British cause. He wasn't even sure about the slaves. In an effort to ensure their loyalty, Sonthonax issued an emancipation proclamation for the whole colony. As a result, thousands of black men headed into the mountains to join their armed brothers in freedom. "Thus," said Sir John, "the most formidable of all the forces in Haiti [the black insurgents] were multiplied many-fold at the very moment of the British occupation." These men formed the nucleus of the force that later defied and defeated the best troops of Napoléon himself.

Still, Whyte, who succeeded Whitelocke, now had an army that numbered five thousand regulars and a militia of French planters led by Baron de Montalambert. Hovering offshore was Commodore Ford's powerful naval squadron: four ships of the line, three frigates, and three sloops. With this considerable force at their disposal, the British commanders sat down at the Mole, their naval base, to decide what to do next. This, after all, was the time. The choice, essentially, was to attack Le Cap and Port-de-Paix, the French military and naval bastions on the north shore, or the colony's commercial center, Port-au-Prince, far to the south. Drawn by dreams of booty—the harbor at Port-au-Prince was filled with forty-five fully loaded merchant ships—they marched for money. "Any principle of national policy never entered into [their] heads," Thomas Maitland complained later to his superiors in London. Their decision to attack Port-au-Prince and those forty-five ships in the harbor was "contrary to every idea of military principle," said Maitland, who would be Britain's last general in Haiti.

Whyte captured the town, but the republican troops managed to slip away quietly, perhaps with the help of General Whyte in return for promising they wouldn't burn the ships or set the town on fire. Whyte made no effort to run them down, presumably too busy in securing his prize money from all those captured merchant ships to get on with the war.

(Whyte wasn't alone in aggressive cupidity. Grey felt that by taking command of the expedition to these rich islands he would finally make a fortune for himself and his large family. He granted a captaincy to his seventeen-year-old son, William, and sent two more of his sons, Henry and Thomas, home with victory dispatches, guaranteeing their promotions. Another son, George, won quick advancement in the navy. Even Grey's twelve-year-old son, Edward, still at home in England, was provided for; he was given half the profits from the Collector of Customs at Fort Royal, in Martinique. Almost everyone in the family won some kind of administrative appointment, carrying with it a handsome payment for little or no work.)

Forced to flee from Port-au-Prince, Sonthonax and the French republicans were also feeling pressure in the north. There, an army of fourteen thousand Spaniards, Britain's allies, led by Captain-General Joaquin García y Moreno, marched from the eastern section of the island, which they controlled, for Le Cap. Spain ultimately would hold most of the north except for Le Cap, which was held by the republicans, and the Mole, the British stronghold.

Toussaint, for reasons never made very clear by Toussaint or anybody else, joined the Spanish cause, accepting a commission in the Spanish army and becoming a knight in the Order of Isabella. He led his own black army, and won crucial victories. "There can be no doubt about his skillful fighting ability. Within a short period his forces had conquered Dondon [seizing an armory loaded with muskets and gunpowder], La Marmelade, Plaisance, and Gonaïves," the historian Thomas Ott wrote. Possessing Gonaïves, at the southeastern corner of the northern peninsula, gave Toussaint an outlet to the Bight of Léogâne (or, sometimes, the Gulf of Gonaïves) and severed the French forces, Laveaux and Sonthonax commanding in the north, the mulatto André Rigaud commanding in the south.

In May of 1794, in another of his surprising switches, Toussaint abandoned the Spanish and joined the French republicans. No one has ever explained that satisfactorily, either. At San Raphael on May 6, he ambushed the Spanish as they emerged from church, killing dozens of them before fleeing to Gonaïves. His loyal troops—four thousand of them—came with him, and soon he was pushing his old comrades, the Spaniards, back in the direction from which they had come.

To the south, Rigaud, who had served with French troops in the American Revolution, was giving serious problems to the British commanders. He stormed Léogâne and forced its British defenders to run for the walls of Port-au-Prince. He then attacked the capital, but was turned away. Undeterred, he sailed with his own little fleet and three thousand men "of all descriptions," and fell on Tiburon on Christmas Day. He blew up a small armed vessel in the harbor with a red-hot shot and then turned his guns, including a huge mortar that fired a fifty-pound shell, on the fort in the town. The fort was garrisoned by a detachment of black troops and some regulars from the Twenty-third Foot. The commander, a Lieutenant Bradford, led his men, many of them wounded, out of the fort and tried to make his way to Jérémie. Sir John Fortescue reckoned that three hundred men were killed or wounded and that most of the survivors were massacred. "The war," he said, "was rapidly becoming a savage contest in which quarter was neither given nor taken."

As Grey departed, rich but physically drained by repeated bouts with dysentery, Whyte malingered in the swampy Haitian capital. While his troops sat idle, the mosquitoes went about their deadly work. Within two months, forty officers and six hundred men were dead from yellow fever, the cost of camping in such a pestilential place.

Indeed, the cost in life throughout the West Indies was appalling. "It is to be gathered," Sir John said, "that of Grey's original seven thousand men at least five thousand had perished. The losses of the navy also were enormous, but it is impossible to reckon them even approximately. The transport vessels suffered even more severely than the men-of-war, their casualties being reckoned at forty-six masters and eleven hundred men dead, chiefly of yellow fever." Added all together, Sir John reckoned—he did a lot of reckoning—"it is probably beneath the mark to say that twelve thousand Englishmen were buried in the West Indies in 1794."

They had set out, he said, to destroy the power of France "in these pestilent islands . . . only to discover, when it was too late, that they practically destroyed the British army."

Surely that's an exaggeration, for Pitt and Dundas were now prepared to try it all over again—with an even bigger expedition. They called it "the great push." It would become, at the time, the largest overseas expedition Britain had ever assembled.

With Spain out of the war—she handed over Santo Domingo, the eastern part of the island, to France—Dundas saw even greater possibilities. Santo Domingo was twice as large as Haiti, and almost entirely undeveloped. The whole island, Dundas figured, could be subdued in four months by a naval blockade and an attack by twelve thousand troops.

Dundas set to work to pull the expedition together. "The countryside around Southampton [in England] and Cork [in Ireland] blazed with red uniforms, and bell tents mushroomed row upon row in farmers' fields, as an army of 30,000 men was assembled," David Geggus wrote. Though shipping was short, Dundas managed to round up two hundred vessels to carry the troops. Officers in the West Indies were instructed to build barracks and hospitals, and horses were purchased in the United States.

Grey had sailed off with some of Britain's finest soldiers. His successor, Major General Ralph Abercromby, a tough, sixty-year-old Scot in his first major command, would lead poorly disciplined, inexperienced troops. The naval command was given to Rear Admiral Hugh Cloberry Christian, a transport specialist.

Picking the commanders was one thing; rounding up the troops was another. By now, almost everyone knew that the West Indies was a killing ground. Even George III recognized that; when asked to permit his three thousand royal footguards to join the expedition, he said no. In Dublin and Cork, soldiers from the 104th, 105th, 111th, and 113th regiments rioted in the streets when they heard they were being sent to the Caribbean.

Dundas was forced to turn to mercenaries in Europe to make up the shortfall. But they didn't like the idea any better than the British regulars in Ireland. More than a third of the Prince of Salm's regiment deserted on their way to embarkation. Those who remained had to be merged with other foreign troops to form what was called—wonderfully English—the Royal Foreigners. Dundas was also forced to pad the rolls with cavalrymen who could not be ordered to fight on foot, but who generally lacked mounts to fight any other way.

Looking back, Sir John Fortescue viewed it all, once again, with apoplectic distaste. "A service," he wrote, "which calls men to certain and ignoble destruction without offering a chance of honour, or even the comforting sense that death may be of benefit to their country—such a service is not calculated to conciliate affection." The troops, he concluded, were "victims of imbecility."

The expedition finally set sail from Portsmouth on November 16, a sight so breathtakingly beautiful that thousands of people lined the shore to watch it. The armada stood down channel with a light breeze and every stitch of canvas set.

Once round the Isle of Wight, the fleet spread out—8 ships of the line and 10 smaller warships escorting 110 transports (carrying 18,742 soldiers), along with 25 ships carrying provisions and guns, shot, and powder. And then disaster—recalling the destruction of the Spanish armada—struck. The wind changed to the southwest, roaring up to the force of a hurricane—so strong it blew a sentinel off the ramparts at Portsmouth citadel. When dawn broke, Admiral Christian could see that five of his ships were ashore and breaking up on Chesil Beach alone. Other ships ran aground for miles up and down the coast. "For a week," said Sir John, "the shore from Portland to Abbotsbury was strewn with corpses, of which very many were those of soldiers. . . . " Geggus estimated 600 soldiers drowned.

The fleet put back to Portsmouth for repairs, sailing for the second time

on December 9, with even more ships. By the twelfth, the clouds had begun to gather once again, and the armada's 218 vessels were whipped by
another powerful storm. This time, they were far enough at sea to weather the worst of it, though the formation was broken up and 30 or 40 ships
disappeared (only to turn up weeks later in the Caribbean).

Even as the great armada was setting sail, Pitt and Dundas were changing their minds about what it was supposed to do when it arrived in the
Caribbean. The British situation had taken a turn for the worse: Guadeloupe had been lost to the canny mulatto, Victor Hugues, along with Saint
Vincent and Saint Lucia. Grenada, a British colony, was barely hanging on.
What was left of the British detachment on Haiti was under severe pressure, too.

What next? Haiti? Saint Lucia? Guadeloupe? Saint Vincent? Demerara?

The navy wanted to attack Guadeloupe, "placed centrally to threaten
sea operations in both the Leeward and Windward islands," according to
John Ehrman, Pitt's biographer. The soldiers, though, always preferred
Haiti as the first target, and Dundas tended to side with the army.

In any event, with all the confusion getting to sea—"incredible,"
groaned Sir John—the politicians threw up their hands. Abercromby, they
said, would have to decide what to do on the scene. He arrived at Barbados on March 17, 1796, with most of his army stretched out behind him in
ships that had been scattered for hundreds of miles. He pulled together
what troops he could round up and dispatched them to relieve Grenada,
which was secured after bloody fighting and a loss of 150 lives. He moved
on next to Saint Lucia; there, in a disastrous struggle, he lost 39 officers
and 520 men. Abercromby confessed, Sir John wrote, that it was "a barren
conquest," for "the island except as a military post had ceased to be of any
value."

Haiti, presumably, was still a rich prize, but it remained the secondary
theater in the campaign. The command had fallen upon Major General
Gordon Forbes by default, for neither Dundas nor Abercromby could find
anyone else. But it shouldn't have been hopeless; reinforcements, in fact,
had been drifting in, and would eventually number twelve thousand men.

Forbes opened his campaign on March 17, before the yellow fever season, by embarking two thousand soldiers at Port-au-Prince—fresh troops
from Gibraltar—and sending them south to attack Léogâne, where a number of his colonial supporters worried about the security of their plantations. The attack was a fiasco.

"No one seems to have discovered that the republicans had surrounded Léogâne with a deep palisaded ditch since capturing it just over a year before. Consequently, Forbes had brought no siege artillery with him, since his engineering officer . . . thought he could take the town with a regular approach," Geggus wrote. Forbes had not reckoned on Alexandre Pétion, either; he was a brilliant artillery commander, and he knocked out two of Admiral Hyde Parker's three ships of the line with his well-directed fire, and then proceeded to dismount the British field artillery. At that point, the republican troops sallied from the town and put the entire British force to rout. Parker called it a day, took in the survivors, and sailed back to Port-au-Prince.

Waiting for him was the deadliest foe of all—yellow fever. Two new regiments, the Sixty-sixth and the Sixty-ninth, suffered the most. By June 1, only 198 out of 1,000 men were fit in the Sixty-sixth, and only 515 out of another 1,000 in the Sixty-ninth. Forbes had no choice now but to wait for reinforcements.

They began arriving in April and May. But these new troops were sickly; Abercromby had taken a look at them and predicted they would all be dead by November. They were followed by ten thousand more troops that put the garrison in its strongest position yet, even though six thousand of the new troops were cavalrymen, and of these more than half were foreign mercenaries.

A more adventurous commander than Forbes might have done something with these reinforcements, but Forbes was a cautious man. All he ever did was march in the heat of broad daylight against republican positions at Bombarde, near the Mole, and watch as his troops, in their heavy wool jackets, dropped by the side of the road, dying of thirst and heat exhaustion. The 350 republicans manning the position surrendered when the British soldiers still on their feet approached, and Forbes allowed them to retire in safety.

After that, Abercromby cut Haiti off with no more reinforcements (except for a four- hundred-man Irish brigade from Jamaica in August). Forbes decided he would be unable to take the field again without significant relief. Historian Michael Duffy argued that even though he now had a sick list of twenty-five hundred European troops, he still had seven thousand Europeans fit for fighting and as many as ten thousand colonial troops and militia. The cavalrymen didn't have as many excuses, either: horses had finally arrived.

But Forbes was finished. His troops went into barracks, and when there weren't enough barracks, they were housed aboard ships in the harbor. Either way, one by one, they died. They died all over the Caribbean, and London did nothing about it. Pitt's government left them in the West Indies in the worst of the sickly season, and Great Britain lost an army.

The government "left in the Caribbean all the fittest and best troops of the great expedition; 18,000 European rank and file of all arms in the Windwards and Leewards, 10,600 in Haiti, and nearly 2,500 on Jamaica," Duffy said.

"At length," Duffy quoted a surgeon in Grenada as writing, "the mortality, particularly of officers, became frightful . . . the first question put on an officer entering the coffee room was—who died since yesterday? and almost always several well-known names of officers were announced."

"Men were taken ill at dinner who had been in the most apparent health during the morning," Duffy quoted an officer serving with a European regiment in Haiti as saying. "The putridity of the disorder at last arose to such a height that hundreds almost were drowned in their own blood bursting from them at every pore. Some died raving mad, others forming plans for attacking. . . ."

But Forbes still held on in Haiti, spending heavily to maintain his position there. With the costs rising so rapidly, doubts about the entire operation began to be raised in Commons. Maybe, some said, it would be better to abandon Haiti altogether. But if they did that, how could they keep faith with the French colonists they had sworn to protect? What else but mount a *third* expedition. This one would be aimed at Puerto Rico, a Spanish-held island—Spain had entered the war again, against Britain—where the French colonists could be resettled. It was an absurd idea from the start. "Neither the Government nor Abercromby," Sir John complained, "possessed the slightest trustworthy information as to the strength of the Spaniards at Porto Rico." And even if Puerto Rico were taken, he noted, sarcastically, "it might be a little difficult to transport some tens of thousands of people with their goods and property for some 500 miles in the teeth of the trade wind." Sir John never got off Dundas's case, and he certainly didn't now. "These practical matters," he wrote, "naturally escaped the notice of Dundas."

Abercromby arrived off San Juan on April 17 with four thousand troops he had compared earlier "to the condotierri [professional mercenaries] of the sixteenth and seventeenth centuries," only to discover that "the town itself lay at the point of a small island, covered by powerful fortifications both to seaward and landward"—they stand there today—"with two redoubts to guard the principal access to it across the narrow channel that parted it from the mainland, and a swarm of gunboats to hinder the passage at any other point." Nevertheless, Abercromby landed his nondescript detachment, but failed to make much headway against overpowering enemy gunfire. He gave it up for a bad idea, and sailed away to Martinique on April 30.

But what about Haiti? The British simply couln't decide what to do. "The colony, it seemed, could not be conquered, but neither could it be abandoned," Geggus wrote. Forbes was finally replaced, in February of 1797, by Lieutenant General John Simcoe, whose orders were to gradually withdraw the remaining British troops to the safety of the Mole, leaving the colonial troops to maintain control of the rest of the colony.

On April 11, an extraordinary event occurred—an intelligent English officer, Lieutenant Colonel Thomas Maitland of the Sixty-second Foot, arrived in Haiti. Two months later, he wrote his brother, the Earl of Lauderdale, a prescient letter. Both the British and the French, he said, were wasting their time in Haiti. "St. Domingo will end up being a Brigand Republick, connected only with America . . . a Negroe free government arising out of the ruins of European Despotism." The British forces, he wrote, had been "annihilated," and "the dreadful scene of mortality exhibited there exceeds every idea of human credibility."

Maitland had arrived on the island with six hundred men from the Fortieth, or Irish Brigade, and a number of other small detachments. Simcoe now used these fresh troops to drive Toussaint and his increasingly competent black forces from their positions overlooking Port-au-Prince. But Toussaint, now commanding twenty thousand men, and Rigaud, leading as many as twelve thousand, struck back, with Toussaint capturing the fortress at Mirebalais and winning the title of lieutenant governor of republican Haiti for his prowess. On June 7, Toussaint led his elite corps against Fort Churchill, defending Saint-Marc. "With ladders in hand," fifteen hundred of them "stormed the fort through a hail of lead shot. For half an hour their bodies piled up beneath its walls. Four times they fought their way through a breach and were driven back," Geggus said. They finally withdrew, leaving five hundred dead behind. It was an astonishing battlefield performance by soldiers who now fought with the kind of tenacity and valor the European commanders could only secretly admire.

In mid-July, discouraged by what was happening, Simcoe and Maitland sailed to explain the problems in Haiti to government officials in London. Maitland, a man with powerful connections, was so eloquent that the politicians sent him back to Haiti in March of 1798 to extricate Britain from the mess. He met Toussaint personally on May 10 to negotiate a withdrawal of British forces from Port-au-Prince. "Toussaint met him in a very friendly spirit," wrote Sir John, "agreeing to respect the lives and properties of the inhabitants; and on the 10th of May a suspension of arms was agreed to for five weeks."

"This historic surrender . . . by a representative of the British government" to an ex-slave "culminated in high farce when two grenadiers of the 69th Foot, standing guard on Government House, were forgotten in the confusion of the embarkation," Duffy wrote. Toussaint discovered the muddle and, after much haggling, sent the two grenadiers under escort to join their departing comrades.

By the eighteenth of May, the British had left Port-au-Prince forever.

But the fighting in other parts of Haiti rumbled on, as Maitland—down to eight hundred British troops, twenty-three hundred European mercenaries, and perhaps six thousand colonial troops, many of whom were already deserting—sought to withdraw in safety. It was over, and Maitland knew it. He decided, unilaterally, to evacuate Haiti "without delay . . . ," according to Sir John, "knowing the outcry that would probably be raised by the planters in Jamaica over the triumph of the negroes, by the navy over the loss of Mole St. Nicolas, by the West India Committee in London, and even by certain members of the Cabinet."

Maitland, now a general, met with Toussaint again on August 31. It was an extraordinary scene. The two generals—one white, the other black—were both dressed in full ceremonial uniforms. They signed a secret agreement in which Toussaint agreed that he would not meddle in the affairs of Jamaica and Maitland agreed that the British naval blockade would be loosened to allow a renewal of trade.

"Thank God I have at length got Great Britain rid of the whole of the incumbrance in this island," Maitland wrote to a friend in London.

"Thus," wrote Sir John, "by the supreme strength and courage of a single subordinate officer, England was plucked from the awful morass of confusion, extravagance, death and disaster into which she had been plunged by the thoughtless incapacity of Pitt and Dundas."

Sir John, in summation, admitted that "the amount of blood and treasure drained from England by that miserable island of St. Domingo will never, I think, be truly known." Haiti alone, he reckoned, cost the British treasury four million pounds, sterling. And, he added, "after long and careful thought and study I have come to the conclusion that the West Indian campaigns, both to windward and to leeward, which were the essence of

Pitt's military policy, cost England in army and navy little fewer than one hundred thousand men, about one-half of them dead, the remainder permanently unfitted for service." England, he said, had sacrificed her soldiers, squandered her fortune, and weakened her influence in Europe. Indeed, for the next "six fateful years," her arm was "fettered, numbed, and paralyzed."

✦

Bidding farewell to the English, Toussaint now turned his attention to a pressing domestic problem—André Rigaud and his mulatto army. To win that struggle, he would need to get help from an unlikely quarter, the infant United States Navy.

The Americans had been feuding with France's ruling Directory for years, but their anger rose to fury when the French renounced the principle of "free ships make free goods" on March 2, 1797, and turned their privateers loose on American commerce in the Caribbean. In the first year alone, they seized more than three hundred American ships; by the time they were finished, the total would surge past two thousand, 40 percent of all the American ships involved in foreign trade.

This wouldn't do. And so the Americans built a little navy and sent it to sea, concentrating it in the West Indies with orders "to seize take and bring" into American ports French vessels committing depredations against the American merchant fleet. It would be called the Quasi-War with France, lasting between 1798 and 1801.

The Americans knew pretty much what to do with French ships—but what about Toussaint-Louverture? President John Adams, along with almost everyone else, was confused. "Toussaint has evidently puzzled himself, the French government, the English cabinet and the administration of the United States," he said in a letter to his able secretary of the navy, Benjamin Stoddert. "All the rest of the world knows as little what to do with him as he knows what to do with himself. . . ."

Stoddert, a Marylander, was a slave owner, and he probably had private doubts of his own about working with Toussaint. But "the lure of renewed trade" with Haiti carried the day, according to American historian Michael Palmer, and in March 1799 the United States sent a consul general to Le Cap. The United States would work with Toussaint.

Patrolling these same seas was a huge squadron of the British navy, led by the irascible Sir Hyde Parker in his great ship of the line, *Queen*, carrying ninety-eight guns. But unlike the Americans, Sir Hyde was unwilling to deal with Toussaint; the admiral was still steaming about Maitland's surrender of the Mole, his splendid advance naval base. Moreover, he remained convinced that Toussaint was simply a puppet of the French Directory.

The British ships were there when Toussaint led ten thousand troops south to Jacmel, a small port on the southern coast, to lay siege to Rigaud and his army. "The struggle would be the decisive battle of the [civil] war, for both sides soon found themselves short of supplies—facing starvation and destruction," wrote Palmer. But thanks to Sir Hyde, Rigaud was doing marginally better, for the British ships refused to cut off supplies arriving for Rigaud by sea. Parker went a step further; he seized four of Toussaint's ships, and carried them off to Jamaica.

What the British navy wouldn't do, a single American ship, the frigate *General Greene*, armed with thirty-two guns and commanded by Captain Christopher Perry (the father of future navy heroes Oliver and Matthew Perry), accomplished alone. Perry, going well beyond his orders, agreed to provide artillery support as Toussaint, with his ragged army, made a final attack on the walls of Jacmel.

"We engaged three of Rigaud's forts warmly for 30 or 40 minutes, in which time we obliged the enemy to evacuate the town and two of the forts, and repair to their strongest hold . . . ," wrote one of Perry's officers. Rigaud and what was left of his army fled, and Toussaint took over the mulatto commander's last bastion the night of March 11, 1800. "It is impossible for me to describe to you the manner in which Toussaint expressed his gratitude to Captain Perry on the occasion," noted the American naval officer. (Washington was not so pleased: Perry had become too deeply involved, and gone well beyond his orders; he was suspended from his command and dropped from the service when the war with France ended.)

But the bombardment by the *General Greene* was decisive and historic. It "marked the beginning of an era of Caribbean interventionism [by the United States]. Gunboat diplomacy was born," wrote Palmer. Toussaint didn't need historic interpretations; he was simply happy that the *General Greene* had shown up in the right place at the right time. Rigaud was finished; he fled Haiti in a French schooner, *La Diana*, only to be captured by the American schooner *Experiment*, commanded by a young Charles Stewart (a future skipper of *Old Ironsides* in the War of 1812).

The black slave armies had triumphed, against overwhelming odds, and

Toussaint was pleased. Paris, still maintaining the fiction that it controlled affairs on the island, was not. After Napoléon overthrew the Directory and seized power in 1799, he vowed to do something about it.

And so, on January 29, 1802, Toussaint watched in dismay from the hills above Samaná Bay, on the island's east coast, as the French began disembarking nine thousand soldiers, the first detachment of their mighty Army of Saint-Domingue, from an armada of ships.

Napoléon had seen enough of this "gilded African" in his fancy uniforms and his independent ways. He disliked blacks generally—he was, in fact, a bigot—and it didn't take the creole landowners much time to convince him that the only way to restore the Haitian economy (and give them back their property) was to restore slavery.

That's why that Army of Saint-Domingue was landing at Samaná Bay; that's why Napoléon had trusted its command to his own brother-in-law, General Charles-Victor-Emmanuel Leclerc, the thirty-year-old husband of the ravishing and promiscuous Pauline Bonaparte. She was only twenty-two, and she had held up the armada's departure so she could load her infant son, Dermide, his nursemaids, plus "musicians, artists, and all the paraphernalia of a court" aboard the giant 120-gun flagship *Ocean*, which would take her and her lovers to Haiti. "Slavery would be re-established, civilization re-started, and a good time would be had by all," said a sardonic C. L. R. James.

It was at the time the biggest overseas expedition ever launched by France (just as the English "great push" had been that nation's biggest overseas undertaking, for its time). The moment was right for Napoléon to make his move. France and England, both exhausted, had decided to take a rest, and so they declared peace. Pitt, exhausted as well, had stepped down, to be replaced by Henry Addington. And in Haiti, the slave rebellion was running into problems. In his attempts to rebuild the shattered Haitian economy, Toussaint had sent his black followers back to work their old plantations, and they resented it.

Like Toussaint, James said, "Bonaparte did everything himself and he wrote out the plan of the campaign in his own hand." He divided it into three periods. In the first, Leclerc was to promise Toussaint everything he asked for, in order that Leclerc might establish himself in the principal points of the country. That done, "you will then be firmer," Bonaparte had written. "Command him [Toussaint] to reply without equivocation to me. . . ." Toussaint was to be summoned to Le Cap with all his principal supporters, black and white, where, in a great double cross, they were to be seized and shipped to France. With honor, of course.

But if they refused to make fools of themselves—Napoléon reckoned they wouldn't show up at Le Cap—they were to be declared traitors and hunted down in "a war to the death"; and, if captured, were to be shot within 24 hours. That completed, Leclerc was instructed to move on to the third phase, the general disarming of the entire population. The notion of reintroducing slavery was to be kept a secret—even Leclerc's second in command, the notorious, Negro-hating Donatien de Rochambeau (son of the man who served at George Washington's side during the climactic moments of the American Revolution), wasn't told.

Toussaint was bewildered. "I found the colony dismembered, ruined, over-run by [bandits], by the Spaniards and by the English, who fought over the bits," Toussaint wrote. He believed he was on his way to the restoration of its economy and the pacification of its bloody countryside. He simply couldn't bring himself to believe "that the French ruling class would be so depraved, so lost to all sense of decency, as to try to restore slavery," James said. But now, here in Samaná Bay, they were preparing to do just that. "We are lost!" Toussaint cried, as he watched the French troops come ashore. "All France has come to St. Domingue!" And then, with an inkling of the kind of battle cry that might inspire his followers, he added, "And they have come to enslave the blacks!"

It wasn't until February 2 that the French fleet appeared off Le Cap, where one of Toussaint's most successful black officers, Henry Christophe, a sophisticated man fluent in both English and French, was in charge. Le Cap was Christophe's home; he owned a mansion there, and he had watched with pleasure as the city rose from the ashes of its earlier destruction. "New buildings had sprung up along the beautiful wide streets, the flourishing plantations had brought new trade and bustle to the docks and business houses," Hubert Cole, his biographer, said.

Leclerc sent a message ashore demanding that Christophe surrender the town, and warned that if the fort and coastal batteries were not abandoned he would put ashore fifteen thousand men at daybreak. Christophe refused, and when the French ships opened fire, he set Le Cap aflame, throwing the first torch into his own home. He retired with most of his army into the protecting hills, burning everything behind him.

So much for phase one. "These people have become convinced that we have come to murder and burn them," Leclerc wrote on February 9. He reported that so far he had received only 9,400 men—the rest were still on the way—and these were scattered from Le Cap to Port-au-Prince. Leclerc pleaded with Toussaint. "Have no worries about your personal fortune," he said. "It will be safeguarded for you, since it has been only too well earned by your own efforts." Don't worry, either, he said, "about the liberty of your fellow citizens." Lies, all lies.

By February 17, Leclerc had had enough. "General Toussaint and General Christophe," he declared, "are outlawed; all citizens are ordered to hunt them down and treat them as rebels against the French Republic."

Begin phase two. Toussaint no longer labored under any delusions. This was war, and he would fight it. It would be "his last campaign, and his greatest," James said. By now, Toussaint's troops were "far different from the ill-armed, untrained bands of field hands who had risen to fight against their masters in the early days, trusting to vaudau [voodoo] charms to bear down a volley of grapeshot or to change it to water, plunging their arms into the mouths of guns to hold back the cannon balls," Cole said.

Captain Marcus Rainsford, a British army officer posing as an American, went ashore at Le Cap to watch them train. "At a whistle," he wrote, "a whole brigade ran three or four hundred yards, and then, separating, threw themselves flat on the ground, changing to their backs and sides, and all the time keeping up a strong fire until recalled. . . . This movement is executed with such facility and precision as totally to prevent cavalry from charging them in bushy and hilly countr[y]."

Toussaint sketched his plan for the campaign in a letter to another of his principal commanders, the bloodthirsty Jean-Jacques Dessalines. "Do not forget," he said, "while waiting for the rainy season which will rid us of our foes, that we have no other resource than destruction and fire. Bear in mind that the soil bathed with our sweat must not furnish our enemies with the smallest sustenance. Tear up the roads with shot; throw corpses and horses into all the fountains, burn and annihilate everything in order that those who have come to reduce us to slavery may have before their eyes the image of the hell which they deserve."

Dessalines never got the letter, for he was already on the move. He smartly avoided a French column, falling on Léogañe. He burned it to the ground. "Men, women and children, indeed all the whites who came into his hands, he massacred. And forbidding burial, he left stacks of corpses rotting in the sun to strike terror into the French detachments as they toiled behind his flying columns," James said.

The French were appalled. "They heaped up bodies," Pamphile de Lacroix, one of the French generals (there were forty of them in Haiti, more than Napoléon had taken with him to Egypt), declared in his memoirs. The bodies "still had their last attitudes; they were bent over, their hands outstretched and beseeching; the ice of death had not effaced the look on their faces."

Leclerc had his own plan. He ordered his subordinates to concentrate on Gonaïves, once again Toussaint's principal headquarters. They would march in several columns; one would set out from Port-au-Prince, a second from Plaisance, a third from Dondon. Rochambeau would lead a fourth, from Saint-Raphael. Toussaint tried to make a stand against Rochambeau in the Ravin-a-Couleuvre, a narrow gully in mountainous territory. He chopped down trees to block the narrow road and fought the French regulars hand to hand for six hours, in what James said, surely incorrectly, was the fiercest fight of the war. That was yet to come, at an old British-built fort called Crête-à-Pierrot. But it was fierce enough. Toussaint charged, again and again, at the head of his troops. "Men threw away their arms and grappled for life and death. . . . At last, late in the afternoon, Toussaint put himself at the head of his grenadiers, [and] with a final attack drove Rochambeau over the river," James wrote. Both sides claimed the victory, though in fact Rochambeau had won the day. After losing eight hundred men, Toussaint retired from the battlefield.

Crête-à-Pierrot was next, an extraordinary—truly a heroic—struggle. It is to black Haitians what the Alamo is to white Texans. Toussaint had ordered Dessalines to hold this mountain fortress while he took his troops and circled to the north, seeking to cut off the French line of communications with Le Cap. From its ramparts Dessalines could see the approaching French army on the plains below. He was joined by his courageous second in command, Lamartinière, whose wife, Marie-Jeanne Lamartinière, would become a legend for her own fighting skills.

The French general Jean Boudet arrived first. Dessalines stood on a parapet with a lighted torch and a barrel of powder. "We are going to be attacked," he said—hardly news to the fort's defenders—"and if the French put their feet in here, I shall blow everything up." With one voice, the defenders replied, "We shall die for liberty!" Something like that, almost surely.

The blacks screening Boudet's advance fell back as the French advanced, until they reached a ditch that Dessalines had dug in preparation for the battle. They jumped into it and let loose with a tremendous burst of artillery and musket fire, cutting the French to pieces. Boudet was wounded, and Lacroix ordered a retreat.

As these troops retired, Charles Dugua's column reached the bloody field, accompanied by Leclerc himself. They led the fresh troops in another attack, but they too were broken by the fierce artillery and musketry fire. As they began to retreat, the black defenders, shouting hurrahs, threw planks across the ditch and ran after the fast-moving French soldiers.

Dugua was hit twice, mortal wounds, and Leclerc suffered a scratch. In one day's fighting the French had lost eight hundred men.

The next column to arrive—hours later—was Rochambeau's. His artillery silenced, finally, the fort's guns, and a worried Dessalines abandoned the post to look for help. Rochambeau launched a third attack, only to be beaten back with the loss of three hundred more men. Lamartinière raised red flags at each corner of the fort, notice that no quarter would be given, and the fighting raged on, day after day.

During the quiet moments between bombardments and attacks, the blacks could be heard singing the patriotic songs of the French Revolution. "Choked with emotion, many French soldiers seemed to be questioning their role in Saint-Domingue," Ott wrote.

Short of food, water, and ammunition, the eight hundred surviving defenders—there had been twelve hundred to start—slipped out of the fortress the night of March 24 and escaped through the French lines. They had held off twelve hundred French troops, some of the finest in the world, for twenty days. "Their retreat—this miraculous retreat from our trap— was an incredible feat of arms," Rochambeau would write later. From that time on, the French honored every black man who had defended Crête-à-Pierrot.

It was a famous victory for Leclerc, but two thousand French troops had died assaulting the mountain fortress. And now columns under Toussaint, Christophe, and Dessalines, reverting to hit-and-run tactics, were recapturing territory from Le Cap south through the Artibonite valley. Moreover, the rain had begun to fall—and the mosquitoes to collect. By the end of March, five thousand French soldiers were dead and five thousand more were sick. "The rainy season has arrived," Leclerc wrote. "My troops are exhausted with fatigue and sickness. . . ."

At this crucial point, when victory seemed so close, Christophe defected to the French, taking twelve hundred seasoned troops and one hundred cannon with him. It was April 25. A few days later, on May 6, Toussaint himself rode into Le Cap with his staff and an escort of more than three hundred dragoons. The guns on the fortress ramparts and the warships in the harbor joined to salute the black general. Toussaint met briefly with the young French general and accepted his invitation to dinner the following night. "The dinner was not convivial," Cole wrote. "Toussaint refused all food and drink until the meal was finally over. Then, cutting a small piece of Gruyère from the middle of a cheese, he trimmed off all the sides and ate the small cube that remained, accompanying it with a glass of water from a carafe from which one of the other diners had already served himself." It was hard to tell which of these men, Toussaint or Leclerc, was victor and which vanquished. Yet, for all of his proud ways, Toussaint had come to Le Cap to surrender. Leclerc, in turn, guaranteed the freedom of the island's blacks, acknowledged that black officers could serve in the French army without demotion, and permitted Toussaint and his bodyguard to retire to a plantation at Ennery, near Gonaïves.

Why did Toussaint give up? His biographer, Ralph Korngold, argued that it was simply a delaying tactic, to await the deadly sting of yellow fever. James said that it was actually a victory, because the blacks were allowed to maintain their army. Ott insisted that it was because Toussaint felt his cause was doomed, with so many French reinforcements on the way. He hinted at another reason—that Toussaint was simply bone-weary. It makes the most sense.

A few days later, the blood-stained Dessalines rode into Le Cap at the head of his column, and submitted to Leclerc. He was appointed military commander of Saint-Marc, where he was just as cruel in repressing black resistance as he had been in leading it.

But if the great men of the revolution—Toussaint, Christophe, Dessalines—had given up, secondary commanders fought on. What had been cruel now became depraved. According to two Polish historians, Jan Pachonski and Reuel K. Wilson, who chronicled the performance of Polish units in the fighting, the French used firing squads, the gallows, and drowning in bags. They also used "the truly modern technique of mass gassing by sulphur in the holds of old ships—a technique Rochambeau called 'fumigational-sulphurous baths,'" the Polish historians said. The insurgents roasted prisoners on spits; hanged them; chopped them to pieces with axes; tied them between boards and sawed them in half.

Through it all, Leclerc's wife, the empty-headed Pauline Bonaparte, partied on. She set up lavish residences on Tortuga Island, just off Port-de-Paix on the north coast, and in Le Cap itself. "Her boudoir she dressed out in blue satin with silver fringes, her bedroom in white and gold. On an altar-shaped table beside the bed an alabaster figure of Silence held a candle in one hand and placed a finger to its lips with the other," Cole said.

She entertained her lovers one after another, with some of them lining up outside her boudoir. When she was on Tortuga she "sought carefree diversion in lavish parties and banquets," according to Pachonski and Wilson. "The blare of music drowned out the groans of the dying; instances are recorded of officers suddenly expiring on the ballroom floor, whereupon the band would recommence playing, no sooner had the dead man's comrades taken his corpse from the room."

The yellow fever was everywhere, just as Toussaint had said it would be. It reached epidemic proportion in mid-May, and by mid-July over ten thousand French soldiers were dead. By September, Leclerc could count on only eight thousand soldiers fit to take the field.

Some of these troops were, in fact, Polish. Though Poland no longer existed—it had once again been dismembered by its neighbors—its army lived on, as a mercenary unit. Two Polish demi-brigades—about five thousand men in all—became a part of the expedition, and four thousand of them never came home. They were sacrificed in the vain hope that Napoléon might be impressed by their valor, and therefore be more sympathetic to the restoration of the Polish nation.

Many of them died of yellow fever. "Ten days after the landing of these two beautiful regiments," a French planter wrote, "more than half their number were carried off by yellow fever; they fell down as they walked, the blood rushing out through their nostrils, mouths, eyes . . . what a horrible and heart-rending sight!"

Sometimes they died in brief engagements with small insurgent groups. The Third Battalion took part in an action against about two hundred insurgents near Port Salut. Confused and exhausted, the Poles announced themselves, beating their drums and loudly shouting. The insurgents showered them with musket fire and an avalanche of boulders. Summoned to attack, "the Poles, rather than spreading out, each man for himself, slowly advanced in a tightly packed mass which afforded an ideal target for the well-protected insurgent riflemen," Pachonski and Wilson said. Then they stopped moving at all; they stood there, in block formation, and died. Certainly, said Rochambeau when he heard about it, they met death without flinching.

The black troops generally admired the Polish units—the ornate, shako-style Polish caps were very popular as trophies—and some of the Poles came to sympathize with the rebels. A number of them deserted, and formed an insurgent Polish corps.

Toussaint, in retirement on his plantation, saw that things were now going badly for the French, and began conniving. On June 7, a French general named Brunet asked to meet him at a plantation near Gonaïves to discuss a number of mundane matters. Brunet guaranteed Toussaint's safety. But, of course, he lied; it was a trap. The unsuspecting Toussaint was seized, tied up, and packed aboard a French frigate. He reached Brest in

July and was thrown into a dungeon in Fort-de-Joux, near the Swiss border. He had fought his last campaign; he died there on April 7, 1803. He was fifty-seven years old.

If Leclerc thought that getting rid of Toussaint would break the back of the revolution, he was wrong: it was "a cold shock to the entire population," James said, "and the black insurgency grew, as field hands put down their tools and hiked into the mountains to join the fast-moving guerrilla bands." By now, too, the French were openly talking about the restoration of slavery on Guadeloupe, and rumors were spreading that Haiti was next. That kind of talk might even have affected Dessalines and Christophe, for they now began holding secret talks with the rebels. Leclerc's black generals mutinied the night of October 13, and began to march on Le Cap. Leclerc, a dying man—yellow fever, of course—rose from his deathbed to organize the town's defense. He was so fearful of even the faithful blacks who had remained at his side that he ordered hundreds of them drowned in the harbor, along with their families.

Le Cap was saved, but by the end of October, only it, Port-au-Prince and Les Cayes remained in French hands. Leclerc died on November 2, in Pauline's arms. Rochambeau assumed command, and with twenty thousand reinforcements, renewed the attack. It was a campaign of extermination; he drowned so many blacks in the Bay of Le Cap nobody would eat fish there for months. He imported fifteen hundred man-eating dogs from Jamaica and turned them loose to run down blacks and mulattoes (it was said he hated mulattoes even more than blacks). Dessalines, the new insurgent leader, struck back. When Rochambeau hanged five hundred blacks in Le Cap, Dessalines mounted the heads of five hundred whites outside the town on spikes so the French inside could see them.

Britain and France had been at peace for a short time; such lulls occurred periodically so that the two combatants could get ready for the next round. Britain was now ready again, and declared war against France on May 18. That meant reinforcements for Dessalines by mid-June, in the shape of British warships blockading Haiti's ports and delivering arms and supplies to Dessalines and his growing army.

With everything collapsing about him, Rochambeau seemed to lose his senses (his father, a marshal of France, had warned Napoléon not to send him to the West Indies). He "amused himself with sexual pleasures, military balls, banquets, and the amassing of a personal fortune," James wrote. But he was forced to close down those parties and evacuate Port-au-Prince on October 8, concentrating what was left of his army at Le Cap.

Dessalines marched into Port-au-Prince, received a welcome from about one hundred whites who had elected to stay behind—and then hanged them all.

The blacks and mulattoes concentrated for the final assault on Le Cap and the forts guarding it on November 16. Clairveaux, a mulatto, was in direct command, seconded by Capois Death, a Negro. They led their troops again and again against the French blockhouses. A bullet knocked over Capois's horse; "boiling with rage," James wrote, "he scrambled up, and, making a gesture of contempt with his sword, he continued to advance. The French, who had fought on so many fields, had never seen fighting like this. 'Bravo! Bravo!' There was a roll of drums. The French ceased fire. A French horseman rode out and advanced to the bridge. He brought a message from Rochambeau. 'The captain-general sends his admiring compliments to the officer who has just covered himself with so much glory.'" He rode back, and the battle resumed. By now, "all in Santo Domingo were a little mad, both white and black."

That night, Rochambeau held a council of war and reached the same conclusion Thomas Maitland had years before—to escape from this place of death. Rochambeau opened negotiations on the nineteenth with Captain John Loring, commanding the British blockade squadron, for the surrender of his army and the remaining white residents of the town. On November 30, twenty ships sailed from Le Cap packed with eight thousand soldiers—all that were left of the mighty Army of Saint-Domingue—and hundreds of refugees.

◆

Jean-Jacques Dessalines crowned himself emperor in October of 1804 and made his grand entry into Le Cap in a six-horse carriage supplied to him by English merchants. The crown came from America, the coronation robes from Jamaica. The victorious leaders of the world's only successful slave rebellion proclaimed Saint-Domingue's independence on December 31, 1804. They named their country Haiti. Then, perhaps to celebrate the New Year, Dessalines ordered the massacre of all the whites.

Dessalines himself was assassinated in 1806, and was succeeded by Henri Christophe, who crowned himself Emperor Henry I and built his great citadel, La Ferrière, in the mountains. Abandoned by his own followers, he committed suicide in 1820. With the plantations in ruins, Haiti, the onetime "Pearl of the Antilles," slipped into anarchy, with blacks and mulattoes constantly struggling for control. Just as Maitland had predicted, the United States interceded, taking control of the Haitian economy in 1905 and sending in the marines to make it function. They weren't withdrawn until 1934. By 1994, the marines were back, still trying to impose democratic institutions on a primitive society that never recovered from the awful events that began the night of August 22, 1791, when slaves rose to challenge their masters.

FOUR

General Charles MacCarthy
and the First Ashanti War
(1824)

Consider the various titles used almost two hundred years ago in the households of the "civilized" kings of England, in London, and the "barbarous" kings of Ashanti, in their capital, Kumasi:

English	*Ashanti*
King	King
Lord chamberlain	Chamberlain
Gold stick	Gold horn blower
Keeper of the privy purse	Captain of the market
Keeper, the king's archives	Keeper, burial ground
Equerry	Captain of the messengers
Peers of the realm	Caboceers
College of Chaplains	Royal fetish house

Yet, until about 1800, Great Britain and the Ashanti kingdom barely knew of each other's existence. In their own way, both were great warlike powers, one white, one black, each with its own imperial trappings. Britain, over the course of seventy-five years, would ultimately destroy the Ashanti empire and burn Kumasi, its once-glittering capital, to the ground.

But Britain didn't succeed without a fight that, among other things, included the beheading of Brigadier General Sir Charles MacCarthy, and the display thereafter of his skull as a highlight of the annual Yam Festival.

The prime reason for European ignorance—for England was not alone—about the proud Ashanti kingdom was the fact that it was an inland empire, deep in the West African forests, joined by a few lonely paths to waterside, or the so-called Gold Coast.

The Gold Coast was much more familiar to Europeans than the Ashanti kingdom—most of all to adventurers and merchants. The appeal was simple enough: gold, in profusion (it is still being mined), and slaves, a plentiful supply. The Portuguese were the first to arrive, in the fifteenth century, and began building small forts. By 1700, the Portuguese were gone, but new arrivals included the English, the Dutch, the Danes, the French, the Swedes, and even Prussians from Brandenburg. They built thirty-five forts in all on the coastline of what is now Ghana and the Ivory Coast.

The key British post was Cape Coast Castle. Britain's chief European rivals, the Dutch, were headquartered in their own fort and castle, Elmina, just to the west. The Europeans dealt, most of the time, with a coastal tribe called the Fantis, who were described in 1809 by an English governor at Cape Coast as "a bad bullying people." The Fantis were, in fact, as events would show, no match for the Ashantis.

Britain abandoned the slave trade in 1807 and a mission was sent out from London in 1811 to see what steps had been taken to suppress it. The commissioners were shocked—*shocked!*—to discover it was still flourishing. "Our forts on the Gold Coast do not appear to be of any further use than merely to prevent its [slave trading] being carried on within their own walls," the commissioners said. "Outside that small range they either have not, or do not, exercise any jurisdiction." The commissioners said they watched as a brig, *Anna*, from Havana, under Spanish colors, "anchored in the road off Cape Coast where she took in a cargo of slaves. . . . She received her slaves from a mulatto, educated in England, possessed of property, and carrying on a considerable trade, who lives a short quarter of a mile from the castle, and would undoubtedly receive its protection in case of danger."

The commissioners found, in fact, that almost all of the Gold Coast forts were useless, with the exceptions of Cape Coast, Elmina, Accra, and Anamabo. The Dutch fort at Elmina, they reported, is "the best on the coast for trade, defense, and landing, and the castle itself is much larger than that of Cape Coast." The commissioners gave some thought to simply attacking it, and making it an English fort, but then concluded it might be more trouble than it was worth. Better, they said, to "lop off" some of the smaller Dutch forts. They urged that the Danish fort at Accra be left alone because its governor, a man named Schonning, was conducting promising agricultural experiments, including a "great perfection" of coffee trees.

Surely the best solution would have been to close down the forts and retire from the Gold Coast altogether, for without the abhorrent slave trade it wasn't worth the trouble to remain. But the local English businessmen, organized as the Committee of the Company of Merchants, objected, arguing, in essence, that they had been shortchanged by London in favor of the West Indies. "It is a lamentable but certain fact," they told the Lords of the Treasury in 1812, that "all endeavours to promote cultivation and improvement in agriculture have been discouraged by the Government of this country, lest her products should interfere with those of our more favoured colonies. . . ." Slavery, they said, could only be abolished "by the occupation by this nation of the whole of the Gold Coast . . . stationing good and respectable garrisons in the most commanding situation, [and], at the rest, establishments sufficient to mark our possession."

"The history of British relations with the people of the Gold Coast and Ashanti, rightly viewed, is the story of an attempt to secure our merchants' profits at the least possible cost to ourselves . . . ," wrote Sir Hugh Clifford, who years later was governor and commander in chief of the Gold Coast, in his introduction to Dr. W. Walton Claridge's monumental history of that region. "The Ashantis never knew what to expect from us—which was only natural, seeing that we were living, so to speak, from hand to mouth, and never knew from year to year what to expect of ourselves."

Maybe that was because the Gold Coast was, career-wise, as they say, the end of the line. This was no place to make a military reputation and no place to make a name in the civil service. And, for the merchants, it wasn't much of a place to make lots of money.

Governor Clifford understood that. That's why, wisely, he suggested that it might be unfair to blame colonial officials for all the "shame and horror" that accompanied the British occupation of the Gold Coast. "Exceptional men," he wrote, "are rare at all times, and few indeed found their way to the West Coast of Africa."

The Gold Coast merchants, fighting hard to keep in business, got their way. They were allowed to stay, dealing with natives bringing them gold dust and ivory, and starting up some agricultural enterprises along the lines of those coffee trees near Accra. Somehow, though, they were deaf to the drums of the warriors in faraway Kumasi. Like Russia, Ashanti was seeking an outlet to the sea. This shouldn't have been a great mystery, for Ashanti warriors had emerged from their wooded empire once before, in

1805, in a drive that ultimately led to an attack on a small British fort at a place called Anamabo, to the east of Cape Coast Castle.

The Ashantis were constantly mounting expeditions to put down rebellions by kings and chieftains in their vassal states. It happened all the time, because the Ashanti kings "established no garrisons in the conquered territories, appointed no governors or residents, and did not attempt in the least to blend with the people," according to Lieutenant Colonel Alfred B. Ellis, a British officer with a West India regiment who wrote an early history of the Gold Coast. "The Ashanti kingdom resembled a loosely united bundle of sticks, which any severe shock might cause to fall to pieces."

The stick causing the shock in 1805 had been a disturbance in the vassal state of Assin, south of Kumasi, where a chief rifled gold ornaments from the grave of another chief. Relatives of the dead chief complained to the Ashanti king, Osei Bonsu; in the turmoil that followed, a number of Ashanti messengers were murdered, their mutilated bodies suspended from trees, and a golden axe of Ashanti was stolen. The Ashantis mobilized a huge army and marched against the rebellious Assins, killing thirty thousand of them before it was all over. The coastal Fantis gave refuge to some of the Assin survivors, including two chiefs, Chibu and Aputai, who stood at the top of Osei Bonsu's most-wanted list, causing the Ashantis under their general, Tutu Kwamina, to march against them, too. "Nearly the entire Fanti force was slaughtered, and only about 100 men were said to have escaped from the fatal field," Colonel Ellis reported. The handful of survivors, including Chibu and Aputai, made their way to the little British fort at Anamabo, where the British took them in (they were soon transferred to the bigger fort at Cape Coast).

The British commander at Anamabo, Edward William White, under a flag of truce, asked the Ashanti general what he was up to, then offered himself as a mediator in the dispute between the Ashantis and the Fanti nation. "This appears to have been the first serious attempt made by the [British] officials . . . to open negotiations with the invading force, and their previous apathy is incomprehensible," wrote Colonel Ellis. The Ashantis were now in possession of a seacoast Dutch fort, surrendered without a shot being fired, just three miles from Anamabo, and "to expect the Ashantis to be moderate in their hour of triumph . . . was to show a lamentable ignorance of savage character."

White had spent twenty-seven years on the Gold Coast, and he had never seen Ashantis, until now. He ordered two or three guns to be fired from the parapets, to give them "some idea of the destructive effects of artillery." White thought the Ashantis were like the tribes "with which he was acquainted, and he was confident that a few discharges of cannon would suffice to put them to route."

It would not suffice. Early on June 15, Claridge wrote, "the Ashantis advanced to the attack on Anamabo, and every coastal tribesman who could carry a musket took the field, while the old men, women, and children crowded into the fort, the gates of which, as soon as it was full, were closed and barricaded. . . .

"To intimidate the enemy, Mr. White ordered one or two guns to be fired over the town, but this did not produce the slightest effect, and by 11 o'clock the Ashanti bullets were whistling about the fort. From all directions the Ashantis poured into the town, and the wretched [Fantis] fled 'like a flock of sheep' to the beach, hoping to be able to escape to sea in their canoes, but the enemy pursued too closely, and a terrible slaughter took place on the sands. The garrison of the fort did their best to check the pursuit. A 24-pounder that pointed to the west, along the seashore, swept down dozens of Ashantis with each discharge of grape, while a 3-pounder that flanked the eastern gate did great execution. But on this [eastern] side the Ashantis pushed on over the heaps of dead, and actually seized and carried off the terrified and shrieking women who were standing close to the fort walls for protection."

White was shot in the left arm and the mouth, losing four teeth, and was forced to turn over the command of the garrison to Henry Meredith. The entire garrison consisted of White and Meredith, along with F. L. Swanzy, a Mr. Barnes, T. A. Smith, and twenty-four soldiers, company slaves, and boys. Their defense of the fort, Dr. Claridge wrote, "furnishes one of the finest chapters in the history of the English on the Gold Coast."

"The whole force of the Ashantis was now directed against the fort, which they imagined to contain a rich booty, and thousands of black warriors swarmed around it," Colonel Ellis said. They pressed on, but the walls were too high to be scaled and the two gates were too heavily barricaded to be forced. They finally broke off at 6 P.M., by which time only eight men in the garrison were still standing.

"Day dawned upon a horrible scene of bloodshed and devastation. Eight thousand Fantis had perished, most of them in the vicinity of the fort," Claridge wrote. "Heaps of dead encumbered the beach in every direction, or were washed hither and thither in the surf, and the sands were red with blood." Dr. Claridge estimated that "of the number the town contained, and which we will calculate to have been at least 15,000 souls, we may suppose that two-thirds of that number perished."

The fort was jammed with two thousand refugees and two hundred more were clinging to a rock a few yards from shore.

Soon after daybreak, the Ashantis attacked again, but perhaps with less fury than the day before. The defenders "fired till their shoulders were so bruised they could no longer bear the recoil of their muskets," Claridge said. Just when the end seemed certain, deliverance for the desperate garrison arrived in the form of two vessels from Cape Coast Castle. Three officers, a corporal, and twelve men were landed under the smoke from the guns, and managed to reach the fort without being attacked.

A truce was arranged, after which two of the garrison's soldiers were lowered over the wall with a Union Jack and a white flag, to be greeted with "unmistakable signs of joy and satisfaction by the Ashantis." The Ashanti king received them politely, and made them a present of a sheep. Efforts were made to induce the king to go to Cape Coast to arrange terms of the truce with the fort's commander, a Colonel Torrane.

Torrane, unforgivably, agreed to give up the two most-wanted chiefs, Chibu and Aputai, in what Dr. Claridge called a "dastardly" effort "to curry favor with the Ashanti king and pave the way for a favorable conference." It was a breach of faith, and the remaining chiefs of the Gold Coast were properly outraged. Aputai managed to escape, but Chibu, "old, feeble, and blind," was taken to Anamabo, "where he was put to death with the most excruciating tortures and his jaw-bone suspended as a trophy from the king's 'death horn.'"

The king and Torrane haggled over what to do with the two thousand refugees inside the fort. They finally cut it in half—1,000 for the king, one thousand to remain protected in the fort. Many of those who fell to the Ashantis were offered up as human sacrifices, the rest were sold as slaves.

The despicable Torrane took his one thousand prisoners and began selling them to the slave traders. When John Swanzy, the governor at Accra, heard what Torrane was up to, he climbed out of his sickbed and traveled by canoe to Cape Coast to protest. A few of the refugees remained, unsold, and Torrane, frightened by Swanzy's threat to expose his dealings, released them. Swanzy returned to Accra, but the canoe ride had been too much for him; he died a few days later. Torrane died in 1808; his personal papers showed he had pocketed the money he received for selling the refugees to the slave traders.

The price paid for Torrane's treachery, wrote Dr. Claridge, was "the loss of British honor . . . " and it "lingered for many years."

Torrane, though a scoundrel, sometimes was an astute observer. "The Ashantis," he said, "fight both with muskets, bows and arrows. . . . Their bravery I have more than once . . . highly extolled; 'tis not to be surpassed. They manifest a cool intrepidity" that Europeans "would look at with surprise and admiration." He was impressed, too, with the Ashanti king. "I look on King Zey [Osei Bonsu, in fact, the Ashanti king from 1800 to 1824] to be a high character. He is of middling stature, remarkably well built, and of a handsome open countenance. Indeed all the Ashantis seem half a century advanced in civilization to those people on the waterside [the coast]." Torrane noted the king was attended by a number of Moors, and that "every Ashanti man has a gregory, or a fetish, which is a little square cloth, enclosing some little sentences from the Alcoran [the Koran]; some have many."

The Ashantis fought one more battle with the Fantis, destroying that nation as a fighting unit forever, and then—their troops weary and sick from smallpox—withdrew to Kumasi.

It wasn't until a decade later, in 1817, that the British decided it might be a good idea to send a peacemaking mission from the coast to the mysterious capital of the Ashantis at Kumasi. The officers employed—they wore full diplomatic uniform, complete with scarlet jackets and swords—were Frederick James, commander of Fort James at Accra; Thomas Edward Bowdich, a nephew of Cape Coast's governor, John Hope Smith; William Hutchison; and Henry Tedlie, a surgeon. If all went well, Hutchison expected to take up residence as the British consul in the Ashanti capital.

Diplomatically, the mission accomplished very little; much more importantly, it gave us Bowdich's extraordinary book, *Mission from Cape Coast Castle to Ashantee*, an unrivaled look at the magnificent Ashanti empire at the very pinnacle of its power and grandeur.

Bowdich and his colleagues set out on April 22, 1817, with three interpreters, two native soldiers, a number of hammock-men (people carriers) and carriers for their luggage and presents for the king (including a nine-foot scarlet umbrella that cost more than one hundred guineas). The party totaled about 130 in all. Day after day, as they traveled north, they saw nothing but devastation, the consequence of the Ashanti scorched-earth fighting strategy. Even Mansu, once the biggest slave mart in West Africa, had been reduced to a few desolate sheds and a small group of "natives gaunt with famine."

"We entered Coomassie [Kumasi] at two o'clock [on May 19], passing under a fetish, or sacrifice, of a dead sheep, wrapped up in red silk, and suspended between two lofty poles," Bowdich wrote. "Upwards of 5,000 people, the greater part warriors, met us with awful bursts of martial music, discordant only in its mixture; for horns, drums, rattles, and gong-gongs were all exerted with a zeal bordering on phrenzy, to subdue us by the first impression."

They were the first Europeans to see Kumasi, and subdued by their first impression they must have been.

> The smoke which encircled us from the incessant discharges of musquetry, confined our glimpses to the foreground; and we were halted whilst the captains performed their Pyrrhic dance, in the centre of a circle formed by their warriors; where a confusion of flags, English, Dutch, and Danish, were all waved and flourished in all directions; the bearers plunging and springing from side to side, with a passion of enthusiasm only equalled by their captains. . . . The dress of the captains was a war cap, with gilded rams horns projecting in front, the sides extended beyond all proportion by immense plumes of eagles feathers. . . . Their vest was of red cloth, covered with fetishes and saphies [scraps of Moorish writing] in gold and silver . . . intermixed with small brass bells, the horns and tails of animals, shells and knives; long leopards tails hung down their backs. . . . They wore long cotton trousers, with immense boots of dull red leather, coming half way up the thigh, and fastened by small chains to their cartouch or waist belt. . . . They were also ornamented with bells, horses tails, strings of amulets, and innumerable shreds of leather; a small quiver of poisoned arrows hung from their right wrist, and they held a long iron chain between their teeth. . . .

Subdued? Bowdich and the rest of these Englishmen were overwhelmed. Next to these warriors, the king's own household regiments dressed like Quaker merchants. But there was more to come. As they made their way down the wide central avenue, their attention was focused on what Bowdich called "a most inhuman spectacle, which was paraded before us for some minutes."

> It was a man whom they were tormenting previous to sacrifice; his hands were pinnioned behind him, a knife was passed through his cheeks, to which his lips were noosed; one ear was cut off and car-

ried before him, the other hung to his head by a small bit of skin; there were several gashes in his back, and a knife was thrust under each shoulder blade. He was led with a cord passed through his nose. . . . The feeling this horrid barbarity excited must be imagined.

There was still a lot more to come. As they continued their slow march to the palace, a scene "burst upon us" that far exceeded "our original expectations."

An area of nearly a mile in circumference was crowded with magnificence and novelty. The king, his tributaries, and captains were resplendent in the distance, surrounded by attendants of every description, fronted by a mass of warriors which seemed to make our approach impervious. The sun was reflected, with a glare scarcely more supportable than the heat, from the massy gold ornaments, which glistened in every direction. More than a hundred bands burst at once on our arrival, with the peculiar airs of their several chiefs; the horns flourished their defiances, with the beating of innumerable drums and metal instruments, and then yielded for a while to the soft breathings of their long flutes, which were truly harmonious. . . . At least a hundred large umbrellas, or canopies, which could shelter thirty people, were sprung up and down by the bearers with brilliant effect, being made of scarlet, yellow, and the most shewy cloths and silks, and crowned on top with crescents, pelicans, elephants, barrels, and arms with swords of gold. . . . The state hammocks, like long cradles, were raised in the rear, the poles on the heads of the bearers; the cushions and pillows were covered with crimson taffeta, and the richest cloths hung over the sides. . . .

Gold and silver pipes, and canes dazzled the eye in every direction. Wolves and rams heads as large as life, cast in gold, were suspended from [the caboceers', or peers of the realm's] gold handled swords . . . the blades were shaped like round bills, and rusted in blood. The large drums supported on the head of one man, and beaten by two others, were braced around with the thigh bones of their enemies, and ornamented with their skulls. . . . The executioner, a man of an immense size, wore a massy gold hatchet on his breast; and the execution stool was held before him, clotted in blood, and partly covered with a cawl of fat.

Bowdich reckoned that the king, Osei Bonsu, was about thirty-eight years old, "inclined to corpulence, and of a benevolent countenance."

Bowdich thought "his manners were majestic, yet courteous." He was seated on a low chair, ornamented with gold, and surrounded by attendants presided over by the royal eunuch, "wearing only one massy piece of gold about his neck."

The royal stool—the celebrated throne of the Ashanti, supposed to have been lowered to earth from heaven—"was displayed under a splendid umbrella," surrounded by drums, horns, and swords of state, all made of gold.

Bowdich and the rest of his party were conducted eventually to their own apartments, located in "forlorn and dreary" buildings that required "much repair to defend us from the wind and rain, which frequently ushered in the nights."

After days of haggling, during which Bowdich collected an extraordinary amount of information about Ashanti geography and customs, the party returned to Cape Coast Castle with a treaty declaring "perpetual peace and harmony" between the two nations and that no "palavers" (disagreements) stood between them. But they never really worked out their basic palaver: the Ashanti contended that they controlled all of the Gold Coast, by right of conquest, and that the British should pay them "notes," a kind of rental, for occupying Ashanti property. The British thought that was blackmail, and refused to pay.

Hutchison remained behind, but not for long. The king sent him on his way so he could launch an attack, unobserved by outsiders, on the neighboring Gaman territory with a large army. He closed the paths to "waterside," and for months no one on the Gold Coast knew what was happening. Some stragglers drifted in and told elated Gold Coast natives that the dreaded Ashantis had been defeated. But it was just the other way around; the Ashantis had won a great victory. Later, when tribesmen from Komenda, west of Elmina, refused to come up with a contribution to help pay for the Ashanti army's triumphant return to Kumasi, Ashanti agents descended upon Cape Coast Castle and said they had been insulted, and that this somehow was a violation of their treaty with the colonial authorities. The British, wanting no part of this tribal argument, insisted it was none of their business.

In an effort to straighten things out, another delegation—this one led by Joseph Dupuis, an officer of the crown dispatched to the Gold Coast from London—was sent off to Kumasi. But Dupuis was a prickly man, "very conscious of his superior status as a Government servant," and he raised the hackles of almost all the company officials he met, including the governor, John Hope Smith.

Dupuis reached Kumasi on February 28, 1820, where he and his party were once again greeted with an impressive display of warriors and bands and caboceers—the peers of the realm—with their "massy" gold decorations. But this time there was an undercurrent of anger, and the king himself became enraged when Dupuis tried to adjust—downward—the amount of gold dust the coastal people should pay the Ashantis for having insulted the king. In signing a new treaty, Dupuis went well beyond his instructions by agreeing that the Cape Coast natives were no longer entitled to protection and that the king of the Ashantis was "resolved to eradicate from his dominions the seeds of disobedience and insubordination" that had been displayed by these coastal people. "It was," said Colonel Ellis, "a complete sellout."

When Governor Smith saw that Dupuis had left "the inhabitants of Cape Coast, who had committed no offense," to the "tender mercies of the king," he repudiated the treaty. Dupuis, in a snit, sailed for home on April 15.

Conditions on the Gold Coast were now in a proper mess, and the arrival of Commodore Sir John Yeo with a squadron of His Majesty's warships didn't help. First of all, Commodore Yeo reported in a blistering report to the Admiralty, the physical condition of most of the forts, still operated by the company of merchants, continued to deteriorate. "I maintain on the honor of an officer," he said, "that they are a positive burlesque as to real defence and nothing can cause them to be respected by the natives but their being sensible that it is in their interest to live under them to protect them from their more powerful neighbors the Ashantees."

Yeo saw war with the Ashantis coming, and he warned that the Ashanti capital was only two hundred miles from the coast. He said "it is not improbable at a future period they may approach the coast. Consequently, it behooves us, if we have forts here, that they should be in a proper state of defence."

The commodore also complained that the company officers seemed to be cooking the books and slyly encouraging the illegal slave trade. He took a swipe at the school at Cape Coast, too. It was a travesty. "All the boys read English pretty clear & direct, but you soon understand that they do not understand one word that they utter, neither does the schoolmaster understand their language, the Fantee."

Yeo was a cautious man—he had spent most of the War of 1812 on Lake Ontario in a shipbuilding race with his American opponent, Commodore Isaac Chauncey. Neither commander ever felt he had enough ships to challenge the other, and so they never fought a battle. With that background, his uncharacteristically emotional report raised eyebrows, and the government decided it was time to set things right. On May 7, 1821, the House of Commons abolished the African company, "transferring to and investing in His Majesty all the Forts [eight of them], Possessions, and Property now belonging to or held by them." The Gold Coast, by that order, was made a dependency of the British colony at Sierra Leone, nine hundred miles away.

Enter, then, Brigadier General Sir Charles MacCarthy.

MacCarthy was one of those obscure British officers perpetually assigned to the periphery, a decent, proud, but stupid man. He began his career with black regiments in the West Indies and was given a lieutenant colonelcy in the Royal African Corps in 1811. The next year, he was named governor of Sierra Leone.

Tall and gray-haired—he seemed a fatherly figure to many who knew him (he was fifty-two years old)—he arrived at Cape Coast Castle, resplendent in his scarlet jacket and plumed helmet, aboard HMS *Iphigenia* on March 28, 1822. "The new governor," Colonel Ellis wrote, was "a stranger to the Gold Coast and its politics" who had "no ordinary difficulties to contend with, for the servants of the late company [of merchants], almost to a man, refused to take office with him. They also withdrew themselves from all participation in native affairs, and Sir Charles MacCarthy was left to grope in the dark, without a single responsible or reliable adviser."

His instructions from Earl Bathurst, in the African office in London, were to shut down some of the old forts, make sure that trade with those that were left was conducted in British ships, and continue to suppress slavery.

He did what he could, complaining early on about the widespread incidence of domestic slavery. He discovered that all the ground surrounding the native *krooms*—small farming communities—was worked by black slaves. Just four miles away, he said, he had heard reports of a "man of color who had cruelly flogged several of his slaves." He didn't know what to do about it, and neither did the authorities in London.

MacCarthy wasn't sure what to do about the Dutch, either. They still maintained forts at Elmina and Accra, without receiving much benefit from either. The problem for both the Dutch and the British, he said, was that American ships were monopolizing the trade, because, under no obligation to pay duty, they could sell their goods cheaply. Helpful to the Yankee traders, too, was the fact the natives much preferred "American rum, which by the natives is preferred to any other, in the proportion of four to five." MacCarthy said he was convinced the Danish government, and maybe Dutch authorities too, would hand over some of their forts, if asked. Bathurst was properly skeptical: "I fear the powers to which those possessions belong will not be so ready to relinquish them as you seem to anticipate." MacCarthy, it seems, was also naive.

What he should have been anticipating was another Ashanti invasion. But all he did, before heading back to Sierra Leone in early May, was pull together some of the native troops who had been employed by the company of merchants into three companies of what he called, portentously, the Royal African Colonial Corps of Light Infantry. He also organized a native militia, the Royal Cape Coast Militia and the Royal Cape Coast Volunteer Corps. He left two officers behind, Captain James Chisholm and Lieutenant Alexander Gordon Laing (who would one day achieve fame as an explorer, the first European to reach Timbuktu), both of the Second West India Regiment, to whip the new force into shape. MacCarthy also threw up a small redoubt on a hill—known for many years thereafter as M'Carthy's Hill—to the east of town. And that was pretty much it.

"Sir Charles MacCarthy seems to have had no idea of the critical condition of affairs," Colonel Ellis wrote, "and apparently thought that everything would go smoothly."

It is a little curious that all the contemporary references to MacCarthy mention this lack of knowledge about West Africa. Yet, as MacCarthy pointed out himself in a letter to Earl Bathurst, he had been employed on the coast of Africa since 1812, and even if he had spent most of his time in Sierra Leone, he still—if he had been curious at all—must have heard something about the Gold Coast and the Ashanti army.

A mulatto sergeant in MacCarthy's newly formed Royal African Colonial Corps, Kujo Otetfo, touched off the inevitable explosion by becoming embroiled in a quarrel with an Ashanti trader inside the fort at Anamabo, scene of the gallant defense in 1805. As tempers flared, the sergeant "grossly abused the King of Ashanti," Dr. Claridge wrote, "and it was this insignificant event that provided the spark that set the whole country in a blaze of war." Sergeant Otetfo mentioned the unmentionable, the awful words, "Cormantine and Saturday." Those are fighting words to the Ashanti, because they refer to a Saturday in 1731 when Atoa tribesmen circled to the rear of an Ashanti army at a place called Cormantine and shot the king in his hammock. To repeat those words is akin to mentioning the word "Tamai" to a soldier in the Black Watch, for it was at Tamai (see chapter seven) that the dervishes broke a British square defended by the Highlanders. But this was much worse: mentioning the words "Cormantine and Saturday" carried with it the death penalty.

Weeks later, in retribution, Ashantis seized the sergeant near Anamabo and took him to Dunkwa, a village some fifteen miles inland. He was put "in log"—secured to a log with an iron staple. Futile negotiations for his release followed, until February 2, 1823, when Cape Coast Castle learned that a state executioner had been sent from Kumasi, attended by two hundred or three hundred warriors, and that the bad-tempered Sergeant Otetfo had been beheaded. His skull, jawbone, and part of one of his arms were taken back to the Ashanti capital, and put on public display.

News of Sergeant Otetfo's capture had brought MacCarthy back from Sierra Leone, on the double. He landed at Cape Coast in December 1822 "and at once went over to Anamabo to investigate on the spot the circumstances in which the sergeant had been seized," Dr. Claridge wrote. "His journey was a triumphal progress. The Anamabos and the people of the other villages through which he passed hailed him with enthusiasm, while, on his return to Cape Coast on the 10th, he was accorded a perfect ovation and the streets and hills were thronged by crowds of Fantis who showed every sign of delight and vied with one another in cheering, firing guns, drumming and blowing horns to do honour to him whom they now regarded as their deliverer."

News of Sergeant Otetfo's death led MacCarthy to take the field against the Ashantis. As he wrote Bathurst, he sent "a military force to Dunkwa [to] make prisoners of those Ashanti caboceers who had been the principal instruments in the whole transaction." It was "the first [offensive] enterprise of that nature by British soldiers [and] it has had the happiest effects. It has dispelled the terror of the Fantee and other native tribes, who had, for many years, been held under the most abject state of oppression by the Ashantees and, in hopeless despair, considered them as invincible."

MacCarthy also told Bathurst that he believed the Ashantis had been "blustering" all along and that "they were not prepared for war, but depended solely upon the terror of their name to bring us to seek a compromise, and, I suppose, to extort from the native people under our fort . . . a contribution of six hundred ounces of gold."

Why MacCarthy thought his expedition to Dunkwa had been a success remains a mystery. One of his officers, Major H. J. Ricketts, in his own narrative of the war, said it was a disaster. The guides, Ricketts said, were either traitors or imbeciles, for the troops "lost the right road, and, after excessive fatigue, and want of every sort of provisions, were suddenly attacked under a heavy fire by a numerous force of Ashantees, ambushed in a thick covered wood, on both sides of a very rugged path." They never did reach Dunkwa, falling back on Anamabo with six men dead and thirty-eight wounded.

MacCarthy was sensible enough to understand he needed to reinforce his native companies on the Gold Coast. When he took command, the only regular troops in all of West Africa were five companies of the Second West India Regiment, and they were spread out between Sierra Leone and the Gambia River. Earlier, a unit called the Royal African Corps, six companies of white troops and three companies of black troops, had served in West Africa. These white soldiers were what Colonel Ellis called "a disciplinary corps," meaning they were men of "bad character" who had been sent out to West Africa as punishment. But, like the white troops England sent to the West Indies, they succumbed to disease. In one year alone, half of all the white troops sent to Sierra Leone died. They were finally withdrawn from West Africa and sent to the more salubrious Cape of Good Hope, in South Africa. MacCarthy now asked that these white troops be returned, and that additional recruits be sent out from England to bring the force up to one thousand men. These reinforcements began arriving in April of 1823. They would ultimately go into battle in scarlet jackets and be accompanied by their own brass band.

As a result, when the Ashantis began their attack, MacCarthy commanded five hundred regulars and several thousand non-Ashanti natives. These native allies included Dankeras, with their brave chief, Kwadwo Tibo, and the "masculine" queen of the Akims, the redoubtable Dokuwa. The Dutch at Elmina promised they would remain neutral, and some of the Danes at Accra actually joined MacCarthy's army.

MacCarthy never seemed to hold any doubts this tatterdemalion force was sufficient. The question remains, is it possible he had any idea what an Ashanti army looked like? Did he understand the odds he faced? The answer seems to be, almost surely not.

Heading his way was a vast army of ten thousand or more highly disciplined Ashantis, most of them carrying their six-foot-long "Long Dane" muskets, manufactured—cheaply and badly—in Birmingham and purchased over the years with Ashanti gold. Each army corps had its own set of drums, and they quite literally "talked." Each drum band—and there were sometimes twenty-two of them in all—"had its own symbolical mottoes for beating the drum," wrote Carl Reindorf in his Gold Coast history.

Bands had names: the attacking band, the kicking band, the invincible band, the fraud-detesting band, the black kingfisher's band, the stand-no-trash band.

"What keeps the warriors together in time of war," Reindorf wrote, "are the flags and drums of the bands, or the tune of the [elephant-tusk] horn of the king or chief."

Before marching off to battle, the Ashanti army assembled in Kumasi, "where gunpowder and shot from the king's apparently huge armory [no European is known actually to have seen it], located three miles outside the city, were distributed to the men," according to the anthropologist Robert B. Edgerton. The powder was often inferior and, instead of real bullets, the Ashantis generally rammed nails or metal slugs down the barrels. On the march, the ordinary soldiers went barefoot, and wore a simple cotton cloth tied around the waist. They carried gunpowder and shot in gourds and slung a skin bag filled with dried beans, cassava, ground nuts, and other provisions over their shoulders. Edgerton wrote that when close to the enemy, "they ate only maize meal mixed with water and ground nuts in order not to reveal their positions by lighting fires."

In battle, said Edgerton, Ashanti troops "marched in perfect order, their guns carried at exactly the same angle, before they turned toward the enemy and fired volleys on command, the only African army that was known to do so."

The commanding general usually took up a position in the rear of his army, in a hammock under a great umbrella, and waited for his troops to bring him the heads of his vanquished foes, which he used as footrests.

After a third company of white Royal African Corps troops showed up from England in November 1823, MacCarthy made a triumphant tour of his outposts, inspecting the camp at Jukwa, visiting the bullet-scarred old fort at Anamabo, and promising Fanti chiefs he would make no peace with the Ashantis without their permission. When he heard that a huge Ashanti army had crossed the Prah River and was moving toward the coast, he sent a Captain Laing to Assin with the Fanti levies, while he proceeded with most of the regulars to reinforce his position at Jukwa, where the Royal African Corps and a detachment of the Second West India Regiment were encamped.

But on January 9, 1824, on receiving news that the Ashantis had crossed into western Wassaw, he set off to meet them at the head of 80 Fantis, just recently enrolled in the Royal African Colonial Corps, 170 men from the Cape Coast Militia, and about 240 other Fantis under their own chiefs. He was accompanied by Major Ricketts, the brigade major, Ensign Wetherell,

Mr. Williams, his private secretary, and Surgeon Tedlie, the same man who had accompanied Bowdich to Kumasi. "With only 20 rounds of ammunition for each man and some loose powder and slugs, most of which was soon spoiled by rain or in fording streams, Sir Charles, falling into the too common error of underrating his enemy and deaf to the remonstrances and advice of the king of Dukwa and other chiefs, now purposed defeating the advance of an Ashanti army of unknown strength, composed of men who were not only inured to bush fighting, but were also confident of success," Dr. Claridge wrote.

Not only had MacCarthy split up his available force into several divisions, "he must needs select the weakest of these with which to meet the enemy." Dr. Claridge concluded that "nothing more foolhardy can well be imagined."

MacCarthy's "miserable little handful" crossed the Prah in eight small canoes on January 13. They reached a village called Insamankow on the fourteenth, where they halted for five days to allow local tribesmen to rally around and to permit Mr. Brandon, MacCarthy's immensely incompetent storekeeper, to come forward with provisions and more ammunition. On the seventeenth—why the delay?—he sent a messenger ordering Major Chisholm to join him with the main body of his army, "but by some extraordinary blunder the letter was entrusted to a man who knew nothing of this part of the country, and who was so long in finding his way to [Chisholm] that it was not until the 22d that it was delivered."

The Ashantis continued their advance, with the Dankera and Wassaw tribesmen falling back in full retreat. MacCarthy sent Mr. Williams forward in an effort to rally them, and he managed to bring them to a halt and make camp on the banks of the Adamansu, a small tributary of the Prah, where he was soon joined by MacCarthy and the rest of the force. Tibo, the Dankera chief, took a look around him, and concluded there weren't near enough men to resist the Ashanti army. He said his soldiers would stand, but he said he was "quite sure that the Fantis cannot stand; that the whole charge will fall upon the Governor and his small force, and the consequence will be the ruin of Dankera!"

MacCarthy barely had time to inspect his positions—Wassaws on the right, Tibo and his Dankeras on the left, and the regulars and the Fantis in the center—when the Ashantis began their attack. Up to that moment, according to Colonel Ellis, "he seems to have been of opinion that there was but a small force of Ashantis at hand, and that the main body was at the distance of two or three days' march," refusing to credit reports from his own scouts that the entire Ashanti army, probably ten thousand men, was on top of him. Chisholm, with six hundred regulars and militia and three thousand unorganized natives, was still twenty-five miles away, and Captains Laing and Blenkarne, with four hundred more regulars among them, were too far away as well.

At about 2 P.M. on January 21, the Ashanti army, blowing their horns and beating their drums, advanced to about a half-mile of the river bank. One of the single most ludicrous incidents in colonial warfare now occurred: MacCarthy called his brass band, from the Royal African Corps, forward, and told them to strike up "God Save the King." The buglers were told to add to the din, the whole idea being that MacCarthy was convinced, "from some strange source of information," that the Ashantis only wanted an opportunity to come over to him.

The Ashantis, though briefly nonplussed, were willing to join this game too. They played in return, "and this musical defiance was kept up for some time, after which a dead silence ensued," Colonel Ellis reported. A few moments later, the drums began beating again, and the Ashantis advanced and lined up on their side of the river, which was about sixty feet wide. "This movement," said Colonel Ellis, "was executed with the greatest regularity, the Ashantis advancing in a number of different divisions under their respective leaders, whose horns sounded their calls; and upon hearing them, a native who had been in Kumasi was able to name nearly every Ashanti chief with the army."

"The action now commenced on both sides with determined vigour, and lasted till nearly dark," wrote Major Ricketts, who was there. "It was reported about four o'clock that our troops had expended all their ammunition, consisting of twenty rounds of ball cartridges . . . " Application was made to Mr. Brandon, who had arrived in the middle of the action, to supply more, "he having received his excellency's orders to have forty rounds of ball cartridges packed in kegs for each man ready to be issued . . . " But Mr. Brandon said they had not yet arrived, "and that he had only a barrel of powder and one of ball with him, which were immediately issued."

The wretched Brandon, it turned out, had left his base with about forty native carriers, but had gone ahead of them to join MacCarthy. The unsupervised carriers, seeing the Wassaws, their countrymen, hurrying to the rear, threw down the kegs they were carrying, and joined the retreat. "On this circumstance being reported to Sir Charles," Major Ricketts wrote, "he [MacCarthy] desired to see Mr. Brandon, with whom he was exceedingly angry, and if he had not suddenly disappeared either into the woods or to look after the ammunition, it is probable that if Sir Charles had had the means at the moment he would have put his threat into execution of suspending him to a tree."

The Ashantis had tried several times to cross the rain-swollen river, but had been driven back by gunfire. Now, "the enemy perceiving our fire had slackened," Ricketts noted, they succeeded. They "rushed in all directions on our gallant little force, who still defended themselves with their bayonets." The Ashantis "instantly beheaded nearly every one of those who unfortunately fell into their remorseless hands."

MacCarthy, already wounded, worked his way to the side of Tibo, the Dankera chief, who, surrounded by his people, was still fighting bravely. MacCarthy wanted a bugler to sound the retreat, but none was to be seen; they were all dead or wounded, or had joined the rest of their unit at the river's side. A small brass cannon was wheeled into place, still lashed with ropes to the poles on which it had been brought on men's shoulders, and aimed through the dense underbrush at the enemy. Mr. DeGraft, "a man of colour, linguist at Cape Coast and lieutenant in the militia, went round and obtained some power from the King of Dankera, [along] with some loose musket balls that had been left in a keg . . . and fired, in hopes to impede, in some measure, their advance. But they immediately rushed forward, and killed and wounded two men of the 2d royal West India regiment."

Ricketts, himself wounded, tried to follow MacCarthy, who had left the side of the king, and was making his way through heavy woods. All Ricketts could see were the feathers in his plumed helmet. "Soon after," he said, "there was a general rush back of those who were with him, after which no more was seen of him."

It was now every man for himself, and Major Ricketts and Mr. DeGraft seized a Wassaw tribesman, bribing him with a silver whistle and chain on the promise he would guide them to safety. When it became too dark to go on, they halted, and hid themselves in the woods. "The rejoicing of the Ashantees on their success, and their attempt to sound some of the instruments of the band which they had taken, was distinctly heard, not being distant half a mile."

An exhausted and bedraggled Ricketts finally crossed to the friendly side of the Prah River, encountering two of his own European soldiers. He asked if they knew him, "to which they answered in the negative."

MacCarthy's fate remained a mystery until late in March, when Mr. Williams, who had been captured by the Ashantis, was released. "He explained that he had left the field of battle with the Governor [MacCarthy], a Mr. Buckle, and Ensign Wetherell and retreated along the path towards Insamankow," according to Dr. Claridge. "They had not gone far, however, when they were attacked by a party of the enemy. One of Sir Charles' arms was broken at the first volley and he almost immediately afterwards fell with a second wound in the chest. He was carried to one side and laid at the foot of a tree," which Dr. Claridge said was "reverenced by the people of the district for many years thereafter."

Mr. Williams remembered seeing Ensign Wetherell "cutting with his sword at some of the enemy who were trying to tear off Sir Charles' uniform, when he himself received a wound in the thigh and lost consciousness. He was brought to his senses by the clumsy attempts of one of the Ashantis to cut off his head. He had already received one gash in the back of the neck when an Ashanti captain, to whom he had once done some kindness on the coast, recognized him and ordered his life to be spared.

"Lying near him he saw the headless trunks of his three companions."

Williams was taken to an Ashanti village, and "shut up each night in a hut with the heads of Sir Charles and the other officers. These heads had been so well preserved that the features of the governor especially presented almost the same appearance as they had done in life."

Williams also reported that the principal Ashanti chiefs "ate Sir Charles' heart in the belief they would thus derive a portion of his indomitable courage, and that pieces of his flesh were smoke-dried and carried on their persons as talismans to protect them in battle."

After two months of sharing his hut with the heads of his three companions, living on a twice-daily serving of as much snail soup as he could hold in one hand, Williams was released, and made his way back to Cape Coast Castle.

In a later engagement, British troops recaptured what they thought was Sir Charles's much-traveled head, which they sent to England. But it was all a mistake; the head, it turned out, had once belonged to a native chief.

MacCarthy's real head was taken to Kumasi, where—now a well-polished skull—it was brought out each year, in early September, as a highlight of the Yam Festival.

◆

The British general, Sir Garnet Wolseley, seems almost ubiquitous in the colonial warfare that was fought in the nineteenth century. In fact, he even put in an appearance on the Gold Coast in 1873. Acting as both the governor and the military commander, he vowed to destroy Ashanti power once and for all. He put his troops in gray homespun uniforms and told his officers they could bring only fifty pounds of personal gear. With an army that included the Welch Fusiliers (their mascot goat dropped dead on the beach) and the Black Watch regiments, they pushed north towards Kumasi. After heavy fighting, including a decisive bayonet charge, they entered the Ashanti capital on February 4, 1874, looted all the gold from the great palace, and then blew it up. His punishing expedition finished, Wolseley returned to the Gold Coast with his army. Back home in London, he was weighed down with honorary swords and university degrees.

The unhappy Ashantis rebelled in 1900 and laid siege to a stockade fort in Kumasi filled with British troops, as well as their women and children. Another relief column was sent, relieving the garrison, and the great Ashanti kingdom was made a British crown colony. The British formed a Gold Coast Regiment, and asked Ashanti warriors to join it. They said no.

The old kingdom is now part of the independent state of Ghana, and the new capital is at Accra.

FIVE

Major General William George Keith Elphinstone and the First Afghan War (1839–1842)

On the morning of November 25, 1838, the two most powerful armies on the Indian subcontinent gathered in a grand encampment at Ferozepore. On one side of the parade ground was Ranjit Singh's mighty Sikh army, the pride of the Punjab, turned out in scarlet tunics and blue trousers. On the other side was the army of the Honourable East India Company, a colorful mixture of native Indian regiments and regular regiments from Great Britain.

They had come together to celebrate the creation of the Grand Army of the Indus, which was soon to march through mountain passes in an effort to put Great Britain's own man, the ill-starred Prince Shāh Shuja, on the Afghan throne in the Bala Hissar, the great citadel, in Kabul.

It was a magnificent sight. The British had erected tents in the middle of a wide street, and lined it with dozens of highly decorated elephants. As the Punjabi maharaja approached at the head of his army, the elephants lumbered forward to greet him, the British statesmen and generals bumping along in their howdahs on top of the great beasts. Sir Henry Fane, commander in chief of the company's army, wore the uniform of a major general in the British army. Lord Auckland, India's governor-general, was "habited in a blue coat embroidered with gold, and wearing the ribbon of the Bath," remembered Captain Henry Havelock of Her Majesty's Thirteenth Light Infantry Regiment, who was there.

Rushing towards them, preceding Ranjit Singh, the fabled "Lion of Lahore," was "a noisy and disorderly though gorgeous rabble of Sikh horse and footmen, shouting out the titles of their great sirdar [general], some habited in glittering brocade, some in the *busuntee*, or bright spring yellow

109

dresses, which command so much respect in the Punjab, some wearing chain armor."

Following them were the Sikh elephants, and seated in the howdah of the lead elephant was the Lion of Lahore himself, described by Havelock as "an old man in an advanced state of decrepitude, clothed in faded crimson, his head wrapped up in folds of cloth of the same color. His single eye still lighted up with the fire of enterprise. . . ." Emily Eden, Auckland's sister, was there, too, and she thought the Lord of Lahore looked "exactly like an old mouse with gray whiskers and one eye."

The trick was to bring the two lines of elephants together and to transfer the fragile old Sikh from his howdah to the one occupied by Lord Auckland. "The shock of elephants at the moment of meeting is terrific," noted Havelock. "More than a hundred of these active and sagacious, but enormous animals, goaded on by their drivers in contrary directions, are suddenly brought to a standstill by the collision of the opposing fronts and foreheads," all of this accomplished "amidst the roaring, trumpeting, pushing, and crushing of impetuous and gigantic animals."

Luckily, no one was killed. That would happen later, for no army was ever defeated so completely, so perfectly, as the Grand Army of the Indus. Ultimately, what was left of it would march out of Kabul, forty-five hundred soldiers and twelve thousand camp followers in disorderly retreat, but only one man, Dr. William Brydon, wounded and frostbitten, would stagger through the deadly mountain passes and collapse in the welcoming arms of British soldiers in the garrison at Jalalabad. All the rest, with the exception of a few deserters and prisoners, died.

It was "the most unjust, ill-advised, and unnecessary [war] that had ever engaged the energies of a British army, or risked the honorable reputation of the British name throughout the East," Havelock concluded.

It was all part of the Great Game, the effort by Britain to deny competing European powers a route to India, its sprawling prize colony. The land route to India led from Persia through Afghanistan, and by 1830, the real concern was imperialist Russia. Herat, a fortified Afghan city west of Kabul in a plain so fertile it was called the "Granary of Central Asia," was thought by nearly everyone to be the gateway to India. With Russian help and encouragement, Persian troops invested Herat in 1837 and 1838; the city held on only because of the military prowess of Lieutenant Eldred Pottinger, a British officer serving with the East India Company's Bombay Horse Artillery who just happened to be visiting Herat when the Persians showed up.

Not only were the Russians helping in the siege of Herat, they had also sent a political agent, Captain Ivan Viktorovich Vitkevich, a Lithuanian-born aristocrat, to stir up trouble in Kabul. A British agent, the celebrated Captain Alexander Burnes, was already in residence in Kabul, and he invited Count Vitkevich to Christmas dinner in 1837. "We are in a mess here," he concluded in a letter to a friend. "The emperor of Russia has sent an envoy to Kabul to offer . . . money [to the Afghans] to fight Rajeet Singh!!!! I could not believe my eyes or ears."

The Afghan ruler, an extraordinarily intelligent and competent man named Dōst Mohammad Khān, preferred to deal with Great Britain, but only if he could get Peshawar, once an Afghan city and now ruled by the hated Sikhs, back. Burnes sympathized with the Afghan ruler, but his government wasn't prepared to take Peshawar away from the Sikhs. The British faced a kind of Hobson's choice—they wanted to create a buffer state to block Russian penetration to the Indus River, where British India began, and either Afghanistan or the Punjab would do. But they couldn't have both. So they chose the Sikhs, and foolishly decided to put Shāh Shuja on the Afghan throne. The fact was, the British worried more about the Sikhs and that huge, French-trained Sikh army, than they did about the Afghans. After all, they reckoned, the Afghans didn't have a real army; the country was broken up into tribal fiefdoms and the highly independent Afghan warriors carried ancient matchlock rifles, called *juzails*.

Shuja, a grandson of the founder of the Afghan empire, the great Ahmed Shāh, had succeeded his brother, Zemaun, as ruler of Afghanistan in 1803. Zemaun's career had come to a ghastly end when his enemies, "with delicate skill," punctured his eyeballs with a lancet. Blind men cannot rule. Shuja himself was toppled from power by rebellious chiefs in 1809 and ultimately took up residence with his dozens of wives and concubines in British-controlled India in 1818, losing his most prized possession, the Kohinoor diamond, to Rajeet Singh along the way. The British paid him a comfortable pension, figuring he might come in handy one day.

And so the Grand Army of the Indus gathered at Ferozepore, presumably to meet the Russian threat posed by the siege of Herat and Count Vitkevich's dangerous diplomacy in Kabul. The Lion of Lahore, old but still no fool, understood what invading Afghanistan entailed, and he wanted no part of those dark passes on the way to Kabul, and the rifles and knives of those bloodthirsty Afghan tribesmen. He wished the British-led army good luck and took his army home to Lahore.

As the British-led army was about to get underway, staggering news arrived: the Persians had lifted the siege, and Herat was saved. Moreover, the emperor at St. Petersburg had turned his back on his envoy to Kabul. It was too much for Vitkevich; he committed suicide.

British intentions had been spelled out on October 1 in the Simla Declaration, issued by Lord Auckland and signed by Chief Secretary William Macnaughten. In it, the British declared that the Afghan ruler, Dōst Mohammad Khān, had made an "unprovoked attack" on the troops "of our ancient ally, Maharaja Ranjeet Singh." That, of course, was patent nonsense, other than the observation that the old maharaja, the one-eyed mouse with whiskers, was a little on the ancient side. The declaration said, too, that Shāh Shuja was "popular throughout Afghanistan," and that he would enter Afghanistan "surrounded by his own troops, and would be supported against foreign interference and factious opposition by the British army." That was absurd, too. Shāh Shuja was only dimly remembered by most Afghans, and those memories were anything but positive. Moreover, he wouldn't lead his own troops into Afghanistan. He didn't have any troops of his own, and those that marched under his name were recruited by the British from all over India.

The manifesto was not well received, either in India or in Britain. "What! Lord Auckland and Macnaughten gone to war," thundered Lord William Cavendish Bentinck, a former governor-general of India. "The very last men in the world I should have suspected of such folly." The Duke of Wellington, still a power in London, observed that the army's difficulties would commence when its military successes ended. He meant that it would be one thing to put Shāh Shuja on the Afghan throne; it would be another to keep him there. Lord Wellesley said it was stupid to occupy a land of "rocks, sands, deserts, ice and snow."

Now was the time to reconsider the entire enterprise. Persia's failure to seize Herat "cut from [under] the feet of Lord Auckland all ground of justification, and rendered the expedition across the Indus at once a folly and a crime," wrote Sir John William Kaye, the campaign's chief historian. But Auckland, backed by the British government in London and supported by the hawks on his own staff, led by his chief secretary, Macnaughten, was committed, and there would be no turning back.

Auckland's Grand Army of the Indus was a mind-boggling mixture of races, cultures, and traditions. Under the governor-general, appointed by the East India Company but in fact subject to government approval, India was divided into three basic parts, or presidencies: Bengal, Bombay, and Madras. One of this army's divisions, it was decided, would come from

Bengal, the other from Bombay. Attached to each were regiments from the British army.

The East India Company maintained its own army, with field headquarters at Simla, and trained its own officers, all of them British, at its own military academy at Addiscombe, a country estate near London. The troops were mercenaries, drawn from all over India. Their officers were always British. It was inevitable that the queen's officers, serving with European troops, would look down their patrician noses at company officers, serving with native, or sepoy, units.

Because of the Persian withdrawal from Herat, Auckland and his commanders agreed to cut back on the size of the army they would send to Kabul. Sir Henry Fane, the commander in chief, drew lots to see which units would go ahead and which would not. The result was that the best British regiment, the Third Foot, known as "the Buffs," was left behind, and the worst, the Thirteenth Light Infantry, a sickly lot, went forward.

The Bengal contingent included native units with names like Skinner's Horse, the Second Light Cavalry, and the Forty-third Native Infantry. The regular units were the Thirteenth Infantry and the Sixteenth Lancers.

The Bombay unit, known as the "Bombay Ducks" because it would be moved into position by sea from Bombay to Karachi, included the Poona Local Horse and the Nineteenth Native Infantry. The regular units were the Fourth Dragoons and two infantry regiments, the Coldstream Guards (Second Foot) and the Seventeenth Foot.

The Bengal unit numbered ninety-five hundred men; the Bombay division, fifty-six hundred. Shāh Shuja commanded six thousand men, all of them hastily recruited mercenaries from India. The British commanders took with them thirty-eight thousand camp followers and 30,000 camels. It was going to be a *promenade militaire*, Captain Havelock was told, and so the officers took everything they thought they might possibly need on the line of march. One brigadier, it was reported, needed 60 camels to pack all his provisions; General Sir John Keane took 260 for himself and his immediate personal staff. One British regiment (the Sixteenth Lancers) took its own pack of foxhounds. Another needed two camels to carry its cigars.

Not so lucky was the ordinary infantryman. He was weighed down with his ten-pound musket, and a bayonet and sixty rounds of ammunition weighing an additional thirteen pounds. Added to that was a light coat and a heavy coat, a pair of trousers, a shirt, an extra pair of boots, and an extra pair of socks, totaling still another thirteen pounds. He was expected to carry all of this in "such a succession of marches as few armies in any quarter of the globe had ever attempted to complete," in some of the hottest weather of the year.

Havelock, traveling with the overland Bengal division commanded by the fat and stupid Major General Sir Willoughby Cotton, set off with his regiment on December 8, the first time in twelve years the Thirteenth Light Infantry had been summoned "to the duties of actual service." They marched southwest, on a line paralleling the Indus River, heading for Hyderabad, capital of the semi-independent state of Sind. That was curious, for Hyderabad was in the opposite direction from Kabul, presumably the army's actual destination. But this was a political decision; the army's political officers hoped to bully the ruling emirs of Sind into declaring their allegiance to Shāh Shuja, and at the same time to extort twenty-five lakhs of rupees—some £250,000 sterling—to line the pockets of both Ranjit Singh and Shāh Shuja.

Hyderabad was supposedly filled with rich booty, and the troops were beginning to lick their chops in anticipation of getting their hands on it. To their delight, Cotton began licking his chops, too. He decided he would loot the city, even though that wasn't in the plan at all. Cotton excused his decision by saying it had something to do with joining up with Sir John Keane's Bombay Ducks, already beginning to come ashore at Karachi, south of Hyderabad where the Indus River empties into the Arabian Sea.

When Macnaughten heard what Cotton was up to, he stepped in and countermanded the decision. "If this goes on," he wrote, " . . . what is to become of our Afghan expedition?" Good point. And so Hyderabad would be spared and the army would turn around and move northwest to Kalat, push through the Bolan Pass, seize Kandahar, capture the great Afghan fortress at Ghazni, and then march triumphantly into Kabul.

By February 18, Cotton and his Bengal column had reached Shikarpur, two hundred miles north of Hyderabad, where they crossed the Indus River on a bridge of boats. There, Sir Henry Fane, the commander in chief, said good-bye to his troops, and headed back to Bombay—and retirement. The new commander would be General Keane, a foul-mouthed Irishman, who had been commanding the Bombay Ducks. But he was still working his way up the Indus, by riverboats now, and was one hundred miles below Shikarpur on the twentieth. Without waiting for Keane to come up, Cotton set out for the dreaded Bolan Pass on the twenty-first.

The army began moving into rough country partly controlled by the ruffian Mehrab Khān, from Kalat, who kept himself and his followers busy by plundering anyone foolish enough to try to work their way through the sixty-mile-long Bolan Pass. Sir Alexander Burnes—he had been recently knighted for his services—rode ahead to talk Mehrab Khān and his greedy chieftains into allowing free passage of the British army through his jurisdiction, and to supply the soldiers and camels with food and forage. Mehrab Khān promised to do his best, and he really did try, but this was barren country without very much in the way of supplies, and 1838 had been a bad year for what crops his people could produce. They barely had enough to feed themselves. Worse, the army was now being tracked by wild Beluchi tribesmen, owing allegiance to no one, and they were beginning to steal camels bearing provisions and to pick off stragglers with their long-range, highly accurate matchlock rifles.

The army's camels started dropping by the side of the road, and there was no one to take care of them, for most of the *surwars*, the Sikh grooms hired to keep track of them, had deserted weeks earlier. Before the army reached Kabul, thousands of them died.

By March 10, Cotton's Bengal division was at Dadur, at the mouth of the Bolan Pass, the camp followers on half rations, provisions for the army running low. Macnaughten unfairly blamed the army's problems on Mehrab Khān, and vowed to get even with him later. The chieftain didn't help his cause by warning the British of what lurked up ahead. "Wait till sickness overtakes your troops," he said. "Wait till they are so exhausted with fatigue from long and harassing marches, and from the total want of supplies. Wait till they have drunk of many waters, and wait, too, till they feel the sharpness of Afghan swords."

The wind blew out of the pass with such force that it threatened to knock down the tents of the British officers. Havelock solved that problem by stationing "four of the stoutest of my domestics with strict charge to hold up the wooden support of the dwelling, and having thus provided against the worst, slept or tried to sleep until the cavalry trumpets sounded [the beginning of the day]."

It took the column six days to clear the sixty-mile-long pass, with more baggage cattle and camels dropping dead. "The way was strewn with baggage—with abandoned tents, and stores, and luxuries which, a few weeks afterwards, would have fetched their weight twice counted in rupees," Sir John Kaye wrote.

When they emerged from the pass on the twenty-sixth, they camped in the clear at a village called Quetta. Cotton met Macnaughten and General Keane on April 4, and described to them his column's sorry plight. Macnaughten was unimpressed. "Sir Willoughby," he wrote Auckland, "is a sad croaker [a grumbler]; not content with telling me we must all inevitably be starved, he assures me that Shāh Shuja is very unpopular in

Afghanistan and that we shall be oppposed at every step of our progress. I think I know a little better than this."

It was at Quetta that the Bombay Ducks finally caught up with Cotton's division, thus bringing the marching Grand Army of the Indus together for the first time. Keane assumed overall command, with Cotton in command of the Bengal division and Major General Sir Thomas Willshire, a queen's officer, in command of the Bombay division. That outraged Major General William Nott, a company officer, who believed he should have been given a divisional command.

With Shāh Shuja and his mercenary army in the lead, the Grand Army of the Indus marched into Kandahar, one of Afghanistan's major cities, on April 25, 1839, with a paid claque of Afghans shouting his praises. Keane lingered in Kandahar for two months, waiting for crops to ripen and for a convoy with fresh supplies to make its way to him through the Bolan Pass. The convoy came in on June 23, and the march to Kabul resumed on June 27, with Keane foolishly leaving his siege guns—four big eighteen-pounders—behind. (The date was important for another reason: back in the Punjab, Ranjit Singh, the Lion of Lahore, the old mouse with whiskers, was dead, and Britain was now without a significant friend in the empire the great man had created.)

Leaving the siege guns behind was a foolish mistake because lying between Kandahar and Kabul was the mighty fortress at Ghazni, ninety miles south of Kabul, defended by three thousand Afghan tribesmen under Hyder Khān, one of Dōst Mohammad's sons. The fortress "certainly far exceeded our expectations," wrote Captain Havelock. With its "soldity, lofty profile and state of repair of its wall and citadel, . . . we now saw that we had at last before us an enterprise worthy of our best efforts."

The Afghans believed Ghazni was impregnable, so impregnable the British would never be foolish enough to attack it. Shāh Shuja urged Keane to forget it. Bypass Ghazni, he said, and continue the march on Kabul. Keane wouldn't hear of it; he insisted on taking the place. But how could it be done? He couldn't blast the thick mud walls apart, because he didn't have siege guns, and he couldn't starve the garrison out, because he didn't have enough food himself to conduct a siege. The answer was supplied by a deserter from the fortress, Abdul Rashed Khān, a nephew of Dōst Mohammad. One of the fortress's great wooden gates, the Kabul gate, was weaker than the others, the traitor told Keane. Maybe it could be blown open with a gunpowder charge.

But before the bags of powder could be touched off, the Grand Army of the Indus was forced to deal for the first time with a force of *Ghazis*, Moslem warriors dedicated to fighting to the death to destroy the despised *harajis* (foreign infidels), and to destroy most especially the *farangis*, a pejorative term reserved exclusively for the British. Hundreds of these Ghazis swooped down on Shāh Shuja's encampment, supported by artillery from the ramparts of the fortress. They were finally driven off by British troops, and fifty of them were captured. The prisoners were hauled before Shāh Shuja and one of them, in a daring display of *lèse-majesté*, stabbed a supporter of the king. Shāh Shuja was incensed, and he ordered his royal executioners to behead them all. Sir John Kaye, the campaign historian, was so outraged by the "wanton barbarity" he could hardly contain himself. On the day of reckoning, he said, "the shrill cry" of the Ghazis would be sounded as the "funeral wail" of his government's "unholy policy."

The assault began early the morning of July 23. The field guns opened up on the walls of the fortress, and the guns of the fortress promptly replied, making a huge din as the engineers crept up to the Kabul gate. Waiting for the gate to be blown open were companies from three British regiments—the Second, Thirteenth, and Seventeenth—all of them led by Colonel William Dennie. Backing them up was another force of British regulars, commanded by Brigadier Robert Sale.

The engineers piled nine hundred pounds of gunpowder, in twelve bags, against the gate, and touched off the powder line attached to them. Two minutes later, the powder exploded, "shivered the massive barricade in pieces, and brought down in hideous ruin into the passage below masses of masonry and fractured beams," according to Captain Havelock. The buglers sounded "Charge!" and Colonel Dennie's storm troops rushed forward into the "smoking and darkened opening," where they found Afghans barring their way. "The clash of sword blade against bayonet was heard on every side."

Resistance was slowly overcome. "But, oh! the fugitive character of human success, even in its brightest moments!" wrote Havelock. Just as victory was almost won, an engineering officer, clearly confused, met the advancing column of Brigadier Sale and told its commander that Dennie's troops had failed to break through. Sale ordered the retreat to be sounded, and the whole force began falling back. Other officers appeared, however, and told Sale that Dennie's men had forced the passage and were inside the fort. Sale reversed the retreat order and resumed the advance.

As Sale began climbing over the gate's broken timbers, he was attacked by a saber-wielding Afghan, who cut him across the face. As he began falling to the ground, "the Afghan repeated his blow . . . but the pommel, not the edge of his sword, this time took effect, though with stunning violence." The two men "rolled together among the fractured timbers" and Sale was beginning to faint away from loss of blood when another officer turned up and "passed his drawn saber through the body of the Afghan." But even that wasn't enough, for "the desperado continued to struggle with frantic violence." Finally, Sale worked himself clear and dealt the Afghan "a cut from his own saber, which cleft his [enemy's] skull from the crown to the eyebrows. "Ue Ullah [Oh, God]," the Afghan said. "and never spoke or moved again," Havelock wrote. Sale would eventually earn the title of "Fighting Bob" and his wife, the resourceful Florentia (soon to be Lady Sale following a knighthood for her husband), would write the best chronicle of the last days of the Grand Army of the Indus.

It was all over at 5 A.M., as Ensign Frere of the Thirteenth Light Infantry hoisted his regiment's colors over the citadel. The attackers had lost 17 men killed and 165 wounded. Afghan casualties amounted to more than 500 men.

Dōst Mohammad's oldest son, Afzul Khān, had been lurking near the fort with five thousand horsemen, hoping to waylay the British column. When he saw British colors flying over the citadel—a sight neither he nor any other Afghan warrior had believed possible—he turned in despair and took his men back to Kabul, leaving all his baggage, including several elephants, behind. Hyder Khān, Dōst Mohammad's son who had defended the fortress, was captured a few days later hiding in a house near the Kandahar gate.

Keane's army collected a huge amount of booty—vast stores of *ottah* (ground wheat), *ghee* (clarified butter the Afghans slathered over their food), powder, shot, chain armor, shields, powder horns, muskets and rifles, and nine cannon, including the mighty *Zubur-Zun* (the "hard-hitter"), an ornamented brass forty-eight-pounder.

Dōst Mohammad tried to rally his supporters, and finally succeeded in marching an army out of Kabul to challenge the advancing Grand Army of the Indus. "But the battle was never fought," said Sir John Kaye, for " . . . it became too manifest there was treachery in his camp." The "venal" Kuzzilbashi tribesmen (their ancestors had come to Afghanistan from Persia, and they had never been completely accepted) had always showed more sympathy to the British invaders than anyone else. Now they began to desert, and soon "there was scarcely a true man left in [Dōst Mohammad's] ranks. . . . He looked around him and saw only perfidy on the right hand and the left." He pleaded with his troops to make one last stand, "like true believers." But it was hopeless; the fall of Ghazni had taken the heart out of them. During the night of August 2, the Dōst, with a handful of loyal followers, took flight, taking refuge, finally, beyond the mountainous Hindu Kush.

The Grand Army of the Indus, in full ceremonial uniform, bands blaring, triumphantly approached Kabul on August 7, with Shāh Shuja, the new king, in the lead. "On the left," said Havelock, "we saw in the plains little eminences, crowded with forts and towers . . . but it wasn't until we nearly approached the town that we perceived wherein the true beauty of the site of Kabul consists. Above us, indeed, on our right, was only a bare mountain crowned with an almost useless wall, but in the vale below were stretched out to such an extent that the eye vainly endeavored to reach the boundaries of them, the far-famed orchards of Kabul."

The army passed through a "suburb" filled with handsome houses, crossed a "paltry" bridge, and was soon "wedged together in narrow streets, which had been choked before we arrived with the dense files of the Afghan population. Never was any town seen more closely thronged by men, [and] of women, glimpses only could be caught as they peeped furtively from the tops of houses."

Historians have argued for years about the Afghan reaction to the arrival of Shāh Shuja. Most of them have said he was unwelcome, and that the crowds that turned out to see him on August 7 were unenthusiastic. James A. Norris, the latest in the line, developed a revisionist view, arguing that "there was great public satisfaction in the change of government" and that Shāh Shuja "saw ready acceptance, or something more, in the faces of the many spectators of [his] entry into Kabul." Norris concluded that the people of Kabul were willing to give Shāh Shuja a chance.

But the problem wasn't so much Shāh Shuja. It was the people he brought with him, the farangis, the British-led Grand Army of the Indus. They were never welcome in Kabul. The wonder of it is, most of them didn't even know it. ("Why is it," one of the political officers, himself a Scot, asked, "that Englishmen everywhere are rough, overbearing, without tact and address, and more disliked by foreigners than any other people?")

By September 1, the war seemed to be over, and it was time to break up the Grand Army of the Indus by sending most of the soldiers home. First, though—what else?—a grand parade. More than thirty thousand troops assembled for it on September 7, thirteen thousand regulars under Keane, the rest native troops. The troops were told they could wear a special Ghazni medal awarded to them by Shāh Shuja. Keane relinquished his command to Cotton, and headed home. The queen made him Lord Keane of Ghazni, but he was not a happy man. Before leaving, he told an aide: "I cannot but congratulate you on quitting the country; for, mark my words, it will not be long before there is here some signal catastrophe."

On the way back to India, a British detachment under General Willshire paused at Kalat to get even with Mehrab Khān, the guardian of the Bolan Pass who really had tried to be helpful. Willshire's troops blew the gates open and stormed into the chief's citadel. He died, sword in hand, and Kalat, on Auckland's orders, was added to Shāh Shuja's dominions.

The army's only worry was the whereabouts of Dōst Mohammad. For a while, he pulled some tribesmen around him and fought a series of guerrilla-style skirmishes. Later, he took refuge with a truly nasty human being, Nasrullah Khān, the emir of Bukhara, who in time tossed him into a dank dungeon filled with human bones, animal filth, and nasty vermin and reptiles. There, he joined a British political officer, Colonel Charles Stoddart, who had been sent to Bukhara to arrange a treaty of friendship. Stoddart was later joined by an Englishman sent to rescue him, Captain Arthur Connolly. He was thrown into the dungeon, too, and in 1842, the crazy emir executed both of them.

The Dōst was luckier—he managed to escape in the summer of 1840, to begin his campaign against Shāh Shuja and his farangi army. The British routed Dōst Mohammad in several skirmishes, but he always managed to escape. "I am like a wooden spoon," he said. "You may throw me hither and yon but I shall not be hurt." Then, on November 2, 1840, he unexpectedly routed some native cavalrymen in a skirmish with a small force commanded by Sir Robert Sale in Kohistan, north of Kabul. Two days later, an Afghan rode into the courtyard of Sir William Macnaughten's residence in Kabul (he had received a knighthood too), and announced he had come to see the Envoy—Macnaughten was known now, always, as the Envoy—to surrender. Unbelievably, it was Dōst Mohammad himself. He was worn out, and tired of the fighting. The British exiled him to Ludhiana, in India, and the same comfortable mansion that had been reserved so long for Shāh Shuja.

Now, surely, the British position in Afghanistan was secure. Lady Sale was busily at work in her garden, cultivating flowers "that were the admiration of the Afghan gentlemen who came to see us." Her sweet peas and cauliflowers were much admired, too, and the potatoes were doing surprisingly well. In August of 1841, her daughter, Alexandrina, was married to Lieutenant John Sturt of the Royal Engineers, and the honeymooners moved into the Sales's home.

On the social ladder, though, Sir Robert and Florentia ranked second. At the top of the ladder were the Macnaughtens. The Envoy had brought his wife to Kabul late in 1839, along with crystal chandeliers, choice wines, and hundreds—no mistake, hundreds—of servants. The British infantrymen couldn't bring their families from home, but the sepoy soldiers were urged to send for theirs, and in no time at all hundreds of them had arrived from India.

Captain Havelock gorged himself on five different kinds of grapes, and apples of a brilliant rosy red, along with melons, almonds, pistachio nuts, walnuts, quinces, small black cherries, and red and white mulberries. The shops in Kabul's great bazaar were filled, overflowing with delicacies.

The British officers raced horses and played cricket. And, when the lakes froze over, they went ice skating, to the astonishment of the natives, who had never seen such a thing before.

Shāh Shuja, roaming his citadel and remembering that it seemed so much bigger and so much better furnished when he lived there as a boy, was nominally the ruler of Afghanistan. But that, of course, was increasingly a joke. He made little effort to win over the Afghans—"dogs," he called them—and relied more and more on the British to make the decisions and keep the country going. Afghanistan, Sir John Kaye noted, again and again, was ruled by the bayonet and the money bag, meaning the British army and the payment of huge bribes to keep the native chieftains in line. These payments extended to the Ghilzye chieftains, whose fierce tribesmen controlled the mountain passes that represented the only way to get into Afghanistan from British India—and out.

To this day, no one has ever determined who was responsible for positioning the British forces in and around Kabul. "It must always remain a wonder," said Lieutenant Vincent Eyre, who was there, "that any government, or any officer or set of officers, who had either science or experience in the field, should, in a *half*-conquered country, fix their forces (already inadequate to the services to which they might be called) in so extraordinary and injudicious a military position."

The main body of the occupying British garrison had been assigned to newly built cantonments on a piece of low-lying, swampy ground to the northeast of the city—the Kabul River a mile to the east, the main road to

Kohistan at the edge of the camp to the west—and commanded by hills on either side. The cantonments ran nearly a mile in length, north to south, and perhaps a half mile east to west. Just to the north of the cantonments was the mission compound, with houses belonging to the military and political officers. The cantonments were surrounded by some of the famous Kabul orchards, and the land was broken up by irrigation canals, making movement of horses and artillery difficult.

The walls, for both the cantonments and the mission, "were beyond measure contemptible," Sir John Kaye wrote. The whole expanse, he said, was planned "as to be swept on every side by hills, and forts, and villages, and whatever else in such a country could bristle with armed men." Kaye said that if the object of those who constructed these works "had been to place our troops at the mercy of an enemy, they could not have been devised more cunningly in furtherance of such an end."

To crown their folly, the men who designed the British position placed the depot for commissary supplies—food to feed the soldiers and camp followers—in a small, partly collapsed fort, undermined by rats, outside the cantonments. At the time this arrangement was made, Captain James Skinner, the chief commissariat officer, had pleaded for room within the cantonments for his supplies. But he was told "no such place could be given him, as they were far too busy in erecting barracks for the men, to think of commissariat stores," according to Lieutenant Eyre.

"The communication between the two places was commanded by an empty fort, and by a walled garden, inviting the occupation of the enemy," wrote Kaye, an apoplectic British military historian in the tradition of Sir John Fortescue. "Human folly," Kaye went on, "seemed to have reached its height in the construction of these works." But that wasn't all. The depot for storing powder and ammunition was outside the cantonments, too, in another tumbledown fort.

The garrison, the whole kit and caboodle, should have been housed in Kabul's great, sprawling citadel, the Bala Hissar, at once the city's royal palace and main fortress. Captain Havelock, soon to depart for India (one of the lucky ones), examined the fortress and found it in a state of some disrepair. But, he said, in a city of sixty thousand, it would have been no problem finding workers to render the defenses respectable. The walls were lofty, he said, the towers and curtains well-disposed, "and a broad stagnant moat runs around the place, which a few strokes of the spade would have filled with water." The fortress, he concluded, "is the key of Kabul."

But, of course, the royal palace was part of the fortress, and it was occupied by the new king, Shāh Shuja, who had filled the place with his extensive harem, dozens of wives and concubines. He wanted the citadel to himself, partly to meet his extensive housing requirements and partly as a point of honor, and he told Macnaughten that the troops should be taken someplace else. Macnaughten agreed.

Macnaughten—the Envoy—was as much responsible for these disastrous conditions as anyone else. By September 1841, he had convinced himself that everything was going beautifully. "Our prospects in this country are brightening in every direction," he wrote to an associate on September 15. "We are all quiet here," he said in another letter, on September 20. "Everything is *couleur de rose*." He was getting ready to go back to India, and that partly explained his unwillingness to listen to bad news. Waiting in line to succeed him as envoy was Sir Alexander Burnes, who had taken up residence in a comfortable, walled manor house in the city itself. The house next door was occupied by Captain Johnson, the paymaster, who had been given permission by the Envoy to keep all the garrison's cash inside.

After talking in his campaign history about the "athletic amusements of our people" in Kabul, Sir John Kaye with great regret turned to a distasteful subject, noting that "there are truths which must be spoken." Things were going on in some of those residences, Sir John said, that involved "temptations which are most difficult to withstand, [and] were not withstood by our English officers." The women of Kabul, he said, finally getting to the point, were exceedingly attractive, and the inmates of the Mohammedan zenanas—women's quarters—"were not unwilling to visit the quarters of the Christian stranger." The scandal, he said, was "open, undisguised, notorious," and Sir Alexander Burnes was one of the chief culprits. The cuckolded Afghan tribesmen, Kaye said, were outraged, and they had begun plotting revenge.

General Cotton, not feeling well, had been succeeded in command of the Grand Army of the Indus by a new man, Major General William George Keith Elphinstone, who was even more sickly, early in 1841. Auckland's sister, Emily Eden, had known him since she was a child, and called him "Elphy Bey." Grandson of the tenth Baron Elphinstone, he came from a distinguished family. His first cousin, Mountstuart Elphinstone, had been governor of Bombay, and had written a well-regarded history of India. Another cousin, the one with the title, was currently serving as governor of Madras. Elphy Bey had entered the army in 1804, and had served in a number of regiments before purchasing the lieutenant colonelcy of the Thirty-third Foot in 1813, commanding the regiment at Waterloo and winning a C.B. (Companion of the Bath) for his conduct. He had gone on half pay in 1822, routinely winning promotion to major general in 1837. But it wasn't until 1839 that he was called back to active service. The Horse Guards (the army headquarters in London) sent him to India to command the Benares division of the Bengal army.

Auckland, in urging him to take the job in Kabul, told him the mountain climate would be "more congenial to your constitution than the hot plains of India." He was now fifty-nine years old, sick and gouty, and his appointment was a military disaster. The man Auckland should have pushed for the job was Major General William Nott, but he was a company officer and he had ruffled too many feathers with his irascible temper. Upon being passed over, Nott grumbled that Elphinstone was "the most incompetent soldier that was to be found among the officers of the requisite rank." Not a good loser, Nott.

Elphinstone arrived in Kabul late in April of 1841 to take up his new command. Cotton, handing over the reins, told him, "You will *have nothing to do here, all is peace.*" New to Kabul, too, was the man who would be Elphinstone's second in command, Brigadier John Shelton. It was to become a match—Elphinstone and Shelton—made in hell. Elphy Bey was a kind, warm-hearted man, constantly trying to please everyone around him. Shelton was a mean, nasty tyrant. He had lost his right arm in an engagement in the Peninsular War, and had remained in a constant state of anger ever since. He had come up to Afghanistan from India with a replacement regiment, the Forty-fourth Foot (yes, the same regiment that had been with Braddock on the Monongahela), in relief of the Thirteenth Light Infantry, which was finally being sent home to England.

By September, five months after his arrival, Elphinstone's health had taken a turn for the worse. He was suffering from gout and rheumatism, and was running a fever. He spent most of his time in bed. "My right wrist is so painful I can't move it," he wrote to one of his cousins. He now wanted to go home. With a new government in London, Auckland was on his way home, too, to be replaced as governor-general by Lord Ellenborough, and even Macnaughten was getting set to leave to take up his new post as governor of Bombay.

Durrani tribesmen north of Kabul and Ghilzye tribesmen patrolling the mountain passes were restless, and even Macnaughten had begun to admit the country wasn't in "perfect tranquillity." Even so, under cost-cutting pressure from London, Macnaughten decided to reduce the traditional stipends, or subsidies—better call them bribes—paid to the Afghan chieftains, including the Ghilzyes, Durranis, and even the usually cooperative Kuzzilbashis. As soon as they got the word, the Ghilzye chiefs mounted their ponies and rode out of town. They "occupied the passes on the road to Jalalabad," wrote Sir John Kaye, "they plundered a valuable *cafila* [caravan], and entirely cut off our communications with the provinces of Hindustan."

Macnaughten still wasn't ready to panic. "The Eastern Ghilzyes are kicking up a row about some deductions which have been made from their pay." he wrote Major Henry Rawlinson, the political officer in Kandahar, on October 7. "The rascals have completely succeeded in cutting off our communications for the time being, which is very provoking to me at this time; but they will be well trounced for their pains." To Macnaughten, this was just another in a series of minor uprisings by the tribesmen. "One down, t'other come on, is the principle of these vagabonds," he wrote Rawlinson a few days later.

Macnaughten's idea was that Sale could deal with these "impudent rascals" on his way home to India with the Thirteenth Light Infantry. But maybe he might need help, and so the Thirty-fifth Native Infantry marched first, on Saturday, October 9, instructed to clear the Ghilzyes from the Koord-Kabul Pass, fifteen miles from the city. The Ghilzyes attacked their camp Sunday night and killed and wounded twenty-four sepoys. Sale, with the Thirteenth, marched out of Kabul on Monday and helped the sepoys clear the pass, though Sale received a slight wound in the ankle. That was it, for now: The Ghilzyes opened negotiations, and, after Macnaughten paid them ten thousand rupees, allowed Sale and his column to proceed on their way to Jalalabad, but not without some recalcitrant tribesmen attacking the rear guard and killing and wounding as many as one hundred men.

The British position began to unravel the night of November 1, while Macnaughten was packing his bags to take up his new assignment in Bombay. It was then the Afghan chieftains met quietly in the home of one of their leaders to plot rebellion.

The tall, energetic Lady Sale, with her daughter and son-in-law, Captain Sturt, had remained behind in the cantonments after her husband's departure with his regiment. Her extraordinary diary remains the best source for the disaster that was now to fall upon Elphinstone's army, and all its camp followers. "This morning, early, all was in commotion in Kabul," Lady Sale wrote on November 2. "The shops were plundered, and the people were all fighting."

A mob, in fact, was besieging Sir Alexander Burnes's house in the city, and he had sent Macnaughten a note asking for help. While waiting for it to arrive, "Burnes was haranguing the mob," Sir John Kaye wrote. Beside him were his brother (Lieutenant Charles Burnes) and a friend (Captain William Broadfoot). "The crowd before his house increased in number and fury. Some were thirsting for blood; others were greedy only for plunder. He might as well have addressed himself to a herd of savage beasts."

Burnes had been warned by Afghan friends that trouble was brewing, and that he should seek the safety of the cantonments, but he had rejected the advice. Even now, as the mob surged in the street below, he refused to allow his small sepoy bodyguard to open fire. But Broadfoot, a practical soldier, had seen enough: he took personal command, and ordered the guards to shoot. He "killed five or six men with his own hand before he was shot down," Lieutenant Eyre reported in his diary.

Burnes and his brother, Broadfoot and the sepoys, and all the women and children in the compound were killed. The mob moved on then to the home of Paymaster Johnson, who, fortunately for him, had chosen to spend the night in the cantonments. They "gained possession of my treasury by undermining the wall . . . ," he wrote later. "They murdered the whole of the guard (one officer and 28 sepoys), all my servants (male, female, and children), plundered my treasury . . . , burnt all my office records . . . and possessed themselves of all my private property."

James Norris, the historian, said that he had lived "through the events of November 2, 1841, many times in his imagination and still finds it impossible to believe that the garrison could have done more that day."

Lieutenant Eyre didn't share that kindly view, and neither did very many other British officers at the time. The riot, after all, had led to the deaths of Burnes and all his companions, and the looting of the garrison's payroll. British-led troops—five thousand of them—were just minutes away, and they did nothing. "The murder of our countrymen, and the spoliation of public and private property, was perpetrated with impunity within a mile of our cantonments, and under the very walls of the Bala Hissar," Eyre wrote, and he was there.

The historian Norris insisted this was Shāh Shuja's problem, and it was up to him to deal with it. In fact, the king was the only one who did take any action on November 2. He ordered out one of his own regiments, commanded by a half-Scottish, half-Indian adventurer named Campbell, to put down the rebellion. But the center of Kabul was a warren of narrow streets, and Campbell's troops, and the two six-pounder guns they had brought with them, soon bogged down. The mob closed in around them, and forced them to make a hasty retreat to the citadel, losing two hundred men dead and wounded. By then, Brigadier Shelton, with a small force of infantry and artillery, had arrived at the Bala Hissar (ordered there by Macnaughten), and covered Campbell's troops as they streamed through the main gate. Shelton's men also recovered the guns. That was about enough for Shāh Shuja. With his favorite regiment cut to pieces, he sank into what Sir John Kaye called "a pitiable state of dejection and alarm."

Lady Sale's son-in-law, Captain Sturt, was sent to the citadel by Elphinstone to see if he could jointly plan some kind of response. "Just as he entered the precincts of the palace," Lady Sale wrote in her diary, "he was stabbed in three places by a young man well dressed, who escaped into a building close-by, where he was protected by the gates being shut." Captain Sturt was sent home with a guard of fifty lancers, to be administered to by his wife and by Lady Sale. "He was covered with blood issuing from his mouth, and was unable to articulate," Lady Sale said (she was not one to spare the details). "He could not lie down, from the blood choking him." Hours later, he was able to swallow a drop or two of water, and faintly utter one word: "bet-ter."

Lieutenant Eyre sympathized with Elphinstone. "No one who knew him could fail to esteem his many qualities both in public and private life," he wrote. The general was kind to everyone, and his "professional knowledge was extensive." But he was old and sick, and Eyre thought he had one serious fault, sick or healthy: "This was a lack of confidence in his own judgment, leading him too often to prefer the opinion of others to his own, until, amidst the conflicting views of a multitude of counsellors, he was at a loss which course to take."

Lady Sale, who seemed to have all the energetic, warlike qualities that Elphinstone lacked, agreed with Eyre's assessment. "General Elphinstone vacillates on every point," she wrote. "His own judgment appears to be good, but he is swayed by the last speaker." Lady Sale said she thought it was "a very strange circumstance that troops were not immediately sent into the city to quell the affair in the commencement, but we seem to sit quietly with our hands folded, and look on."

With the fires of rebellion spreading, with uncertain tribesmen such as the Kuzzilbashis watching, Elphinstone, just as Lady Sale said, sat on his hands and did nothing. Instead of talking to Macnaughten, he began writing him letters, though both men were in the cantonments. "Since you left me," he wrote late on November 2, "I have been considering what can be done tomorrow." He had already given up on doing anything today, and noted that. "our dilemma is a difficult one." He wondered about reinforcing Shelton or assembling near Burnes's house and fortifying that part of the city. He wondered about winning the cooperation of the Kuzzilbashis. It was too much for him. "We must see what the morning brings," he concluded.

Morning did bring some good news. A native regiment, the Thirty-seventh, ordered to reinforce Sale, had been called back, and it marched into the cantonments in good order before daybreak. Macnaughten sent messages to Sale, asking him to break off his march to Jalalabad, and return with his brigade, and to Nott, at Kandahar, asking him to send help. (Nothing would come from either Sale or Nott.) At noon, Elphinstone sent out a small detachment—three companies of infantry and two Horse Artillery guns—in an effort to thrust its way into the city. It was too weak to do any good, and it was forced to retire. No other effort was made the rest of the day, though Sir John Kaye noted there was still enough daylight "to do good execution with adequate force, adequately commanded."

That evening, Lady Sale reported, the rebels began appearing in large numbers near the crumbling old fort that contained the food and provisions for the garrison. "We have only three days' provision in cantonments; should the commissariat fort be captured, we shall not only lose all our provisions, but our communications with the city will be cut off," she said.

The commissariat fort, only two hundred yards from the walls of the cantonments, was defended by Ensign Warren of the Fifth Native Infantry Regiment and eighty sepoy infantrymen. He wrote Elphinstone on the fourth that, unless reinforced, he couldn't hold out. The commissariat officers inside the cantonments pleaded with Elphinstone to send a powerful detachment to rescue Warren and all the army's supplies. Instead, the indecisive old man sent a single company from the Thirty-seventh Native Infantry Regiment; they were driven back, and their commander, Ensign Gordon, was killed. Next, Elphinstone sent two companies of British regulars from the Forty-fourth Foot, under Captains Swayne and Robinson. They were both killed, and that detachment was driven back. Incredibly, another small detachment, a party from the Fifth Light Infantry, was sent out early in the evening, with the same painful results.

After hearing that Elphinstone was now prepared to give up the commissariat fort, Captain Boyd, the assistant commissariat officer, hastened to the old man's side to explain the fort contained not only all the army's food, but all its medicine, rum, and clothing as well. Elphinstone called a council of war at 9 P.M., during which the Envoy, in full alarm, pressed him to hang on to the fort. It was now dark, and those attending the conference received a report that only about twenty Afghans were near the fort, and that they were seated outside, "smoking and talking."

"The debate was now resumed, but another hour passed and the general could not make up his mind," Eyre wrote. Captain Sturt, recovering from his wounds, was the last to get in a word with the general, and he urged waiting until daybreak. Elphinstone agreed, and a force was told to get ready to make a sortie at 4 A.M. They were just getting ready to move out when Ensign Warren showed up with the fort's surviving defenders, saying he had been forced by enemy action to evacuate.

"It is beyond a doubt," Eyre concluded, "that our feeble and ineffectual defense of this fort, and the valuable booty it yielded, was the first *fatal* blow to our supremacy at Kabul, and at once determined those chiefs—and more particularly the Kuzzilbashis, who had hitherto remained neutral—to join in the general combination to drive us from the country."

Lady Sale was able to watch what was going on from the roof of her house, peering out from behind a chimney. She wrote that she could see hundreds of exultant Afghans emptying the commissariat fort of all of the army's food and provisions.

The Afghans also had occupied another fort even closer to the cantonments (the whole area was dotted with old forts, really fortified houses for the feuding chieftains). It was now Eyre's idea to make a move against this fort, called Muhammad Sherif's Fort, "by regular breech and assault." He took part in the attack, which actually succeeded, opening the way to repossessing the nearby commissariat fort. But that, of course, was pointless, because the supplies had all been hauled away.

Elphinstone was by now in dreadful shape. He had lost the use of his limbs and could no longer walk. He had managed to get on a horse the day before the uprising, but he had fallen off, and that just made his condition even more perilous. Macnaughten sent for Brigadier Shelton, still at the Bala Hissar, to give leadership to the garrison. At this point, Elphinstone probably should have surrendered command to Shelton, on his own motion or under pressure from Macnaughten. But he held on, and that only made the already nasty Shelton nastier. Shelton, physically brave enough, was a chronic complainer, a "croaker," and he was croaking now about hanging on at Kabul. He never liked Afghanistan, Lady Sale said, "and his disgust has now considerably increased. His mind is set on getting back to Hindustan," she wrote on November 9.

Elphinstone said Shelton was "contumacious" and "insubordinate," Sir John Kaye wrote. "He never gave me information or advice, but invariably found fault with all that was done. . . . He appeared to be actuated by an ill feeling toward me." Shelton said Elphinstone second-guessed him, and wouldn't allow him to move a single gun without permission, Kaye recounted.

Yet Shelton was a brave soldier. On November 10, in fact, he led some of his regulars from the Forty-fourth Regiment and sepoys from two native regiments against a strong Afghan position called Rickabashee Fort, which was within rifle range of the northeastern corner of the cantonment walls. After a spirited fight, in which Shelton displayed "iron nerves and dauntless courage," the fort was captured. "This was the last success our arms were destined to experience," Eyre wrote.

Lady Sale, getting advice from Captain Sturt, her son-in-law, said that now was the time for the entire garrison, with its camp followers, "to make one bold night march in very light marching order" to the great Bala Hissar citadel, where "we can be lodged (not comfortably, I admit) in the houses of the inhabitants."

The Envoy favored the move and so did Eyre. "I venture to state my own firm belief," he wrote, "that had we at this time moved into the Bala Hissar Kabul might still be in our possession." But, though the distance between the cantonments and the citadel was only two miles, the last half of which was covered by the fortress's guns, Shelton opposed the move, and he got his way; the move was never attempted.

Shelton's conduct truly was shameful. Day after day, Elphinstone would call his officers together and discuss, endlessly, what might be done next. Shelton would bring a bedding roll to these meetings, curl up on the floor, and pretend to be asleep.

Shelton led another sortie on November 23, seeking to flush out Afghan warriors from a village called Beymaroo that had been selling grain to the garrison. With three squadrons of cavalry, seventeen infantry companies, and a single gun, this was the most ambitious offensive move the garrison had taken so far.

The Afghans turned out in force—some said there were ten thousand of them—and took up a position on a hilltop across a gorge from Shelton's hilltop position. From there, they began cutting up the British-led troops with slow fire from their deadly matchlock rifles. Shelton, unbelievably, formed his troops into two squares. Squares were fine for resisting cavalry, Eyre wrote, but this was the first time he had seen squares formed "to resist the *distant fire of infantry.*"

Lady Sale watched the action from her rooftop perch, escaping "the bullets that constantly whizzed about me" by hiding behind the chimney. It was about 10 A.M., she thought, when a party of Ghazis turned up on the brow of the hilltop held by the Afghans on the other side of the gorge. She watched as Shelton's troops fired volley after volley at the enemy, and not one struck home. It was the "old fault of firing too high," she wrote.

The detachment's single cannon served effectively until it became so overheated that it would no longer function. It was then that the Ghazis, encouraged by the gun's silence and by the fact that their enemy couldn't shoot their muskets with very much accuracy, slipped down into the gorge and began climbing up the other side. Shelton offered a reward to any man who would go forward and capture a Ghazi flag, but no one took him up on it. And, when he ordered a bayonet charge, no one responded. Some of his officers became so frustrated that they ran forward and hurled rocks down the gorge at the Ghazis.

It was about 12:30 P.M., Lady Sale reported, when the panic began. "Our whole force, both horse and foot, were driven down the hill, and our gun captured—a regular case of *sauve qui peut,*" she wrote.

November 23 was decisive, Eyre reported. It ended all hope of matching the Afghans on the battlefield. The next day, Elphinstone wrote to the Envoy, asking him to open negotiations with the enemy. The Envoy, reluctant to undertake negotiations, asked Elphinstone to put his case in writing. "I am of the opinion," the general wrote, "that it is not feasible any longer to maintain our position in this country," and that it was time to set terms for a withdrawal.

The problem facing Macnaughten was that the Afghans now had a new leader, Akbar Khān, Dōst Mohammad's second son, and he would turn out to be as mean and treacherous as his father was kindly and straightforward. More than anyone else, he knew Macnaughten's predicament. Food was running low inside the cantonments, and the animals were eating bark from the trees. Even worse, snow was beginning to fall.

Talks began early in December, with Macnaughten promising to remove all the British forces at Kabul to Peshawar, and then back to India if Akbar and the rest of the chiefs would promise not to attack them as they withdrew. The garrisons at Jalalabad (Sale) and Kandahar (Nott) would be withdrawn too, following the Kabul garrison on the road back to India. "It amounted to a complete capitulation," historian Patrick Macrory wrote.

But Macnaughten wasn't being honest himself. He was also talking to other chiefs, trying to play one off against another, and offering all these people huge amounts of cash he didn't have. "He appears to have turned first to one party and then to another, eagerly grasping at every new combination that seemed to promise more hopeful results than the last," wrote Sir John Kaye. "His mind was by this time unhinged."

The morning of December 23, the Envoy breakfasted with his senior officers and said he would meet Akbar Khān that day to save Britain's national honor. Watch out, he was warned, for a plot. "A plot!" he replied. "Let me alone for that—trust me for that."

And so, two days before Christmas, Sir William Macnaughten and a small party rode out of the cantonments to meet the Afghan chiefs. They met near the river, where Macnaughten presented Akbar Khān with a handsome Arab horse as a gift. Seconds later, the Envoy and the men accompanying him were seized, their arms pinned behind their backs. The Envoy's companions were taken away and forced to run a gauntlet through crowds of angry Ghazis. One of them, Captain Robert Trevor, slipped from his horse and fell to the ground. He was cut to pieces on the spot.

In the meantime, Macnaughten and Akbar Khān were rolling on the ground, wrestling one another. Akbar drew a pistol—a gift, earlier, from Macnaughten—and shot him through the body. Macnaughten's last words were said to be "Az barae Khoda" (For God's sake). The Ghazis surged forward, and hacked his body to pieces with their knives.

It had been treachery, though some historians believed that Akbar Khān only meant to take Macnaughten hostage, and killed him in an uncontrollable fit of rage. Even so, the negotiations continued, and the snow kept falling and the temperature kept dropping.

Lady Sale opened her diary entry two days later: "A dismal Christmas day, and our situation far from cheering."

Lady Sale's son-in-law, Captain Sturt, an engineer, was instructed to make a breach in the cantonment walls on January 5 so that the whole force—forty-five hundred soldiers and twelve thousand camp followers—could be marched out and started on its way to Jalalabad, ninety miles away, the next morning.

Thursday, January 6, 1842: "We marched from Kabul," Lady Sale wrote in her diary. "We started about half-past nine A.M. The advance party were not molested; there might have been 50 or 100 Afghans collected about

the gateway to witness our departure. The ladies, collectively speaking"—
she means, of course, the *English* ladies, a dozen of them, with maybe
twenty children—"were placed with the advance, under the charge of the
escort . . . The progress was very slow; for the first mile was not accomplished under two and a half hours."

The advance party, commanded by Brigadier Thomas Anquetil, included the Forty-fourth Foot, the Fourth Irregular Horse and Skinner's
Horse, plus two Horse Artillery guns. The main column, under Brigadier
Shelton, included the Fifth and Thirty-seventh Native Infantry regiments, and two more guns. The rear guard, commanded by Colonel Cham-
bers, included the Fifty-fourth Native Infantry Regiment, the Fifth Light
Cavalry, and the king's Sixth Regiment (though the king himself remained
behind, holed up in his citadel, with hardly a loyal officer left to serve him),
and four more guns.

Baggage was carried on the backs of two thousand camels and Afghan
ponies.

But it was the twelve thousand camp followers—mostly menservants
but including hundreds of women and children, some of them the families of the sepoy soldiers—who slowed everything down. "These proved
from the very first mile," wrote Lieutenant Eyre, "a serious clog upon our
movements." Lady Sale said she set out with forty servants from her own
household, not one of whom was ever named in her diary. Lieutenant
Eyre's son would be saved by an Afghan woman servant, who galloped
through an ambush with the boy strapped on her back, but her name was
never mentioned, either. Reading the old diaries and journals, it is almost
as if these twelve thousand native servants and sepoy wives and children
didn't exist individually. In a way, they really didn't. They would die, all
of them—shot, stabbed, frozen to death—in these mountain passes, and
no one bothered to write down the name of even one of them.

As soon as the British evacuated the cantonments, the exultant Ghazis
stormed in, looting the housing and then setting most of the buildings on
fire. As night fell, said Eyre, "the conflagration illuminated the surrounding countryside for several miles."

Akbar Khān had solemnly promised to protect the army and its camp
followers, and maybe he meant it. But the Ghazis—Ghazis, remember, are
the religious fanatics, Ghilzyes are the mountain tribesmen—weren't prepared to show moderation, even if Akbar Khān had asked them to do so.
Even before the rear guard began its march, Lieutenant Hardyman and
fifty troopers from his Fifth Light Cavalry "were stretched lifeless on the

snow," Eyre wrote. Much of the baggage was abandoned before the march got under way, and scores of exhausted sepoys and camp followers simply "sat down in despair to perish in the snow."

The column made only five miles the first day, settling down for the night at a village called Begramee. "There were no tents, save two or three small palls that arrived," Lady Sale wrote. Everyone "scraped away the snow as best they might, to make a place to lie down on. The evening and night were intensely cold; no food for man or beast procurable, except a few handfuls of *bhoosay* [chopped straw], for which we had to pay five to ten rupees." Lady Sale curled up in a straw chair and wrapped her *poshteen*, her sheepskin jacket, around her.

Captain Sturt had brought some of his books with him; now he was forced to throw them away. Lady Sale picked one up and opened it by chance to a selection called "Campbell's Poems"; one verse jumped out at her, haunting her thereafter day and night. It read:

> Few, few shall part where many meet,
> The snow shall be their winding sheet;
> And every turf beneath their feet
> Shall be a soldier's sepulchre.

By morning, almost all of the king's troops, including the whole of the Sixth Regiment, had deserted, returning to whatever fate awaited them in Kabul. The advance guard moved off at 7:30, forcing its way through the baggage train and the camp followers. "Discipline," wrote Lady Sale, disapprovingly, "was clearly at an end." Even the six hundred regulars from the Forty-fourth Foot began to show a lack of spirit. When tribesmen attempted to seize two of the army's guns, the regulars "*made themselves scarce,*" Lady Sale said. In the midst of the confusion, Afghan horsemen charged into the center of the baggage train and rode off with vast quantities of plunder.

All this time, Akbar Khān was tracking the line of march up on the ridges, on horseback. Captain Skinner even managed to talk to him, and the Afghan chief said the attacks were taking place only because the army had marched prematurely, before its Afghan escort could be organized. The next morning, the "treacherous" Afghans attacked again, Eyre said, until Major Thain led some of the Forty-fourth regulars in a bayonet charge that put them to route. Skinner met with Akbar Khān again, and this time the Afghan chief demanded that three British officers be turned over to him as hostages for General Sale's evacuation of Jalalabad, and three officers were sent to him.

Akbar promised again to provide protection, and the column resumed its march for the first of the great mountain passes, Koord-Kabul, five miles long and "so narrow and so shut in on either side that the wintry sun rarely penetrates its gloomy recesses," according to Sir John Kaye. Akbar told Skinner that he would ride ahead and tell the Ghilzyes—the Ghilzyes now replaced the Ghazis as the chief threat to the column—to let the army through.

"Bullets kept whizzing by us," Lady Sale wrote, as the column entered the pass. Some of the artillerymen managed to get drunk after breaking open a regimental store of brandy. Lady Sale said she knocked down a tumbler of sherry herself, "which at any other time would have made me very unlady-like, but now merely warmed me." The Ghilzyes were swarming everywhere, and soldiers and camp followers were dropping in heaps on the snowy ground.

"Poor Sturt," Lady Sale wrote, rode back down the column to look after a friend, but his horse was shot out from under him, "and before he could rise from the ground he received a severe wound in the abdomen." The indomitable Lady Sale said that, fortunately, she was wounded by just one bullet—it lodged in her wrist—but "three others passed through my poshteen near the shoulder without doing me any harm."

Sturt was put down on the side of a bank, "with his wife and myself beside him. It began snowing heavily." He was examined by a doctor, "but I saw by the expression of his countenance that there was no hope. He afterwards cut the ball out of my wrist, and dressed my wounds." That night, said Lady Sale, near-frozen sepoys tried to force their way into her tent, and even into her bed. "Many poor wretches died round the tent in the night."

The next day, January 9, was Lady Sales's last on the deadly march. Akbar told the three British hostages that he would be willing to take all the British ladies, and their families, under his wing, and guarantee them safety. With her pregnant daughter, Alexandrina, Lady Sale agreed to accept Akbar's offer. "Poor Sturt" was dead by now, and he had been given a Christian burial. The English ladies, with their families, were taken to an old fort, where three rooms were cleared out to receive them. "All that Mrs. Sturt and I possess," she wrote, "are the clothes on our backs in which we quitted Kabul. At midnight some mutton bones and greasy rice were brought to us."

Lady Sale was one of the lucky ones. The army, without her and the rest of the English ladies, pushed on, and the native women and the wives of the sepoys died in the pass, just like everyone else. The army left three thousand dead there, Eyre estimated, including women and children.

Eyre was also one of the lucky ones. As a wounded officer with a family—he was shot in a place that made it difficult for him to climb on a horse—he was now told to join his wife and son and the other ladies and their families being handed over to Akbar Khān. He sought Elphinstone out "to hear it from his own lips." The "poor general was greatly distressed," but, pressing Eyre's hands warmly, told him to be on his way. And so he rode off into captivity with Lady Sale and all the rest; in the nearly nine months he was in Akbar Khān's hands, he polished his journal, with an eye to publication.

The deluded Elphinstone continued to speak of Akbar Khān as his "ally," thinking the Afghan chief was seriously attempting to save his column. On the chief's promise that supplies were on their way, Elphinstone halted the column all day on January 9. The supplies, of course, never showed up, and Shelton, grumpy as ever, said in effect, "I told you so."

The column resumed its march the next morning, January 10, in the snow, in freezing cold, the sepoys now mingled with the camp followers. All that was left of the fighting army were 250 regulars from the Forty-fourth, 50 Bengal horse artillerymen with a single gun, and perhaps 150 cavalry troopers. They trudged on, behind the mass of the camp followers, until they entered the deadliest place of all, the gorge of Tunghee Taree-kee. It was only fifty yards long, the historian Patrick Macrory reported; the problem was that it was only four yards wide. The Ghilzyes slaughtered the camp followers first, until the dead and the dying began to choke the narrow defile. Not a single sepoy survived, and all the baggage was destroyed. Elphinstone's "ally," Akbar Khān, watched the slaughter from a nearby peak, and when Elphinstone sent Skinner to remonstrate, he said that the Ghilzyes were out of control, and neither he nor their chiefs could do anything to restrain them.

The surviving troops had to climb over the bodies of the camp followers to get through the defile, with Shelton's rear guard under heavy attack. Leading a handful of soldiers from the Forty-fourth, he held off wave after wave of shouting tribesmen. "Nobly and heroically," he said later, "these fine fellows stood by me."

In desperation, the column's remaining officers decided they would attempt a night march to reach Jagdalak, twenty-two impossible miles away.

They set off at 7 P.M., encountering no resistance for several miles. But, at a place called Seh-Saba, shots were fired at the rear of the column. The camp followers surged forward. Shots were then fired at the front of the column. The camp followers surged to the rear. Thus, wrote Sir John Kaye, ebbing and flowing, "these miserable camp followers, in the wildness of their fear, overwhelmed the handful of soldiers who were still able and willing to show a front to the enemy, blocked up the road, and presented to the eyes of the Afghan marksmen a dark mass of humanity, which could not escape their fire even under cover of the night."

The column was ten miles from Jagdalak when dawn broke on the eleventh. Shelton, still performing deeds of extraordinary valor, fought off attacks all day, until the advance party staggered into the village at 3 P.M. There, they took up a defensive position on top of a small hill behind some crumbling walls, and cheered as the rest of the column straggled in. Captain Johnson, the paymaster and commissary officer, found three bullocks among the camp followers, seized them, cut them up, and fed the pieces—raw—to the soldiers.

They halted at Jagdalak all that day and through the night while Skinner resumed negotiations with Akbar Khān. Then, at the chieftain's invitation, Elphinstone, Shelton, and Captain Johnson attended a conference. Akbar Khān received the three officers with kindness, gave them food and hot tea, and told them they were now hostages. Elphinstone gallantly insisted that he should be allowed to return to his men—otherwise, he might be accused of desertion. Akbar Khān refused his plea. The treachery became complete when Captain Skinner was shot in the face by one of Akbar's tribesmen, a mortal wound.

Brigadier Thomas Anquetil was now in command of the column, reduced to 120 soldiers from the Forty-fourth and 25 artillerymen; they resumed their march about 8 P.M. on the twelfth. "The curse of the camp followers clung to them still," Sir John Kaye wrote. "The teeming rabble again came huddling against the fighting men, and the Afghans, taking advantage of the confusion, stole in, knife in hand, amongst them, destroying all the unarmed men in their way, and glutting themselves with plunder."

The brave men of the Forty-fourth shook loose from the camp followers and attacked the plundering Afghans with bayonets, chasing them away. The column set off again—but lying just ahead was still another terror, the Jugdulluck Pass. They marched up a long incline to the mouth, and there they found that the Afghans had blocked the defile with tree branches and prickly holly oak, twisted together and six feet high.

What had been the mighty Grand Army of the Indus died in Jugdulluck Pass on January 12, 1842. "The massacre was something terrible to relate," wrote Sir John Eyre, who talked to survivors. "Officers, soldiers, and camp followers were stricken down at the foot of the barricade." Now it was time for the officers to die. Brigadier Anquetil, sword in hand, was one of the first to fall. Captain Thomas Nichol, commanding officer of the First Troop, First Brigade, Bengal Horse Artillery, died a little later. His men had fought hardest of all, and they were all killed. The one-legged Captain William Dodgin held the Forty-fourth together, in the regiment's last stand, until he too was cut down.

A handful of men scraped their way through the barricade, and were trampled as the remaining officers, on horseback, galloped over them. Perhaps as many as fifty men managed to reach Gundamuck at daybreak on the thirteenth. Their refusal to surrender infuriated a mob of villagers, and they were set upon. In the hand-to-hand fighting that followed, only Captain Souter of the Forty-fourth, his regimental colors wrapped around his waist, and a few rank and file, survived. They were taken prisoner.

Several other officers had taken a different road on the way to Gundamuck, and, late in the day on the thirteenth, found themselves in the clear, only fifteen miles from Jalalabad. The party included Captains Bellew, Hopkins, and Collier, three lieutenants, five or six British soldiers, and two doctors. One of them was Dr. William Brydon.

Bellew was a fool; when his party approached a village called Futtehabad, he paused to talk to the villagers and seek food from them. It was, of course, a trap, and Bellew was the first to be killed. "It became a case of utter rout," Dr. Brydon wrote in a brief journal, "out of which all that got clear were Captains Hopkins and Collier, Dr. Harper, Lieutenant Steer, and myself."

Dr. Brydon galloped away on his Afghan pony, and suddenly found he was alone. He managed to cut his way through a party of about twenty tribesmen drawn up in the road. They opened fire, and one of the bullets broke Dr. Brydon's sword; another struck "the poor pony, wounding him in the loins." He lurched on until the fort at Jalalabad came in sight, and Captain Sinclair of the Thirteenth Light Infantry and others came out to greet him. He was the only person to complete the entire death march.

"I was taken to the Sappers' mess, my wounds dressed by Dr. Forsyth, and after a good dinner, with great thankfulness, enjoyed the luxury of a sound sleep," Dr. Brydon wrote. The pony was taken to the stables, "lay down and never rose again."

Dr. Brydon, then, could say he was the only living creature, man or beast, to survive the entire march from Kabul to Jalalabad.

Sir John Kaye was prone to hyperbole, but he wasn't far off when he wrote in 1851: "There is nothing, indeed, more remarkable in the history of the world than the awful completeness—the sublime unity—of this Kabul tragedy."

✦

Akbar Khān kept at least one of his promises, providing safety, if not much comfort, for his English prisoners. But Elphinstone, blaming himself for the tragedy, died in captivity the night of April 23, 1842, his head cradled in the lap of his orderly, a man named Moore. "Lift up my head, Moore," he is supposed to have said. "It is the last time I shall trouble you." The other prisoners were released.

The siege at Jalalabad was lifted by forces commanded by a fighting general, Major General George Pollock, in early April. He and his army pushed on to Kabul, passing the rotting corpses of Elphinstone's column along the way, and then defeating Akbar Khān's army in two decisive engagements. Pollock occupied Kabul on September 15, and the British flag once more flew over the Bala Hissar. But Shāh Shuja, the puppet king, was no longer in residence; he had been murdered by his own soldiers. Pollock blew up Kabul's great bazaar as a form of punishment for destroying a British army.

The British then withdrew their armies from Afghanistan, and released Dōst Mohammad. He returned to Kabul and took his throne once again, retaining power until his death in 1863. His son, Akbar, died in 1845. He was only twenty-nine.

Sale, saluted as a hero for commanding the "Illustrious Garrison" at Jalalabad, returned to India after being reunited with Lady Sale. He died in battle in 1845, leading British troops in the first of two wars the British fought against the Sikhs, who had turned contentious after the death of their great leader, Ranjit Singh, the Lion of Lahore. Lady Sale was given a modest pension and spent her declining years in a villa near Simla. She died in 1852. Her daughter, Alexandrina, was remarried to an artillery major, but both of them were slaughtered in their carriage at the start of the Sepoy Mutiny in the Bengal army in 1857. Henry Havelock, a general, won fame for relieving Lucknow during the mutiny. Dr. Brydon was there, too, and he was seriously wounded. He was made a Companion of the Bath for his gallantry and died in his bed in his native Scotland in 1873, one of life's legendary survivors.

Brigadier Shelton survived a court martial, and resumed command of a new Forty-fourth Regiment in Dublin. When his soldiers heard he had died after falling off a horse in 1845, they cheered. Vincent Eyre became Sir Vincent Eyre, and retired, full of honors, as a major general.

A British army under the redoubtable General Frederick "Little Bobs" Roberts returned to Afghanistan in 1879. Russia had been causing trouble again, and another mob had risen in Kabul, killing a second British envoy, Sir Louis Cavagnari. Roberts won a decisive victory over the Afghans at Kandahar in 1880.

But, once again, the British army was withdrawn, leaving Afghanistan to the proud Afghans. Since then, the Afghans have resisted every effort to subdue them, including a disastrous Russian invasion in the late twentieth century. They continue to fight each other, as tribal and as contentious as ever.

SIX

Major General Sir George Pomeroy-Colley and the First Boer War (1880–1881)

Everybody agreed the smartest general in the British army was Major General Sir George Pomeroy-Colley, K.C.S.I., C.B., C.M.G., Her Majesty's High Commissioner for South-Eastern Africa, Governor of Natal, and Commander in Chief of all British troops in Natal and the Transvaal.

Everybody was wrong.

When General Colley (the hyphenated Pomeroy-Colley was an affectation) led British forces in the First Boer War from 1880 to 1881, he lost not one, not even two, but three battles, and in the final disaster at Majuba Hill he was shot in the forehead, just over the right eye, as his panic-stricken Highlanders and Green Jackets raced down the slopes of the mountain pursued by farm boys dressed in corduroy.

"Another fearful defeat," Queen Victoria wrote in her diary, "and poor Sir G. Colley killed."

Poor Sir George. He was supposed to have been something of a prodigy, or as close to one as Queen Victoria's army was apt to stomach. Like so many other Victorian generals (Garnet Wolseley, Frederick Sleigh Roberts, Horatio Herbert Kitchener), Colley was born in Ireland of Anglo-Irish parents, into an old army family. He entered the Royal Military Academy at Sandhurst at thirteen, and graduated first in his class. He played the flautino (a small flute) and read the classics, painted in his sketchbook, and wrote bad poetry. He spoke several languages and contributed articles to the *Encyclopaedia Britannica*. The papers called him the "Pillar of Empire." His fellow officers may have found him a little insufferable.

141

South Africa, his final resting place, was a key part of the British empire. The British had seized Cape Town from the Dutch East India Company as early as 1806, and, moving into the interior, had made Natal and Griqualand West crown colonies by mid-century. The descendants of the Dutch colonists—the Boers—had watched in dismay as thousands of English settlers staked out homes in their ancestral territory. Starting about 1835, as many as twelve thousand of these Dutchmen simply pulled up stakes, abandoning their homes and their land, and set out on the so-called Great Trek to the vast interior of southern Africa, settling in what came to be known as the Orange Free State and the Transvaal. There, living in complete isolation on ranches of six thousand acres or more, they read their Bibles, tended their cattle, and reared their huge families. Their boys were accomplished horsemen by the age of six and crack rifle marksmen by the time they were twelve. They may have been the toughest pioneers in history.

Little did they know they were sitting on top of some of the richest diamond and gold fields in the world.

The British were contemptuous of them. Wolseley said they were "the most ignorant white people in the world. . . . They are given to more tall talk than the Americans, but at heart they are cowards. . . .They know they could not stand up against our troops for an hour." One Boer, the English joked, asked if he could see England from Cape Town.

H. Rider Haggard, the author of *King Solomon's Mines* and *She*, raised ostriches (for the decorative feathers) on a farm in Natal and came to have strong feelings about the Boers. The men, he thought, were ugly, while the women tended to "get very stout as they grow older." The typical Boer "has no education, and does not care that his children receive any. . . . He has no romance in him, nor any of the higher feelings and aspirations that are found in almost every other race."

The Boer, the English believed (with justification), was a racist, too, still maintaining slaves to work the fields and perform the household chores. The Transvaal, in fact, already maintained a primitive form of apartheid, with the races clearly separated. The Boers believed it was God's will. The queen despised them. "The Boers are a horrid people," she said, "cruel and overbearing."

Maybe worst of all, Boers were so *dirty*. "The dress of the Boer," one journalist wrote, "is of the roughest material . . . corduroy and flannel for the body, a soft felt hat for the head, and soft leather-soled boots suited to walking on the grass. . . . The clothing sometimes never comes off his body till it drops off through old age, not of the man, but of the material."

Perhaps, Haggard thought, "the most striking of all his oddities is [the Boer's] abhorrence of all government, more especially if that government be carried out according to English principles. . . . It is not liberty they long for, but license."

British bureaucrats in London, led by the colonial secretary, Lord Carnarvon (Henry Molyneux Herbert), better known to his friends as "Twitters," became convinced the only way to bring order out of the chaos in South Africa was to federate all the colonies and territories, including the Transvaal, into one manageable unit. Twitters dispatched Sir Garnet Wolseley, perhaps the army's most accomplished general, to Natal to start the ball rolling.

Wolseley didn't like the place much—"wretched little colony," he called Natal, in private—but he gave dinners and dances two or three times a week, and almost "drowned the independence of the colony with sherry and champagne," historian Joseph Lehmann wrote in his reliable history, *The First Boer War*. He brought with him as chief of staff his favorite officer, Colonel George Pomeroy-Colley, and sent him into the Natal legislative pit to argue the government's case for giving the Crown—that is to say, General Wolseley, the governor of the colony—more power. Colley rose to his feet, drew in a deep breath, and choked. Not a word. He stammered, he mumbled, his eyes bulged, but he couldn't think of a word to say. "He cracked under the strain," wrote Lehmann in his history. It was perhaps an omen of things to come.

The man assigned to annex the Transvaal was Sir Theophilus Shepstone, who interrupted his honeymoon to take up his new post. Accompanied by twenty-five mounted police, Shepstone rode into Pretoria, the Transvaal capital, on April 12, 1877, and raised the Union Jack at Government House. Performing the flag-raising honors was his private secretary, young Haggard, the novelist–ostrich breeder. Shepstone cabled Twitters: "Great majority of Boers welcome change."

They may not have welcomed it, but they seemed to accept it, because the British promised, in Sir Theophilus's proclamation, to allow the Boers to maintain "a separate government, with its own laws and legislature." But that promise was never kept, and British soldiers and native police were brought into the colony to keep the peace.

Shepstone was replaced by Sir Bartle Frere ("Bottle Beer" to his critics), who soon concluded that all the unrest in the white colonies was being stirred up by Cetewayo, the powerful Zulu chief. In no time at all Lieutenant General Frederic A. Thesiger, the second Baron Chelmsford, known to his men as "that old fool," was marching against the Zulu impis, or columns. On January 22, 1879, a British force camped at a place called Isandhlwana was attacked by a spear-carrying Zulu army. At the end of the day, 52 British officers, 806 British soldiers, and 500 of their native allies lay dead, almost all of them disemboweled. It was a staggering defeat. Six companies in the Twenty-fourth Regiment were wiped out.

Chelmsford survived—he had been leading another column off in the wrong direction at the time the Zulus attacked his camp—and he managed to redeem himself, in part, by defeating the Zulus in a second engagement, at Ulundi. Wolseley succeeded Chelmsford, and finished off the campaign with the capture of the Zulu chief. But the Boers had taken notice; maybe the redcoated British army, they concluded, wasn't so formidable after all.

It was at about this time that London named Colonel Sir William Owen Lanyon as governor of the Transvaal, a disastrous selection. He had no sympathy for the Boers and was interested only in collecting taxes from them. "Colonists are like a glass piano," he said. "They require most careful playing, but a skillful operator can get harmonious touches out of them by gentle touches."

The Boers were convinced that because of his swarthy complexion, and the fact he had commanded black troops in the West India regiment, he was partly black himself. They wondered, too, about the fact that he was thirty-seven years old and unmarried. Unnatural. He wrote his father he expected to stay single for a while, because a Boer wife would almost surely be "flabby, limp, and draggle-tailed."

With Wolseley on his way home, London made another appointment—Colley as high commissioner for all of Southeast Africa, with Lanyon more or less still in charge at Pretoria.

The trouble began at Potchefstroom, where a farmer named Piet Bezuidenhout challenged an order to pay back taxes amounting to a little more than twenty-seven pounds. He proved, in court, that he owed no more than fourteen pounds. The *landdrost*—the town magistrate—agreed, and then ordered Bezuidenhout to pay the fourteen pounds plus thirteen pounds in court costs, putting him right back where he started.

Acting on his lawyer's advice, Bezuidenhout refused to pay the costs. In retaliation, Mr. Goetz, the landdrost, seized one of Bezuidenhout's ox wagons and announced it would be put up for public auction at 11 A.M. on November 11, 1880, in the public square. At the appointed hour, the sheriff climbed up on the wagon and began reading out the terms of the sale. One of the Boers, Piet Cronje, jumped up on the wagon, grabbed the sheriff, kicked him, and announced: "Away with you, you government officials, we don't acknowledge you."

The Boers hitched some oxen to the wagon and drove off in triumph. The sheriff, with no force to compel compliance, watched as the Boers and Piet Bezuidenhout's wagon disappeared in the dust.

"I do not anticipate that any serious trouble will arise out of the affair," Lanyon told Lord Kimberley, the colonial minister in London, on December 5.

But, even as the message was being sent, more than four thousand Boers were massing, rifles oiled and bandoliers jammed with cartridges, at a place called Paardekraal, where they established a new government, choosing three men—Paul Kruger, Marthinus Pretorius, and Piet Joubert—to lead them. To show their solidarity, in their own traditional way, each Boer picked up a small stone and threw it on a large heap. Even for Lanyon, this suggested serious trouble.

Because there was no printing press in Paardekraal, the Boers descended on Potchefstroom, where there was a press, to publish their declaration of independence. But, in response to the trouble over Piet Bezuidenhout's wagon, there were two hundred soldiers in town from the Twenty-first Regiment, now officially (it was about this time army reformers shifted from numbered regiments to regional or county designations), the Royal Scots Fusiliers. They had been sent from Pretoria to enforce the tax laws.

The Boers rode right up to the little fort, and jeered at the British garrison. "Why don't you fight, you damned cowards!" one of the Boers shouted in English. A small detachment of mounted infantry rode out to meet with the Boers, and, according to journalist Thomas Fortescue Carter of the *Natal Times*, were fired upon by five or six Boers "who lay concealed behind a wall."

The war had commenced.

Lanyon was astonished. "I cannot conceive what can have so suddenly caused the Boers to act as they have," he told Colley. He pleaded with Colley for reinforcements. But there were almost none to be had. As a cost-saving device, troops had been pulled out all over South Africa, including the Transvaal. The only available cavalry regiment, the King's Dragoon Guards, had been transferred just as the trouble was coming to a boil (their horses were sold to the Boers), leaving the British with no experienced mounted troops to face the best sharpshooting mounted infantry in the world.

The British commander at Pretoria, Colonel William Bellairs, had complained about the shortage of troops and had pressed Colley and others to concentrate those who remained at a few well-protected places. Bellairs elaborated his themes after the war was lost in a self-serving book he published under his wife's name. As for Bellairs himself, he hunkered down at Pretoria and endured a siege in which his besieged troops outnumbered the sieging Boer farmers by two- and sometimes three-to-one.

Even so, the nonaggressive colonel had a point. Fewer than two thousand British regulars were spread out all over the Transvaal, garrisoning Pretoria, Rustenburg, Marabastad, Lydenburg, Wakkerstroom, and Standerton.

To make matters worse, these were bad soldiers, poorly trained, poorly led, constantly bored by garrison duty. Desertion—they ran off to freedom in the Orange Free State—was a constant problem. The most remarkable thing about them was they couldn't shoot at all; they would fire thousands of rounds from their state-of-the-art Martini-Henry rifles in this war, and hardly ever hit anyone. This was an army that couldn't shoot straight.

Colley, awakening now to the danger, ordered several of his garrisons to join Bellairs at Pretoria, and most of them made the march without any trouble. But Lieutenant Colonel Philip R. Anstruther, in Lydenburg, commanding two companies of the Ninety-fourth Regiment (soon to be the Connaught Rangers), was unimpressed with the urgency of the situation. He received orders on November 27 to abandon his post and march on Pretoria "without delay." But, because most of his wagons had been withdrawn as another cost-saving device, he figured he needed time to collect transportation from local farmers. He took eight days to round up thirty ox wagons, two mule wagons, one water cart, and one ox-ambulance. The big wagons were drawn by sixteen or eighteen oxen, meaning a span of oxen with its wagon covered as much as thirty yards. "Allowing for a certain interval between each wagon," Carter of the *Natal Times* estimated, "it may be reckoned that the train accompanying the 94th did not cover a less extent of ground than a mile and a quarter, even when in 'close order.'" Anstruther seemed to think he needed all these wagons and carts, driven and handled by sixty native boys and young men called foreloopers, to move 9 officers, 254 rank and file, and 3 women and 2 children.

That the Boers might want to fight never seemed to occur to him. They "will turn tail at the first beat of the big drum," he said, referring to the big drum in his thirty-man regimental band.

He was expected to reach Pretoria by December 12, but on December 18 he was at Middelburg, preparing to cross the Crocodile (Limpopo) River, just halfway to his destination. He had already been warned by Colonel Bellairs, a day earlier, to look out for a Boer ambush. Before leaving Middelburg on the nineteenth, he was warned again, this time by English residents of the area, that the Boers planned to attack him en route to Pretoria. The morning of the twentieth, safely on the other side of the Crocodile, Anstruther and some of his officers joined the family of the local field cornet, the closest thing the Boers had to a professional soldier, at his farmhouse for breakfast. Their Boer hosts said that they might see some mounted (and armed) burghers during the day, but to be reassured that their intentions were entirely friendly. The soldiers, denied breakfast, filled up on ripe peaches from the field cornet's orchard, and stuffed their pockets with more to eat on the long march.

And so, breakfast finished, the column set off for Pretoria. It was now close to Christmas, and the troops were in a good mood. The band, just behind Anstruther and the other mounted officers, led the column, blaring away at one of the regimental favorites, "Kiss Me, Mother, Kiss Your Darling."

Anstruther had been told to deploy some of the native foreloopers as scouts, but he didn't think it was necessary. The troops had been issued thirty rounds of ammunition, instead of the standard seventy. Lids of the reserve boxes of ammunition hadn't been unscrewed, and the members of the band were unarmed, their rifles stored away in one of the wagons.

The colonel, with four of his officers, was riding at the head of the column at about 1:20 P.M., near a place called Bronkhorst Spruit, when one of the bandsmen spotted a troop of 150 mounted Boers about three hundred yards away, to the column's left. "My God," he said, "look there." The music died away. The colonel called a halt, and ordered his long wagon train to close up. One of the Boers, Paul de Beer, approached the British line with a white flag. Conductor Ralph Egerton (he had nothing to do with the band; in those days a conductor was a senior noncommissioned officer functioning as a kind of quartermaster), who survived the action, said de Beer gave the colonel a letter written in English warning him that the Boers had now formed a republic and that any advance into their territory by British troops would be considered a declaration of war. Anstruther, the Boers said, "must be responsible for the consequences."

According to Egerton, "the messenger said verbally that two minutes were allowed for the colonel's decision. The colonel replied his orders were to march to Pretoria, and he should go there." As the band played "God Save the Queen," "each party galloped back to his own force."

De Beer said that when he reached his lines he told his commanding officer, Commandant Frans Joubert, that the British intended to continue their march to Pretoria. "Our burghers were all this time within 330 yards of the [British] troops; then the order was given to advance, and they advanced within 130 yards, whereupon firing commenced." De Beer estimated that thirty or forty minutes had elapsed between the time he was told by Joubert to deliver the letter to the British commander and the time the Boers opened fire.

"I asked him [de Beer] to let me know the result, to which he nodded assent," Anstruther wrote in an official report before he died. "Almost immediately, however, the enemy's line advanced. I ran back as fast as I could, ordering the leading company to skirmish, but before they could open out to more than loose files a murderous fire was poured upon them, which was hotly returned."

Anstruther thought he had been attacked by anywhere from twelve hundred to fifteen hundred men. It might have seemed like that, so accurate was the Boer musketry. Most of the Boers were armed, here and in all these battles, with .45 caliber Westley Richards rifles, a percussion cap, breech-loading weapon with a curious "monkey tail" lever for opening and closing the breech. These powerful rifles used paper cartridges containing half an ounce of powder, and the Boers could fire them rapidly and accurately, on horseback and off, at distances exceeding seven hundred yards, a feat no other soldiers could accomplish anywhere in the world.

The British officers went down first, then the soldiers, and finally the oxen. It took about ten minutes for these 150 Boers to kill 77 officers and men and wound 7 officers, 91 men, and 1 woman. Anstruther, struck by five bullets himself, called on his bugler to play the cease fire. The red-coated regulars raised their cork sun helmets, covered with white canvas, in the air and waved white handkerchiefs. The Boers, a little shocked at their own success, stopped firing. In this brief engagement, they had killed or wounded every British officer on the field.

"The carnage was sickening," historian Lehmann wrote. "The entire column was a shambles. Dead and dying men, horses and oxen were strewn all about and there were pools of blood in the white road. The little band boys and drummers had the appearance of lifeless red dolls."

Boer casualties were two dead, four wounded.

This was the last war in which British troops carried their regimental colors into combat, and in this action Conductor Egerton emerged a hero for wrapping the Ninety-fourth's colors under his tunic and taking it with him when he was given permission to walk forty miles to Pretoria to seek medical assistance for the wounded.

The British surgeon, a Dr. Ward, wounded himself in the battle, commented in his report on the accuracy of the Boer rifle fire. The average number of wounds was five per man, he said, and he singled out one of the regulars, a Private Duffy, who lived to fight another day with eighteen holes in him, where bullets had either entered or exited.

Another of the day's heroes was Mrs. Marion Smith, wife of the dead bandmaster, who "was most unremitting in attendance on the wounded, and did much to alleviate suffering," Dr. Ward said. When she died, back home in England years later, she was given a full military funeral.

Colonel Anstruther died the night of December 26. "Words fail to describe a scene so sad and unique," Dr. Ward said. "The remains were placed on a stretcher, and carried by four sergeants, three out of the four being wounded; while the majority of those who followed were wounded, some on crutches, others with bandaged heads, and some—unable to walk—were carried on the backs of their more fortunate comrades. At the grave not a dry eye could be seen, and one and all seemed to think that a friend—a good man and a soldier, in the widest and best sense of the word—was gone from their midst."

The soldiers were buried where they died, and because their pockets and haversacks were still filled with peaches, peach trees grew from their graves, eventually becoming, one officer who returned to the battlefield years later said, "uncommonly fine orchards."

The Boers, in victory, were almost always gracious and helpful, and this first action at Bronkhorst Spruit was no exception. They sympathized with the survivors and offered them food and shelter. Some of them, though, may have begun to wonder if their conduct had been completely honorable. A century after the battle, George R. Duxbury, director of the South African Museum of Military History, wrote an account of the action, and wondered about it all over again. "One can argue," he said, "that the matter was still subject to negotiation and that the Boer attack was premature. This might be correct, but, in tense times such as these, as anyone who has awaited an order to advance into battle will know, finer points of this nature are inclined to be overlooked."

The British insisted that it was a massacre—but if that's what it was, Colonel Anstruther had himself to blame. Because of his foolish confidence in the power of the British infantry—the idea that the enemy would flee at the beat of the big drum—he died, and so did dozens of men under his command, who deserved better.

It was still not too late for the British to put an end to the Boer uprising: all the Gladstone government had to do was carry out the prime minister's campaign promise that he would give the burghers a form of limited self-rule. But he refused, breaking his promise, and on January 6, the queen, in her Speech from the Throne, said: "A rising in the Transvaal has recently imposed upon me the duty of taking military measures with a view to the prompt vindication of my authority; and has of necessity set aside for the time any plan for securing to the European settlers that full control over their local affairs, without prejudice to the interests of the natives, which I had been desirous to confirm."

It was, of course, nonsense; the speech contained an outright lie, and the queen was forced to deliver it. No plans had been made to grant self-rule, and the outbreak of hostilities had nothing to do with postponing the drawing up of such plans. "The queen's words," historian Joseph Lehmann wrote, "only confirmed the mistrust and contempt that the Boers felt for British statesmen."

No army anywhere could match the Boers in mobilizing for war. Every healthy burgher "was expected to provide himself with a rifle, for which he was at all times to have fifty rounds of ammunition, a horse, saddlery, and, on being called out, eight days' rations," according to George Duxbury, the South African historian. "He wore the clothes he possessed or which he thought were best suited to local conditions. These were often adapted to special purposes and pictures reveal an odd assortment of ammunition pockets and pouches sewn on to, or attached to, shirts, waist-coats, and jackets."

Colley had actually gone out with a commando unit—the Boers had always maintained self-defense units—five years earlier, and was unimpressed. "Camp discipline was amusing," he wrote. One example he cited was when "the bugle sounded 'lights out.' A field cornet on duty passing a wagon with a light in it, calls out, 'Now, then, put out that light there.' Answer from within: 'If you want to put this light out you had better bring a precious big stick with you.'"

"It was perhaps this sort of rejoinder," Duxbury pointed out, "that misled Colley and others into thinking the enemy was completely undisciplined, whereas in fact his strength lay in his friendly outspokenness and ability, when called upon in an emergency, to think and act for himself."

It wasn't until much later, too, that the British came to understand for the first time that at least some of the Boer field commanders were extremely able. Piet Joubert, the principal commander, was a tall, muscular man of French Huguenot extraction in his mid-forties; he was often described as "patient, crafty, and cautious." He was also a gentle man, with a strong distaste for bloodshed. Self-taught, he took most of his inspiration from the Bible and believed the British had been sent to the Transvaal by the devil.

His deputy, Nicholas Smit, was a military prodigy, and had no aversion to bloodshed. He loved to fight, and he loved, in particular, to fight the pompous, overbearing British. One of his opponents, General William Butler, called him "one of the ablest leaders of mounted infantry that have appeared in modern war."

It was poor Colley's misfortune to take on these troops, and these generals, with a mere fifteen hundred men.

"This is a sad and anxious New Year for us all here," he wrote his sister. " . . . I start in a few days to take command and try to bring the Boers to battle. . . . Now I feel considerable doubts whether the force I am taking up [to the front] is sufficient, and it is possible I may have to wait further for the reinforcements from India and England."

That, of course, is exactly what he should have done, but he had recently married a much younger woman, Edith Hamilton, daughter of Colonel Meade Hamilton, one of the most bellicose officers in the British army. Edith herself was known throughout the service as "Tiger," and thought nothing of taking the throttle of a locomotive on ceremonial occasions. Time, Tiger told her husband, was wasting.

As soon as the fighting commenced, the Boer leaders dispatched units to lay siege to the five isolated British garrisons, and then sent a larger force, the heart of their army, to fortify a low-lying, six-mile-long spur of the Drakensberg Mountains that blocked the way from Natal into the Transvaal. It was summer in South Africa, and the ridge "was colored in infinite variations of green and brown. . . . Its crest was bare of trees, but little tongues of brushwood grew from the dark forest at its foot and mounted the ravines which indent the southern face," historian Oliver Ransford wrote.

In the center of the six-mile-long ridge was a saddle called Lang's Nek. It was into this funnel that Colley would lead his little army. Overlooking the funnel, standing to the west of the saddle, was Majuba Hill, rising six thousand feet above sea level and deserving to be called a mountain.

Colley gathered his troops at Newcastle; Rider Haggard wasn't far away, tending his ostrich farm. "The little town of Newcastle was at this time an odd sight," he wrote, "and remained so throughout the war. The hotels were crowded to overflowing with refugees, and on every spare patch of land were erected tents, mud huts, canvas houses, and every kind of covering that could be utilized under the pressure of necessity."

Haggard called on the colonial secretary, a Colonel Mitchell, to offer his advice "of the Boers and their shooting powers, and the inevitable result" should Colley move against them with such a small force. But he never really thought the British general would be so foolish. "Nobody dreamt he meant to attack the Nek with such an insignificant column."

But on the morning of January 28, 1881, Haggard wrote that he and "anyone listening attentively in the neighborhood of Newcastle could hear the distant boom of heavy guns."

Colley, Tiger urging him on, advanced on Lang's Nek with a small, nondescript force, consisting of five companies of the Fifty-eighth Foot (soon to become the Northamptonshire Regiment); five companies of the Sixtieth Rifles (soon to be the King's Royal Rifles), in their distinctive green jackets; a small detachment, maybe fewer than 100 men, from the Twenty-first Regiment (Royal Scots Fusiliers); a naval detachment (120 men in all), dragging with them three Gatling guns and three rocket tubes; a mounted squadron with volunteers from the infantry units, numbering 120; and 70 splendid troopers from the Natal Mounted Police, along with an artillery detachment serving two seven-pounders and four nine-pounders.

Colley had set up camp on the twenty-sixth at Mount Prospect, an open plateau about midway between the Ingogo River to the south and Lang's Nek to the north. He began his advance on the Boer positions at 6 A.M. on the twenty-eighth, with his mounted squadron and the Sixtieth Rifles in the lead, followed by the naval brigade, the regulars from the Fifty-eighth, and the artillery. The cannon opened up about 10 A.M., but the gunners weren't any more accurate than the riflemen. The artillery fire was ineffective, and Colley put a halt to it after thirty minutes.

The mounted squadron, led by Major Brownlow and Sergeant Major Lunnie, moved against a hill forming the most advanced position of the Boer line of defense, but the Natal Mounted Police unit was left behind, perhaps another example of British contempt for the abilities of colonial soldiers.

Brownlow's pitiful mounted squadron—many of these soldiers barely knew how to ride a horse—began the attack prematurely, and Brownlow mistakenly veered away to the right and began galloping up the steepest part of the hill. His and everyone else's horse was blown by the time they approached the enemy. The result was predictable. The moment they "gained a level which exposed them to the view of the Boers on the summit of the hill, a terrible volley emptied half the saddles," wrote the journalist Carter, who was there. "Horses were galloping here and there. Those who remained mounted were staggered by this first reception, but manfully reformed, still under fire, and charged again. The hail of lead they were again met with was one that the weak force could not stand." Sergeant Major Lunnie actually jumped into the enemy trenches, only to be killed by fire from six Boer marksmen. One of the last to go down was a Lieutenant Linmitte. "I got up," he said later, "and, seeing no one about, I turned and legged it down the hill. My helmet had fallen off, my sword dropped out of my hand, and I lost my field glasses. It was a dashed expensive day."

Seventeen men were killed and wounded, and thirty-two horses were lost.

Making their way up an even steeper hill were the redcoated regulars from the Fifty-eighth Regiment, the Northamptons known proudly as the "Steelbacks" for their unflinching acceptance of flogging. It is a moment to mark—probably the last time a line of scarlet-coated British soldiers advanced against an enemy, and probably the last time, too, they advanced with both their own and the queen's colors flying.

They appeared in the Boer sights minutes after the repulse of the mounted squadron, perfect timing for the burghers with their slower-firing Westley Richards rifles. Leading the infantrymen was Colonel Deane, a staff officer who failed to give the order to his men to deploy right and left, spreading out, before making the climb. They arrived at the crest crowded together, forming—just as Braddock's troops had done in 1755 (see chapter 1)—another terrible red bull's-eye.

Deane called on his men to "fix bayonets," and they paused to execute the order. "Charge!" Deane bellowed. The Boers, hunkered down in defensive positions brilliantly planned by General Smit, could hardly believe their eyes. "Volley after volley was delivered into [the British] ranks," and the officers began falling fast. One of them, a Lieutenant Elwes, Colley's aide-de-camp, turned to Lieutenant Monck, an old mate from boarding school, and shouted "Come along, Monck! *Floreat Etona!*" just before he was cut down (the moment, romantically rendered by the artist Lady Butler, became a Victorian favorite). Deane's horse was shot from under him, but he jumped to his feet, crying out, "I am all right." Not for long, though. Another heavy Boer slug tore into him, knocking him to the ground. The wound was mortal. Major Poole was the next to die, followed by Lieutenant Dolphin. Captain Lovegrove and Lieutenants Baillie and O'Donel were badly wounded. Running out of commissioned officers, the Boers turned their fire on noncommissioned officers, and the sergeants began to fall.

Lieutenant Baillie had been carrying the regimental colors, and when he was struck down, Lieutenant Peel, carrying the queen's colors (the Union Jack), offered his assistance. "Never mind me, save the colors," the dying Baillie said. Peel moved down the hill with both colors, and when he fell into a large ant hole, Sergeant Bridgstock seized the standards, and took them to safety. A third lieutenant named Hill rushed back up the hill, picked up Baillie, and tried to carry him to safety. Baillie died in his arms. Hill rode his horse back up the hill again and again, seeking to rescue the wounded. He won the Victoria Cross for his bravery and two of his horse's hooves ultimately were plated in silver and used as ashtrays by officers of the regiment.

When it was over, a Private Brennan said he had killed a Boer with his bayonet, and produced the bloody weapon to prove it. Later, though, he admitted he had stuck the bayonet in a dead horse. British troops prided themselves on their work with the bayonet, and the Boers admitted that they didn't care for bayonet attacks, but not once in any of the fighting in this brief war did a British bayonet draw burgher blood.

The survivors of the Fifty-eighth fell back, covered by the green-jacketed riflemen of the Sixtieth Rifles. Losses among the Steelbacks were 73 dead and 100 wounded, bringing British losses for the day to 83 dead, 111 wounded, and 2 taken as prisoners. The Boer losses for the day, almost entirely from cannon fire, were 14 dead and 29 wounded.

"The moral effect of our defeat on the Boers was very great," Rider Haggard wrote. "It gave them unbounded confidence in their own superiority, and infused a spirit of cohesion and mutual reliance into their ranks which had before been wanting."

It was the first time since the Crimean War that British soldiers had been routed by troops with European roots, the historian Lehmann pointed out. "What made it worse was that the Boers were considered a primitive enemy, one which had barely attained that level of civilization which could avail itself of the advantage of modern rifles." The British soldiers called the Boer infantrymen "pinheads."

Like so many others, Haggard wondered why Colley had made the attack in the first place. "It was said at the time in Natal that he was a man with a theory; namely, that small bodies of men properly handled were as useful and as likely to obtain the object in view as a large force. Whether or no this was so, I am not prepared to say.

"But"—and this is a perceptive point—"it is undoubtedly the case that very clever men have sometimes very odd theories, and it may be that he [Colley] was a striking instance in point."

Colley called the survivors of his little army together the evening of the defeat, and gave a short speech. "I wish everyone present to understand," he said, "that the entire blame of today's repulse rests entirely upon me, and not on any of you. . . . We have lost many gallant men, [but] we have not lost one atom of the prestige of England." He told his troops that owing to the day's losses, he would be forced to wait until reinforcements under the command of the experienced General Sir Evelyn Wood arrived before resuming his offensive.

The British withdrew to their camp at Mount Prospect, to lick their wounds and await the fresh troops that would permit them to resume their march to Pretoria. But now, giddy over their victory at Lang's Nek, the Boers became more daring and their highly mobile mounted columns began threatening Colley's line of communication to his base camp at Newcastle. The road was little more than a dirt track that meandered up and down over hills and valleys, passing through several streams and *dongas*, or ravines.

The brilliant General Smit was one of the raiders, and he quickly caught on to the fact the British soldier's lack of mobility made him an easy target. Colley, still unconvinced the Boers posed any special kind of military problem, decided a show of force would frighten off these roving burgher bands playing havoc with his lines of communication. And so, at first light on February 8, he took personal command of a column escorting some ambulances and mail wagons to Newcastle. It was a job for a major, or maybe, at the outside, a lieutenant colonel. But here was a British major general, escorting the mail, with a column of 270 Green Jackets under Colonel Ashburnham and 38 mounted infantry under Major Brownlow, along with four cannon. Thinking it would be a fine parade, he took staff officers (including his brother-in-law, Lieutenant Bruce Hamilton, a future general) and even some personal friends along; he didn't bother with rations or a water wagon for his men.

"The morning was fine and bright," wrote Carter of the *Natal Times*, who went along on the off-chance there might be a story in it. "Everyone was in good spirits at the prospect of an outing."

Carter was an early believer in one of the cardinal rules of every traveling correspondent: never miss a chance to tuck away a decent meal. There was a small inn where the road crossed the Ingogo River, and Carter hustled into the dining room for a full breakfast. "The cloth was spread," he wrote, "and I prepared to obey the law of hunger, when a shot or two was heard from the direction of our mounted men, who were scouting a mile ahead of the main body, and simultaneously the advance [bugle call] sounded. Forgetting all about breakfast, I saddled up and overtook the column."

Colley, once again, was in deep trouble.

The road descended gradually to the river, which could be easily waded at two points, and then began slowly climbing to a plateau called Schuins Hooghte ("slanting heights" in Dutch). The wily Smit, with a force of maybe two hundred men at the start of the fighting (and more as the day wore on), opened fire as the British troops reached the high plateau.

This was Carter's first time under fire, and he found himself right in the middle of it. His horse was hit twice, and he "promptly 'took to earth' in the center of the plateau." He tried to squeeze himself behind a small boulder, keeping the rock between himself and the hard places where the bullets were coming from. But then they began coming from other directions, too. "I might have dodged around and around that stone all afternoon if I had not come to the conclusion that one place was as safe as another on that plateau."

The Boers, scurrying from boulder to boulder, "formed a line of individual huntsmen, sleuthing and stalking, and moving often to fire from an unexpected place," historian Joseph Lehmann wrote. The Boers were supposed to live in terror of cannon fire, and one of the reasons Colley felt so comfortable on this patrol was that he had brought nine-pounders with him. But guns are operated by gunners, and the British gunners were more exposed to the astonishingly accurate Boer rifle fire than anyone else. "They had no cover except when behind the guns," Carter said, "and that was miserable shelter, seeing the determination with which the enemy shot from close quarters incessantly at the gunners. Captain Greer, [the artilleryman] who was directing the fire on the southern edge of the plateau, was killed very early in the day. Taking the fuse from the hand of one of his men, who was not moving as smartly as his commander wished, he was on the point of inserting it in the vent when a bullet, glancing off the broad arrow on the gun, killed him on the spot."

Lieutenant Charles Parsons took Greer's place, and began moving his two guns "as if on parade." But, one by one, the gunnery officers, the gunners, and the drivers who directed the horses that brought the cannon into action went down, either dead or wounded. Of the total gunner strength of twenty-seven men, two officers and thirteen men were killed or wounded. The moment the guns were fired—and the gunners complained they never saw very much to aim at—Boers popped up "and pelted the gunners terribly as they sponged and reloaded," Carter reported. Parsons was one of the few survivors. By mid-afternoon, the two guns were silenced, a rare instance of cannon being put out of action by concentrated rifle fire.

Colley, frustrated by the Boer marksmanship, ordered Major Brownlow to lead the mounted infantry in an attack on a position on the right flank from which most of the gunfire seemed to be coming. Brownlow, with a Lieutenant Collinson, "led the troop cheerily to the edge of the plateau," Carter said, "and over the side of the crest." But "before the order to charge could be given, the Boers in this quarter, now not more than 150 yards distant, gave them a terrible volley," killing, intentionally, most of their horses. Brownlow led his troop back to the main lines, on foot.

By now the sun was baking the plateau, and the British troops were running out of water. One poor fellow, Carter said, his foot smashed, crawled to where the journalist was crouched behind his rock and begged for water. "That I could not give him; already every water bottle had been exhausted, and now was a time when the heat was terribly intense." Colley, of course, hadn't brought a water cart with him; no need for it, he had said.

The "hospital," Carter found, was a place in the center of the plateau protected only by the bodies of six or more dead artillery horses. It was rapidly filling up with the wounded, all crying out for water.

By mid-afternoon, Colley realized his situation was desperate. He sent two mounted messengers back to Mount Prospect to bring up three companies of Steelbacks to reinforce the Green Jackets; then, in an effort to halt the steady advance of the Boer marksmen up the shoulder of the hill on his left flank, the eastern side of the four-acre plateau, he ordered another attack. This time, Colley gave the job to seventy men from the Green Jackets' I Company, and once again he placed a staff officer, Captain J. C. MacGregor, his private secretary and a Royal Engineers officer, in command. MacGregor was directed to take his riflemen from the right flank across the road to the other side of the plateau, to keep the Boers from turning his left flank.

MacGregor, of course, was mounted (British officers still went into battle on horseback), and he led his troops to an exposed position. "Poor MacGregor," Bruce Hamilton (Colley's brother-in-law) later wrote. He "had gone with one of the companies of the 60th [the Green Jackets] to show them where to post themselves, but unluckily for him and the whole company with him, he took them too far below the brow and they got detached from the rest of our line, and being on the side of the hill the Boers could see them from the top of the one opposite." MacGregor, an easy target on his horse, was killed right away. Others were shot down as they ran and crawled six hundred yards across the open plateau to a position among a clump of rocks, barely sixty yards from the forward position of the enemy. The survivors were now commanded by Lieutenant Francis Beaumont, who, it is said, hid behind a rock eight-by-ten inches in size for four hours. (Beaumont, a former coxswain for the Oxford crew, was a very small man.) By nightfall, most of the Green Jackets were either dead or wounded. They were shot, the Boers said later, by three burghers skillfully positioned to rake the British line.

These brave Green Jackets probably prevented Colley's column from being annihilated. They held out all afternoon, into the evening, and slowed the Boer advance. "I believe [their] conduct saved the Ingogo fight from being a ruinous reverse," Carter wrote.

By 7 P.M., the Boer fire slackened off, and rain began pelting the thirsty British soldiers on the plateau. Colley huddled with his officers, lightning flashing around them, and debated what to do next. Some of the officers thought the troops should fortify their position and fight the Boers again the next day. Colley worried about the security of his camp at Mount Prospect, and decided to withdraw, even if it meant—as it did—leaving his wounded behind.

"Everyone was moody and sad," said Carter, who now "felt ready to eat or drink anything." He watched as the six surviving horses were hitched to the two guns and a single ammunition wagon, and asked Colley what was going on. Colley told him he was withdrawing, and Carter said he would tag along. Colley "added he only thought it fair to warn me that there might be some 'rough work' on the way home."

But the Boers, convinced the British would still be there the next morning, had pulled back, the only major mistake they made the whole war, and the British retreat went ahead unopposed. Carter, after fording the river, now running fast and deep from all the rain, made his way back to the inn. "I gained admission at Fermistone's hotel," he said, "after being duly cross-questioned through the keyhole of the door. Some hot tea and whisky was recommended by the host, and palatable it was." Thomas Fortescue Carter was an ornament to his profession.

The British called the Ingogo River engagement a draw, but they lost four officers and sixty-two men killed and four officers and sixty-three men wounded. Nine men drowned attempting to cross the swollen river. One of them, Lieutenant O. H. Wilkinson, had returned all by himself to the battlefield the following day, hoping to rescue some of the wounded. He was swept away fording the river. Boer casualties were ten dead and six wounded—evidence, once again, of poor British marksmanship.

Rider Haggard, who had heard the gunfire at his ranch house near Newcastle, said "the result of the battle was to make the Boers, whose losses were trifling, more confident than ever, and to greatly depress our soldiers. Sir George had now lost between 300 and 400 men out of his column of little over a thousand. . . ." Only two members of Colley's staff were still alive—Lieutenant Hamilton, the general's brother-in-law, and the amazing Major "Lucky" Essex, who had also managed to survive the Zulu massacre at Isandhlwana.

Back in camp, Colley gave another speech to his troops, some of whom were now openly grumbling about the man's competence. "One or two more Pyrrhic victories like that," Lieutenant Percival Marling of the Green Jackets wrote in his diary, "and we shan't have any army left at all." Once again, Colley said it was all his fault. He was right about that.

But help was finally on the way. General Wood arrived in Newcastle on February 23, fifteen days days after the disaster at Schuins Hooghte, with the Gordon Highlanders (the Ninety-second Regiment under the old system), fine troops fresh from active service in Afghanistan; two squadrons of the aristocratic Fifteenth Hussars, splendid cavalrymen; two more companies of the Green Jackets; and a naval brigade with two guns. Wood was actually senior to Colley, but he had agreed to serve under his old friend—a serious mistake. Wood was an extraordinary figure. He had been a hero in the Zulu War in 1879 and the winner of a Victoria Cross in the Sepoy Mutiny in India in 1857. He was also an odd character. He was a hypochondriac, constantly fidgeting, and his uniform, except for his medals, which he outlined in black to make them show up better (some said he wore them on his pajamas), was a rumpled mess. His nose was memorable: it had been smashed to a pulp by a giraffe the old cavalryman had tried to ride, without much success, years earlier.

The key contingent was the Highland regiment. They had arrived in Durban with a band playing "The Blue Bells of Scotland," the first kilted troops ever seen in Natal. They were veterans from the old unreformed army—serving twelve years on active service at a hitch (instead of six years on active duty, six in the reserves, in the new reformed army). They were supposed to be the best marksmen in the army. The historian Lehmann said that the regiment took pride in the fact that none of its officers had ever been to staff college.

After discussions with Colley, Wood agreed to turn back to Pietermaritzburg to hurry up more reinforcements. These included three entire infantry regiments (the Eighty-third, Ninety-fourth, and Ninety-seventh), the Sixth Dragoons, and the rest of the Fifteenth Hussars. Wood passed Melton Prior, a combat artist and war correspondent hurrying to observe the fighting, on his way south, and told him there was no rush: "I have just left Colley, who has given me his word of honor that he will not move out of camp until I return."

But he didn't really know his man. Colley was now obsessed with redemption. "You will also, I am sure, understand that I mean to take the Nek myself," he had written Wood. He worried, too, about peace negotiations, now beginning to get serious. "I am daily expecting to find ourselves negotiating with the [Boer] 'Triumvirate' as the acknowledged rulers of a victorious people," he wrote his friend Wolseley on February 21, "in which my failure at Lang's Nek will have inflicted a deep and permanent injury on the British name and power in South Africa which it is not pleasant to contemplate." He felt time was running out; surely, his wife, the terror, Tiger, still felt that way.

Armistice feelers actually were sent to Paul Kruger, the most important member of the Triumvirate, but before he could reply Colley made another incredibly stupid move. He and some of the best soldiers in the world climbed to the top of Majuba Hill and one of the most celebrated disasters in the history of the British army.

The ever-alert Carter figured something was up when he noticed Colley and Lieutenant Colonel Herbert Stewart, the new chief of staff, "taking a very long survey of the Nek through their field glasses . . . one would have thought they had never seen it before." Stewart was so absorbed in it that he lay down on his back, with a pillow propping his head, "and gazed and gazed at the enemy's position. . . ." He said he was trying to figure out if the Boers had any guns on the summit.

Majuba Hill, a square-topped extinct volcano rising two thousand feet from the valley, fascinated the two officers. Colley and Stewart, with a few escorting Hussars, had examined the reverse slopes of the mountain on the morning of the Twenty-fourth. They had also interviewed a Zulu servant from a local farm—a "kaffir," in South African terminology—who said he had been on the mountain the previous night, and that there were no Boers to be seen.

"I may have to seize some ground which has hitherto been practically unoccupied by either party, lying between the Nek and our camp," Colley wrote the War Office in London.

But why would he want to occupy the summit of the mountain? Unquestionably, it provided a fine view of the Boer positions in the saddle below, but the sides of the mountain were too steep for cannon and the distance from the summit to the Boer lines too great for rifles. Even the Gatlings were too heavy to haul up the mountain. That left the three rocket tubes, which probably could have been manhandled to the summit. They might have reached the Boer trenches, barely. But they were left behind, too.

"Military leaders and historians have argued the pros and cons of Colley's actions in occupying Majuba for the past 100 years without reaching a sound conclusion," George Duxbury, the South African historian, noted in 1981. "It is my belief that Colley had no sound plan."

"The enterprise was that of a madman," David Cromb, coauthor of a history of the Gordon Highlanders, concluded. And maybe it was. Even General Sir William Butler, Colley's sympathetic biographer, questioned the "balance of his mind" in the hours leading up to the disaster. Haggard said the soldiers he talked to after the engagement remarked that the general was "not himself."

Lehmann, the most careful historian of the campaign, disagreed. The general's letters and dispatches were calm and dispassionate right to the end, he argued. Colley was simply extending his lines, just as the Boers were extending theirs, and that was a perfectly obvious thing to do. His mistake was in believing the Boers wouldn't try to recapture the mountain. "After all," said Lehmann, "the Boers were committed to fighting on the defensive . . ."

Perhaps. Yet, it is hard to believe that Colley really considered this to be an unexceptional move. His final letter to Tiger strongly suggested he knew it was a daring toss of the dice. "Don't let all things be dark to you if I don't come back to you," he said. Generals don't talk about death in letters to their wives when they are making conventional extensions of their lines.

Duxbury believed that Colley's "sole intention was to make a show of troops on this 'unassailable' feature [the top of Majuba Hill]," believing "the Boers would be taken by surprise at his feat, in fact staggered at the immensity of his night achievement," to the point where they would hitch up their wagons, "mount their horses and depart for their farms as quickly as they could." It would be "a bloodless military settlement of the war that would vindicate his previous defeats and the great loss of lives which must, from all accounts, have weighed heavily on his mind."

But if he believed it was going to be bloodless, why did he worry Tiger with suggestions he would be killed atop Majuba Hill?

It remains, after all, a conundrum.

Mysterious, too, was why Colley picked a mixed force of 554 rifles— two companies of the Northamptons (170 men), two companies of the Green Jackets (140 men), three companies of the Gordon Highlanders (180 men), and one company of the Royal Navy Brigade (64 men). "Colley would have been far wiser to have taken a single battalion rather than this composite force to seize Majuba," historian Oliver Ransford wrote. "It lacked homogeneity and *esprit de corps;* there was no hierarchy of officers down which command would automatically pass in the event of casualties; nor was there a single regimental commander known to all the troops, round whom they could rally in a crisis." Ransford speculated that the outcome might well have been different if the battle-hardened Highlanders, under their own colonel, had been assigned the job.

Colley's excuse, if he had lived to give one, probably would have been that he wanted to give the Northamptons, the Green Jackets, and the sailors a chance to redeem themselves for earlier defeats.

Naturally, Carter of the *Natal Times* accompanied the force. The soldiers had been told to take rations for three days. Carter said he filled his pockets with enough to last four. "It would be ten o'clock before a start was made," he wrote. "There was no moon, but the night was not very dark. . . . The general and his staff rode in front, just behind the Zulu guides, followed, in turn, by the Northamptons, the Green Jackets, the Gordon Highlanders and the naval brigade."

Halfway to the mountain, two Green Jacket companies were detached and ordered to cover the line of march. A company of Highlanders fell out at the foot of Majuba and was told to dig in. The rest of Colley's force, about 375 men, each of them loaded down with fifty-eight pounds of rations and equipment, stumbled on, the kilted Highlanders scraping their knees as they climbed over rocks and boulders. Colley took off his boots and put on soft leather shoes. "Crawling on hands and knees, and laying hold of the grass," Carter wrote, the column finally came in sight of the top of the hill. A file from the leading company of the Northamptons was sent ahead to reconnoiter the summit, with Colley and his staff close behind.

"The first thing we did [when we reached the summit]," Carter wrote, "was to lie down and rest for five minutes, then to take a survey of the ground." Carter peered over the side of the mountain at the Boer positions

Sir George Colley at the Battle of Majuba Hill, as illustrated by Melton Prior in the *Illustrated London News*, May 14, 1881. (Library of Congress collections)

far below. "Very little could we see before four o'clock," he said, "a solitary light here and there in the darkness. In a very short time, however, the change was marvelous. The Boer army had risen from sleep, and in every tent and wagon there was a light. The valley, into which it seemed we could throw a stone, was a mass of light. . . . It was a thrilling sight from our point of vantage; there was our enemy *at our mercy*, and unaware of our proximity to them."

Carter thought there was more to Colley's plan than occupying the top of Majuba Hill. He said he expected to see the artillery from Mount Prospect advance on the Nek, and begin to pound away at the Boers. He expected to see the Hussars and the rest of the British infantry advance to the assault, "and at the same time part of our force would descend from the position we held, and our movement [would] spread dismay and terror among the enemy, and there would then be a general stampede of the enemy."

But Carter was just a journalist from an obscure colonial newspaper; everyone said Colley was the most brilliant general in the British army.

Colley did nothing. Even though his troops had hauled eighty picks and eighty spades to the top of the mountain, no effort was made to erect breastworks, and no effort was made to scout the sides of the mountains facing the Boer positions. These were fatal mistakes. "The idea of the enemy creeping from terrace to terrace, or up the gullies, and reaching the crest, occurred to no one," Carter said.

Colley said the men were too tired from their long climb to dig in. Others argued the men were full of enthusiasm, ready to fight at a moment's notice. Lieutenant Ian Hamilton of the Gordon Highlanders (he would one day command the disastrous Gallipoli expedition in World War I) said his troops were "too excited to feel fatigue and I saw no signs of it."

"We could stay here forever," Colley told Stewart as he settled down for a brief nap.

Discipline apparently was slack. Soldiers wandered around the ten-acre top of the hill, still separated from their units. Carter said he saw twenty Highlanders standing up on the ridge in "full view of the Boers on the Nek below."

"Come up here, you beggars!" they shouted. This was foolhardy, and Carter recognized the point, even if the brilliant Colley didn't. "Had orders been issued for every man to lie close, we might have captured the first arrivals"—the Boers put a small patrol on the top of the mountain during daylight hours—"without firing a shot." One of the Northamptons, a Lieutenant Lucy, actually borrowed one of his soldier's rifles and fired a shot in the general direction of the Boers down below. "Stop that firing," the lethargic Colley ordered. But the shooting continued.

The Boer commander, Piet Joubert, was first informed the British were on Majuba Hill by a Boer housewife named Mrs. de Jager. She galloped into camp on her pony early Sunday morning and pointed to some of the stragglers making their way to the summit. Joubert said they looked like mountain goats to him. "Since when," huffed Mrs. de Jager, "have mountain goats been dressed in red tunics?"

By most accounts, Joubert was reluctant to storm the mountain, fearful the British had hauled cannon to the summit. Reassured they only had rifles, with which, he knew by now, they couldn't shoot very well, he ordered his best general, Nicholas Smit, to make the attack.

What Smit knew, and what Colley hadn't bothered to discover, was that the north and west faces of the mountain were broken by terraces and gullies and covered by deep grass, good cover for the agile Boers. They knew, too, that once they reached the terraces at the top, they would be totally concealed from the British, and invulnerable to their rifle fire. The key to the British position, if they had only known it, was a grassy knoll projecting from the plateau at its northern angle. Colley did know enough to post a handful of Gordon Highlanders on it. It has been known ever since as Gordons' Knoll.

A second knoll projected from the plateau near the southwest angle "like a miniature Gibraltar," Carter said. It was a perfect defensive position, and if men had been posted there, and if they had dug in, perhaps, just as Colley had said, the British could have remained on Majuba Hill forever. But, of course, no such preparations were taken.

Joubert delivered a short, emotional speech to his burghers and asked for volunteers to storm the hill—a traditional invitation—and 350 men stepped forward. The older men were positioned at the bottom of the hill, to give cover to the younger men, many of them farm boys, as they zigzagged up the slopes from boulder to boulder. "It was a perfect example of fire and movement as taught even today," Duxbury wrote, "except that their supporting fire was from rifles and not from flanking machine guns [or artillery fire] as it would be in modern warfare."

From the top of the mountain, the British could see the Boers preparing to make an attack. "The ground below the mountain was dotted all over with them," Carter wrote. Too late, the British began digging in. "But such cover!" said Carter. "Each man cast about for a few stones, made a breastwork for himself on the ridge by piling them loosely one on top of the other. . . . Anything more trumpery and miserable against a bullet could not be conceived." Carter asked several of the men what was the use of it. "Oh, it's all right, sir," they replied, "it's good enough for what we shall want up here."

Colley, awake at last, walked the perimeter of his lines talking quietly to his troops. He, Stewart, and Commander Romilly, leader of the naval brigade, peered down the mountain into a ravine. "See," said Romilly, "there's a man who looks as if he were going to try and shoot us." Stewart looked at him through his binoculars, and estimated the range at nine hundred yards. The Boer marksman, at that point, fired at the three officers silhouetted on the ridge. The bullet entered Romilly's abdomen and came out the back of his neck. "I am all right," he said. But he wasn't; the wound was mortal.

"What military genius possessed these burghers!" Ransford burbled. "What instinctive aptitude they had for war! Here were a few hundred men prepared to assault a position which any professional soldier of the time would have insisted was impregnable. Yet everything was planned by Smit that morning with Napoleonic facility and speed; it was carried out with an exact precision scarcely equaled in the annals of warfare."

The Boers attacked the British from three directions. Two commando units scaled the hill from the east and the west. The main force, under Commandant Stephanus Roos, "approached Majuba from the north using the cover of a wooded ravine which points like a dagger at Gordons' Knoll," Ransford wrote. They rested under a hanging cliff halfway up the mountain, drank a little water, and then continued the climb in a highly professional skirmishing order. By 11 A.M., they began gathering in a rocky gully just below the knoll. Colley had no idea they were there, having sent a heliograph message at noon saying that he had broken up the Boer attack and that the burghers had "begun to move away."

At 1 P.M., Colley stretched out for another nap, asking Stewart to waken him if anything developed.

The Boers already had begun a steady fire on Gordons' Knoll, and Lieutenant Ian Hamilton, commanding the fifteen Highlanders holding the outpost, could see that trouble was developing. He ran across the plateau to tell Colley about it, and to seek permission to charge the Boers with bayonets. Colley, unbelievably, was still asleep, and Stewart, his chief of staff, told Hamilton to stop worrying.

Carter remembered talking to an English officer who had removed a glass eye, "held it in the palm of his hand, and from a water bottle poured water over it to wash it." He was replacing his glass eyeball when "there came of a sudden a terrific outburst of fire from the Boers, just on the other side of the slope of the basin on which we were at this time talking."

It was, of course, the Boers attacking Lieutenant Hamilton and his Highlanders on Gordons' Knoll. The Boers, huddled below the knoll, had watched as the Highlanders stood up every few moments to fire at Boers at the foot of the mountain, well out of range. "This was the criticial moment of Smit's plan," wrote Ransford. "At a signal the waiting burghers below the knoll stood up, stepped back, and . . . fired a volley" at the exposed Highlanders above. A dozen were killed; the rest, three or four men, dropped their rifles and ran away. Hamilton tried to stop them, without much luck.

Carter said one of the officers, possibly Colonel Stewart, raced by to call up reserves to assist the panic-stricken Highlanders. "The reserves obeyed the order," Carter said, "but my impression at the time while looking on was that there was a want of alacrity shown by the men which was not altogether reassuring."

The reserves from the Steelback and Highlander regiments, along with sailors from the naval brigade, "disappeared in skirmishing order over the ridge to meet the enemy," Carter wrote, "and returned the fire rapidly." Carter felt the Boer fire slacken, and "thought our men had driven them back." He was about to gather up his personal belongings—field glasses, clasp knife (for opening sardine cans), remains of a loaf of bread—when the reserves, in pell-mell retreat, "came rushing straight over me, making for the ridge nearest Mount Prospect." Without stopping to pick up his belongings, Carter "ran with the rest at a moment's notice into the bottom of the basin."

"Rally on the right! Rally on the right!" the officers shouted, and slowly some order was established. But, by now, the units were all mixed up, "a Highlander next to a 58th man, a sailor next to him." If it wasn't exactly that fatal red bull's-eye all over again, it was simply because the only redcoated troops were the Steelback regulars.

The Boers "reopened fire with a fury that could not be excelled. Between the ridge of boulders behind which we sheltered and the enemy there was thirty yards of flat, covered only with grass, then the ground sloped down. Lying on their faces on the slope, and peering across the space which separated us, the Boers kept up a terrific fire, aiming as low as they could at our line of defense without exposing themselves," Carter said.

Now, if ever, was the time for a bayonet charge. Carter heard officers crying out, "Fix bayonets!" and he could hear the bayonets as they rang into their rifle sockets. Colley's response was: "Wait a while."

The British line was anchored on the right at Hay's Knoll, but its defenders, under heavy fire, were already deserting their post. Anchoring the British position on the other side of the plateau was Macdonald's Knoll, and its defenders should have been in a good position to stop the Boers from crawling forward in the center of the plateau. But another column of Boers had climbed the mountain and was now positioned on the western edge. They brought Macdonald's hill under a barrage of accurate rifle fire. "They could see us from all sides," one British officer noted.

Ian Hamilton (no relation to Colley's brother-in-law, Bruce) approached Colley again. "I do hope, general," he said, "that you will let us have a charge, and that you will not think it presumptuous on my part to have come up and asked you."

"No presumption, Mr. Hamilton," said Colley, "but we will wait until the Boers advance on us, then give them a volley and a charge." It was Colley's last decision, and, as Ransford suggested, it almost surely was the wrong one, once again.

Carter was sitting next to another war correspondent, J. A. Cameron of the *London Standard* (he would be killed later in the Sudan), a couple of yards behind the British fighting line. "'There's going to be a disaster here,' I said to him. 'Oh, I don't know,' he replied. 'See, the men are standing well up to it with the bayonet.'" Sure enough, said Carter, "'but why doesn't the general let them go at it . . . while the men have their blood up?'" Cameron said he was certain that the Highlanders would attack any moment.

Carter didn't think so. "Discipline was on the wane," and he watched as some of the finest soldiers in the British army refused to deploy as that new column of Boer farmers appeared on the summit. "I saw blue-jackets, red coats, and brown coats [Highlanders] moving in ones and twos on their faces to where they were called from; but an insufficient number were willing to obey the command. There was a hanging back . . . which neither entreaties nor threats could move."

The Boers, when they first arrived at the summit, had feared a bayonet attack. "My courage sank for a moment," Commandant Roos said later, as he peeked over the ridge. But the Highlanders were just standing there. Roos said he lied to his men, crying out that the British were on the run. "Come on now, you chaps," he said. "Come quickly. The English are flying." They weren't, but one volley from Roos's Boers, and they were.

Carter looked to the left, where the new attack was coming from, and saw Colley directing a handful of men to meet the threat. "It was the last time I saw him alive. A sudden piercing cry of terror, which will ring in my ears for many a long day, rose from the line or group of infantry." The men stopped firing; the headlong, panic-stricken retreat had begun.

"What the devil are you doing?" an officer shouted above the din and through the smoke. "Come back! come back!"

"It was not long," Carter said, "before I was on my feet and running with the rest," shoulder to shoulder with a stout Highlander. Another Highlander was hit in front of him. "Oh, my God," he cried out, and Carter had to jump over his fallen body.

Carter was faced with a precipice and a sheer drop of forty feet. Two Steelbacks were at his side. When one of them was cut down, Carter decided he "might as well die of a broken neck as to be shot in the back." He jumped, and landed safely on his feet.

One of the British soldiers said it had taken him five bloody hours to get up Majuba, but he touched the ground only five bloody times on the way down.

Only one British soldier was still advancing—Colley, with a revolver in his hand, "firing rapidly at the Boers some 20 yards away." It didn't last long: he was struck by a Boer bullet that some survivors said seemed to lift him off the ground. His last words may have been: "Oh my men, do not run."

Ian Hamilton was still standing too, his kilt and jacket riddled with bullets. He was finally struck in the wrist, and knocked to the ground. When he regained consciousness, two Boer boys, twelve or thirteen years old, were removing his possessions. The Boers especially treasured sporrans—the Highlanders' decorative pouches—as souvenirs. Hamilton eventually wandered in a daze away from the battlefield, collapsing in a marsh at the bottom of the hill. He was discovered at dawn by a search party; his fox terrier, Patch, licked his face, and brought him back to life.

A young Boer, firing down at the retreating, panic-stricken British troops, said it was just like killing deer. "*Al te lekker*," he said—very nice.

Poor Colley was dead, and the battle—soon to become a Boer legend, the Bunker Hill, the Bastille in white South African history—was over. British losses were 92 killed, 134 wounded, and 59 taken prisoner. Boer losses—an incredible indictment of British marksmanship—were 1 dead and 5 wounded (one of whom died several days later). The Boers reported that the British rifles picked up on the battlefield were sighted at four hundred yards; most of the fighting took place at distances of less than two hundred yards. Rider Haggard called the British marksmanship "villainous."

Generals Sir Evelyn Wood and Piet Joubert met on March 6, midway between Lang's Nek and Mount Prospect, and signed a temporary armistice. The Boers, the despised "pinheads," had won, and the reputation of the British army—the army that couldn't shoot straight—plunged to a new low.

◆

Incredibly rich deposits of gold drew thousands of *Uitlanders* to Boer territory starting in 1886, alarming the Boer leaders. Old Paul Kruger, now president of the Transvaal, denied the newcomers, most of them British, citizenship or even basic civil rights. War was inevitable, and it was touched off when a mad adventurer named Doctor Leander Starr Jameson invaded the Transvaal with 470 Rhodesian policemen late in 1895. He and his small force were easily subdued, but Boer opinion was aroused. Kruger demanded the British give up all claims to the Transvaal; when they refused, Boer commandos from both the Transvaal and the Orange Free State invaded Cape Colony and Natal on October 11, 1899, laying siege to several towns garrisoned by British troops, including Kimberley.

The British found another incompetent general, Sir Redvers Buller, to take command of their army, and he promptly led it to one crushing defeat after another. In one week—called black week—the British managed to lose three times. They even found a way to duplicate the disaster at Majuba Hill in the First Boer War on another hill called Spion Kop. Seventy men were shot dead in one trench, each of them with a bullet in the head.

Buller was replaced by a better general, Frederick Sleigh "Little Bobs" Roberts, who quickly lifted the siege at Kimberley, and freed the richest Englishman in the world, Cecil Rhodes. British troops marched into Pretoria on June 5, 1900, and Kruger slipped away to Holland.

It had been a big war, with British losses set at more than twenty-two thousand dead. Boer losses in fighting men came to seven thousand, and hundreds of Boer women and children died in British-run concentration camps. The British were generous in victory, paying millions to reconstruct the ravaged Boer territory. Boers fought at Britain's side in both world wars and the English maintained a naval base in South Africa until 1955. In 1961, Boer leaders took South Africa out of the British Commonwealth and set up the racist apartheid state that outraged world opinion.

But in an almost miraculous series of events, the ban on the African National Congress was lifted in 1990 and its leader, Nelson Mandela, was freed, after spending twenty-seven years in prison. A year later, apartheid laws were repealed. And, in 1995, the democratically elected leader of a peaceful South Africa was none other than Nelson Mandela himself.

SEVEN

Major General Charles "Chinese" Gordon and the Fall of Khartoum (1884–1885)

To this day, no one can be quite certain why William Gladstone's government sent Great Britain's most eccentric general, Charles George Gordon, to Khartoum, capital of the Sudan, in 1884.

Sir Garnet Wolseley, adjutant general at the War Office, carried Gordon's kit bag to Charing Cross Station on January 18. Lord Granville, the foreign secretary, bought his ticket. And His Royal Highness, the Duke of Cambridge, Queen Victoria's cousin and commanding officer of the British army, held open the carriage door.

And so Gordon, a major general whose greatest exploit, leading the imperialist Ever-Victorious Army in China, had earned him the nickname Chinese Gordon, embarked on the final journey of his life, accompanied by a single British officer, Colonel J. D. H. Stewart of the Eleventh Hussars. He was ten days shy of his fifty-first birthday.

The queen, with better instincts than almost anyone else, wrote in her diary: "His attempt is a very dangerous one."

Very dangerous indeed. Gordon would die—widely admired as a splendid Christian hero to the end—at the top of the stairs outside the governor's palace, pierced in a dozen places by the spears of the dervishes, the foot soldiers of a great Muhammadan army led by a man so devout he believed he was the Mahdī, the second coming of the Prophet himself. Belatedly, Gladstone sent an army to rescue Gordon, and a small part of it was only hours away when the climactic moment arrived. On hearing the terrible news, all of Great Britain burst into tears. "Too late!" cried a famous *Punch* drawing, as Britannia grasped her fevered brow in grief.

"What enterprise, . . ." Winston Churchill once asked, "is more noble and more profitable than the reclamation from barbarism of fertile regions and large populations? To give peace to warring tribes, to administer justice where all was violence, to strike the chains off the slave, to draw the richness from the soil . . . what more beautiful ideal or more valuable reward can inspire human effort?"

The Sudan, a dependency of Egypt and its nominal ruler, the khedive, surely was a challenge.

The land wasn't a fertile region at all. It was undeveloped and poor, Churchill wrote in *The River War*. "The arbitrary and excessive taxes were collected only at the point of a bayonet [by the khedive's undisciplined soldiers]. . . . The ability of the Arabs to pay depended on their success as slave-traders. When there had been a good catch, the revenue profited. . . . In the miserable, harassing warfare that accompanied the collection of taxes the Viceregal commanders [serving the Egyptian khedive] gained more from fraud than force. No subterfuge, no treachery, was too mean for them to adopt." It was a volcano, in which "the Arab tribes obeyed, and the black population cowered."

Gordon was no stranger to this mysterious corner of the world. He had served as the khedive's governor-general in Equatoria, in the south of the present-day Sudan. He had traveled almost everywhere by camel. "Those marvelous camel rides," John Buchan, the novelist/historian/diplomat wrote. He "sped like a flame across the deserts and surprised his enemies while they were still conspiring." In one year, Gordon estimated, he traveled close to four thousand miles on camelback. He was not without a sense of humor. "The Gordons and the camels are of the same race," he said. "Let them take an idea into their heads and nothing will take it out. I have a splendid camel—none like it; it flies along and quite astonishes the Arabs." Later, he again represented Ismail, the Egyptian khedive, as governor-general of the Sudan, a job in which he attempted, with limited success, to destroy the slave trade. He also abolished torture in the prisons and put an end to public floggings with a buffalo hide whip called the *kourbash*.

The mobs loved him, but real reform was always elusive. Discouraged, thinking his life was over, Gordon resigned and came home to England. He moved restlessly from place to place, testing once again his Christian beliefs. He had always been suspicious of the Anglican Church, but now he discovered the meaning of Holy Communion. "Through the working of Christ in my body by His Body and Blood, the medicine worked," he wrote to his spinster sister, Augusta, his closest friend and his principal religious confidante. "Ever since the realization of the sacrament," he said, "I have been turned upside down."

He was "a type without comparison in modern times," Churchill said, and potentates from all over the world competed for his services—the emperor of China, the king of the Belgians, the premier of Cape Colony, the khedive of Egypt. And yet, Churchill said, he contained so little "mental ballast. . . . Mercury uncontrolled by the force of gravity was not on several occasions more unstable than Charles Gordon. His moods were capricious and uncertain, his passions violent, his impulses sudden and inconsistent. The mortal enemy of the morning had become a trusted ally before the night." His temperament, Churchill thought, was "naturally neurotic," a condition that became exaggerated "by an acquired habit of smoking . . . he was rarely seen without a cigarette." He was never married, and never, as far as anyone knows, showed any interest in sex. Some of his biographers suggest—inevitably—that he was a repressed homosexual.

His appeal may be puzzling to those of us living at the dawn of the twenty-first century. But in the age of Victoria, Gordon was so "unlike other men," Buchan concluded, "that he readily acquired a spiritual ascendancy over all who knew him well and many who did not . . . " Yet, Buchan agreed with Churchill. There was a "dualism" there; "the impression of single-heartedness was an illusion, for all his life his soul was the stage of a conflict."

Perhaps most important of all, he had no fear of death. Quite the opposite: as a devout evangelical Christian, he welcomed it. He set off to Khartoum joyously prepared to meet his Maker.

Britain felt it needed to do something. With the opening of the Suez Canal in 1869, Egypt, simply by its location, assumed an important role in world affairs. But the khedive—Egypt's nominal ruler—borrowed so much money from European bankers that his country went broke trying to pay off the interest. Economic conditions reached such a low point in 1881 that Ahmed Arabi, a colonel in the army, launched a coup that was only put down by the British navy and seventeen thousand British troops commanded by Queen Victoria's busiest general, Sir Garnet Wolseley. He routed Arabi in a night attack (he had discovered the Egyptians didn't post sentries when it was dark) at Tall al-Kabīr, between Cairo and Port Said, and Egypt became, in consequence, a British protectorate.

Now trouble began boiling up in the Sudan, where the Mahdī and his devout, but ragged, Muhammadan army were inexorably advancing, imperiling the outposts maintained by 20,000 soldiers from the Egyptian army and 11,000 civilians employed by Cairo bureaucrats. An aging British officer, Colonel William Hicks, was put in charge of an expeditionary force in 1883 to suppress the Mahdī's insurgency. At the head of 8,000 Egyptian soldiers—sometimes described as the worst professional army in history—he set off in pursuit, stumbling through the desert for two months. Some of his troops were in chains to prevent desertion. Officers openly feuded with each other. The guides were traitors. At a village called Kashgil, near El Obeid, the principal town of Kordofan, they were attacked by 50,000 dervishes—known, to themselves, as Asmar—and only 250 soldiers survived. "The European officers perished fighting to the end, and the general [Hicks] met his fate sword in hand, at the head of the last formed body of his troops, his personal valour and amazing strength exciting the admiration even of the fearless enemy, so that in chivalrous respect they buried his body with barbarous honours," Churchill wrote. Muhammad Ahmad—the self-professed Mahdī—"celebrated his victory with a salute of 100 guns, as well he might, for the Sudan was now his. . . ."

It was against this appalling background that Gladstone's government decided to send Gordon to Khartoum. No army, just Gordon himself, plus Colonel Stewart.

Why? The government already knew his views on the subject, for he had expounded them at great length in an interview in W. T. Stead's *Pall Mall Gazette.* The interview, picked up by every other paper in the country, left no doubt that Gordon and the government did not see eye to eye. The government favored abandoning the Egyptian garrisons; Gordon wanted to save them. "You cannot evacuate," he told Stead. "You must either surrender absolutely to the Mahdi or defend Khartoum at all hazards."

Only Sir Evelyn Baring, the British consul in Cairo, objected to hiring this opinionated unemployed general. He didn't like Gordon and he didn't need him now. But Wolseley did like Gordon, and Gordon liked Wolseley (Gordon prayed for him every night). Wolseley called Gordon to the War Office to talk about the Sudanese mission. It was during that meeting, wrote historian Julian Symons, that Gordon came to understand "that he was called in the Sudan to carry out the work of God."

The national press was now in full cry too. They wanted Gordon sent to Khartoum, to do something, anything. So, not for the first nor the last time, a government succumbed to public opinion. Still, Gladstone's ministers believed they had set markers. The mission would be one of inquiry; Gordon and Stewart would go to Suakin, a Sudanese port on the Red Sea, "to report on the military situation in the Sudan and . . . consider the best move of evacuating the interior of the Sudan and of securing the safety and good administration of the Egyptian government of the ports on the Red Sea coast."

"I understand," said Gordon, "H.M.G. [Her Majesty's government] only wish me to report and are in no way bound to me."

But then the Egyptian minister of war, Abd el-Kader, changed his mind. More than just a study mission, he now wanted "a qualified British officer to go to Khartoum with full powers civil and military to conduct the retreat." Baring gave in, too, agreeing to Gordon getting the job "if he will pledge himself to carry out the policy of withdrawal from Sudan as soon as possible, consistently with saving life."

Instead of moving on to Suakin, Gordon was persuaded to go to Cairo and sit down with the new khedive, Tewfik. Unexpectedly, the two hit it off famously, and the khedive gave Gordon two important *firmans* (edicts), one naming him governor-general of the Sudan, the other saying he was going to evacuate the garrisons and—this was new—establish some kind of government based in Khartoum.

Baring, who would one day rule Egypt, began expressing doubts about Gordon almost at once. "A man who habitually consults the Prophet Isaiah when he is in a difficulty is not apt to obey the orders of anyone," he wrote. What, after all, was a rational man to make about Gordon and his feelings for Zobeir Pasha, perhaps the most notorious slave trader in all of Africa? Gordon had despised Zobeir for years, and had in fact been at least partly responsible for executing the slaver's son, the rebellious Suleiman, during his earlier stint as governor-general. As soon as he set out on his new mission, he cabled ahead suggesting that Baring should exile Zobeir to Cyprus. But then, in the Cairo anteroom of an old friend, the two men met, accidentally. "They had a long talk about the Sudan," Churchill wrote, after which Gordon told Baring that Zobeir "must accompany him to Khartoum at once." Baring, in fact, rather thought it was a good idea, but he couldn't believe Gordon was serious. Think about it, Baring urged. Gordon said that wasn't necessary, for he had undergone a "mystic feeling" that Zobeir was the one man in all of Egypt who could put things back together in the Sudan. The anti-Mahdists, Gordon reasoned, would rally to Zobeir in ways they would rally to no one else, least of all a devoutly Christian general from England.

Thus, said Churchill, "the 'Christian hero' asked for the help of the 'abandoned ruffian.'"

Ministers in London—more sensitive than Gordon to the lobbying power of the Anti-Slavery Society—were appalled. Under no circumstances, they said, should the old "ruffian" be put to work for the Egyptian or the British governments. Gordon thought it was a great mistake—Churchill agreed—and stewed about it for weeks .

"With their refusal to allow Zobeir to go to the Sudan began the long and miserable disagreement between the government and their envoy," Churchill said. " . . . Gordon considered that he was personally pledged to effect the evacuation of Khartoum by the garrisons and civil servants. . . . He therefore considered that his honor was involved in their safety. Henceforth he was inflexible."

He knew what he was doing. "I own to having been very insubordinate to Her Majesty's Government and its officials, but it is my nature, and I cannot help it," he wrote in his extraordinary Khartoum journals, all of which were smuggled to safety before the city fell. "I fear I have not even tried to play battledore and shuttlecock with them. I know if *I* was chief I would never employ *myself* for I am incorrigible."

There was more going on than thoughts of playing a game of battledore and shuttlecock, concluded Anthony Nutting, the Gordon biographer. Locked in Gordon's mind now was "the ever-present, constantly repeated desire for martyrdom and for that glorious immortality in union with God and away from the wretchedness of life on this earth. 'I feel so very much inclined to wish it His will might be my release. Earth's joys grow very dim, its glories have faded,' he had recently written to his sister."

The night he took a train from Cairo en route to the Sudan, he telegraphed Khartoum: "Don't be panic-stricken. Ye are men, not women. I am coming. Gordon."

He and Stewart arrived in Khartoum, surely an earthly expression of the wretchedness of life, on February 18. If he was going to meet his Maker, he would do it with an extraordinary burst of energy. "He gave every power of mind and body to the task of performing the impossible," Buchan wrote. "In all the history of war there are few records in which the spirit of man shines so triumphantly as in Gordon's desperate toil at the defense of a sprawling city and a scared people, with dwindling supplies and raw troops that drew their only virtue from his courage."

At the start, Alan Moorehead pointed out in *The White Nile*, "Gordon's plight . . . in Khartoum was not absolutely desperate. He had with him in the town about 34,000 people, of whom some 8,000 were soldiers" and perhaps as many as 20,000 black slaves. The soldiers weren't very reliable, but they were armed with Remington rifles; during the course of the siege, they managed to fire off millions of rounds. Most of all, Gordon had his beloved little paddle steamers, not very different from the penny steamers that took day-trippers for outings on the Thames. Using the city's old Egyptian arsenal, he slapped enough armor plate on their sides to ward off dervish rifle fire. "My beautiful steamers," he wrote in his journal weeks into the siege, "which used to be comparatively sweet, now stink like badgers." The *Ismailia*, he said, was a "cess-pit." But they remained his most dependable link to the outside world and, with their brass cannon, his best artillery battery.

Gordon had been trained as a military engineer and he put that experience to work to improve his position. "His first duty," wrote Buchan, "was to strengthen the ramparts so that the place could not be taken by a sudden assault." The city was located on the south side of the Blue Nile. The White Nile was a mile or so to the west. They joined to the north of the city to form the Nile itself, flowing north almost two thousand miles to the sea. He built fortifications both to the east of the city—Fort Buri, on the Blue Nile—and to the west—Fort Mukran, near the White Nile. He then ran a parapet and ditch in a half-moon formation between the two Niles. He also garrisoned a fort in Omdurman, an Arab village on the west side of the White Nile.

"Gordon excelled in this kind of situation," Julian Symons said. "His nature was autocratic, his mind ingenious, and he enjoyed fighting against odds. . . . He had telegraph stations placed at all outlying posts, communicating with a central point, and the defenses were strengthened by placing . . . wire entanglements outside the lines, and by putting beyond them mines made of old water tins filled with dynamite. . . ." Like the fictional Beau Geste, he even made wooden dummy soldiers and put them up on the east bank of the Blue Nile as targets for the dervishes.

He printed his own paper money, and personally signed the ones with the big denominations. He cast decorations for soldiers—silver gilt for commanders, silver for majors, and tin for everyone else. He held church parade on Sundays and his band entertained soldiers and civilians in concerts in the square every Friday and Sunday after sunset.

He despaired of his troops, though, especially the twenty-three hundred Arab tribesmen, the Shaggyeh (one of the rare tribes that didn't join the Mahdī). "Those Shaggyeh!" he wrote in his journal. "I will back them to try a man's patience more sorely than any other people in the whole world, yea, and in the Universe!" He returned to his anti-Shaggyeh theme again and again. "Dreadful lot," he said. "How I look forward to their disbandment!" The bashi-bazouks, Turkish irregulars from Cairo, weren't much better. He had nineteen hundred of them. He also had about fourteen hundred "white" Egyptian troops, and they were a sorry lot. His best troops were the black regulars, many of them former slaves; he had twenty-three hundred of them.

The toughest creature in town might have been the palace's nasty turkey cock. "I think the turkey cock is a bird worth studying," Gordon wrote in his amazing journal. "I would give him the palm over all other birds for pluck." His own turkey cock, he said, kept a harem of five and managed to be angry most of the time. If only his soldiers, he may have thought, shared some of his turkey's fighting qualities.

There was no doubt he expected England to do its duty, and rescue him and the Egyptian garrisons (smaller outposts were holding out, too) with a relief expedition. His chronicler in Khartoum, Frank Power, the British consul and the London *Times*'s correspondent, reported to his paper in March that "we are daily expecting the British troops. We cannot bring ourselves to believe that we are abandoned by the government."

London dithered; it wouldn't agree to send Zobeir; it wouldn't agree to send two hundred troops to Berber to create a diversion. The government, most of it anyway, simply wanted Gordon to get on with the evacuation (Gordon actually did send four hundred sick and infirm members of his garrison downriver, but that was all). On March 12, communication stopped: four thousand Arabs attacked Halfaya, nine miles downstream from Khartoum, and cut the telegraph line. From that point on, the only messages from Gordon were written on slips of paper and carried by native runners. Most of them failed to get through.

Things had been going badly along the Red Sea, Britain's gateway to India, too. Colonel Valentine Baker, a disgraced British officer (he had been convicted of assaulting a young woman in a railway carriage) who commanded the semimilitary Egyptian gendarmerie, set out with 3,500 men to relieve the Egyptian garrison at Tokar. At a place called Al-Teb, 1,000 dervishes led by Osman Digna, armed with spears and clubs, attacked Baker's square. The Egyptian troops abandoned their artillery and their Gatling guns and ran, "allowing themselves to be killed without the slightest resistance," Baker reported. All together, he lost 2,225 men and 96 officers.

Suakin, the principal British and Egyptian base on the Red Sea, vital for maintaining the Suez Canal, now came under threat, too. London wouldn't help Gordon, but it responded to the Red Sea crisis by dispatching three British battalions under Lieutenant General Sir Gerald Graham. Graham marched right back to Al-Teb and defeated a dervish army of some six thousand men. Later, at Tamai, he took them on again; this time, the dervishes were Hadendowa tribesmen with their fuzzy hair. These "fuzzy-wuzzies" charged with "reckless determination" and actually broke a British square partly defended by the famous Black Watch regiment. ("And 'ere's to you, Fuzzy Wuzzy," Kipling wrote, in Cockney dialect, "with your 'ayrick 'ead of hair—You big black boundin' beggar—for you bruk a British square!") The embarrassed British pulled themselves together, reformed the square, and the dervishes were driven off with heavy casualties.

The question now was whether this force, which included some of the best troops in the British army—the Black Watch, the Gordon Highlanders, and the Nineteenth Hussars among them—would be used to help Gordon. Out of the question. The whole force, except for a small garrison at Suakin, was pulled back to Cairo. Gordon, wrote biographer John H. Waller, "denied military relief, without telegraphic communications and completely surrounded by hostile tribesmen, could only now await the Mahdi with his grand army of Baggara horsemen and Dongolowi zealots. The siege had begun."

"Gordon is in danger," Queen Victoria told her war minister, Lord Hartington. "You are bound to try and save him. Surely Indian troops might go from Aden; they could bear the climate. You have incurred fearful responsibility." The government was not moved. "It would be unjustifiable to send a force as proposed," Lord Granville told the queen.

Even Baring, the one man who hadn't wanted Gordon, pleaded his cause. He wrote his superiors in London that "having sent Gordon to Khartoum, it appears to me that it is our bounden duty, both as a matter of humanity and policy, not to abandon him."

Wolseley, too, pressed hard for an expedition to relieve Gordon. Time was running out, he declared, and it will be "an indelible disgrace if we allow the most generous, patriotic, and gallant of our public servants to die of want or fall into the hands of a cruel enemy because we would not hold out our hands to save him."

But Gladstone still wouldn't move. "The debates," he told the House of Commons, "are out of all proportion to the pressure and urgency of the question, and have the effect of offering immense obstruction to important public business." The prime minister even had the temerity to say that sending a relief army to Khartoum would amount to "a war of conquest against a people struggling to be free. Yes, these are people struggling to be free and rightly struggling to be free." This was the same man, of course, who had agreed to Graham going to the Red Sea, where he had killed hundreds—thousands—of these same people struggling to be free.

Talking nonsense became contagious. Gordon, reeling from the government's inaction, said that three thousand Turkish troops could be hired for £300,000 and sent to the Sudan. If the British government couldn't afford that much money, maybe American and British millionaires could come up with it. He even made an appeal to the pope for help.

But did he really need the pope, or anyone else? Was it really too late for Gordon to pull out of Khartoum? The fact is, he wasn't completely blockaded. His steamers went up and down the river, without much trouble. Gordon himself wrote off the force arrayed against him as "some 500 determined men and some 2,000 rag-tag Arabs." He had 8,000 men under arms inside Khartoum.

Gordon, historian Anthony Nutting argued, "could have withdrawn at almost any moment between March and May," and even as late as September, his precious steamers could still get past the Turkish positions downstream at Berber. But instead of following instructions, he stayed put, longing for martyrdom. It wasn't exactly fair to the Egyptian garrisons he had been sent to evacuate; they had no death wish.

In London, Gladstone's position began to unravel, finally, on July 25, when for the first time a majority of the Cabinet came around to the idea of sending a relief expedition. Gladstone still objected. But faced with a vote of censure he knew he would lose, the old man finally yielded. On August 5, the House of Commons authorized an expenditure of £300,000—a ridiculously low amount that the army would disregard—"for the relief of General Gordon." Gladstone made the motion himself.

Lord Wolseley—cartooned in Gilbert and Sullivan's *Pirates of Penzance* as "the very model of a modern major general"—arrived in Cairo on September 9 to take command of the expedition. That same day, Gordon sent Colonel Stewart, *Times* correspondent Power, and the French consul, a man named Herbin, down the Nile aboard the little steamer *Abbas* to communicate Khartoum's plight to the outside world, taking with them Gordon's cipher key and detailed reports on the strength of the garrison. Two other steamers, *Safia* and *Mansura*, were sent along as escorts. The little convoy—they also had two sailboats under tow—went swimmingly, passing Berber without any trouble. It was all so easy that Stewart sent the escorting steamers back to Khartoum and cut himself loose from the sailboats. It was a big mistake; nine days out of Khartoum, little *Abbas* missed a turn in the river and ran aground. Offered help by an Arab waving a white flag, Stewart, Power, and Herbin went ashore. They were promptly set upon by dervishes and put to death. The papers were sent to the Mahdī, and the cipher key was destroyed.

Now Gordon, alone in Khartoum, could still receive coded messages, but he couldn't read them. "I think cipher-messages are in some countries, like this, a mistake," he wrote, sensibly, in his celebrated journal, after he first heard that the *Abbas* might have been captured, along with the cipher key. Writing his journal became a kind of substitute for conversation with educated Europeans. It rambles, and even Gordon thought it would need "pruning" should it be published. Yet, as biographer John H. Waller noted, "Gordon's stream-of-consciousness style provided insights which no biography or history of the time has been able to equal."

What troubled Gordon most, as he surveyed his defenses from his perch on the roof of the palace and as he scribbled in his journal, was what people would make of the purpose of the relief expedition. His conscience was troubling him. "I altogether *decline* the imputation that the projected expedition has come to *relieve me*. It has come to SAVE OUR NATIONAL HONOUR in extricating the garrisons, etc., from a position our action in Egypt has placed these garrisons. . . . I am not the *rescued lamb*, and I will not be." He protested too much, and too frequently, to be believed.

Meanwhile, he took the offensive. His steamers foraged up the Blue Nile and his soldiers marched out of Khartoum, inflicting a number of defeats on the Mahdī's forces, to the point that crop-growing land southeast of Khartoum was cleared, and provisions began flowing into the city. "We are going to hold out here forever," Gordon wrote. But on September 4 disaster struck. Gordon's best commander, Mohammed Aly, and his best troops, close to a thousand of them, wandered into a trap and were destroyed. During the fighting, Gordon said, Mohammed Ali caught "a lad of 12 or 14 years of age, and the little chap spoke out boldly, and said he believed Mohammed Ahmed was the Mahdi, and that we were dogs. He was shot! Before I heard of our defeat I heard of this, and I thought, 'THAT will not pass unavenged.'"

It was in September, too, that Count Edward Gleichen, a lieutenant in the Grenadier Guards stationed in Dublin, learned that he "was to go out to the Sudan at once with the Camel Corps detachment of my battalion," the government "having suddenly taken into its head the idea that it was necessary to rescue General Gordon from his perilous position at Khartoum. . . ."

The government's problem was how it was going to get Gleichen and the rest of the troops streaming to Egypt to relieve Khartoum. One possibility was to send them to Suakin on the Red Sea and then cross the desert to Berber, on the Nile, a distance of 245 miles, and then march south (and upriver) to Khartoum. The other was to send the expedition up the Nile by train and boat to Wadi Halfa, some 760 miles, and then continue to Khartoum in boats, another 650 miles.

No one in London could reach a decision, and so there was more dithering. Wolseley's chief rival for command of the expedition, Lieutenant General Sir Frederick Stephenson, wanted to transport the army in native boats handled by five thousand loyal tribesmen; that would be quicker, he said, and cheaper. But Wolseley finally carried the day—up the Nile it would be, and he had his own notion about how to get around the cataracts. Years earlier, he had led an expedition up the Red River in Canada with the help of French-speaking voyageurs. He would hire them for this job, and give them twenty-eight-foot-long whaler gigs (complete with two masts, sails, and yards) to do the job. That was going to take even more precious time.

Lots more precious time. When the eight hundred boats and the men serving on them finally reached their destination, they found that the Nile wasn't the Red River. "However zealous the men might be, they could not prevent the light craft being battered against the rocks and having to undergo constant repairs," wrote Bernard Allen, the historian. "Nor could they prevent the heart-breaking delays that occurred owing to the breakdown in the organization of the transport steamers that had been chartered to tow the boats up to the foot of the cataracts and were marooned in the lower reaches of the Nile owing to the lack of coal. . . ."

The army had contracted with Thomas Cook & Sons, the travel agency, to get the army to Egypt and to supply the steamers with coal. But the shortage of coal wasn't Cook's fault; that problem was laid directly at the doorstep of Sir Redvers Buller, the chief of staff. "I should not have relied upon my trust in him on such a vital question, and ought personally have gone into it," Wolseley wrote. Thirteen more days were lost.

Another problem: Cook's had put the oars in one ship, the whalers in another. Getting them back together took time. And when they finally did get the boats into the water, it became apparent that not all the voyageurs were really voyageurs; eight of them, in`fact, were deskbound Canadian lawyers. Their commander was a Toronto alderman. They had come along for the sport of it.

So, as it turned out, if Gordon was to be saved at all, he was going to be saved by the Camel Corps—eighteen hundred young men at full strength, drawn from some of the finest old regiments in the British army. They would be joined by a small detachment of marines that would include a young subaltern named Charlie Townshend, who would eventually lead an entire army to destruction in World War I (see chapter 10).

Young Gleichen met his camel—"a great upstanding white beast of some 22 hands" which he named Potiphar—at Wadi Halfa late in October. Potiphar would carry Gleichen twelve hundred miles before their campaign was over; Gleichen would live through it, Potiphar and thousands of other camels would not ("the last time I saw him," said Gleichen, "the poor beast had holes in his side you could put a cocoanut in").

Camels, Gleichen found, were nasty brutes. "A camel's hind legs will reach anywhere—over his head, round his chest, and on to his hump; even when lying down, an evil-disposed animal will shoot out his legs and bring you to a sitting position. . . . He will chew the root of his tail, nip you in the calf, or lay the top of his head on his hump. He also bellows and roars at you, whatever you are doing. . . ."

The biggest disappointment was in the camels' much-advertised qualities of endurance. Overrated, Gleichen found. They get "a sore back after four days, or less," and "as for trotting, it was only by a vigorous application of the koorbash that I could succeed in making mine go that pace for more than 50 yards at a time." They got colds in their noses, too, a sloppy business. "Altogether they are a sad trouble." Yet, he said, they weren't spooked by gunfire; they simply paid no attention to it. He finally figured out why: "It was want of brains, *pur et simple.*"

Stupid or not, there simply weren't enough of them. That was mostly Buller's fault, too. Because of the shortage, they had to be sent back and forth, in relays, to bring up supplies. They weren't in very good condition to start with—the Arabs held back on selling their healthy beasts—and so they were quickly worn out.

Wolseley issued his marching orders on December 27. There would be two columns—the river column, under Major General William Earle, and the desert column, under Brigadier General Sir Herbert Stewart. The river column, with the Staffords, the Gordons, the Duke of Cornwall's Light Infantry, the Royal Highlanders, and the Egyptian Camel Corps, was to push upstream in the whalers through the remaining cataracts, recapture Berber, and move on to Shendi, below Khartoum, by March 10. The desert column—the Camel Corps—was supposed to make a shortcut dash across the Bayuda Desert, from Korti to Metemma, where Wolseley hoped to communicate with Gordon by river steamer. If he found Gordon was in "in extremis," he planned to use the camel corps to come to his help. Otherwise, the two columns would be joined, and the siege would be lifted at a more leisurely pace. The desert column was comprised of the camel regiments, the Nineteenth Hussars on their amazingly tough little Egyptian ponies, and three seven-pounder screw guns carried in pieces on camelback.

A messenger from Gordon managed to get through the Mahdī's sentries on December 30. A note, dated December 14 and written on a piece of paper the size of a postage stamp, said "Khartoum all right. C. G. Gordon." But the messenger had memorized another, more ominous message from Gordon: "We want you to come quickly."

It was on that same day that Gleichen and Potiphar and the Camel Corps set out across the desert. Stewart, in command, led the way, "his tall figure topped by a shining Guards' helmet with a distinctive puggaree [scarf] of orange silk," Julian Symons wrote. Second in command was an adventurer, Colonel Frederick Burnaby, a giant of a man with a loyal following in London. Wolseley sent him along—he set off on a polo pony—in case anything happened to Stewart. Lord Charles Beresford, a favorite of the Royal Family, commanded a small naval contingent that was supposed to man Gordon's steamers. Beresford, a noted horseman, had purchased three racing camels soon after his arrival in Egypt; he named them Bimbashi, Ballyhooly, and Beelzebub. But his problem in this campaign was something else: Boils. He could barely sit down on his little white donkey. His detachment dragged with them a Gardner machine gun, a competitor to the Gatling and Nordenfeldt guns. Great things were expected from it. The other ranking officer was Colonel Sir Charles Wilson, an intelligence officer with no experience commanding troops in battle.

It must have been a brave sight, all these soldiers in their light gray uniforms and white pith helmets, perched atop their camels on red saddles, flags flying, the band sending them on their way by playing "The Campbells Are Coming."

For Gleichen and the rest of these aristocratic officers, it was something of a lark. They had enjoyed shooting crocodiles and chasing dogs, and now they hoped to pot some "niggers."

They would surely get their chance. Because of the delays, the Mahdī had been able to organize a resistance, and by the time the Camel Corps troopers got under way, ten thousand tribesmen were waiting for them near the wells at Abu Klea, all of them wearing their distinctive *jibbas* (long flowing white robes with colorful patches) and white cotton skullcaps. The more patches (plus straw caps), the higher the rank.

The two sides met the afternoon of January 16. "Eagerly we watched the niggers dancing about on the hills, some 2,000 yards off," wrote Gleichen. "This looked like business." But it was too late in the day to advance, and so the Camel Corps made camp, building a simple zareba, a low-walled stockade of stones and thorn bushes. All night long, the Arab snipers—the elite Jehadiya—lobbed rounds into the camp, keeping the nervous troopers awake. Off in the distance they could hear the rising, falling beat of the tom-toms. "I do not know a more curiously deceptive sound than that of tom-toms," Colonel Wilson wrote in his journal. "It is almost impossible to localize it, especially when any wind is blowing."

The troopers awoke at dawn, ate breakfast—bully beef and biscuits—and formed a square. By now, the enemy's rifle fire was intense. A Major Dickson went down first, shot in the knee. A bullet grazed the temple of Major Gough, commanding the mounted infantry, and "knocked him senseless," young Gleichen recalled. This was no longer a lark.

As it became evident "that the enemy intended to keep up a harassing fire on us, and not deliver an attack, Stewart determined to march out and give battle," Colonel Wilson wrote. "The square was then formed up, and we marched down the valley towards the row of flags which stretched across it. . . ." The British troops halted from time to time and returned the Arabs' fire with their little screw guns and their Martini-Henry rifles. Two hundred yards from what appeared to be the main enemy position, another force—much larger—"rose from the ravine in which they were hidden, in the most perfect order," Colonel Wilson said. "It was a beautiful and striking sight, such a one as Fitz-James must have seen when Roderick Dhu's men rose out of the heather [in Sir Walter Scott's poem *The Lady of the Lake*]. The Dervish formation was curious, a sort of variety of the old phalanx with rows of men behind. At the head of each rode an emir or sheikh with a banner, accompanied by personal attendants, and then came the fighting men, armed only with spears, swords and hatchets. They advanced at a quick pace as if on parade, and our skirmishers had only just time to get into the square before they were upon us: one poor bugger who lagged behind was caught and speared at once."

Gleichen was stunned by the enemy's disciplined movements. "With wild yells the Arabs (still about 500 yards off) moved across our left front, in *column of companies*, and disappeared for a moment behind the rocks and grass in the wady. In half a minute they reappeared, close on the left rear, *left wheeled into line*, and charged. . . . I found myself lifted off my legs amongst a surging mass of Heavies (Heavy Camel detachment) and Sussex, who had been carried back upon the camels by the impetuous rush of the enemy. Telling the men to stand fast, I forced my way through the jam to see what had happened. Heavies, Sussex, and camels of all sorts were pressing with terrific force on our thin double rank, and it seemed every moment as if it must give, but it didn't."

"I remember thinking," said Colonel Wilson, "'By Jove, they will be into the square!'" At almost the next moment he witnessed a sight he would never forget: "I saw a fine old sheikh on horseback plant his banner in the center of the square, behind the camels. He turned out to be Musa, Emir of the Duguaim Arabs, from Kordofan. I had noticed him in the advance, with his banner in one hand and a book of prayers in the other, and never saw anything finer. The old man never swerved to the left or the right, and never ceased chanting his prayers until he had planted his banner in our square. If any man deserved a place in the Moslem Paradise, he did."

Colonel Wilson drew his revolver just as the old sheikh fell, and opened fire on three Arabs attacking General Stewart. "I was close to his horse's tail, and disposed of the one nearest to me, about three paces off, and the others were, I think, killed by the Mounted Infantry officers close by."

Beresford wanted desperately to get his Gardner machine gun into action, and so he wheeled it up at a point where there was a break in the line. He now made the break even bigger, something a regular infantry officer never would have tolerated. He trained the gun and began cranking the firing lever himself. "As I fired," he wrote later, "I saw the enemy mowed down in rows, dropping like ninepins." He had fired about seventy-five rounds when the gun jammed. He and the two sailors with him tried to free the jammed round from the gun's chamber. Within moments, Symons wrote, the enemy was on them. His two sailors were killed instantly; Beresford was spared when he was knocked under the gun's feed plate. "He caught a spear blade that was being thrust at him, got to his feet, and then was borne backwards" by a crush that he compared to a theater crowd alarmed by a cry of fire.

Many of the Martini-Henry rifles jammed too, and the bayonets, apparently made from inferior steel, bent. In the confusion, British soldiers killed British soldiers. What saved the day were the camels in the middle of the square. They were packed so close together the dervishes couldn't get through them, to fight their way across the square.

That was the high point—perhaps the finest showing ever made by

spear-carrying dervishes against British regulars. The dervishes began retiring, "and loud and long cheering broke out from the square."

As the victors began collecting the dead, a young private in the Bays,
part of the Camel Corps, discovered poor Burnaby. "Oh, sir," he reported-
ly told Lord Binning, a lieutenant in the Blues, "here is the bravest man
in England, dying, and no one to help him." Burnaby died moments later,
one of nine officers and sixty-five men killed in the attack. Another nine
officers and sixty-five men had been wounded. The Arab losses were
eleven hundred killed, hundreds more wounded.

Gleichen couldn't believe the variety of weapons strewn on the field:
"arms of all sorts and broken banner-staves," he wrote, "spears in hundreds, some of enormous length, javelins, knobkerries, swords and knives,
but no shields of any sort." Gleichen even found a Birmingham billhook,
a pruning instrument, "with the trade mark on it, in an Arab's hand; how
it got there I know not, so I confiscated it for the use of our mess."

"How was the square broken?" Sir Charles Wilson asked in his journal.
"Well, there are various opinions; one is, that it was a mistake to turn cavalry into infantry, and make them fight in square with an arm they were
not accustomed to. Add to this, the cavalry were detachments from different regiments, only brought together a few days before we left Korti. A
cavalry man is taught never to be still, and that a square can be broken.
How can you expect him in a moment to forget all his training . . . ?"

By five in the afternoon, the fighting was finished, and the British troops
were tired and very thirsty. But the wells, Gleichen said, "were nowhere
to be seen." The Hussars on their little ponies finally found them, what
Colonel Wilson called "a series of pits in the sand in the valley-bed, with
little basins at the bottom into which water trickles." When man and beast
"had drunk their fill," said Gleichen, "a large square was formed for the
night on some rising ground close to the wells, for the chances of another
attack were not yet by any means over."

It was the coldest night the Camel Corps would experience, and sleep
was hard to come by. Wilson curled up under a prayer carpet looted by one
of his friends, but it didn't help much. Gleichen tried to sleep between two
camels, "but directly I began to get warm the brutes would feel me and
lurch over on top of me, till I was driven into the open again."

After burying their dead and eating their first decent meal in days, they
formed up the next day at 4:30 P.M. and set out for Metemma on the Nile,
twenty-five miles away. They marched on into the night, Stewart determined to reach his destination. "Progress was very slow," Wilson said, "not

a mile an hour." And the confusion of marching in the dark was very great. "I cannot think [the night march] was necessary, for the days were not hot, and the men would have fought better after a night's sleep and a good breakfast," Wilson wrote.

By 8 A.M. on January 19, they were still four miles from the Nile and the Arabs. Stewart ordered a brief halt and the construction of a modest zareba. By now, the Arabs were closing in again. "I had scarcely settled down to eat something when bullets began to whistle overhead," Wilson noted. "Bullets kept spattering in on us from invisible marksmen in the grass all the time," said Gleichen, "and many was the 'Fft, fft' into the mass of camels."

Gleichen said the "terrible disaster" happened about 9 A.M. Wilson put it at about 10:15. They were both talking about Sir Herbert Stewart being shot in the groin. He "dropped mortally wounded," said Gleichen. "It was a fearful blow to us all, when we heard of it." The command then devolved upon Colonel Wilson, who had never led troops in battle. It was just what Wolseley had worried about most.

"Every one of my men was extended flat on his stomach," said Gleichen, "potting anything in the shape of niggers or smoke." Gleichen tried to stretch out the same way, but he couldn't bring his field glasses to bear that way. So he sat up. "Suddenly," he said, "I received a violent blow in the pit of the stomach. . . . My wind was entirely gone, so I lay and gasped." On further examination, he found the bullet had struck one of his brass buttons, then carried away his watch and compass. He had been "potted" himself, and "it was as near a squeak as I ever wish to have."

There were several journalists traveling with the Camel Corps. One of them, J. A. Cameron of the *London Standard* (he had already survived the awful disaster on Majuba Hill in the First Boer War), was killed as he got up to collect a box of sardines from his servant. The camels were the easiest targets of all, and they died by the score. "You would see the poor brute patiently lying there, with a stream of blood trickling from his shoulder or neck," Gleichen wrote. "After a time his head would drop lower and lower, till the neck got that peculiar kink in it that betokens the approach of the end, and over he would roll, quite silently."

The troops formed up in a square once again—the force was now down to nine hundred bayonets—and resumed their long march to the Nile, constantly under the unexpectedly accurate fire of the Arab marksmen. Once again, though, the Arabs foolishly chose to make a frontal assault with their spears and swords. They "came running down the hill at a great pace," Wilson said. "It was a relief to know the crisis had come." Gleichen agreed: "Thank God," he wrote.

This time, said Wilson, "all the leaders with their fluttering banners went down, and no one got within 50 yards of the square. It only lasted a few minutes; the whole of the front ranks were swept away, and then we saw a backward movement, followed by the rapid disappearance of the Arabs in front of and all round us."

"Metemmeh, and the river was won!" wrote Gleichen. Potiphar, he reckoned, "remained fourteen minutes with his nose in the water, and then began eating the green cotton plant all around as if he would never stop."

Khartoum's plight was now desperate. A last crop of *dhoora*, a kind of millet, had been harvested, still green, on Tuti Island in early January, and, John Waller wrote, "what few donkeys and horses remained were soon butchered for meat. . . . Rats, cats, and dogs were chased down for food; even leather was soaked and eaten. . . . Corpses littered the streets, victims of starvation and flux. Garrison soldiers, many too weak to function, stood listlessly at their posts waiting to die."

Gordon invited the town's civilians to leave, even to join the Mahdī if that's what they wished. Maybe as many as half of them, fifteen thousand or so, accepted the offer.

The situation in the fort at Omdurman, on the west side of the White Nile, was even more precarious. Its commander, Faraj Bey Allah, signaled Gordon he was out of food and ammunition, and Gordon ordered him to surrender. The starving survivors marched out of the fort under a white flag, probably in the second week of January. The Mahdī's guns now moved closer to Khartoum.

Gordon, Waller wrote, "received a last appeal from the Mahdi—his final terms: 'We have written to you to go back to your country. . . . I repeat to you the words of God, Do not destroy yourself. God, himself, is merciful to you.'" These two extraordinary men, both deeply religious, had by this time each "recognized the other as a brave soldier and a man of God. Neither wanted to destroy the person of the other."

On the roof of the palace, Gordon maintained his vigil, vainly looking downriver for the smoke from his steamers.

Wilson and the steamers had joined forces on the twenty-first. There were four of them—*Bordein, Telahawiya, Safieh*, and *Tewfikieh*—now even dirtier than badgers but still flying the khedive's huge Egyptian flag. The crew members, mostly coal-black former slaves, still had plenty of fight in them, and they joined Wilson in trying to subdue the Arab garrison behind the loopholed mud walls of Metemmeh. "The blacks were most amusing," Wilson wrote, "just like children." But the attack was botched, turning into what one historian called "comic relief." The withdrawal, Sir Charles was forced to admit, "gave the enemy fresh heart."

What about Gordon? Wilson talked to the commanders of Gordon's four steamers and inexplicably came to the conclusion that the situation at Khartoum wasn't so pressing after all, and "that a delay of a couple of days wouldn't make much difference." So, of all things, he sent the steamers up and down the Nile on reconnaissance missions, going along himself on the *Telahawiya* with Beresford, whose boils were so painful he had to be helped aboard. They accomplished nothing worthwhile.

It was not until the morning of January 24—having wasted three days—that two of the steamers, *Bordein* (with Sir Charles) and *Telahawiya*, set off for Khartoum. By this time, Wilson wrote, he knew that Omdurman had fallen to the Mahdī.

"Now what was it we were going to do?" Wilson wrote in his journal. "We were going to fight our way up the river in two steamers of the size of 'penny' steamers on the Thames, which a single well-directed shell would send to the bottom, with crews and [240 Sudanese] soldiers absolutely without discipline, with 20 English soldiers [Sussex regiment], with no surgeon, and with only one interpreter. . . . " He didn't think much of his odds. "The outlook was not bright," he concluded, with typical English understatement. His forlorn hope was that once Gordon, from his post on the roof of the palace, saw the steamers approaching, fifteen or twenty miles off, he would create some kind of diversion that would allow the steamers to push through.

It was now late January and the water level of the Nile was falling; that meant a slow, rough passage through gorges and around sharp, jutting rocks. The night of the twenty-seventh, Wilson dined aboard *Bordein* with his handful of officers in what he called, somewhat mysteriously, "high spirits," looking forward to "at last meeting General Gordon after his famous siege."

They set off at 6 A.M. on January 28—it would have been Gordon's fifty-second birthday—for the final run into Khartoum, blazing away with every gun they had. Under steady fire from Arabs on shore, they rounded a bend and for the first time could see the large Government House—Gordon's palace—at Khartoum, "plainly above the trees." But where was the Egyptian flag? Gordon, Wilson was told, always flew it, but he couldn't "see a trace of one anywhere."

They ran in closer, halfway up Tuti Island, and tried to ask people on shore if they had any news. But, instead, they were fired on. The old steamers, belching smoke, sides and funnels riddled with bullet holes, plunged ahead, and "we got into such a fire as I hope never to pass through again in a 'penny steamer.' Two or more guns opened upon us from Omdurman fort, and three or four from Khartoum or the upper end of Tuti; the roll of musketry from each side was continuous; and high above that could be heard the grunting of a Nordenfeldt or a mitrailleuse [machine gun], and the loud rushing noise of the Krupp shells. . . .

"We kept on to the junction of the two Niles, when it became plain to everyone that Khartoum had fallen into the mahdi's hands; for not only were there hundreds of Dervishes ranged under their banners, standing on the sandpit close to the town ready to resist our landing, but no flag was flying in Khartoum and not a shot was fired in our assistance. . . .

"I at once gave the order to turn and run full speed down the river. It was hopeless to attempt a landing or to communicate with the shore under such a fire."

Too late!

It wasn't until weeks later that Wilson learned how close—just forty-eight hours—he and the two little steamers had come.

The Mahdī and his closest advisors had held a war council the evening of January 24. The Mahdī himself was reluctant to attack Khartoum, weak as he knew it now to be. He remembered a similar attack on a fortified Egyptian garrison at El Obeid, where his troops had suffered terrible losses. But, his uncle, Muhammad Abd al-Karim, argued it was now or never. Attack, he said, before the British reinforcements arrived. The way was open; the river was so low that it could be crossed on the exposed mudflats. He carried the argument, and the attack was set just before dawn on January 26, 1885.

"Riflemen from Kordofan and Darfur led the way over the marshy ground, followed by spearmen, and then by more men with rifles," Symons, the historian, wrote. "Many of the defenders were too weak to respond. . . . Within an hour resistance had collapsed and the Arabs were in the town, killing, looting, and raping. . . . The killing lasted about six hours, and several thousand people died." After 317 improbable days, Khartoum had fallen.

Most accounts agree that Gordon, with a few loyal men, was in his regular post on the roof of the palace. He went to his room, put on his uniform, and strapped on his sword. He went to the top landing of the outside stairs that led from the ground to the second floor. There, holding his revolver at his side, he watched as the Arabs advanced. The Mahdī had re-

The death of General Charles "Chinese" Gordon at Khartoum, shown in a print after a painting by J. L. G. Ferris. (Library of Congress collections)

quested that he be taken alive, but these frantic dervishes wanted him dead. Four of them ran up the stairs and stabbed him again and again; he made no resistance as he—no doubt joyously—began his long-awaited trip to the Kingdom of Heaven. They cut off his head and took it across the river to Omdurman, as a gift for the Mahdī. It was mounted on a pole outside the Mahdī's tent, and remained there for several days.

Rudolf Slatin, an Austrian prisoner in the Mahdī's camp with a close connection to Gordon, said that he "gazed silently at this ghastly spectacle. His blue eyes were half-opened; the mouth was perfectly natural; the hair of his head and his short whiskers were almost quite white."

"Is not this the head of your uncle the unbeliever?" Slatin was asked. "What of it?" he replied. "A brave soldier who fell at his post. Happy is he to have fallen; his sufferings are over."

The last installment of the journal Gordon had carefully written for three months was discovered aboard his steamers. The final entry was dated December 14. "Now MARK THIS," Gordon had written, "if the Expeditionary Force, and I ask for no more than two hundred men, does not come in ten days, *the town may fall;* and I have done my best for the honour of our country. Good bye. C. G. Gordon."

Tennyson would say of him:

> Warrior of God, man's friend, not here below,
>   But somewhere dead far in the waste Sudan,
> Thou livest in all hearts, for all men know
>   This earth has borne no simpler, nobler man.

◆

Sir Charles Wilson managed a narrow escape himself; both his steamers were wrecked, and he and his shipmates were rescued from an exposed island by another steamer sent to look for him. The expeditionary force marched back across the desert, Gleichen saying farewell to poor Potiphar, and the army, including the river column, was sent home. The nation wept, and Queen Victoria fired off angry, critical letters to her ministers. Gladstone, who had been G.O.M. (for Grand Old Man), now became M.O.G. (Murderer of Gordon). He was forced to step down, in favor of the Marquess of Salisbury, in 1885. Wilson was never publicly criticized, but he was immediately replaced in command of the desert column by Sir

Redvers Buller, who could have been blamed for a lot of things. It's easy to criticize Wilson for arriving too late to save Gordon. But even if he had reached Khartoum in time, would that have helped? Churchill didn't think so, and not many modern historians do, either. Twenty British regulars against one hundred thousand dervishes? Too late was part of the problem; too little was a much bigger part. It wasn't until 1897 that another British army, under Sir Horatio Herbert Kitchener, returned to the Sudan to avenge Gordon. The Mahdī, grown enormously fat, had died on June 22, 1885, but his army was still intact, led by the resourceful Khalifa Abdullah; he and his loyal troops weren't vanquished until the battle of Omdurman. British and Egyptian flags were raised over the palace at Khartoum on September 4, 1898.

EIGHT

General Oreste Baratieri and the First Ethiopian War (1895–1896)

Augustus B. Wylde, an English adventurer and part-time correspondent for the *Manchester Guardian*, arrived in Massawa, the Italian outpost in Eritrea on the Red Sea, in April of 1896. "What struck me most," he said, " . . . was the happy-go-lucky way in which the Italians worked."

Though Italy was at war with Ethiopia, which was a neighbor of Eritrea, "the government offices were closed from eleven till three, and again at six o'clock. . . . Clearing the transport and store ships was left to the agent of the steamers, and there were seven men of war in the harbor and not a fatigue party of sailors were employed to clear the stores. . . ."

What, Wylde wondered, must their working habits have been like six weeks earlier, *before* an Italian army of fifteen thousand men had been annihilated by the Ethiopians near a market town called Adowa?

The defeat—almost half of the Italian army was killed, wounded, or captured—was immensely humiliating, and when the survivors, many of them on crutches, came home, they were hissed and booed as they straggled down the gangplanks of their troopships in Naples. It rankled so badly that the loathsome Mussolini and the Fascists would return to Ethiopia, determined to wreak vengeance, in 1935.

That the Italians should have taken up a position on the Red Sea is itself an anomaly. This, historically, was a British sphere of influence. In 1868, a British army under Sir Robert Napier had landed near Massawa and marched inland to rescue a handful of English bureaucrats and missionaries at Magdala, held hostage there by the crazed Emperor Theodore of Ethiopia. The expedition had its comic aspects—the British forgot, for example, to bring scaling ladders—but it worked out in spite of all that. Theodore committed suicide and the hostages were freed.

In 1884, Egypt controlled, in theory, what is now the Eritrean province of Ethiopia and its port at Massawa. But Egypt was rapidly unraveling under dervish pressure from the Sudan (chapter 7), and Britain wanted to do something to provide a buffer state along the Red Sea coast (they chose not to occupy the place themselves—too bloody hot). The British idea was to prevent their rivals, the French, from moving towards the Nile basin from their base at Djibouti. Britain, Egypt, and Ethiopia signed the Treaty of Adowa on June 3, allowing the Ethiopians to recover some lost territory and giving them free transportation of goods in and out of Massawa.

John, the Ethiopian emperor, believed the treaty opened the way to Ethiopian control of the port city. But in seeking a buffer state, Britain refused to take Ethiopia seriously as a regional power. As a result, the British—perfidious Albion—sold the Ethiopians out, and encouraged the Italians to fill the vacuum by developing a colony of their own. "England made use of King John as long as he was of any service," Wylde wrote, "and then threw him over to the tender mercies of Italy. . . . It is one of our worst bits of business out of the many we have been guilty of in Africa . . . one of the vilest bits of treachery."

Napier, now Lord Napier of Magdala, raised a lonely voice of protest in the House of Lords. "No good will come of it," he said.

The first Italian troops arrived at Massawa on February 5, 1885.

Italy, one of the last European powers to build a modern empire, was delighted to accept Britain's invitation. It had already secured a commercial beachhead in Eritrea at a port called Assab, south of Massawa, where an Italian company had purchased land from a local sultan and opened a coaling station for its steamships in 1869, soon after the Suez Canal began operations. The Italian government purchased the property early in 1885.

By then, jingoism was rampant. "Italy must be ready," the newspaper *Il Diritto* said. "The year 1885 will decide her fate as a great power. It is necessary to feel the responsibility of the new era; to become again strong men afraid of nothing, with the sacred love of the fatherland, of all Italy, in our hearts. . . ."

The British, not sure they actually wanted the Italians and the Ethiopians at war, sent a small mission to Ethiopia to attempt to bring about a reconciliation. It was led by a classically English figure, Gerald (later Sir Gerald) Herbert Portal, formerly consul-general at Zanzibar, accompanied by a veterinarian, a Mr. Beech, and his manservant, Hutchisson. Both Mr.

Beech and Hutchisson behaved throughout, he said later, with the "greatest pluck."

The delegation set out on October 17, 1887, and made the last sea leg of the voyage aboard an Egyptian vessel, the *Narghileh*. Portal wrote that it was "a small, dirty, greasy steamer bound [from Alexandria] for Jeddah [Jidda], Suakin, and Massawa, in which we very soon discovered that our travelling companions consisted of cockroaches and other smaller animals innumerable, a flock of sheep, a few cows, many cocks, hens, turkeys, and geese, a dozen of the evil-looking Greek adventurers who always appear like vultures around a dead carcass whenever there is a possibility of a campaign in North Africa. . . . The crazy old tub," he noted, "rolled solemnly down the Gulf of Suez at her extreme speed of five knots an hour."

Once safely arrived in Eritrea, the Englishmen set off in a mule caravan for the interior of Ethiopia. On the morning of November 11, they met the most intriguing—and surely the most successful—of all the Ethiopian generals, the man who would do more than any other to humiliate the Italian empire builders, Ras Alula. Portal may have been a failed diplomat, but he was a fine travel writer and a keen observer:

> The beating of the tom-toms and the shouts of the populace announced the approach of the great Ras Alula, and a few minutes later a vast crowd of cavalry and infantry, all dressed in the picturesque white-and-red toga, began to swarm into the plain, and to speed along towards the immense earthen or mud pyramid, on the summit of which are the two large huts which constitute the Ras's headquarters, and from whence he looks down on the plain of Asmara like an eagle from his eyrie. . . .
>
> Imagine a circular hut, perhaps forty-five feet in diameter, its lofty dome-shaped roof supported by numerous poles, its walls composed of the split trunks of young trees, and its earthen floor covered partly with skins and partly with rushes. About two feet from the wall, immediately opposite the door by which we entered, was a large divan covered with crimson cotton-cloth; on this sat, in Turkish fashion, i.e., with his feet drawn up and crossed under him, a striking-looking man whom we had no difficulty in recognizing at once as the dreaded chief, who by courage, ferocity, unscrupulous cruelty, and considerable military ability, had risen from the ranks of private soldier to the position of generalissimo of the Abyssinian frontier. . . .
>
> His complexion was darker than most of the men of the Tigre mountains, being of a rich chocolate colour; but, whatever the

colour, the owner of that powerful, cruel, and intelligent face
would be bound to make his name known in any country, either as
a leader or a destroyer of men. But . . . attention at first was rivet-
ed to one striking peculiarity—a pair of gleaming tawny eyes of a
much lighter colour than the skin of the face. To these flashing yellow orbs, whose effect was aided by a brilliant row of white teeth,
was no doubt due much of the terror with which Ras Alula was generally regarded. I had seen such eyes in the head of a tiger (at the
"Zoo" only) and of a leopard, but never in that of a human being.

The faithful Beech came forward with a present for the old ruffian—a
handsome Winchester repeating rifle, with eight hundred rounds of ammunition. But the Ras "scarcely looked at it," and ordered Portal and his
little party to return to their hut, to which he sent them two large jars of
ciderlike tedge, Portal's favorite local brew. They were, in fact, prisoners;
Ras Alula was convinced they were in cahoots with the hated Italians, and
had in mind disposing of them in traditional (and always fatal) ways. But
the King of Kings, the emperor himself, ordered him to send the Englishmen on their way.

Once again, Portal gave a marvelous description of the raw power of the
Ethiopian empire that was soon to shock the so-called civilized world:

> At last, at nine o-clock on the morning of the 4th of December
> [1887], we rode into the camp of Emperor John, the King of Kings
> of Ethiopia (near the shores of Lake Ashangi), and a wonderful
> sight it was. As far as the eye could reach the plain was thickly dot-
> ted with small black tents and with little grass huts; tens of thou-
> sands of horses, mules, and cows were grazing on every side, while
> the whole district seemed to be alive with moving swarms of armed
> men, and of women and slaves. In the centre of the plain were two
> large circular white tents, standing in an open space . . . these were
> the head-quarters of the great King Johannis [John].

The next morning, on instructions, Portal and his little delegation took
up position "in a field at a little distance from the road which the King and
his army would follow, with their thousands of animals. . . . " Portal's journal continues:

> Beech and I made a most careful calculation of the number of per-
> sons who marched past us that morning, counting first the num-
> bers who passed a certain spot in a minute, and then taking the

time in which the whole army passed; at a very low estimate we calculated the numbers to be not less than between 70,000 and 80,000 persons.

About the middle of the throng rode the king himself, surrounded by a picked body of cavalry. He was mounted on a handsome mule, and was dressed in the usual Abyssinian red and white "shamma," or toga, a fold of which concealed all the lower part of his face, the only distinguishing mark of royalty being the fact that he kept the rays of the sun from his august head with a red silk umbrella.

Portal, summoned to the king's presence, hastily put on his "diplomatic finery" and then slowly rode up with presents, including a telescope, for the king and letters from Queen Victoria urging reconciliation with the Italians. Too late. "What might have been possible in August or September," Portal said in his official report, "was impossible in December, when the whole of the immense available forces of the country were already under arms; and that there now remains no hope of a satisfactory adjustment of the difficulties between Italy and Abyssinia until the question of the relative supremacy of these two nations has been decided by an appeal to the fortunes of war."

With the King of Kings blessing, Portal undertook the long journey home. But he had seen enough—he was observant—and he wrote some final impressions. "No one," he said, "who has once seen the nature of the gorges, ravines, and mountain passes near the Abyssinian frontier can doubt for a moment that any advance by a civilized army in the face of the hostile Abyssinian hordes would be accomplished at the price of a fearful loss of life on both sides." Abyssinians, he said, might well be "savage and untrustworthy," but they were also "redeemed by the possession of unbounded courage, by a disregard of death, and by a national pride which leads them to look down on every human being who has not had the good fortune to be born an Abyssinian."

The Italians, he reckoned, were making a big mistake in preparing to fight these people. "It is the old, old story," he said, "contempt of a gallant enemy because his skin happens to be chocolate or brown or black, and because his men have not gone through orthodox courses of field-firing, battalion drill, or 'autumn maneuvers.'" It is hard to think of anyone who has said it better.

Ras Alula had already defeated Egyptians and dervishes, and, starting a year earlier, he had begun skirmishing with the Italians as they moved into his frontier territory from their Eritrean beachhead. He churned with anger as the Italians seized a village called Saati and wells at a place called Uaa. He called up his army and attacked Saati, defended by two companies of Italian regulars, three hundred irregulars, and some artillery, on January 18, [1887]. George Fitz-Hardinge Berkeley, a pro-Italian Englishman, in his thorough but biased campaign history, wrote that the Italians saw Ras Alula coming, thereby eliminating any chance of surprise, and sent a Lieutenant Cuomo with a small detachment forward to meet him. The Ethiopians rose out of the underbrush, overpowered poor Cuomo (he was mortally wounded) and advanced on the fort, where they were repulsed with serious losses. It was a minor victory—Berkeley called it a "brilliant success"—and the papers back home were ecstatic.

The Italian general, Gene, worried about his garrison at Saati, ordered reinforcements from Monkullo, consisting of a five-hundred-man white battalion under Colonel de Christoforis with fifty irregulars and two machine guns. The first eight miles were uneventful, but then the detachment came to a little town called Dogali, a name that lives on in a special place of honor in Italian military history. Here the Italian advance guard was suddenly attacked by Ras Alula, who had set a trap.

The Italians hurriedly took up a position on a hill along the side of the road, and during the action they moved back to a higher hill, where, like Custer, they made their last stand. Alula employed traditional Ethiopian tactics; his troops, many of them armed with spears, worked around the Italian flanks, aiming to encircle the enemy. The Italians fought bravely enough, but after the first half hour—so soon?—their machine guns began to jam, and they had to rely on their rifles. Ras Alula gave the order to charge at about 1 P.M. The Italians had opened the engagement at long range, so that by this time they had expended most of their ammunition. The fighting became hand to hand. Throughout the Ethiopian campaign, again and again, the Italians ran out of ammunition, even though it seems obvious that an army outnumbered five, ten, and even twenty to one should carry more ammunition than the other side. The Italians never caught on.

Now, said Berkeley, "each man defended his life with bayonet or sword. To the last they struggled against an enemy twenty times their number, falling one by one on the position that they were holding: 23 officers killed and one wounded, 407 men killed and 81 wounded. Such is the death toll of that sad but glorious day."

Sad, surely; but glorious, hardly. The Italians shouldn't have been this deep in contested territory in the first place, and Ras Alula had warned them they faced consequences. Saati, during the next twenty-four hours, was evacuated, and the troops made their way back to Monkullo in safety. The Italian newspapers called it a "massacre," and the government fell.

Dogali was the only major action fought between the Italians and the Ethiopians during John's regime. The emperor died on March 10, 1889, from wounds received in a glorious victory over the dervishes at Metemma. On his deathbed, he acknowledged that twenty-five-year-old Ras Mengesha was his natural son by the wife of his own brother, and recommended him to the chiefs crowding his tent as his heir. Menelik, though, would have none of that: the powerful ruler of central Ethiopia, he proclaimed himself King of Kings on March 26, and his claim would soon take precedence by right of force.

The Italian premier throughout most of this period was Francesco Crispi, who believed that Italy's recently won national unity—achieved with the help of Giuseppe Garibaldi's Red Shirts in 1861—required "the grandeur of a second Roman empire." Crispi was a fool, a bigot, and a very dangerous man.

The Eritrean-based Italians had minded their own business for several years following the "massacre" at Dogali. Crispi, though, wanted action, and chose General Oreste Baratieri, fifty-one years old, to resume the Italian takeover of Ethiopia. One of the great Garibaldi's "thousand" revolutionaries in Sicily, he was an authentic Italian hero. Baratieri took up his position as colonial governor in Eritrea (the eighth in just six years) on February 28, 1892.

By then the die had already been cast. One of Baratieri's predecessors, Baldissera, had occupied Asmara and Keren, key towns in the Tigrean highlands, in December of 1889. His successor, Orero, occupied Adowa in January of 1890. Key to their good fortune was the fact they had a powerful ally in Ras Mengesha, the chieftain who had challenged Emperor Menelik II for Emperor John's throne. But, in June 1894, Mengesha and most of his key lieutenants from Tigre (including Ras Alula) showed up in Addis Ababa, Menelik's capital in Shoa, and, each man carrying a large stone in token of submission, proclaimed their loyalty. Ethiopia, finally, was unified, and the common enemy was Italy. The country was swept by a popular refrain: "Of a black snake's bite, you may be cured, but from the bite of a white snake you will never recover."

In mid-December of 1894, a midlevel Ethiopian chief, Batha Agos, a longtime Italian ally, rose unexpectedly against his erstwhile Italian

Menelik II, King of Abyssinia, as shown in *Harper's Weekly*, 1896. (Library of Congress collections)

friends in what some historians declared was the opening shot in a war of liberation. Baratieri sent a Major Toselli, fifteen hundred men, and two guns to slap him down. Toselli found the Tigreans besieging a small Italian garrison at Halai, and launched a quick and successful attack on their rear. Totally surprised, they fled in disorder, and the body of Batha Agos was left on the field. The Italians lost just eleven killed and twenty-two wounded, and marked the minor action as a great victory. The revolt had lasted just three days.

Mengesha, surprised himself by the quick flow of events, rushed forward to sustain the Tigrean rebels. Baratieri moved to meet him, and they faced off for the first time at Coatit. Baratieri commanded just 3,900 men, of whom only 180, officers and men, were Italians (the rest were native Eritrean troops called Ascari). Mengesha commanded as many as 12,000 riflemen and about 7,000 irregulars armed with spears and swords. Baratieri, from his perch on Mount Tocule, could see the dust rising as they advanced against him.

"The moon shines over us, and the great extension of the Tigrean camps reveal their numbers and their carelessness," the Italians' official battle report, written by Baratieri, said. He continued:

> In an hour and a quarter all our men are at their posts and the movement of offense begins, with the first gleam of the morning, by a general advance wheeling slightly to the right, pivoting on the artillery.
>
> All goes well. A little after 6 A.M. the two battalions of the first line have some of their companies deployed, and the rest under good cover. With the first rays of the sun, Captain Cicco di Cola's battery from its skillfully chosen position on a height, sends the first shrapnel at 2,100 yards into the rebel camp, while I betake myself with my staff and the banner of Italy, to the high conical hillock . . . at the center of the line. . . .
>
> A great commotion is visible in the hostile camp. . . . They offer us only a small mark as they disappear from time to time, and gather in greater numbers under the cover of the defences. The rifle fire runs along the whole of the 3d and 4th battalions, which keep well under control of their officers in spite of the élan of the attack, as is proved by the frequent volleys, and the bayonet charges of individual units, on that broken, furrowed, and thickly covered ground.

But just when Baratieri thought he had everything under control, he saw another cloud of dust, representing a new hostile force, led by Mengesha himself, attacking his left wing. Companies on the right were ordered to reinforce the left, suffering losses in the process. With his retreat to Coatit threatened, Baratieri was forced to fall back, barely escaping himself from his headquarters post on what he called Commando Hill. The day's work, he said, was ended. The next day, to the Italians' surprise, Mengesha and his army withdrew. Baratieri saw his chance, and ordered a hot pursuit, chasing the Ethiopian hordes for more than thirty miles the next few days. An Italian gun actually lobbed one or two shells into Mengesha's tent at a place called Senafe, before the Tigrean army escaped in the mist.

The Italians exulted: it had been so easy, with such a small loss of life (324, total); and, best of all for the miserly Italian government, it had cost only 500,000 lire, or about £19,000. A nice house in London, it was said, cost no more. The Italians now controlled almost all of Tigre, a province about the size of Ireland. Baratieri was hailed as the new Garibaldi, and promoted to lieutenant general "per merito di guerra." The king, Umberto I, and the politicians vied with one another in sending him extravagant telegrams and letters of congratulation.

The emboldened politicians now wanted more, still more—but the government was virtually bankrupt, and insisted it couldn't pay for it. The government already had sent Baratieri two new white battalions and had authorized him to form two more Ascari battalions and a native mountain battery. After defeating Mengesha, Baratieri had moved forward in April to occupy Adowa (allowing the native troops to loot the place), and said he needed more money to maintain this forward position. Crispi told him he could not, under any circumstances, spend more than 9 million lire. Baratieri said 13 million lire was absolutely the lowest sum he could work with. Told he couldn't have that much money, he offered his resignation, but the cabinet refused to accept it. He tried twice more, warning each time that Menelik was preparing a large army to attack him, and twice more he was rebuffed.

He went home, to Rome, in early July of 1895, to consult with the cabinet and to make the argument for increased spending. With promises of support, he returned to Massawa late in September and massed his forces at Adigrat, slightly northeast of Adowa, early in October. He now commanded over 8,800 men (116 officers, 672 white soldiers, and 8,065 natives), twelve hundred animals, and ten mountain guns. Mengesha, meanwhile, was eighty miles away at Debra Aila, with no more than 5,000 men.

With the odds, for once, in his favor, Baratieri put his army into motion, reaching a point near Debra Aila on October 9. The scenery, as usual, was spectacular. "The height of Debra Aila," Baratieri wrote in his report, "rises to the south west . . . like a fortress—the peaks dotted here and there giving the effect of towers and steeples, amidst the other projecting blocks."

The Ethiopians' resistance, Baratieri said, was "brisk," but the Italian artillery, followed by an infantry charge, put the enemy to route in short order. It was a meaningless action, but it had some symbolic importance:

It was either the last skirmish of the campaign against Tigre Province, or the first skirmish in the Abyssinian war.

One of the Tigrean prisoners was prophetic: "For the present, you have been victorious, because God so willed it; but wait a month or two and you will see the soldiers of Menelik, and they are as many in number as the locusts."

Baratieri and his woefully inadequate intelligence service never believed that Menelik would be able to put more than thirty thousand men in the field. Nor did they consider the fact that, in some ways, Menelik's army would be equipped with more modern guns than their own. Menelik was getting his new weapons from the French; the arms were pouring through Djibouti, the French port on the Red Sea. The French figured, with indisputable Gallic cunning, that these guns would be used against either the Italians or the British, and either way that was just fine. Cartridges for the French-supplied rifles contained nearly smokeless powder, making it difficult for the Italian marksmen to determine the enemy's position. The Italian rifles were older models, and they made lots more smoke when they were fired. Another key weapon was the Hotchkiss quick-firing cannon, using both solid and percussion shells, which was more accurate and had a much longer range than the slow-firing mountain guns that would be used by the Italian batteries. Menelik's artillerymen would be more than adept in handling these guns.

And then, finally, there was the individual Italian soldier. The *Manchester Guardian*'s Wylde, who traveled with two cooks and several other servants, saw these soldiers on the march, and—with exasperating English arrogance—was unimpressed. "It is a most painful sight for a civilian who has been accustomed to see English troops campaigning to see these poor fellows struggling along, overladen, dirty, and ragged, without what we in England should call any discipline or the *amour propre* of a soldier. The officers keep themselves neat and tidy, but then again they have little with them, and I do not know what English officers would do under the circumstances that the Italian officers are placed in.

"The Italian soldier has to carry his greatcoat, blanket, cooking pots, water bottle, a fourth part of a tent, and 186 rounds of ammunition . . . and often a couple or three days' rations as well. Clothes besides which he has on, he has none."

In the days that followed his victory at Debra Aila, Baratieri proclaimed that Tigre had been annexed to the Italian colony, and set about fortifying three strong points: Adowa, Mekele, and Adigrat. Then he returned to Massawa and left his deputy, a General Arimondi, with whom he had been feuding, in command.

Menelik issued a mobilization proclamation on September 17, 1895. "An enemy is come across the sea," he said. "He has broken through our frontiers in order to destroy our fatherland and our faith. I allowed him to seize my possessions, and I entered upon lengthy negotiations with him in hopes of obtaining justice without bloodshed. But the enemy refuses to listen. He undermines our territories and our people like a mole. Enough! With the help of God I will defend the inheritance of my forefathers and drive back the invader by force of arms. Let every man who has sufficient strength accompany me. And he who has not, let him pray for us."

Major Toselli, with a small force of 2,150 men, was working his way south, advancing beyond Amba Alagi to a place called Belego. If attacked, he was under instructions to fall back on Amba Alagi, and if that didn't work, retire to General Arimondi's stronghold at Mekele. Baratieri had even insisted that if Mekele came under serious threat, everyone should fall back all the way to Adigrat, so he could consolidate his forces in one easily defended place.

On the twenty-ninth, Toselli, just to make sure, asked Arimondi to confirm his orders, and Arimondi sent a telegram the next day that read—the words are crucial—"I leave you the choice of maintaining your position at Belego or of retiring to the foot of Amba Alagi or, according to circumstances, still further."

But the telegraph office garbled the message. Like the ammunition shortages, garbled telegraph messages would become a habit in the Italian campaign. The message went out this way: "I leave you the choice of maintaining your position at Belego or of retiring to the foot of Amba Alagi according to circumstances." Nothing was said about retiring "still further," and so Toselli, naturally, presumed he had been ordered to make a stand at Amba Alagi. It was a death sentence.

Arimondi at one point wanted to move south to support Toselli; they were, after all, only thirty-five miles apart. But Baratieri flatly forbid it. So Toselli dug in, posting Ras Sebat with 350 irregulars on his left flank on Falaga Hill, covering the center with Captain Persico and his Ascari regulars (together with four mountain guns, all Toselli had), and deploying more irregulars on his right flank, near the mountain slope.

With only 2,150 men, Toselli never had a chance. He now faced thousands of Ethiopian warriors, led by the King of Kings himself, and with the best general in either army, Ras Alula, at his side. They began advancing from—wonderfully appropriate name—Boota Hill the morning of December 7. They first attacked those 350 irregulars on Toselli's left flank, causing them to retreat. This forced two companies of regulars to change front left and meet the charge. "By brilliant counterattacks," wrote Baratieri, "they kept in check an enemy twenty times their number."

Just as Toselli seemed to be checking the enemy's advance on his left, he received word that a huge Shoan force, led by Mengesha and Ras Alula, was descending on his right flank. It was hopeless. "They were many, many," wrote a survivor. "The plain did not seem sufficient to contain them . . . it seemed as if they sprang up out of the earth. The infantry fired and killed some of them [but it was] useless. The enemy continued to increase."

Toselli ordered a general retreat at 12:40 P.M., but the road to Mekele was cut off, leaving only a narrow mountain path running along a precipice four hundred feet high as an escape route. But sitting on top of the hill, waiting for them, was—who else?—the sly Ras Alula. Seeing the path blocked, the Italians turned around on the narrow path and, with their mules and guns, began to file carefully back down the way they had come. It was at this precise point that Ras Alula ordered his men forward, and the ragged Italian column was torn to pieces.

"They fired from above us, from our flank, from the rear," another survivor said. "What confusion! Mules rolling over the precipices . . . wounded men calling for help, and everywhere Abyssinians who were following to fire at us. . . . I left the road and, making a circuit through the mountains, placed myself in safety."

The survivors, including an exhausted Toselli, who was crawling on his hands and knees, reached a crossroads called Bet-Mariam. "I am at the end of my strength," Toselli said. "Now I will turn about and they can do what they like." His second in command, a Lieutenant Bodrero, rounded up the three hundred soldiers who were still ambulatory—including Ras Sebat—and made his way to tell General Arimondi the terrible news.

Amba Alagi was a nasty defeat: starting with 2,150 men, the Italian column lost 1,300 native Ascari soldiers and 20 Italian officers.

Worst of all, the battle broke the spell of Italian military supremacy. "The whole political edifice," Baratieri himself admitted, "indispensable to our colonial defense, was shaken to its foundation, and to some extent fell to the ground, increasing the boldness, confidence, strength, and pretensions of the enemy."

But it was just the beginning. With the defeat of Toselli at Amba Alagi, General Arimondi with his relief column of fifteen hundred men was threatened. Ras Alula—he had been leading his men for more than twelve hours—appeared out of nowhere and began pressing an attack on Arimondi's right. He fought his way to within one hundred yards of Arimondi and his staff, at the top of a hill, before being forced back. Now it was General Arimondi's turn to order a general withdrawal, and the column began falling back on the fort at Mekele.

They arrived exhausted—they had been marching for more than twenty-four hours, with only brief resting periods—and that may explain the kind of thinking that now took place. The decision facing Arimondi was whether to make a stand at Mekele, filled with tons of precious stores, or to continue the retreat, joining the rest of the army at Adigrat. But Arimondi came up with a third solution: he would leave a garrison at Mekele—20 Italian officers, 150 Italian soldiers, 1,000 Ascari, and two guns, under the command of a Major Galliano—and would push on with what was left for a safe haven with Baratieri at Massawa.

Arimondi defended his insane decision by arguing that it would have been demoralizing to abandon the fort, that he wasn't sure he had time to blow up all the supplies inside the fort, and that he didn't think he had enough food to feed his whole force on its line of retreat.

No one bought Arimondi's arguments, least of all General Baratieri. Even Berkeley, the Italian army's apologist, said that "one cannot help feeling it was a pity to allow these 1,200 men to be cut off and surrounded." A pity? It was a tragedy that should have led to a court-martial.

The siege began early in December 1885. The fort was actually an old church—Ethiopia was, and is, a Christian nation—and the outer defenses were made from the tombstones in the cemetery. It commanded the village of Mekele, once the site of one of Emperor John's palaces, to the northwest, and a smaller village, Enda Jesus, to the south. The whole position, in turn, was commanded by a ridge that was part of nearby Mount Gargambessa.

The fort and its defenders would depend for water on two streams—one running south of the fort, not more than 100 yards from its walls, and the other, to the north, running at the bottom of Mount Gargambessa, about 150 yards away. Toselli, perhaps the brightest of all the Italian officers, had started to build a blockhouse to defend the stream on the north side of the fort. Major Galliano, one of the stupidest Italian officers, ordered it to be torn down. In its place he built a small reservoir inside the fort, but it contained only enough water for ten or eleven days. He could have filled the scores of bottles inside the fort with water, too, but he broke them up and scattered the pieces outside the fort's walls, hoping they would cut the bare feet of the enemy soldiers.

Once again, there wasn't enough ammunition—only three hundred rifle rounds per man and even less for the guns—and no adequate excuses to explain why.

On the morning of January 7, the fort's defenders spotted a huge red tent on the plain to the southeast. That meant only one thing: the King of Kings had arrived, and he was just seven thousand yards away. Later in the day, Menelik's artillery opened fire from a distance of about five thousand yards. That represented a problem, too, for the range of the Italian guns was only forty-two hundred yards.

The Ethiopians, almost all of them Menelik's Shoans, attacked the fort's south front on the morning of the eighth. They captured the water supply, the small stream not far from the walls, and nothing the defenders could do would dislodge them. That night, the defenders found that they couldn't safely reach their water supply on the north, either. As a result, the rank and file were limited to a pint of water a day; the officers, magnanimously, said they would share the wine.

The fort was under fire from both the rapid-firing Hotchkiss guns and now, even more ominously, two machine guns.

Major Galliano raised the white flag over the fort on the nineteenth, ending a forty-five-day siege. The garrison marched out and, of all things, was allowed to go free. The King of Kings said he did it "to give proof of his Christian faith." Cynics suggested that he had been bought off, but that was never proved. Others argued that the garrison was released on the promise they would take no more part in the war. But, if that were so, the Italians didn't keep their end of the bargain, for the troops from the garrison—poor souls—participated six weeks later in the decisive battle at Adowa.

No one, in fact, had an answer, and it remains a mystery.

Mekele was more bad news for Baratieri. By the end of December, he had lost almost all of Tigre Province, and so far he hadn't even met the main Ethiopian army. But it was on its way—115,000 men, four times the number the Italians had anticipated.

Baratieri faced an impossible situation, and he was surely smart enough to appreciate it. He should have stayed where he was, waiting out the enemy. He knew that an Ethiopian army traveled without foragers or quartermasters. No one was assigned to bring in food or anything else. Ethiopian soldiers simply lived off the land, and when there was nothing left to eat, they had no choice but to move on. They would have done so now, if Baratieri had given them the chance.

But the politicians in Rome wanted a quick solution; they voted more money for the campaign and began sending reinforcements. The first contingent arrived on Christmas Day of 1895, and by March 1896 almost forty thousand men and nine thousand mules had been disembarked at Massawa. Most of them arrived too late to do any good.

Their equipment was awful. The uniforms were heavy and poorly made. They were soon in rags. The boots fell apart in a matter of weeks. Everyone connected with the disaster seems to remember the soldiers' headgear. "Helmets, anything of all shapes," wrote Wylde. "Many common sola-type hats from India, with or without the badge of the regiment, as the case may be." When the soldiers lost their caps, and most of them did, they were issued a Moorish tarboosh, a kind of fez with a blue tassel at the end of a long string. A few of them even wore navy straw hats.

Most of these reinforcments had no idea which battalion and which regiment they had been assigned to, and their officers had to write the new designations in ink on their hats and helmets. That didn't solve the problem entirely, because the soldiers, when asked to which unit they belonged, invariably replied by naming "the regiment and battalion of Italy from which they came."

Some of the soldiers had been issued old Remington rifles, and had to be taught how to work them. The idea, apparently, was that the government had a surfeit of Remington cartridges and wanted to use them up.

Baratieri seemed to dither, and the Italian government began to sense he was losing his edge. The cabinet even went so far as to name his successor (it was, in fact, his predecessor, Baldissera) secretly, on February 22, 1896. Crispi sent Baratieri an insulting telegram three days later. "This [campaign]," he said, "is a military phthisis not a war. . . . We are ready for any sacrifice in order to save the honor of the army and the prestige of the monarchy." (Phthisis is a wasting disease, like tuberculosis.)

Menelik, faced with his own problems—food, predictably, was running low—fell back on Adowa on February 17. But Baratieri was running short, too. Two armies, then, were facing each other, and both were running out of food.

Baratieri called a war council with his four generals the night of February 28, and gave every indication he thought a withdrawal was the right thing to do. "Retire? Never!" roared General Dabormida, commanding the Second Infantry Brigade. Retreat, he said, would be dishonorable. General Albertone, commanding the Native Brigade, agreed. Arimondi, commanding the First Infantry Brigade, was all for an attack, too, and he had the nerve to suggest that several opportunities already had been missed. General Ellena, commanding the Third Infantry Brigade and lately arrived from Italy, deferred to the three other generals.

The next day was February 29—this was leap year—and Baratieri made the fateful decision to order 14,519 men and fifty-six guns to start a night attack, in the mountains. They might have had some more seasoned regulars at their side, except for another garbled telegram. It sent the unit, numbering 1,200 men commanded by a Major Ameglio, in the wrong direction. When the mistake was discovered, a second telegram was sent, but it was garbled, too, and Major Ameglio, thoroughly confused, missed the battle.

Ranged against the Italians were fighting men drawn from every corner of Abyssinia—the army of Menelik and his warlike queen, Taitou, mostly Shoans and southwestern Gallas; Ras Michael's Wollo Galla army; the Tigrean troops under Ras Alula; King Tchlaihaimanout and his Godjam army; and even two generals, Ras Sebat and Hagos Tafreri, both from Agame, who had been in the pay of the Italians up until six weeks earlier. Sebat, in fact, had survived the Italian defeat at Amba Alagi. His defection was especially crucial: he came to Menelik's camp with a detailed knowledge of the Italian battle plan and line of communications.

Menelik would put eighty thousand infantrymen and eighty-six hundred cavalrymen, all of them armed with rifles, in the field, along with forty-two guns, many of them quick-firing Hotchkisses. Most of the rifles were modern breechloaders, including Martinis and Remingtons. These frontline regulars—many of them adequate marksmen—were backed up by twenty thousand more Ethiopians carrying lances, spears, and swords, and prepared to pick up the rifles of their fallen comrades.

The two armies were sixteen miles apart, with a series of three hills—the Spur of Belah, the Hill of Belah, and Mount Belah—in between, a barrier straddling all the paths leading from one position to the other. Baratieri intended to take up a position on these three hills, dig in, and tempt the enemy to make an attack. But there was another hill, a little farther to the left, which Baratieri's incompetent intelligence officers put down on their maps as Kidane Meret. In fact, though, it seems to have had no name at all. Four miles further on, there was still another hill, which was known to almost all the natives as the Hill of Kidane Meret. Baratieri ordered Albertone to occupy Kidane Meret; predictably, acting on the advice of his native scouts, he marched his men to the other Kidane Meret, the real one, and put his entire division four miles in advance of the rest of the army, exposed and—eventually—cut off.

Still, for all their bumbling, the Italians might have achieved the surprise they sought if it were not for one man. He was, of course, their nemesis: Ras Alula. Of all the Ethiopian generals, he was alone in believing the Italians might risk a night march. He positioned his own scouts on the mountaintops, where they watched, in the moonlight, as the Italians slowly began their advance. They sent word back to Ras Alula, and he alerted Menelik: the Italian army was moving against Adowa.

The Italians fanned out at a place called Entiscio, where the narrow mountain path split off in three directions. Albertone, with 4,000 rifles and fourteen mountain guns, headed for the wrong mountain, to the south; Dabormida, with 3,600 rifles, most of them Italian regulars, and eighteen mountain guns, marched for the Spur of Belah and the Hill of Belah, to the north; and Arimondi, with 2,500 rifles and twelve mountain guns, proceeded in the direction of Mount Belah, in the center. Ellena, with 4,150 rifles and all the new quick-firing guns, was held in reserve.

It was dark, of course, and the terrain was all rugged slopes, ravines, gorges, and clefts. One of the Italians said that "the surface seems like a stormy sea moved by the anger of God." A European-style army could hardly have picked a worse place to fight a battle against an enemy who could move quickly and silently from crag to crag, and who knew every ravine and every cleft.

The Ethiopians opened their attack against Albertone, simply because—being lost in the mountains—he was the first to show up, posting his Native Brigade on the real Kidane Meret, only three miles from the King of Kings and Queen Taitou, headquartered in what had been the house of one of the most famous monks in Ethiopian history. As the sun came up, Albertone looked hopefully for Arimondi's column, which was supposed to have taken position on his right. But he was supported there only by a small detachment of Ethiopian irregulars, in the pay of the Italian army. They didn't like this much more than Albertone, and—knowing that if they were taken prisoner they would be mutilated, losing their right hand and left foot—they understandably retreated at the first sign of trouble. As masses of Ethiopians advanced, Albertone caused considerable havoc by firing his mountain guns into their dense ranks. Soon, though, the Ethiopians' Hotchkiss guns were wheeled into position to reply to the slow-firing Italian guns. Within less than an hour, the Italian guns were silenced, from want of men to serve them or shells with which to load them. Once again, limited to ninety rounds, the Italians were running out of ammunition.

General Albertone, said Major Gamerra, one of the Italian survivors, sat "immovable on his horse near the batteries" and "gazed fearlessly at the whirlwind that was approaching." At a crucial moment, he ordered his reserves to attack, "and immediately afterwards the . . . battle cry which has sent its terrible notes over so many battlefields . . . the avanti! avanti! of the old Bersaglieri . . . ," rang out. But these were Ascaris, not Bersaglieri, and "a storm of lead" greeted their charge. "The 8th battalion no longer exists, it is destroyed! All the captains are dead, and the commander [Major Gamerra himself] no longer has a command and becomes a soldier. He follows, stupefied with grief, the remnants of his splendid battalion. . . . All is lost, all is lost, and the few survivors are trying to save their lives." The major turned out to be one of the lucky ones; he was taken prisoner and remained a captive of the Shoan army for ten months. Albertone was taken prisoner too, and was reduced, in his prison hut, to washing his linen without soap.

With the surrender of Albertone's isolated Native Brigade on the left, the victorious Ethiopians were able to turn their attack to the Italian center. Baratieri, at least, knew where the center was; he was with it. But now he couldn't find Dabormida, either; he and his Second Infantry Brigade were supposed to be securing the heights of the Spur of Belah, but they were nowhere to be found. Baratieri was in the unenviable position of having lost touch with both his left and his right flanks, and he reckoned things were getting serious.

Dabormida, in fact, had taken the wrong path, and had led his entire brigade into a narrow valley, some three miles from where he was supposed to be. It seemed peaceful enough. Standing on a slight rise, Dabormida could hear distant gunfire, and he and his staff officers made small jokes about it—until Major Bolla was shot in the right elbow. Dabormida didn't know it, but he had run into fifteen thousand Ethiopians, including a detachment from Ras Alula's army.

Dabormida was the best general the Italians had at Adowa, and with cool precision he deployed his thirty-six hundred men from one side of the valley to the other. They had barely taken up their positions when they were attacked by the Galla cavalry, shouting "Ebalgume! Ebalgume!" (The

Italian officers just before the Battle of Adowa, as shown in the *Illustrated London News*. (Library of Congress collections)

word means to mow or to reap, to cut down enemies like grass.) "How fine, how superb was that charge of the Gallas, with their strange and rich trappings glinting in the sunlight, bending low over the small horses that dashed headlong forward, and coming stoically onward to be massacred by our own guns," wrote Captain Menarini, one of the Italian survivors.

The Second Brigade even managed to launch a spirited charge of its own, with cries of "Savoia! Savoia!" and "Viva il nostro generale!" They sent the Ethiopians in their front flying. But no sooner had they won this piece of the battle—the highlight of the Italians' day—when they were attacked by a huge mass of Ethiopians from the rear. Captain Menarini remembered seeing his general, Dabormida, standing in the shade of a solitary sycamore fig tree in the middle of the valley, shaking his head. "'It is a serious thing, a serious thing,' he mutters to himself. 'No message, no order, no reinforcement. Nothing.'"

Dabormida tried one last counterattack, and when it failed he ordered a general retreat. "Cover us with your regiment," he told Major Airaghi. "Yes, general," the major replied. After that, silence. General Dabormida simply disappeared.

The final attack that had forced the Second Brigade to retreat was led by—no surprise—Ras Alula.

That left Arimondi, with Baratieri at his side, trying to hold the center, and he was in terrible trouble, too. One of his problems was that an entire battalion, the Fourth, commanded by a Major De Amici, had somehow joined forces with the right wing under Dabormida (and was, in fact, unexpectedly in a position to help secure his line of retreat). That meant Arimondi commanded only 1,773 riflemen and two artillery batteries. About 10:30, his little command was attacked by another swarm of Ethiopians, who pierced the center of his line and spilled over into the reserves' camp. Belatedly, Baratieri and Arimondi called on General Ellena to bring the new quick-firing guns forward, but it was too late. The guns simply clogged the road the army was beginning to use for its retreat, and never played any role in the battle at all. The generals also called on Major Galliano's Third Native Battalion, reputedly the best in the army, to come forward, but it only took about twenty minutes of close action before all 1,150 of them broke, an event so unpredictable that their Italian officers would attribute it to treachery.

It was at this point in the battle that the Italian army turned into a rabble. "The tail of the column became a confused mass of white men and black men, Ascari of Galliano, and Ascari of the other units, together with the Shoans, who dashed themselves into the middle of them, leaping as if possessed by a madness to kill or to be killed," Baratieri later wrote.

With about one hundred Italian soldiers and a few officers, Baratieri tried to make a stand at what he thought was a graveyard. He said he called out "Viva l'Italia!" and grasped his revolver, but this was not Baratieri's day; the cemetery's walls were too high to allow the Italians to fire over them.

And so, he said, "we continued along our path of sorrow."

The exhausted survivors—they had had no food for more than twelve hours and now were short of water—staggered on, with the enemy lurking on their flanks, taking occasional potshots. Fortunately for the Italians, though, the Ethiopians didn't pursue the defeated army with very much vigor and, after seven or eight miles, pretty much gave up the chase altogether.

Three times, the army lost its way. "A terrible destiny," wrote Baratieri. It wasn't until 9 P.M. on March 3 that they arrived at the little Italian fort at Adi Caje, where the general sent off a coded telegram to Rome describing the disaster.

And what a disaster it was. Of the fourteen thousand men who took part in the battle, more than six thousand died, including almost three thousand Italians. Another thousand were listed as missing, never to be seen again. The wounded totaled about fifteen hundred. The Italians lost almost 50 percent of their total combat strength, an extraordinary figure.

Losses for the Ethiopians were estimated to be seven thousand killed and
ten thousand wounded, a much smaller percentage of the men they committed to the battle.

The *Manchester Guardian*'s correspondent, Augustus Wylde, arrived in
Adowa about two months after the battle had ended. He said he made
"many visits to the battlefield, perhaps the most disagreeable task I ever
had to perform in my life, one position being more foul smelling and dis-
gusting than another. . . ." He passed one pile of thousands of right hands
and left feet, taken from the Ascari prisoners. It was the most terrifying
sight of all. "My faithful [servant] Hadgi Ali and my Abyssinian guides
used to tie their cloths around their nostrils and mouths and ask if I had
not seen enough."

Wylde called on Ras Alula, too. The old villain was still seething over
the fact that the man he hated most, General Baratieri, had managed to
slip away.

◆

When the news reached home, Crispi's government fell; when the troops
came home, they were booed and hissed. The Italians sought peace with
Ethiopia, and signed a treaty at Addis Ababa on October 26, 1896, that restored the old frontier, although Eritrea wasn't finally handed back until
1952. Menelik ruled on and on, holding a grand review for the heroes of
Adowa in 1902; some 300,000 showed up. He died in 1913.

Baratieri was put on trial, but was acquitted of criminal charges; even
so, the tribunal said that Italy regretted trusting "a general who has shown
himself so entirely unfitted to cope with the exigencies of the situation."
Ras Alula, grumpy to the end, attacked—and killed—one of his neighboring princes in 1897, but was mortally wounded in the fighting himself.
Though he looked like an old man, he was only fifty.

The Italians, armed this time with bombing planes and poison gas, returned to Ethiopia in 1935. Emperor Haile Selassie, Menelik's grandson,
put up a stubborn resistance, but he had hardly any modern weapons or
disciplined troops. The world watched, appalled at the cruel Fascist ag-
gression, but did nothing. The emperor fled the country on a British warship on May 2, 1935, to spend six years in exile. He returned to power in
1941 and was himself overthrown in a military coup that wrecked the country in 1974.

NINE

Major General William R. Shafter and the Spanish-American War (1898)

When Teddy Roosevelt went to war in 1898, he emptied out the finest men's clubs in Boston and New York. His troopers included Dudley Dean, "perhaps," in Roosevelt's opinion, "the best quarterback who ever played on a Harvard Eleven"; Craig Wadsworth, the steeplechase rider, and Joe Stevens, "the crack polo player," from Princeton; and Hamilton Fish, the ex-captain of the Columbia crew.

He mixed these Ivy Leaguers with Indian fighters and cowboys from the west, men like Benjamin Franklin Daniels, who had half of one of his ears bitten off during a fight when he was marshal of Dodge City, and little McGinty, the broncobuster from Oklahoma who never had walked a hundred yards if by any possibility he could ride.

In his own book, Roosevelt said he thought all of them—"Easterners and Westerners, Northerners and Southerners, officers and men, cow-boys and college graduates, wherever they came from, and whatever their social position—possessed in common the traits of hardihood and a thirst for adventure. They were to a man born adventurers, in the old sense of the word."

It *was* a great adventure, starting off as perhaps the most popular war in American history. Roosevelt, the greatest adventurer of them all, gave up his job as assistant secretary of the navy to become Lieutenant Colonel Roosevelt, second in command of the First United States Volunteer Cavalry, the most improbable fighting unit in the history of the U.S. Army. Everyone called it the Rough Riders.

"He [Roosevelt] has lost his head to this unutterable folly of deserting the post where he is of most service and running off to ride a horse . . . ," said his boss, Navy Secretary John D. Long. "He is acting like a fool."

While preparing his Rough Rider volunteer regiment for action against sickly Spanish regulars in Cuba, Roosevelt read with approval a book by M. Demolin called *La Supériorité des Anglo-Saxons*, in which the author explained why "the English-speaking peoples are superior to those of Continental Europe."

Roosevelt believed every word of it, so it came as a terrible shock when the army grossly bungled the organization of the expedition, and when the Spanish Mauser bullets began cutting down the pride of the Knickerbocker and Somerset clubs, and when, victory in hand, more or less, the entire army was ravaged by tropical disease.

The fact is, this was a close call: if the Spanish commanders hadn't been even more incompetent than the Americans, the Cuban expedition might have ended in one of the most calamitous defeats in empire-building history. The Americans were lucky.

In 1897, the entire U.S. Army consisted of twenty-five thousand officers and men, spread out across the country at seventy-seven separate posts. Its principal function was still to maintain patrols to deal with restless Indians. Yet modest reform was in the air, and the army was now equipped with the new thirty-caliber, five-shot Krag-Jorgensen rifle, with its smokeless ammunition. The artillery units had turned in their old muzzleloaders for breech-loading steel guns. Professional schools to train officers in the army's various branches had been founded, including one at Fort Leavenworth to teach the science of high command.

But the men who would lead this expedition hadn't been to these schools. Mostly relics of the Civil War, they had been given command of the biggest military expedition ever undertaken by the United States. The general in charge was a massive, three-hundred-pound major general, sixty-two-year-old William Rufus Shafter, known throughout the army as Pecos Bill. He ate mounds of food, drank too much whiskey, was loud and profane, and was heartily disliked by many of the men who served with him. Huffing and puffing, unable to walk as far as a mile, he would collapse in Cuba from heat and exhaustion.

"Not since the campaign of Crassus against the Parthians has there been so criminally incompetent a general as Shafter," Roosevelt wrote his friend, Senator Henry Cabot Lodge.

But no one else seemed to be much better. The army's commanding general was the old Indian fighter—he helped capture Geronimo—Major General Nelson A. Miles. Tall and powerful, he looked the part, but he was impossibly vain and pompous, designing his own fancy uniform. "Seize

Gen'ral Miles' uniform," said the popular comic figure Mr. Dooley. "We must strengthen th' gold resarve."

The secretary of war was Russell A. Alger, a distant relative of Horatio Alger, the chronicler of capitalist success stories. He had served in the Civil War with George Custer, ultimately rising to the rank of major general. Like Miles, he was vain and pompous and constantly at odds with his colleagues. The best officer in the army, Henry C. Corbin, the adjutant general, said Alger was "the most egotistic man with whom I have come in contact."

President William McKinley was no war hawk—he tried to keep the country from drifting into war with Spain—but he had served in the Civil War, too, as a major, and sometimes he believed he knew more about military strategy than his generals, and maybe he did.

Spain, on the other hand, possessed a huge army. As many as 150,000 Spanish regulars had been sent to Cuba to suppress an armed uprising led by poet José Martí that began in February of 1895. Martí was killed early on in an ambush, but the revolutionary forces—25,000 or 30,000 men—continued to fight a hit-and-run guerrilla campaign that took a heavy toll on the Spanish army. The strongest guerrilla army was led by Calixto García in the eastern part of the island. García could bring an artillery battery manned by American volunteers into action.

A British observer who watched the Spaniards march off to war said, "It makes me sad to see the quality of the expeditions packed off in heartless shoals to Cuba, boys, to look at, fifteen or sixteen, who had never held a rifle til this moment, and now are almost ignorant which end it fires, good lads—too good to go to such uneven butchery—with cheerful, patriotic, willing faces, but the very antithesis of a soldier." Thousands of these young men would die in Cuba, most of them from disease.

Early in 1896, the Spanish government dispatched one of its most celebrated soldiers, General Valeriano Weyler y Nicolau, to step up the pressure against the insurgents. His solution was a program called reconcentration, in which Cuban peasants were moved forcibly from their homes to army-maintained outposts. The villagers—known as *reconcentrados*—died by the tens of thousands, and world opinion marked the Cuban program as illegal and immoral. Weyler took on a new first name: he was now known everywhere as "Butcher" Weyler.

McKinley, like President Grover Cleveland before him, squirmed and twisted to avoid war with Spain. And then, early in the evening of February 15, 1898, the second-class battleship *Maine* blew up in Havana harbor, killing 266 of her 354 officers and men. The "yellow press," led by Joseph Pulitzer and William Randolph Hearst, screamed that the ship was sabotaged by the Spaniards, but this was never proved. It remains more likely that it was an accident, touched off by spontaneous combustion in a coal bunker that ignited a nearby ammunition magazine. But, with screaming headlines and detailed drawings of the infernal device that had caused the explosion, American public opinion was inflamed. Two months later, on April 19, Congress passed a joint resolution, calling for a *Cuba libre*, with armed intervention by the American army if that turned out to be necessary. War was formally declared on April 25.

Ordinary Americans, the historian David F. Trask wrote, went to war with an absolutely clear conscience, convinced this was God's work. "Perhaps," said one well-known preacher, "this experience may awaken in us that enthusiasm of humanity by which life is purified. In saving others we may save ourselves."

With Shafter in command—he already was being described as weighing one-sixth of a ton and resembling, in profile, a floating tent—the army was instructed to assemble six thousand regulars at Tampa, on Florida's Gulf Coast, and prepare them to sail to Cuba to link up with General Máximo Gómez, the Cuban resistance fighter, in more of a display of American intentions than a serious invasion.

First to sail, though, was the *Gussie*, an ancient side-wheel steamer painted fire-engine red that set off from Key West on May 10 to deliver arms and ammunition to the Cuban rebels. She was accompanied by two seagoing tugs, the *Triton* and the *Dewey*, chartered by uncensored American reporters who had alerted the whole world they were on their way. *Gussie* sailed with her lights blazing—all American noncombat ships sailed lit up like Broadway, throughout the war—and a navy officer watching her go by wondered "what in Hades kind of lunatic asylum had gone adrift."

When *Gussie* and the tugboats finally arrived in Cabañas Bay, three agents and their horses were dumped overboard to make their way ashore and contact the rebels. One of the horses headed back to Florida, and disappeared. The agents were followed by forty soldiers, including one small detachment commanded by James F. J. Archibald, a reporter for the *San Francisco Post*. The Spaniards, fully alerted, watched in amazement as the soldiers poured ashore. They fired off a few random shots, one of which nicked the *Post*'s Archibald in the elbow. It was the first serious shot in the war.

Gussie herself was now under fire, and the soldiers made haste in getting back aboard. But the anchor was stuck in the mud, and sailors had to chop the hawser with an axe. *Gussie* headed home, the guns and the ammunition undelivered.

As the war fever mounted, military planners in Washington became more ambitious. An army—a big one—would now be mobilized to invade Cuba; another army would be collected on the west coast to attack the Spaniards in the Philippines; a third army would get ready to capture Spanish-held Puerto Rico.

This was no Vietnam; every young man in America, it sometimes seemed, wanted to put on the uniform. Buffalo Bill Cody said he could win the war by invading Cuba with thirty thousand Indian braves. Jesse James's brother, Frank, volunteered to lead a company of cowboys. A woman in Colorado proposed to take the field with an all-female cavalry regiment.

McKinley and his advisors wanted to build an expanded regular army to win the war, perhaps as many as 104,000 men. But they failed to account for the political power of the poorly trained, poorly equipped, badly led National Guard. The Guard's defenders said regular soldiers were little more than mercenaries, recruited from the lower classes of American society. Citizen soldiers, on the other hand, a Guard spokesman said, "fight for the defense of home and country, for principle and glory, for liberty and the rights of man. . . . They do not menace our liberties or the stability of our free institutions."

The government in Washington caved in, and agreed that the regular army would be expanded to 61,000 men and that the rest, 125,000 eventually, would be volunteers drawn largely from National Guard units. But most of the soldiers in the militia units were raw recruits, with no military experience at all. They lacked uniforms and mess kits and tents, and they didn't have modern weapons. For all the boasting of their generals and home-state politicians, they weren't ready for action, and wouldn't be for months.

The regulars, on the other hand, responded quickly and skillfully. Black Americans played a key role in building the new army. Four of the regular army's regiments—two infantry and two cavalry—were black, and most of them had served with distinction in the Indian wars. They all fought courageously in Cuba. As many as ten thousand of the volunteers were black, too, and three of these units had their own black commissioned officers.

The idea was to send this army off to Havana, where most of the Spanish troops were concentrated. But that all changed when a Spanish naval squadron, led by Admiral Pascual Cervera y Topete, crossed the Atlantic and holed up deep inside the harbor at Santiago de Cuba, on the southeastern coast of Cuba. The army was told to come ashore near Santiago, and help the navy destroy Cervera's warships.

The jumping-off point was Tampa. Normally a sleepy port on Florida's Gulf Coast, the city "presented throughout May and June an appalling spectacle of congestion and confusion," noted the historian Graham A. Cosmas. "Tampa lay in the pine-covered sand-flats at the end of a one-track railroad," Cosmas wrote, "and everything connected with both military and railroad matters was in an almost inextricable tangle." No one was ever put in charge, and as train after train arrived with guns and horses and soldiers and crates of canned beef, nobody knew where to put it. Trains soon were backed up all the way to Columbia, South Carolina; on May 18, Cosmas reported, one thousand box cars jammed the yards at Tampa and the nearby Port of Tampa, and only two or three were being unloaded every twenty-four hours. There were no bills of lading and no one had thought to mark on the outsides of the freight cars what was packed inside, so nobody knew what the box cars contained. "The officers are obliged to break open seals and hunt from car to car to ascertain whether they contain clothing, grain, balloon material, horse equipments, ammmunition, siege guns, commissary stores, etc.," General Miles reported to Secretary Alger.

Roosevelt complained that there was no one in Tampa to meet the Rough Riders when they arrived. There was no one "to tell us where to camp, and no one to issue us food for the first 24 hours; while the railroad people unloaded us wherever they pleased, or rather wherever the jam of all kinds of trains rendered it possible. We had to buy the men food out of our own pockets, and to seize wagons in order to get our spare baggage taken to the camping ground which we at last found had been allotted to us."

Railroad service was provided by two private companies, which bickered with each other as they fought to get the lion's share of the government work. At the same time, they continued to run their own trains into town, carrying goods that had nothing to do with the war. Soon, too, passenger trains began showing up, filled with tourists.

Shafter, luxuriously headquartered at the Tampa Bay Hotel, tried to bring order out of chaos, with very little success. He was surrounded at the hotel by a press corps in full exercise of its guaranteed First Amendment rights. The reporters were camped out, Private Charles Johnson Post reported, "with ice water, steaks, eggs, ice cream, highballs—and Scotch whisky, which was just becoming fashionable. To us doughboys, it tasted

Major General William R. Shafter commanding the first expedition to Cuba, 1898, shown in a stereopticon by Strohmeyer & Wyman. (Library of Congress collections)

too much like creosote. We were very common folk." Richard Harding Davis, probably the nation's best-known journalist and a celebrity in his own right, was, from Post's perspective, "busy conning his Social Register on the cool hotel porch, until he knew the elite of the Rough Riders from Teddy on up or down, and keeping himself and his silk undies in perfect condition for the rigors of the coming campaign."

No doubt Davis was a little fastidious, and maybe he was a bit of a snob, too, but he would put himself in the middle of the fighting when the time came. Private Post, on the other hand, would serve with the so-called Gallant Seventy-first, a volunteer infantry regiment from New York, which would turn out to be the only unit in the war that could fairly be accused of malingering under enemy fire.

The navy, which would win all its battles and show a surprising amount of professionalism, had seized every big high-speed passenger liner it could get its hands on to serve as auxiliary cruisers and scouts for the slower warships, leaving nothing but rusty coastal steamers for the army. The Quartermaster Department ultimately collected more than thirty of these old one-stackers, plus—to land the troops—three small steam lighters, two double-decked barges, and one oceangoing tug.

Shafter had twenty-five thousand troops at Tampa; the ships had room for seventeen thousand. The expedition, as a result, would be composed of all the regulars, along with the Rough Riders and two volunteer infantry regiments (including Private Post's Seventy-first). The rest of the volunteers had to be left behind.

When the time came to sail on the night of June 7, it was every man for himself. Roosevelt seized a coal-car train for his Rough Riders, and the engineer backed the train nine miles from Tampa down the single track to the port itself. "We arrived covered with coal dust," Roosevelt wrote, "but with all our belongings." Next challenge: find a ship. Roosevelt and his good friend, Colonel Leonard Wood, the commanding officer of the Rough Riders, spotted the *Yucatan* in midstream, seized a stray launch, and boarded her. They were told the ship was reserved for troops from the Second Regulars and the Gallant Seventy-first, but that didn't impress either Wood or Roosevelt. "I ran at full speed to our train," Roosevelt wrote, "and, leaving a strong guard with the baggage, I double-quicked the rest of the regiment up to the boat, just in time to board her as she came into the quay, and then to hold her against the Second Regulars and the 71st, who had arrived a little too late, being a shade less ready than we were in the matter of individual initiative."

Early on June 8, Shafter reported to Washington that the ships were loaded, and the expedition was on its way. But, late in the afternoon, Washington cabled back: "Wait until you get further orders. . . ." Two American ships had reported sighting two Spanish warships, a kind of "ghost squadron." What the navy ships had actually seen were more American ships; the result was a six-day delay. Roosevelt complained some more: the men, he said in another letter to Senator Lodge, "are down in the lower hold, which is unpleasantly suggestive of the Black Hole of Calcutta."

The convoy finally sailed on June 14—thirty-five transports and support vessels carrying 819 officers and 16,058 enlisted men, of which only 2,465 were volunteers. They were accompanied by 959 horses, including Roosevelt's personal mounts, Little Texas and Rain-in-the-Face, and 1,336 mules.

Conditions on the old steamers were awful. "There were no facilities for the men to cook anything," Roosevelt complained (he complained a lot during the war). "There was no ice for them; the water was not good; and they had no fresh meat or fresh vegetables." Richard Harding Davis, roughing it aboard Shafter's flagship, the *Seguranca*, complained that the table linen in the dining parlor was seldom changed, and that there weren't enough stewards to serve the civilian passengers. The drinking water, he said, smelled like a "frog pond." He drank bottled water, instead.

"The squadron at night, with the lights showing from every part of the horizon, made one think he was entering a harbor, or leaving one," Davis later wrote. "There was really nothing to prevent a Spanish torpedo boat from running out and sinking four or five ships while they were drifting along, spread out over the sea at such distance that the vessels in the rear were lost to sight for fourteen hours at a time, and no one knew whether they had sunk or had been blown up, or had grown disgusted and gone back home. . . . But, as it was, nothing happened. We rolled along at our own pace, with the lights the Navy had told us to extinguish blazing defiantly to the stars, with the bands banging out rag-time music. . . ."

The British navy's observer, Captain Alfred W. Paget, was just as shocked as Davis. "Had any of these [Spanish torpedo boats] made an attack on the fleet spread over an enormous area, each ship a blaze of lights . . . , a smart Spanish officer could not have failed to inflict a very serious loss."

But there were no Spanish naval officers, smart or not, around. Davis reckoned that "God takes care of drunken men, sailors, and the United States. This expedition apparently relied on the probability that that axiom would prove true."

The American flotilla arrived off Santiago on June 22. General Shafter then began conferring with the navy commander, Rear Admiral William T. Sampson, about overcoming the Spanish army defenders—there were maybe thirteen thousand of them—and capturing Cervera's four modern warships in the harbor, which was protected by shore batteries and floating mines. It was a rare meeting, for one of the oddities of the Santiago campaign was the complete lack of cooperation between the American army and navy. The navy's big guns were never used, seriously, in support of the troops ashore (who were never able to bring their own big guns into action), and Shafter simply refused almost all the time to take Sampson into his confidence. The only explanation is that Shafter was jealous of the navy's success—Dewey had already defeated a Spanish squadron at Manila—and wanted to win this one for the army.

The first troops began tumbling ashore at a coastal village called Daiquirí, seventeen miles east of Santiago, on June 22. "At Daiquirí," said Richard Harding Davis, "are the machine shops and the ore dock of the Spanish-American Iron Company. The ore dock runs parallel with the coast line, and back of it are the machine shops and the company's corrugated zinc shacks and rows of native huts thatched with palm leaves. Behind these rise the mountains, and on a steep and lofty spur is a little Spanish block house with a flag pole at its side. As the sun rose and showed this to the waiting fleet it is probable that every one of the thousands of impatient soldiers had the same thought, that the American flag must wave over the block house before the sun sank again."

Fortunately for the Americans, the three hundred Spanish soldiers posted at Daiquirí had retreated into the mountains at the first sign of American hostility. In a very short time, four American soldiers clambered up "the sheer face of the mountain" and seized the abandoned blockhouse. "For a moment they were grouped together there at the side of the Spanish fort," Davis reported, "and then thousands of feet above the shore the American flag was thrown out against the sky, and the sailors of the men of war, the Cubans, and our own soldiers in the village, the soldiers in the long boats, and those still hanging to the sides and ratlines of the troop ships, shouted and cheered . . . , and every steam whistle for miles about shrieked and tooted and roared in a pandemonium of delight and pride and triumph."

That was the easy part. Getting the rest of the army and all the animals ashore was a disaster. Private Post and the Gallant Seventy-first came ashore eight miles down the coast at a place called Siboney, and it was no better than Daiquirí. "The transports were under charter merely," Private Post wrote, "and it was the ship captain who could tell the colonel what he, the skipper, would or would not do with his ship." As a result, Post said, most of the horses and mules "were jumped overboard from a half to a quarter mile offshore—depending upon the skipper's indigestion or his judgment—and then swam. Horses by the hundreds were drowned . . . the deep blue of the Caribbean became dotted with the bodies of drowned horses and mules."

Buglers on shore did what they could by playing calls to which the horses had been trained to respond—"Stables," "Boots and Saddles," "Fours Right," and even "Charge"—to get the animals swimming in the right direction. Roosevelt, landing at Daiquirí with the Rough Riders, watched as his two horses were unloaded. "A huge breaker engulfed Rain-in-the-Face, and drowned her before she could be released from harness," wrote

Edmund Morris, Roosevelt's biographer. "Snorting like a bull, [Roosevelt] split the air with one blasphemy after another," noted a Vitagraph movie cameraman watching the disaster. The terrified sailors took a lot more care unloading Little Texas, Roosevelt's only surviving horse.

The captains of the chartered merchant ships refused throughout the campaign to come too close to shore, for fear of damaging their vessels. It was one of the reasons rations were always short for the men at the front. "These captains knew that the soldiers needed food . . . ," Davis said, "and they allowed the men at the front to starve while they beat up and down as they pleased."

Davis blamed Shafter for allowing them to get away with it, and it is a fair criticism. But an even bigger problem was the lack of landing craft; there weren't nearly enough of them. Making things worse was the fact that the seagoing tug had simply deserted the convoy and gone home, while one of the double-decked barges had broken loose in the night and disappeared. Most of the supplies were brought ashore by a single steam lighter. Davis said the result was that the American army "fought in self-imposed privation."

It hadn't always been this way: the American army, under the leadership of Winfield Scott, one of its most brilliant generals, had landed a twelve-thousand-man expeditionary force, the largest amphibious invasion in history at the time, on the beaches of Veracruz on March 9, 1847, during the war with Mexico. Instead of a single lighter, Scott had provided his army with sixty-five flatboats to take the men ashore. It worked almost to perfection, and could well have served as a model for the Santiago expedition.

But, as far as anyone can tell, no one bothered to examine Scott's success. From the start, this campaign was hell-bent on becoming a disaster, and the press was there to write about it. Davis and the other reporters had wanted to go ashore with the first wave, but Shafter said he needed all the space on the landing boats for his soldiers. Davis collared Shafter on the *Seguranca* and said the general was making a serious public relations blunder. "No reporters will go ashore," the general said, "until we have the beach under control."

"But I am no ordinary reporter," Davis said.

"I do not care a damn what you are," Shafter growled. "I'll treat you all alike." Shafter was never apt to get much good ink from the press corps; now he was certain not to get any at all.

Shafter, a pith helmet shading his head from the sun, simply couldn't cope—with the reporters or with very much else. He had painful varicose veins and the gout was back again. He was exhausted almost before the campaign began, and he was never able to exercise anything resembling disciplined command over his army.

While Roosevelt was supervising the landing of his men at the dock, "a boatful of colored infantry soldiers capsized, and two of the men went to the bottom." One of the Rough Riders' heroes, Captain William O. "Bucky" O'Neill, the ex-mayor of Prescott, Arizona, plunged in, in full uniform, "to save them, but in vain." The dock, Davis reported, was a rickety thing, "covered with loose boards, and the men walked on these or stepped across open girders, two feet apart." When Davis returned three weeks later, the pier was still as rickety as ever. "It was obviously the work of the engineers to improve this wharf," he said, "or build a better one. But the engineers happened to be on the transport *Alamo*, and on the day of the landing General Shafter sent the *Alamo* to Aserrados for three days to build pontoon bridges for the Cubans."

Safely ashore, Roosevelt encountered for the first time the Cuban resistance fighters, whom he described as "a crew of as utter tatterdemalions as human eyes ever looked on, armed with every kind of rifle, in all stages of dilapidation. It was evident, at a glance, that they would be no use in serious fighting. . . ." These, of course, were the same guerrilla fighters who had tied down 150,000 Spanish soldiers for more than two years, but Roosevelt didn't understand that, and neither did very many other Americans involved in the campaign. Roosevelt shared the same misguided view of so many empire-building officers: if they didn't look like real soldiers, they couldn't fight like real soldiers.

The troops and the animals were all ashore, unopposed by the Spaniards, by June 26—two infantry divisions, a dismounted cavalry division (including the Rough Riders), and an independent infantry brigade, plus the usual assortment of artillery, engineering, and signal units.

What now?

Shafter had two options. He could march down the coast road and attack Morro Castle, the fort that guarded the entrance to Santiago Bay, storm it with the navy's assistance, and thus open the harbor to the fleet. Or, he could move his troops along a second road that ran north and west from Siboney toward the city, and attack Santiago that way.

The navy, almost needless to say, favored storming Morro Castle and opening the harbor to its warships. Generals Miles and Shafter, though, both preferred the inland route, in the belief that the Spanish commander, General Arsenio Linares, had concentrated most of his force around Morro Castle, leaving the northern approach to the city weakly defended.

Linares, in fact, was a dithering fool, and couldn't make up his mind whether to concentrate his troops anywhere. Instead, he spread them out, holding too many places with not enough men.

At the outset, at least, the terrain was a bigger obstacle for the Americans than General Linares and his Spanish regulars. Santiago was surrounded by hills and valleys, covered with dense and impenetrable underbrush, and broken by creeks and ravines. Tropical rains—it was now the rainy season—flooded these creeks and ravines, and turned the narrow forest paths into mud. Only the mules could carry provisions to the soldiers at the front; they were, in lots of ways, the real heroes of Santiago.

The general idea was that Brigadier General Henry W. Lawton's infantry division would lead the way towards Santiago, followed by the Second Infantry Division, commanded by Brigadier General Jacob F. Kent. Brigadier General John C. Bates's independent brigade was supposed to support Lawton's infantrymen. The dismounted cavalry division was led by sixty-one-year-old Major General Joe Wheeler, a Confederate cavalry commander in the Civil War, and now a wizened Democratic congressman from Alabama personally recruited for this assignment by President McKinley himself. "There must be a high officer from the South," the President told him. "There must be a symbol that the old days [of a divided nation] are gone. You are needed." (When "Fighting Joe" was buried years later, in his blue Yankee uniform, one of his old rebel comrades was alleged to have said, "Jesus, General, I hate to think what old Stonewall's going to say when he sees you arrivin' in that uniform." It's a nice story.)

Wheeler was supposed to bring up the rear. But he was the senior commander on land—Shafter was still, literally and figuratively, at sea—and Wheeler decided to jump-start the war by sending one of his brigades, commanded by Brigadier General Samuel B. M. Young, forward the morning of June 24 to challenge fifteen hundred Spaniards defending a crossroads called Las Guásimas, three miles from Siboney. The advance was supposed to be supported by eight hundred Cuban insurgents under the command of General Demetrio Castillo Duany, but they never put in an appearance.

"General Wheeler, a regular gamecock," Roosevelt said, "was as anxious as Lawton to get first blood, and he was bent on putting the cavalry division [including, of course, the Rough Riders] to the front as quickly as possible."

With only three hours' sleep, the Rough Riders set off at 5 A.M., climbing the steep ridges above Siboney to a trail that ran to the west about a mile from the route to the east—a road called, grandiloquently, the Camino Real—that was being taken by regulars from the First and the Tenth Regiments. The Tenth was a black regiment, and one of its officers was Lieutenant John J. Pershing, who would go on to command the American Expeditionary Force in World War I. The two columns moved through the dense underbrush with no way of communicating with one another. General Lawton, realizing that somebody else was taking his place in leading the attack, furiously complained to General Shafter, still headquartered on his flagship, but it was too late to do any good. The cavalrymen pressed on, eager to get this war underway. But as the morning progressed, many of them dropped their bundles, or, exhausted, fell out of line, "with the result," said Roosevelt, "that we went into action with less than 500 men."

Marching single file along the narrow trail, they were led by a special "point" of five men skilled as scouts and trailers. "No flankers were placed for the reason that the dense underbrush and the tangle of vines that stretched from the branches of the trees to the bushes below made it a physical impossibility for man or beast to move foward except along the beaten trail," Roosevelt said. Colonel Wood, the commander, and Roosevelt, his second in command, rode at the head of the main body on their horses, with Roosevelt's two favorite reporters, Davis of the *New York Herald* and Edward Marshall of the *New York Journal*, at their side. Roosevelt didn't like Stephen Crane of the *Journal*, the novelist who had written *The Red Badge of Courage* without ever hearing a shot fired in anger, and so he had been assigned to bring up the rear.

It was a lovely day. "The tropical forest was very beautiful," Roosevelt remembered. "Now and then we came to glades or rounded hill-shoulders, whence we could look off for some distance. The tropical forest was very beautiful, and it was a delight to see the strange trees, the splendid royal palms and a tree which looked like a flat-topped acacia, and which was covered with a mass of brilliant scarlet flowers. We heard many bird notes too, the cooing of doves and the call of a great bush cuckoo. . . . It was very beautiful and very peaceful."

Critics said later that the cavalrymen were ambushed, but that isn't true. General Young and all the others knew that the Spanish were waiting for them, and their positions had been properly scouted. But it was nonetheless a shock for these troopers to suddenly find themselves under heavy enemy fire. "The Mauser bullets were singing through the trees over our heads," Roosevelt wrote, "making a noise like the humming of telephone wires. But exactly where they came from we couldn't tell." The reason, of course, was smokeless powder. The Spanish-made Mausers were modern weapons, and they gave off no telltale smoke signals. The firing at first was erratic. "Gradually, however," Roosevelt said, "they began to get the range and occasionally one of our men would crumple up. In no case did the man make any outcry when hit; at the outside, making only such a remark as, 'Well, I got it that time.' With hardly an exception, there was no sign of flinching."

Davis, with binoculars, was at Roosevelt's side—Roosevelt was so excited he kept jumping up and down—and he was the first to see real Spanish soldiers. "There they are, colonel; look over there; I can see their hats near that glade." Roosevelt detailed several of his best marksmen—this, unbelievably, was the first time these men had ever fired their new Krag-Jorgensen carbines—to take aim. Ultimately, the shots began to tell, "for the Spaniards suddenly sprang out of the cover through which we had seen their hats, and ran to another spot; and we could now make out a large number of them," Roosevelt said. He even took a rifle from a wounded man "and began to try shots with it myself."

"It was an exceedingly hot corner," Davis reported.

Men were dying, and this no longer seemed an adventure. Roosevelt said one of the first casualties was Harry Heffner of G Troop. He fell, wounded though the hips, "without uttering a sound, and two of his companions dragged him behind a tree. Here he propped himself up and asked to be given his canteen and his rifle, which I handed to him. He then again began shooting, and continued loading and firing until the line moved forward and we left him alone, dying in the gloomy shade."

Davis reported, "One man near me was shot through the head. Returning two hours later to locate the body, I found that the buzzards had torn off his lips and his eyes." Huge land crabs feasted on the corpses, too.

At one point, Davis found himself all alone on the trail. "I guessed," he said, "this must mean that I was well in advance of the farthest point to which [Captain Allyn] Capron's troop had moved before it was deployed to the left, and I was running forward feeling confident that I must be close on our men when I saw far in advance the body of a sergeant blocking the trail and stretched full length across it. . . . It was apparently the body of the first man killed."

It was, in fact, Sergeant Hamilton Fish, the grandson of President Grant's secretary of state and a member of one of the nation's most energetic political families. "He remained a giant in death," said Davis. "His very attitude was one of attack; his fists were clenched, his jaw set, and his eyes, which were still human, seemed fixed with resolve. He was dead, but he was not defeated."

Now, wrote Davis, those "comic paragraphers" who made fun of "the members of the Knickerbocker Club and the college swells of the Rough Riders organization, and of their imaginary valets and golf clubs, ought, in decency, since the fight at Guásimas . . . go out and hang themselves with remorse."

Roosevelt, hearing cheering on his right, ordered his own men to advance on some red-tiled buildings Davis had spotted. "They came forward with a will," Roosevelt recalled. "There was a moment's heavy firing from the Spaniards, which all went over our heads, and then it ceased entirely. When we arrived at the buildings, panting and out of breath, they contained nothing but heaps of empty cartridge shells and two dead Spaniards, shot through the head."

The shooting lasted about two hours, after which the Spaniards began what was presumably a planned retirement. Old Fighting Joe Wheeler, seeing them fall back, allegedly called out, "We've got the damn Yankees on the run!"—forgetting, momentarily, which war he was fighting. The story's almost too good to be true, but it got a nice play in the papers back home.

When the war was over, Shafter said the brief engagement had had an "enspiriting effect upon our men"; but it didn't amount to much, and Fighting Joe Wheeler could properly be criticized for bringing it on simply so he could say he was the first to engage the enemy in battle.

The Americans lost sixteen men killed and fifty-two wounded; the Rough Riders lost over half of the casualties—eight men killed and thirty-four wounded. The First Cavalry lost seven men killed and eight wounded. The Tenth, the black regiment, lost one man killed and ten wounded.

Shafter, still at sea, sent instructions to Wheeler—"do not try any forward movement until further orders"—and continued to try to deal with the hopeless tangle in getting food and equipment ashore. Meanwhile, the Spanish commander, Linares, could see what was going on, and began making his own plans. He reckoned that the Americans would attack near Morro Castle, and placed almost 5,000 men there to repel it. He scattered

Fighting uphill at Santiago de Cuba, as shown in a wash drawing by William Glackens, 1898. (Library of Congress collections)

the rest of his force helter-skelter, with no point to any of it. Only 137 men were assigned to San Juan and Kettle hills, two crucial positions on the San Juan Heights. Some 500 men were posted at El Caney, an isolated outpost six miles northeast of the city.

On June 30, Shafter was placed on a large, powerful mule and taken forward to a plateau called El Pozo, on high ground, less than three miles from the city of Santiago itself, with a fairly clear view of General Linares's outer defenses. Based on those observations, his first decision—a costly one, predictably—was to send Lawton's infantry division to take El Caney on July 1. It was held by General Joaquin Vara del Ray with no more than five hundred men, including two of the general's own sons. Kent, with the other infantry division and Wheeler's dismounted cavalry, was ordered to move against the San Juan hills, just two miles east of the city. This way, Shafter divided his forces, normally a mistake; but he thought El Caney would fall quickly and easily, within two hours maximum, and that Lawton's men could then join the main attack on the San Juan hills. Shafter's idea was to break through the Spanish lines, occupy Santiago itself, and then proceed to capture the entire Spanish naval squadron, a first for an American, or maybe anybody else's, army. That, he seems to have figured, would put an end to all the rhapsodizing about the glories of the United States Navy.

It wasn't much of a plan in the first place, and it soon fell apart. One of the problems was that this was the sickly season in Cuba, and malaria and yellow fever were soon to be bigger enemies than the Spaniards. Wheeler, frail to begin with, collapsed, and his cavalry command was taken over by General Samuel S. Sumner. General Young, commanding the cavalry division's Second Brigade, became ill, too; he was succeeded by the Rough Riders' Colonel Wood. That meant that Roosevelt now had his Ivy Leaguers and cowboys all to himself.

Shafter, in worse shape than ever, retreated to a position a mile east of El Pozo, where he could see almost nothing. One of his aides, Lieutenant Colonel Edward J. McClernand, was posted forward to serve as Shafter's deputy, relaying messages and orders between the rear-base headquarters and the shifting front line. Another aide, the loyal Lieutenant John D. Miley, was sent forward to the San Juan hills to serve a similar function. Predictably, the arrangement didn't work, and Shafter quickly became a mere onlooker, unaware most of the time of what was happening. This was a battle, everyone said, that "fought itself."

Davis, implacable now in his contempt for Shafter, said the sick old general, spending most of his waking hours on his cot, should have resigned his command. But, as Davis saw it, "his self-confidence was untouched. His self-complacency was so great that in spite of blunder after blunder, folly upon folly, he still believed himself infallible, still bullied his inferior officers, and still cursed from his cot. . . . The truth . . . is that it was not on account of Shafter, but in spite of Shafter, that the hills were taken," and the battle won.

El Caney really should have been a simple affair. The five hundred defending Spaniards had no artillery or machine guns; they would fight with their Mauser rifles alone. Lawton, leading fifty-four hundred men, the pride of the American army, had a battery of four slow-firing 3.2-inch guns. They opened fire at 6:30 A.M., but they were posted too far away from the Spaniards' strongest point, a stone fort called El Viso, which was situated atop a rounded hill and surrounded by rifle trenches. The shots had no effect at all. One of the American officers said the Spanish troops, "in their light blue pajama uniforms and white straw slouch hats," watched the shelling with apparent indifference.

The American artillery performance was inept, even taking into account the fact that the light guns brought ashore were obsolete. The guns were badly served, and, because of it, Americans needlessly died. Unbelievably, too, the American navy was never asked to bring its big guns to bear on the Spanish positions, which were well within their range. Shafter "planned the attack as though the warships were thousands of miles away," historian Graham Cosmas pointed out.

And so, if El Caney were to be taken, it would be up to the infantrymen. Lawton inched forward, encountering unexpectedly sustained enemy fire. He was forced to bring up reinforcements, and still the Spaniards—this was truly heroic—held on. The Americans had assumed these soldiers would run; but here they were, five hundred of them, pinning down five thousand men. Their gallant commander, Vara del Ray, was killed about noon, and his two sons died soon after. The Spaniards held out at El Caney for more than ten hours, making a shambles of Shafter's plan to sweep into Santiago and capture the Spanish fleet.

Shafter began to panic. He ordered Lawton to break off the attack, and move to support the attack on the San Juan hills. "I was fearful I had made a terrible mistake in engaging my whole army at six-mile intervals," he wrote later. Lawton, a stubborn man, refused to obey the order. It was too late to break off the engagement, he said. And so, with Shafter's reluctant consent, he pressed on, until the Spanish position was finally overrun by the regulars from the Twelfth Infantry. They had fought side by side with the black regulars from the Seventh Division, who had, one observer said, "swept up the hill like a legion of demons."

"The trench around the fort was a gruesome sight, floored with dead Spaniards in horribly contorted attitudes and with sightless, staring eyes," an American officer said. "Others were littered about the slope, and these were mostly terribly mutilated by shell fire. Those killed in the trenches were all shot through the forehead, and their brains oozed out like white paint from a color-tube."

Of the 500 Spaniards who entered the fight, only 80 remained on their feet. The Americans lost 81 men killed and 360 wounded.

One of the wounded Americans was James Creelman of Hearst's *New York Journal.* Stretched out on the grass, he felt someone stroking his forehead. "Opening my eyes," he wrote later, "I saw Mr. Hearst, . . . a straw hat with a bright ribbon on his head, a revolver at his belt, and a pencil and a note book in his hand. . . . Slowly he took down my story of the fight. 'I'm sorry you're hurt,' he said, 'but'—and his face was radiant with enthusiasm—'wasn't it a splendid fight? We must beat every paper in the world.'"

Hearst had come ashore from his yacht, anchored off Siboney. The yacht even had its own printing press, which Hearst would eventually use to publish a four-page newspaper for the boys in the trenches.

The attack on the San Juan hills was a hard-fought business, too.

Captain George Grimes opened up on the Spanish positions with his four 3.2-inch guns at about 8 A.M. But these guns used the old black powder, and they instantly gave away their location to the enemy. Linares had two bigger guns on the Heights—one 6.3-incher, the other a 4.7. They had no trouble zeroing in on the slow-firing American guns. Wood and Roosevelt were sitting together, and Roosevelt remembered Wood saying he wished

> our brigade could be moved somewhere else, for we were directly in line of any return fire aimed by the Spaniards. . . . Hardly had he spoken when there was a peculiar whistling, singing sound in the air, and immediately afterward the noise of something exploding over our heads. It was shrapnel from the Spanish batteries. We sprung to our feet and leaped on our horses. Immediately afterward a second shot came which burst directly above us; and then a third. From the second shell one of the shrapnel bullets dropped on my wrist, hardly breaking the skin, but raising a bump as big as a hickory-nut. The same shell wounded four of my regiment. . . . I at once hustled my regiment over the crest of the hill into the thick underbrush, where I had little difficulty in getting them together again into column.

The American guns were silenced in less than an hour. That meant, campaign historian David Trask noted, that eight thousand men had to struggle without artillery support along a narrow, congested road against an entrenched enemy. The army's big siege guns were still deep in the holds of ships offshore; the navy's big guns were idle, no one having asked for their help. "It was like going to a fire with a hook and ladder company and leaving the hose and the steam engines in the engine house," Richard Harding Davis reported.

A British correspondent, John Black Atkins, wrote: "But this hill—the look of it was enough to stagger any man. Was this to be taken practically without the aid of artillery? Artillery should have battered, and battered and battered the position, and then the infantry might have swept up at the run. The infantry stood before the thing alone."

Roosevelt didn't know much about this scandalous situation, or if he did he didn't care. This was to be what Roosevelt would always call "the great day of my life," and he was ready for it. Extra spectacles were pinned inside his sombrero, and he had attached his blue polka-dot scarf to the rim, to protect his head from the sun.

"Three regiments were now on the trail," Private Post of the Gallant Seventy-first reported, "and it was jammed. Companies were mixed up. Officers and sergeants were shouting to keep their units intact. 'Company F—forward!' 'Company C—here!' It was no march, it was a weaving, shuffling mass of men, crouching, halting, crouching again, and always pressing forward over the rough path of the trail. Now and then a man would seem to trip and then sink down, badly hit or killed. Another would give a sudden jerk and the rifle would fall from his grasp while he crowded in the jungle growth to get out of the way. . . . Men did not get hit or die in a dramatic outstretching of clutching hands and arms. They just sat down, crumpled and wilted, and lay still if dead, or crawled to one side."

Private Post failed to point out that it was his outfit, the Seventy-first, that was causing much of the problem. Foolishly, the Seventy-first, with its untested volunteers and its old Springfield rifles, which used black powder, had been ordered to lead the regulars into position. But when the First Battalion came under fire, it fell back, and the whole regiment refused to resume its advance. They were told to get off the trail so the others, regulars from the Sixth and Sixteenth infantry regiments, could get by.

Private Post, caught in the middle of this military logjam, later remembered that "the trail underfoot was slippery with mud. It was mud made by the blood of the dead and wounded, for there had been no [rain] showers that day. The trail on either side was lined with the feet of fallen men and the sprawled arms of those who could not quite make it."

Those who were there remembered it always as Bloody Ford.

The attacking Americans were, in fact, trapped, at the place where the ten-foot-wide trail crossed the shallow San Juan River. Bloody ford.

Captain Bucky O'Neill of the Rough Riders, chain-smoking as always, turned to his sergeant and said, "Sergeant, the Spanish bullet isn't made that will kill me." Wrong. The next moment, a Spanish Mauser bullet entered his mouth and exploded out the back side of his head. An erudite man, he had been Roosevelt's closest companion in the Rough Riders.

It was at this precise point that the army's lone war balloon, manned by Lieutenant Colonel George Derby and Lieutenant Joseph Maxfield, and attended by four soldiers with guy ropes, was raised over the battlefield. Even Lieutenant Miles, Shafter's loyal defender, conceded it was a serious mistake. "The enemy's musketry fire," he said, "was already becoming quite spirited, but when the balloon reached this point it was opened upon by a heavy fire from field guns, and the musketry fire also increased."

Roosevelt was incensed. "Of course," he said, "it was a special target for the enemy's fire. I got my men across before it [the balloon] reached the ford. There it partly collapsed and remained, causing severe loss of life, as it indicated the exact position where the Tenth and the First Cavalry, and the infantry, were crossing."

At 1 P.M., hearing nothing from Shafter—he was too far away to take part in the action—Lieutenant Miles, on his own, ordered a general attack on the San Juan Heights. There were two hills being defended by the Spaniards: San Juan was the big hill, the one the Americans knew all about, but in front of it was a smaller hill, never properly scouted by the Americans, called Kettle Hill, and it was exploding with Mauser fire.

Roosevelt, jumping up and down, was apoplectic. "I sent messenger after messenger," he said, "to try to find General Sumner or General Wood and get permission to advance, and was just about making up my mind that in the absence of orders I had 'better march towards the guns.'" At that precise moment, a messenger turned up and ordered Roosevelt to move forward with the Rough Riders in support of the regulars from the Ninth and First cavalry regiments attacking Kettle Hill.

"The instant I received the order I sprang on my horse and then my 'crowded hour' began."

Some of Roosevelt's troopers were reluctant, briefly, to make the advance, and one of them was lying behind a little bush. Roosevelt told him to get on his feet and join the attack. "Are you afraid to stand up when I am on horseback?" he asked. "As I spoke, he suddenly fell forward on his face, a bullet having struck him lengthwise. I suppose the bullet had been aimed at me. . . ."

The Ninth Regiment was in front of Roosevelt and the Rough Riders; the First was on his left. Partly involved, too, were units from the Third, Sixth, and Tenth regiments, moving up Kettle Hill as a means of joining the main assault on San Juan Hill. Richard Harding Davis wrote:

> I have seen many illustrations and pictures of this charge on the San Juan hills. But none of them seem to show it as I remember it. In the picture-papers the men are running uphill swiftly and gallantly, in regular formation, rank after rank, with flags flying, their eyes aflame, and their hair streaming, their bayonets fixed, in long, brilliant lines, an invincible, overpowering weight of numbers.
>
> Instead of which I think the thing which impressed one the most, when our men started from cover, was that they were so few. It seemed as if someone had made an awful and terrible mistake. One's instinct was to call them back. You felt that someone had blundered and that these few men were blindly following out some madman's mad order. It was not heroic then, it seemed merely terribly pathetic. . . . They had no glittering bayonets, they were not massed in regular array. They were a few men in advance, bunched together, and creeping up a steep, sunny hill, the tops of which roared and flashed with flame.
>
> The men held their guns pressed across their breasts, and stepped heavily as they climbed. Behind these first few, spreading out like a fan, were single lines of men, slipping and scrambling in the smooth grass, moving forward with difficulty, as though they were wading waist high through water. . . . It was a miracle of self-sacrifice, a triumph of bull-dog courage, which one watched breathless with wonder.

Roosevelt, having the time of his life, galloped all over the hill, urging his men forward. Finally, unable to stand it any more, he charged for the crest, with his faithful orderly, Henry Bardshar, trying to keep up with him on foot. "Some forty yards from the top I ran into a wire fence and jumped off Little Texas, turning him loose. He had been scraped by a couple of bullets, one of which nicked my elbow, and I never expected to see him again. As I ran up to the hill, Bardshar stopped to shoot, and two Spaniards fell as he emptied his magazine."

Suddenly, two Spaniards "leaped from the trenches and fired at us, not ten yards away. As they turned to run I closed in and fired twice, missing the first and killing the second." Roosevelt killed his Spaniard, probably one of those poorly trained teenage regulars, with a revolver retrieved from the sunken battleship *Maine* and given to him by his brother-in-law, Navy Captain W. S. Cowles. The Spaniard fell, he said, "neatly as a jack-rabbit."

The Spanish commanders made a lot of mistakes in this battle; one, of course, was not defending the San Juan hills with more men. But even more grievously, they had placed their firing positions at the true crest of the hills, from which they couldn't train their rifles on the Americans coming up the slopes. They should have dug in below the crest, at what's called the "military crest," twenty or thirty feet below the actual crest, where they would have had no trouble taking aim.

Roosevelt looked around him and found that he had seized the hill with a motley collection of troops from several regiments. "There were about fifty of my Rough Riders," he said. "Among the rest were perhaps a score of colored infantrymen, but, as it happened, at this particular point without any of their officers. No troops could have behaved better than the colored troops had behaved so far; but they are, of course, peculiarly dependent upon their white officers." It was, of course, nonsense, and patronizing to boot, but he and most of the rest of the white officers believed it.

From his perch on Kettle Hill, Roosevelt found that he had a wonderful view of General Kent's infantry division attacking San Juan Hill. "Obviously," he wrote, "the proper thing to do was help them," and so for the next few minutes he ordered his troops to fire, in volleys, at the Spaniards in their blockhouse on the top of the hill. But even this wasn't enough. "The wolf rose again in Roosevelt's heart," wrote biographer Edmund Morris, and he raced down Kettle Hill to join the attack on San Juan Hill. But he didn't tell any of his troops to come along with him. He had to run back and accuse them, unfairly, of cowardice. Soon, the Rough Riders, and troopers from the First and Tenth cavalry regiments, were engaged in the fight to take San Juan Hill.

Roosevelt and his reinforcements may have tried to save the day, but the real turning point was provided by a Gatling gun detachment led by Second Lieutenant John H. Parker of the Thirteenth Infantry. He wheeled his three guns into position at 1:15 P.M., and opened fire on the Spanish blockhouse at a range of about six hundred yards. "The gunners poured fire on the hilltop at the rate of up to 3,600 rounds a minute," wrote the historian Trask, "and quickly forced the defenders to abandon their positions." The Gatling fire had lasted for less than nine minutes.

The Spaniards ran down the hill, toward Santiago, to the safety of their main defensive positions. "We have carried their outer works," Shafter reported, "and are now in possession of them. There is now about three-quarters of a mile of open country between my lines and the city." He said he regretted to say that American casualties were 400 or more. That wasn't even close. It had been a hard day for the Americans: 205 men were killed and another 1,180 were wounded. Altogether, the Americans lost about 10 percent of the men they had committed to battle on July 1. The Spaniards committed only a fraction of their force—only 1,700 troops altogether—and they had lost 215 killed and 376 wounded.

It was a victory of sorts for the Americans, but Shafter hadn't seized Santiago, as he had hoped to do. And now he had dead and dying men lying along the road leading to the battlefront, and hardly any decent medical staff to treat them. They were "ghastly in their unstudied positions," a correspondent for *Harper's* magazine reported, "men dying, men wounded, passing back to the division hospital, some being carried, some limping, some sitting by the roadside, all strangely silent, bandaged and bloody. . . . The road was strewn with parts of clothes, blanket rolls, pieces of bacon, empty cans, cartridges. . . ." Roosevelt said that there were only twelve ambulances in the whole army and that conditions were so bad at the large field hospital in the rear "that as long as possible we kept all of our sick men in the regimental hospital at the front."

Shafter—malaria now added to all his other personal afflictions—called a council of war at 7 P.M. on July 2, the day after the fighting, and told his generals that maybe the American army ought to retreat. "I have been told by a great many this afternoon," he said, "that we cannot hold the position, and that it is absolutely necessary for us to retreat in order to save ourselves from being enfiladed by the Spanish lines and cut off from our supplies, as an attack by the Spanish with a few fresh troops would result in our utter defeat."

He worried constantly that Spanish reinforcements would soon be pouring into Santiago, though, in fact, only a few hundred actually got through. What he didn't seem to understand was that the Spaniards were in worse shape than the Americans. Their water supply had been cut off, and they were running short of food. General Linares had been severely wounded in the July 1 fighting, and morale among his soldiers was very low. There was no chance at all the Spaniards would make any kind of meaningful attack on the American lines.

Most of Shafter's generals voted against retreat, yet by now there was no fight left in the American army. The Americans had been brought to this point of desperation by seventeen hundred unhappy, sickly Spanish soldiers, who were inadequately led, foolishly positioned, and never properly supported by the big guns available to them.

Roosevelt was deeply concerned, too. In a letter to his friend Senator Lodge on July 3, he said: "Tell the President for heaven's sake to send us every regiment and above all every battery possible. We have won so far at a heavy cost; but the Spaniards fight very hard and we are within measurable distance of a terrible military disaster. We *must* have help—thousands of men, batteries, and *food* and ammunition."

Shafter, now the very embodiment of a defeated general, cabled Washington that he was "seriously considering withdrawing about five miles and taking up a new position on the high ground between the San Juan River and Siboney . . . so as to get to our supplies . . . " Washington was aghast: this would be political dynamite, and so McKinley and Alger urged their wobbly commander to do all he could to hold the San Juan Heights, because "the effect upon the country would be much better than falling back." They told him help was on the way, and General Miles himself, the commanding general, said he was coming to lend a hand.

Shafter suddenly remembered the navy, and urged Sampson to attack the forts and force his way into the harbor, "to avoid future losses among my men." But Sampson was having none of that; he was still worried about the mines in the narrow channel leading into the city.

The Americans finally got lucky on Sunday, July 3.

The day began with Colonel McClernand suggesting to the tired old general, stretched out on his cot, that he "demand" a Spanish surrender, or else all hell would break loose. "Well," said Shafter, "try it."

Minutes later, at about 9 A.M. on this clear, hot, sunny day, Admiral Cervera led his little squadron—*Infanta Maria Teresa*, *Vizcaya*, *Cristóbal Colón*, and *Almirante Oquendo*, along with two destroyers, *Furor* and *Pluton*—out of the harbor in a desperate bolt for freedom. A melancholy man, he knew he had no chance to pull it off. Waiting for the Spaniards were four American battleships—*Indiana*, *Texas*, *Oregon*, and *Iowa*—along with the armored cruiser *Brooklyn* and a number of smaller ships.

In one of the most one-sided naval engagements in history—only one American, Chief Yeoman George W. Ellis of the *Brooklyn*, was killed—the Spanish squadron was destroyed, with 323 men dead and 151 wounded.

With the Spanish ships beached, in flames, there was now not much reason for the army to be besieging Santiago; destroying the naval squadron had been the whole point of the exercise. But it was too late to draw back. So the army dug in, and still, shamefully, necessary supplies failed to make their way to the front. "For one week," said Private Post, "nothing came through, aside from ammunition, but hardtack. And we lived on it. Then came a one-gallon can of tomatoes for each company . . . and then we went back to hardtack."

Richard Harding Davis said the worst problem of all was the lack of to-bacco—men craved it, in desperation, and for days none was available.

Some of the soldiers actually began to show signs of malnutrition—bloated bellies—and Private Post reported that "even on the short trip to the latrines and back, men would lie down to rest."

The negotiations with the new Spanish commander, General José Toral, seemed to go on endlessly. On July 8, he offered to evacuate Santiago if he and his army could march in safety to a Spanish-held position at a place called Holguín. Shafter was tempted to accept almost any offer that would get his army out of this pestilential place, but Washington told him nothing less than unconditional surrender would be permitted. The talks went on. By July 10, reinforcements had arrived and Sampson's ships had begun lobbing shells into the city. The deadlock was broken when Washington made a face-saving concession to the Spaniards: "Should the Spaniards surrender unconditionally and wish to return to Spain, they will be sent back direct at the expense of the United States Government."

The articles of capitulation were finally signed on July 16, with General Toral agreeing not only to the surrender of the garrison in Santiago, but all the other Spanish troops in eastern Cuba. The American flag was raised over the Spanish palace at noon on the seventeenth. It should have been poor Shafter's defining moment, and maybe it was, at least until he saw the *New York World*'s Sylvester Scovil shimmying up the roof so he could be prominently displayed in all the photographs of the momentous event. "Throw him off!" Shafter roared. Scovil climbed down, walked up to the elderly general, and tossed a punch at him. It was the last blow struck in the campaign, and it apparently missed.

The Spanish surrendered about 23,500 troops, 13,000 of them from garrisons outside Santiago. With them came 100 cannon, 6,800 shells, 15,000 pounds of smokeless powder, 25,114 rifles, and 5,279,000 rounds of small-arms ammunition.

By July 20, there were twenty thousand American soldiers camped in the hills around Santiago, and ships carrying supplies for them soon began arriving at the city's wharves. But for many of the Americans it was too late:

they were already sick. The army's doctors had worried most about the killer yellow fever, but what was destroying Shafter's army was malaria, often joined with dysentery.

The army's solution was to move units to a new location every two days. But this exhausted the already weary men, and made conditions worse. "Whenever we shifted camp," Roosevelt said, "the exertion among the half-sick caused our sick-roll to double the next morning, and it took at least three days, even when the shift was for but a short distance, before we were able to bring up the officers' luggage, the hospital spare food, the ammunition, etc."

Lice became a problem, and the biggest kind were named "Rough Riders." Land crabs crawled into the tents, and tarantulas sometimes showed up. Private Post speared one of the huge land crabs with his bayonet and took it home as a souvenir.

One of the camp songs went this way:

> Snakes as long as Halstead Street,
> Flies and skeeters that can't be beat.
> Oh, how we want to leave Cuba.
> Lord, how we want to go home!

Roosevelt said the army should have been pulled out of Cuba as soon as the capitulation was signed. To leave it in place was to invite its destruction. That led Roosevelt and the other officers to take matters into their own hands. They wrote a "round-robin" letter in which they pointed out the army's ragged condition. "This army must be moved at once or it will perish," the letter concluded. The letter was leaked to the Associated Press, and caused a furor when it was published by newspapers back home on August 4.

Washington had already ordered a withdrawal from Santiago, but the letter nudged the army into moving faster.

The Rough Riders, with their three mascots—Josephine, a mountain lion with an "infernal temper," Cuba, "a rather disreputable but exceedingly knowing little dog," and Teddy Roosevelt, a war eagle—arrived at their mustering-out camp, at Montauk Point, Long Island, on August 15. "Many of the men were very sick indeed," Roosevelt wrote. His orderly, Henry Bardshar, "was a wreck, literally at death's door. I was myself in first-class health, all the better for having lost 20 pounds."

The army sent to Cuba with such great expectations had ceased to exist as a fighting unit, but Teddy Roosevelt was a champion, "the most fa- mous man in America." Thomas Collier Platt, the Republican "Easy Boss" of New York State, knew he had a bull by the tail. "If he becomes gover- nor of New York," the Easy Boss said, "sooner or later, with his personali- ty, he will have to be President of the United States, [and] I am afraid to start that thing going."

But go it did. Colonel Roosevelt was elected governor of New York on November 7, 1898. He was forty years old, and, just as the Easy Boss had predicted, this was only the beginning.

◆

As president, Roosevelt gloried in his country's role as a world leader, building a battle fleet and sending it around the world as a symbol of Amer- ican strength. But in the long run the United States was never really hap- py as an imperial power. It gave Cuba its independence in 1902, while re- taining a naval base at Guantánamo Bay. Puerto Rico eventually became an American commonwealth, and by 1995 was still debating whether it wished to retain that status, become the fifty-first state, or go it alone as an independent nation. The Philippines was a more difficult problem. The insurrection continued there after the war was over, and it took two years for the Americans to put it down. The United States annexed the Philip- pines, paying Spain $2 million, with President McKinley promising "to up- lift and civilize and Christianize" the Filipinos. Annexation of the Philip- pines (combined with the annexation of Hawaii the same year) helped to make the United States a Pacific power. A battleground in World War II, the Philippines was given its independence in 1946.

Cuba, the first to be freed, managed to give the United States more trouble for more time than all the rest combined. The Communist Fidel Castro seized power at the height of the Cold War with the Soviet Union, and the Russians took the opportunity to try to sneak nuclear missiles into the island, "just 90 miles from the American mainland," setting off Presi- dent Kennedy's dramatic missile crisis. Kennedy won that one, but his administration had been embarrassed earlier when forces it had secretly supported failed in their effort to make a landing to overthrow Castro on the beaches at the Bay of Pigs in 1961. In the mid-nineties, the question of what to do with Cuba was still a significant issue in domestic American politics.

TEN

Major General Charles Vere Ferrers Townshend and the Mesopotamian Campaign in World War I (1915–1916)

He lied. He whined. He constantly maneuvered for promotion. He criticized his superiors behind their backs. He thought a lot more of his fox terrier, Spot, than he did of his manservant, Boggis. Major General Sir Charles Vere Ferrers Townshend was a louse.

His commanding officer, Lieutenant General Sir John Eccles Nixon, was an idiot.

Together, these two British generals—Townshend, the Man of Mesopotamia, and Nixon, the Baron of Baghdad—marched thousands of troops up the Tigris River in Mesopotamia in World War I into murderous battles against Germany's allies, the Turks, that never should have been fought at all.

Ultimately, Townshend and his expeditionary force of British and Indian regulars were forced to hunker down in a muddy, flyspecked Arab village named Kut el Amarah, while a relief force desperately tried to come to their rescue. They held out against an encircling Turkish army for 147 days before surrendering in one of the British army's most terrible disasters.

Townshend actually had known better. He didn't have enough troops to march on Baghdad; he didn't have enough ships to transport the troops he did have, and he had no ambulances, no hospital ships, and not nearly enough medical personnel. But, knowing all these things, he had marched anyway, never lodging a formal complaint, never demanding the help he needed. The bumbling Nixon should have stopped him, but he really didn't know any better. The people in Simla who ran the Indian Army—for this began as an Indian Army exercise—should have taken action, too, but the viceroy, Lord Hardinge, and the Indian Army's commander in chief, the elderly Sir Beauchamp Duff, really didn't want to help. With typical colonial myopia, they worried more about Afghans and the troubled Northwest Frontier, hoping World War I would simply go away.

London was diverted, too. The British had a war to fight in Europe, and at about the same time Townshend was taking his army up the Tigris, they were foolishly landing another British force against Turkey at a place called Gallipoli. No one at the time, it seems, thought the Turkish army would stand up to British steel.

Townshend was a serious student of military history, full of ideas about the "principle of economy of force" and the "principle of the mass" and "the adoption of the Napoleonic principles by Moltke." He would spell out his tactical and strategic views in an opening chapter in his two-volume, 719-page book, the egregious *My Campaign in Mesopotamia*, published in 1920.

And he had it right about Mesopotamia (the present-day Iraq): "I was always of the opinion that as Mesopotamia was a secondary Theatre of the War we should have held Basra and its province on the defensive by a disposition similar to the Manoeuvre of a Central Position. . . . I should have occupied the towns of Kurna [Al-Qurna] on the Tigris, in the bifurcation of the Tigris and the Euphrates, Nasiriyeh [An Nasiriya], and Ahwaz [Ahvāz] on the Karun River . . . with minimum forces strongly entrenched and with ammunition and provisions for six months." In short, he said, "in this way I should have secured Mesopotamia at a minimum cost to England, and in absolute security until such time as Government decided that I should take the offensive—preferably when the decisive offensive was assumed in the theatre in France—and gave me adequate forces to do so."

Precisely. The British army's original idea of sending a small force up the Persian Gulf and the Shatt-al-Arab to Basra was a good one. The goal was to protect the oil pipeline—owned by a British company—that ran from Persia down to Ābādān Island. The Royal Navy, switching over from coal, needed the oil to power its warships. That modest goal already had been accomplished, though with great loss, by Lieutenant General Sir Arthur Barrett within three months of the declaration of war against Turkey on November 5, 1914. With two Indian brigades and a handful of British regulars, he had worked his way slowly up the river, taking positions near Shaiba, below Basra.

But he had faced the kind of fight that should have been a warning to those who followed him. On April 14, 1915, Barrett was attacked by twenty thousand Arabs, Kurds, and Turks, along with fifteen to twenty mountain guns. His Sixth Division, wrote campaign historian Russell Braddon, "simply stood in its trenches and, on two consecutive moonless nights, allowed itself to be thrown into such confusion that one unit even fired on another." On the third day, Major General Sir Charles Melliss ordered his troops to attack. But many of the Indians troops in the Sixth Division were Muhammadans, and they had become increasingly worried about fighting a war on soil sacred to their religion. They advanced slowly, and reluctantly. It was the first sign of a problem that would plague the expedition until the end. It was a close, hard-fought battle, and it raged all day, with the Turks breaking off when they thought they saw reinforcements arriving. What they had seen, in fact, was the dust from carts and mules coming up to help carry away the dead and wounded.

"The loss of the British troops was very severe," said Townshend in his postwar history of the campaign, with ". . . 1,000 killed and wounded, including 18 officers killed and 42 wounded. The battle has often been described to me as a 'touch-and-go affair,' and Generals Melliss and [W. S.] Delamain both described it to me as a 'regular soldiers' battle."

Townshend had been at dinner at the Rawal Pindi Club early in April 1915 when he got the joyful news that he had been appointed to command the Sixth Division in Mesopotamia, in relief of General Barrett, who was ill.

An "implacable careerist," according to Braddon, Townshend had drifted from one post to another since joining the Royal Marines in 1884 at the age of twenty-three. He served with Sir Garnet Wolseley's Camel Corps in the Sudan the next year, and was at Abu Klea when the dervishes broke a British square.

He was the son of a railway clerk; his mother came from Australia, without a dowry; his immediate family was poor. But his father's first cousin was a marquis, a peer of the realm, and young Charlie was descended from the Townshend who took command at Quebec following Wolfe's death. The family owned two great estates, Raynham Hall in Norfolk and Balls Park near Hertford. They had to sell off Balls Park (along with a number of paintings in it—by Reynolds, Lely, Kneller, and Romney, among others—as well as most of the flat silver at Raynham Hall) to pay the bills. The old marquis's only son had no children, and Townshend hoped it would stay that way, for it put him in line to take over both the estate and the title.

In his bachelor days, Charlie Townshend was something of a playboy. He hung around music halls, and escorted ladies of the stage to night clubs. He played a banjo himself, and had an extensive repertoire of bawdy songs, some of them unfit even for the London stage. He didn't marry until he was thirty-four, but it was a good choice. He wooed and won Alice, daughter of the Count and Countess Cahen d'Anvers, who maintained a luxurious estate, the Château de Champs, outside Paris. He and Alice had one child, a daughter, Audrey.

He constantly appealed to his friends and relations, especially the marchioness, the Lady Anne, to use their influence to help him win promotion or to be transferred to other regiments. "Anybody who could further his career was invariably called up to help, often in the most pleading terms," wrote Townshend's biographer, A. J. Barker.

He transferred from the marines to the Indian Army in 1886 and finally made his mark in 1895 in a mountain campaign against Hunza tribesmen on the Northwest Frontier when, with four hundred men, he withstood a siege in a primitive fort in Chitral for forty-six days. He was relieved by Captain Fenton Aylmer, who, as a lieutenant general, would be told to lift the siege at Kut twenty-two years later, and save Townshend again. As we'll see, it didn't work the second time around; and Aylmer, after losing thousands of men trying to break through the Turkish trenches to the besieged garrison, must have cursed the day his and Townshend's paths had crossed.

But until 1915, Townshend had never commanded anything as large as a division in combat. As he made his way to his new post in a small mail steamer called the *Dwarka*, his thoughts turned to Belisarius, "the Roman general who gave a last flicker of glory to the expiring Eastern Empire," partially retaking Mesopotamia in A.D. 541. "Who knows," he wrote in his diary, "that I shall not eventually become governor of Mesopotamia?"

He arrived in Basra several days after the battle with the ragtag Arab-Turkish army had ended and sat down for the first time with General Nixon, commanding Expeditionary Force D, which consisted of both Barrett's old division, the Sixth, and Major General Sir George Gorringe's division, the Twelfth. There he learned, for the first time, that he and the Sixth Division had been chosen to "drive the Turks away from their position north of Kurna [Al-Qurna], push northward 90 miles, and occupy Amarah [Amara], a very important town."

Amarah was halfway to Baghdad. This flew in the face of all of Townshend's precious principles. Expeditionary Force D, wrote Ronald Millar, another campaign historian, "was in no condition for a prolonged overseas campaign. . . . The shortage of artillery was acute; there were no heavy guns; although a plan to form an air corps had been approved shortly before the outbreak of war, nothing had yet been done about it. Other deficiencies included such items as wire-cutters, telephones, transport for drinking water, Very lights, signal rockets, tents, mosquito nets, sun-helmets, periscopes, telescopic sights, loophole plates, flares, hand grenades and even blankets and clothing."

But worst of all were the medical arrangements. "There was a lack of drugs, dressings, and splints for broken limbs," wrote Millar. "There was not one hospital ship available for service in Mesopotamia." There were no nurses and not many doctors, and no ice and no electric fans. And when soldiers wrote home to complain about their treatment, their letters were censored. From beginning to end, the generals in command refused to admit there was anything wrong with the medical care being given to their men, and even rejected offers of medical assistance.

Townshend said nary a word. He moved into a comfortable home owned by a Greek merchant, Mr. Antipas, and began to take a look at his troops. He liked the Dorsets and the Oxford and Buckinghamshire Light Infantry and thought the Twenty-second Punjabis appeared especially fit. Then he rode a steam launch upriver to Al-Qurna and clambered up an observation tower, "a rickety structure of wooden scaffolding, like a lighthouse on sands," to get his first look at the enemy.

Floods had overflowed the Tigris, "giving the landscape the air of Lakes Superior or Michigan in the United States. Sand-hill islands appeared in these waters. They were Turkish redoubts." He was not encouraged. "In fact," he wrote, "I had reason to think that Wolfe's job at Quebec was a fool to mine."

He had hoped to employ the Principle of the Principal Mass "in a turning movement against the redoubts from the westward," but the ground was under water. That suggested a frontal attack, "the most unsatisfactory and costly manner of attack," and he wasn't prepared for that at all.

"I saw I was committed," he said, "to a peculiarly difficult operation, with an unknown command under me. It seemed to me that the betting was well in favor of the Turks; and I am quite certain that, if I had been in the position of the Turkish general, I should have inflicted a bloody defeat on the British."

He complained—in his book, after the campaign was over—that he had needed more sapper companies, that he had wanted his signal company returned to his command. He complained that one brigade was being forced to garrison a fort. He complained that the "three trans-Border Pathan companies" in the Indian regiments were disaffected. "All the mistakes and errors of our maritime expeditions during the 18th and early part of the 19th Centuries are here repeated with interest. Even Bonaparte could not have succeeded with methods like this. . . . Truly a heart-breaking affair for one imbued with the importance of the Principle of Force!"

And he started criticizing Nixon, for whom a great deal of criticism was surely deserved. Townshend, Braddon wrote, was "in the habit of criticizing his superiors—had done so in the Sudan, in Chitral, in the Royal Fusiliers, and lately in India—so it is perhaps not surprising to find him, within four days of meeting his new commander, indulging the habit again. . . ."

But he never suggested the job couldn't be done. It was going to be an unusual battle, he figured. "The leading feature . . . was that the infantry must advance in boats, and the only boats available at Basra were the Arab 'bellums,' or 'balams,' on each of which a crew of one NCO and 9 men could be placed." He ordered up 328 for the brigade, the Seventeenth, that would use them in the attack. He ordered the troops to start training in the polling of these bellums, "which is practically the same as punting on the Thames." The idea was to launch the bellums across the marsh to attack the Turkish position upriver.

A full-dress rehearsal took place on May 28. Some of the boats, at General Nixon's insistence, were protected with armored plates. It worked in theory; in practice, the plates, flopping over the gunwales, got tangled in the reeds. Machine guns and mountain artillery were mounted on specially constructed armored rafts, and were added to this curious flotilla.

He climbed up the rickety observation tower again on May 30, "and saw a great sea with small yellow islands here and there, which were redoubts occupied by the Turks. I could see other redoubts at Bahran, men moving about, and the masts of the dhows at Maziblah . . . My attack," he said, ". . . was ripe for defeat." He confessed his doubts that night to his manservant, Whitmore, "who had been with me 14 years. He replied, 'It's all right, sir; you'll have the Townshend luck all right!'" Not so poor Whitmore; he died a few days later, from illness, and was replaced by J. Boggis, a twenty-three-year-old infantryman from the Norfolk Regiment who had worked as a boy at Raynham Hall, the family seat in Norfolk.

He made HMS *Espiegle*, a fifty-year-old sloop originally built to suppress the slave trade in West Africa, his headquarters. The *Espiegle* was part of a small navy squadron that also included two other sloops, *Odin* and *Clio*, and the armed tugs *Shaitan* and *Lewis Pelly*.

The attack began, on time, at dawn on May 31. As Townshend recalled, "Our heavy guns at Kurna began their bombardment of the Turkish curtain position" in support of the Seventeenth Infantry Brigade, "which now set off in its bellums—and an extraordinary sight it was." But the Turks hardly responded, and when the bellums arrived at the Turkish trenches, they discovered the reason why: the artillery barrage had taken a terrible toll. With no supporting timber, the shallow trenches had collapsed, and were now filled with the dead and the dying.

The dreaded Turkish mines hadn't done their job, either. These weren't contact mines, the British discovered, but mines set off electrically from a master keyboard. They found the keyboard "on a little sand island about 20 yards square," and with it an elderly Turkish officer, a kind of naval Wizard of Oz, furiously pumping away at the keyboard but getting absolutely no result. He was taken aboard *Lewis Pelly* where, with what Townshend called "quiet cheerfulness," he proceeded to "point out all the mines remaining in the river."

Townshend and his soggy expedition set off the next morning, expecting to encounter tougher opposition. But a Royal Flying Corps plane—one of three that had arrived in Basra the day before—dropped a canister with a message inside. "Bahran abandoned," it said.

With the Turks in flight, Townshend opened what the troops laughingly called "Regatta Week." It now became, Townshend wrote, "a question of a vigorous and rapid pursuit by the naval flotilla on Amarah." General Nixon—he seems more often than not to make an appearance at the front just as a battle has ended, or just as one is about to begin—made an appearance now, and he approved the rapid movement upriver. With *Shaitan* in the lead, followed by *Espiegle*, *Clio*, and *Odin*, the steam-powered sloops, and *Lewis Pelly* and *Shaitan*, the armored tugs, Townshend took up the pursuit. By evening, after shelling, but not stopping, two retreating Turkish vessels, *Mosul* and *Marmarice*, the flotilla closed in on the blue dome of Ezra's Tomb, twenty miles upriver from Bahran. Townshend was now properly in a positive frame of mind; he pushed on in *Espiegle* at 2 A.M., as the moon came up, accompanied by only two staff officers.

This was the most fun—maybe the only fun—Townshend had in the entire campaign. *Espiegle* was 150 feet long, drawing 9 feet of water, and she was steered, Townshend said, "by the old-fashioned hand wheel between decks," so that the navigating officer on the bridge had to shout instructions down to the helmsman below, out of sight. The result was that *Espiegle* frequently ran aground. Townshend thought the sloops were a grand sight anyway. "They must have made a great impression on the Arabs," he reckoned.

Townshend didn't like Arabs much. When he and *Espiegle* came alongside two abandoned Turkish lighters full of rifle ammunition and equipment, they found Arabs busily at work. "The Arabs from the marshes, who are well armed with rifles and known as great scoundrels and even murderers, had been busy looting rifles and ammunition out of the lighters before we arrived," he said. They were chased away. These marsh Arabs resented the Turkish occupation of their homeland, and some British intelligence officers—T. E. Lawrence, among them—thought that if properly handled they could be recruited for the Allied cause. But men such as Townshend and Nixon, deeply distrustful, weren't interested in such an accommodation. They called the marsh Arabs, derisively, the "Salvation Army."

To speed up the pursuit, Townshend abandoned *Espiegle* and joined a new addition to the flotilla, the armed dispatch steamer *Comet*, and continued the hunt. By 3:20 P.M., little *Comet* was at Kila Salih, chasing off a few cavalrymen with her twelve-pounder. "Kila Salih," said Townshend, "seemed a town as large as Kurna. There was a great display of white flags on all the houses . . . " When the local sheik came on board, Townshend told him that fifteen thousand troops were close behind. The sheik passed the misinformation on to the Turkish commanders, just as Townshend had hoped he would.

At 5 A.M. on June 3, Townshend was underway again, halting briefly at Abu Sidrah to think things over. His instincts told him that he had come far enough; his naval commander, a Captain Nunn, "as is the way with sailors," said go for it. He went for it. With *Shaitan* in the lead, followed by *Comet, Samana*, a launch, and *Lewis Pelly*, and three 4.7-inch guns towed in horse boats, he set off for Amarah, the most important town—population, 20,000—in Mesopotamia between Baghdad and the Persian Gulf.

At 1:30 P.M., Townshend wrote, "I was alongside the custom house at Amarah, where the Turkish commander in the battle at Kurna, Halim Bey, the governor of Amarah, Aziz Bey, three or four colonels and some 30 or 40 officers came on board to surrender." Ready to lay down their arms, too, he was told, were Turkish *pompiers* from Constantinople, a whole battalion of them. (Pompiers were actually firefighters, but they had been sent to Halim Bey in desperation.) Two naval officers from the *Comet* and a British soldier from the Dorsets took their surrender "and marched them down to the quay and [put] them on board one of the big lighters there. . . ."

The campaign was an extraordinary success, and Townshend can be excused for boasting he pulled it off with twenty-five British soldiers and sailors. In celebration, he seized an immense Persian carpet in the custom house, ordered a dozen Arabs to clean it and roll it up, and shipped it home as a trophy. General Nixon, right on schedule, showed up in Amarah when it was safely secured, and tendered his congratulations. He also ordered Townshend to advance on a town called Kut el Amarah, which he had concluded, for reasons of his own, possessed important strategic considerations.

Nixon's headquarters staff believed that Townshend was opposed by two battalions of Turkish regulars, four dispirited Turkish battalions that had fought at Shaiba, two reserve battalions, two newly raised battalions of "inferior material," and the remnants of several other units. Together, intelligence had concluded, "these forces were not sufficiently numerous to be formidable," and it was unlikely that reinforcements could be sent from Anatolia or the Caucasus to arrive in time.

Like so many of his troops, Townshend fell victim to vomiting and diarrhea, and was shipped to Bombay to recover. Al-Qurna was supposed to have been the Garden of Eden; Amarah had been the Garden of Tears, the place where Adam and Eve bid farewell to Eden. No wonder; it was a very unhealthy place, "a thief-ridden incubator of dysentery, sunstroke, malaria and paratyphoid," as Braddon described it. Once again, the hospital couldn't begin to handle all of the sick.

The idiotic Nixon still hadn't provided hospital ships or ambulances or nurses or ice and electric fans. He still had artillery for only one of his two divisions, Braddon noted, still had no wharves at Basra, still had only three airplanes, and still was deficient in all those things he had been deficient in right from the start. He hadn't even asked for them. Yet, on April 11, he had signaled his superiors at Simla, the Indian Army headquarters, that Townshend was continuing his advance, and Simla had replied that "all advantages . . . point to as early a move on Baghdad as possible."

While he was recuperating in India, Townshend wrote a letter to a friend at the War Office in London, in which he made perfect sense. "We have certainly not good enough troops to make *certain* of taking Baghdad, which I fear is being fortified. . . ." He said a retreat from Baghdad would mean an "instant rising of the Arabs of the whole country behind us," and possible problems with the Afghans and Persians as well. In conclusion, he said: "We ought to hold what we have got and not advance any more. . . . All these offensive operations in secondary theatres are dreadful errors in strategy: the Dardanelles, Egypt, Mesopotamia, East Africa!" They violated, he said, one of his fundamental principles of war, the Economy of Force.

He wrote a revealing letter about the same time to his wife. "I told you, darling," he said, "that I only wanted my chance! You should have seen the British and Indian soldiers cheering me as I stood on the *Comet*. I must have the gift of making men (I mean the soldier men) love me and follow me. I have only known the 6th Division for six months, and they'd storm the gates of hell if I told them to. . . ."

To secure Townshend's flank, Nixon had ordered Gorringe's Twelfth Division to seize An Nasiriya, west of Al-Qurna on the Euphrates River. The fighting was unexpectedly ferocious, as a new Turkish commander, Nureddin, took charge, but An Nasiriya fell on July 12. The Turks then retreated toward Kut.

Nureddin, Townshend said, came to the Tigris front with a reputation as "an up-to-date general." He also brought with him the first real Turkish fighting men, the soldiers from Anatolia, and they were the finest trench-digging defensive troops in the world. British troops, watching their spades fly, became convinced they had unusually powerful knees. Ominous, too, was the arrival of a German field marshal, Colmar von der Goltz, author of *Das Volk in Waffen* (The nation in arms), in which he described total, all-encompassing warfare; Townshend considered him to be one of the finest military thinkers in the world. Von der Goltz would soon command all the Turkish forces in Mesopotamia.

Townshend, refreshed—he said he had an "operation" to reduce the fever—was back in Basra the first week in August, ready to take his army to those gates of hell he had talked about in his letter to Alice. It was just seventeen days after he had told his friend in London that the whole business was a huge mistake.

Nixon's position was understandable. He was a fool, and he continued to believe the Turk wouldn't fight, and that marching on Baghdad would turn out to be a riverside stroll. But Townshend knew better. So why did he do it? Ambition, concluded Braddon. Ambition to the point of egomania. What he wanted was a corps; commanding a corps meant promotion to lieutenant general. And if he slogged on towards Baghdad, or even took it, a new division would be his, and so would the promotion.

Perhaps so; the argument makes some sense. But there must have been more to it than that. Perhaps, for all his talk of defeat, he really believed he was invincible. Contemporaries noted that he revered the French commander, Marshal Foch, and sometimes he seemed to think he was Napoléon. His officers called him "Alphonse," because they thought he was so Frenchified (and, of course, his wife was French, and he lived part of the time with her family in France). They even felt he had developed "some of the quirks and mannerisms of the First Consul," according to the campaign historian Millar. So, if Napoléon could march on Moscow, surely Townshend could march on Baghdad. It's a possibility.

"Your mission," he was told on August 23, "is the destruction and dispersal of the enemy," along with the occupation of Kut. He responded that if he routed the Turks, "and stampeded them, as at Kurna," he was "willing to take the responsibility of entering Baghdad." This, of course, was madness. He had no way to maintain a five-hundred-mile-long line of communications; he didn't have enough ships or carts—he admitted being "undermanned as regards land and water transport." And yet he could joke about it. "Sir John Nixon," he wrote, "told me to send him a wire if I intended a rush into Baghdad, as he might be able to come on in time to enter Baghdad with me." Typical Nixon.

Like Napoléon, Frederick the Great, and Moltke, Townshend said, he was prepared to use the Principle of the Principal Mass against the enemy's weakest point. Nureddin, he had been told, was digging in with seven to eight thousand Turkish infantrymen and about three thousand Arab horsemen, on both sides of the Tigris, with a boat bridge connecting his two positions, at a place called Essinn, just below Kut.

Townshend decided to attack the enemy's defenses closest to the left bank—Nureddin's strongest point—with Minimum Force (Column B), and then circle around and fall on the weaker point, the defenses farthest from the left bank, with his Principal Mass (Column A). (Left bank or west bank were used to describe locations, instead of compass positions, because the river twisted and turned so often. Left bank and right bank refer to the situation when looking downstream.) But turning movements, Townshend conceded, can be difficult, and this one turned out to be very difficult. While the Minimum Force launched its diversionary attack, most of the Principal Mass, under a General Hoghton, got lost in the desert. General Delamain, with the smaller piece of the column, attacked the Turkish lines with two battalions, the Dorsets and the 117th Mahrattas. "The whole point of the Mass on the enemy's weakest point was thus lost," Townshend admitted, "and it went near to costing us the battle."

But Hoghton, wandering in the wilderness, saved the day. When the sun came up, on their left hand, he and his command figured out they were marching south. "Blimey," Braddon reported a Cockney saying, "we're lost!" They plodded on until they saw what might have been a mirage—mirages were always causing problems—but in fact it was the main Turkish entrenchments. "They were coming on Johnny Turk, from behind," wrote Braddon. They carried Nureddin's communications trenches, routing his cooks and servants, and then fell on the Turkish firing line, while poor Johnny Turk was looking the wrong way. "Stick and jink," said Braddon, "pitchfork, jump and run out."

It was hot work, and the troops were so exhausted when the Turks began their retreat that they were unable to pursue them. Townshend never did find out what happened to his cavalry. Mostly from India, they more or less disappeared, upset because they were being forced to eat from Arab cooking pots. All in all, said Townshend, "it was a terrible disappointment to me"; made worse, perhaps, by the fact that Nixon actually had shown up and watched the whole thing from that rickety observation tower. "They'll go in the night," Townshend told Nixon. And, sure enough, the next morning they were gone. But it had been a costly battle—1,229 killed and wounded. The wounded were carried from the field on carts without springs and put aboard barges with iron decks. They had almost no water and very little medical treatment, and "they lay," Braddon wrote, "in a mass of their own blood and excreta, assailed by millions of flies. Quite unnecessarily, many of them died." Their broken limbs were often splinted with wood strips from Johnny Walker whiskey boxes, one medical officer reported.

King George V actually worried about them. "I trust," he said in a telegram to Nixon, "the sick and wounded are doing well." Nixon replied: "Sick and wounded well and it is hoped many will be back in the ranks shortly. Spirit of troops splendid."

"The Battle of Kut-el-Amara can be said to have been one of the most important in the history of the British Army in India," Townshend boasted.

But he also thought enough was enough. "It seemed to me," he wrote, "that it was useless to continue the pursuit any longer, so I decided to halt . . . and to report to Sir John Nixon, who was at Kut, that in my opinion we ought to return to that place and consolidate." He said, slyly, that if Nixon thought he should continue to advance, he should be given "two divisions, or one Army corps." And a promotion. But he didn't press his opinion. After all, he concluded, he was a "subordinate general," who could do no more than point out to his superior officer the "rashness" of the enterprise. Nixon wasn't moved; he cabled London that he thought Townshend's army was still strong enough to open the road to Baghdad, and he told Townshend that Nureddin was down to four thousand bayonets, five hundred sabers, and twenty guns, and that his force was inferior in both moral and physical strength to Townshend's. "It seemed to me," said Townshend, "it was useless to argue any longer."

Problems began multiplying. The river was now too shallow for some of the ships in his little flotilla, and he would have to do without them. And his Indian troops were murmuring about fighting a battle on or near the tomb of Suliman Pak, the Prophet's barber. Townshend was forced to send one entire battalion of transborder men back to Basra, "owing to numerous cases of desertion to the enemy." To bring up supplies, Townshend relied heavily on Arab *mahelas*, great ungainly sailing vessels with huge triangular sails. Sometimes, when the wind was wrong, they sailed backwards. They were very slow. Maddening problems, too. "I made repeated efforts to induce Headquarters to send back to my battalions the scores of British soldiers, of the Norfolks, Dorsets, and Oxfords, who were employed in every imaginable kind of billet in Basra—as police in the city, extra clerks, batmen for officers (including officers of the Indian Army, who are not entitled to British soldiers as servants) . . . , all taken from the bayonets of my division." Nixon would have none of it. Townshend marched into battle with fourteen thousand troops, of which only eighty-five hundred were infantry.

Nureddin, digging deep in the shadow of Ctesiphon's great arch, near Suliman Pak's tomb, wasn't brimming with confidence either. Two of his divisions, the Thirty-fifth and the Thirty-eighth, had been cut up badly at Kut. Millar, in his dependable book, *Death of an Army*, which picks up the story at this point in the campaign, reported that Nureddin had two new divisions, the Forty-fifth and the Fifty-first, and worried if they would be enough. All together, he could put eighteen thousand infantrymen, fifty-three cannon, and nineteen machine guns in the field, along with several thousand camel-mounted Arabs commanded by Turkish officers called out of retirement.

He couldn't tell how strong Townshend was because he didn't have a single airplane in all of Mesopotamia to reconnoiter. He had trouble with his telephone cable, too; as soon as his troops would put it down, the Arabs would pick it up and sell it as salvage.

At Kut, Townshend had formed two columns. For Ctesiphon—the Tommies, naturally, called it "Pissed-upon"—he formed four: A, under Delamain, with the Dorsets, the 104th Rifles, and the Thirtieth Composite Brigade with two companies of Gurkhas; B, under Hamilton with the Norfolks, the Seventh Rajputs, and the 110th Mahrattas; C, under Hoghton, with the Oxfords, the Twenty-second Punjabis, the 103rd Mahrattas, and the 119th Infantry; and a flying cavalry column, under Melliss, with the Seventh Lancers, the Sixteenth and Thirty-third Cavalry, and the celebrated S battery of the Royal Horse Artillery. It also included two armored cars and two trucks, making their first appearance in Mesopotamia. Townshend expected the flying column to lead the way into Baghdad, after the battle was won.

The reduced naval flotilla consisted of the gunboats *Firefly* (brand new), *Comet*, *Shaitan*, and *Samana*, along with two towing barges mounted with big guns. The flying corps was down to three airplanes—a converted Short seaplane, a Maurice Farman, and a B.E.2c biplane flown by Major H. L. Reilly, who Townshend called a "brilliant" officer. Flying back to his own lines on the eve of battle, he was hit by ground fire. He landed safely, and had walked three miles, reported Millar, "when the Arabs captured him." That left two planes.

Townshend said that he hoped by means of a turning movement with the Principal Mass "either to throw the Turks into the Tigris or to compel them to a disastrous flight across the Diala river, some six miles behind them."

It was the Principle of the Principal Mass on Nureddin's weakest point all over again. This time, the wayward Hoghton would pin down the Turkish right flank while Columns A and B, the Principal Mass, attacked the left flank. Melliss's flying column would maneuver on the exterior flank of the Principal Mass and eventually come "down like a thunderbolt" on the enemy's rear.

The night before the battle was cold, and Spot, the general's fox terrier, snuggled up to Boggis, the general's manservant. When Townshend found them asleep, he began screaming. Boggis awoke to find the general thrashing the poor dog. "What are you doing that for, sir?" Boggis asked. "He was sleeping with you!" Townshend bellowed. "He's *my* dog and he's got to learn." Townshend was a "harsh bastard," Boggis told Braddon years later.

Hoghton's column led off the attack at dawn on November 22, 1915. The ground was heavy with mist, but this time Hoghton could figure out where he was; rising out of the mist was the great arch. He aimed straight for it. But by 8 A.M., he still had not drawn any enemy fire, and so he sent an officer and three men forward to see if anybody was there. They were killed instantly, reported Millar, "as the enemy's machine guns opened up." Hoghton, completely exposed, ordered his soldiers to dig in.

It was at about this point that reports began circulating—no one knows how they started—that the Turks were in a general retreat. Delamain asked if he could take Column A forward in the direction of a strongly held Turkish position called V.P., for Vital Point, and Townshend agreed. The general—he was unquestionably a brave man—then galloped across two miles of open desert, under constant sniper fire, to take up his new head-quarters near V.P. At the same time, Hoghton resumed his advance, too, and was soon being cut apart by Turkish gunners, who hadn't retreated af-ter all. But it was even worse for Delamain. He ordered his reserves to help Hoghton capture the last of the Turkish positions. "The Oxfords," Millar wrote, probably meaning the Dorsets, "rose from their shallow ditch and charging over the last hundred yards clambered through the wire and captured 'Water Redoubt' but not without grievous losses." Colonel S. H. Climo, commanding the Thirtieth Brigade, finally captured V.P., and most of the Turks began falling back to their second line of entrenchments.

By 1:30, "the whole Turkish front line was in British hands," Millar said, but the Turks were still in the field, and beginning to counterattack with fresh troops. Townshend, now watching the battle from V.P. itself, ordered Delamain to advance with as many troops as he could collect—including orderlies, cooks, and sappers. "In all my experience of war," Townshend recalled, "I have never seen or heard of anything so fine as the deliberate and tranquil advance of the thin chain of Dorsets in extended order . . . making their way towards the Arch of Ctesiphon." Now, Townshend felt, was the moment for the little navy flotilla to show up, and begin shelling the Turkish defenders. But the gunboats were pinned down by enemy guns themselves. "I have no doubt that the difficulties to be overcome were too serious to permit their advance on this occasion," Townshend said, oozing insincerity.

With the battle raging around him, Braddon wrote, Townshend turned to Boggis, and said, quietly, "A change of clothing."

"*Now*, sir?"

"I always change at this time."

And so poor Boggis ran and scrambled a mile or more across a battle-field to the river, picked out the general's new clothes, and made his way back. Townshend stripped off his old uniform, stood naked in the heat, smoke, and dust, and then put on "a silk vest, silk underpants, a khaki shirt, his breeches, boots and sunhelmet, and, picking up his binoculars, eating a piece of plum cake passed to him by a junior staff officer, resumed his inspection of the battle." Townshend was a rare one, right enough.

At least Nixon had shown up, and presumably he had a chance to watch this extraordinary performance. Townshend reassured him that "everything was going well." But everything wasn't going well. The Dorsets were taking a terrible beating, Hoghton was having a bad time, and even Melliss's cavalry was being pressed hard by fresh troops reaching the field under a new Turkish general, Khalil Pasha, described by Townshend as a "thrusting commander." Khalil's arrival "saved Nureddin from defeat," Townshend concluded, "and the Turks now took the counter-offensive in an attempt to throw the British out of the second position, in which our troops were now installing themselves." Townshend wailed that if he had just had "the extra division that I needed—[or] even *another brigade*—we should have swept the Turks into the Tigris. It was hard to stand there and realize that the victory was slipping away from my grasp for want of a few troops."

The Indian troops, he charged, led a withdrawal he had never ordered. The problem, he believed, was that so many of their British officers had been killed or wounded that they didn't know what to do. Townshend pulled the survivors together at V.P., and began reorganizing his shattered troops for a renewed attack the next morning. "If I live a hundred years," Townshend said, "I shall not forget that night bivouac at V.P., amongst hundreds of wounded, who were being brought in, loaded on the commissariat carts, by which they were collected for hours during the night. Their suffering in these small, springless carts can be easily imagined; but the way in which our medical officers worked is beyond all praise." To have allowed this sort of thing to happen in the first place was, of course, beyond belief.

Nureddin was having problems of his own, though news of his losses was slow coming in. It wasn't until midday, for example, that he learned that his Forty-fifth Division had been virtually wiped out. He would have known about it earlier if Arab cavalrymen hadn't stolen his copper telephone cable and rode off with it. His losses the first day totaled nine thousand men—but, of course, with his reinforcements, he could afford to lose more men.

Just as Townshend anticipated, Nureddin fell back during the night, leaving the bloody battlefield to the British. Townshend knew that to reach Baghdad, he should now transfer his force to the right bank of the Tigris, forcing the Turks to fall back on the city. "But daylight on 23d November convinced me still more with the conviction of the hopelessness of resuming the offensive." The Turks, he had finally concluded, were too strong for him to move against Baghdad. He shifted his position slightly to the south, not two thousand yards from the great Arch, and just ahead of what he called the "High Walls" of Ctesiphon. This battle was being fought, in fact, on top of the ruins of the capital of the Parthian kings.

The next day, starting about 4 P.M., while Townshend was still trying to remove his wounded from V.P., the Turks resumed their attack. Hoghton, in command at V.P., held on, repulsing wave after wave of Turkish soldiers. The attack continued all along the line, and reached a frenzy at a mound south of Water Redoubt, defended by three hundred Gurkhas and a hundred Punjabis. Muhammad Amin, one of Nureddin's staff officers, wrote later that this "brave and determined little force" held off an entire Turkish division. Not only did they hold them off, but in the end they "drove back the thousands of riflemen of the 35th Division to the second line of defense." Townshend, quick enough to criticize the performance of his Indian troops, made no reference to this gallant action in his journal.

The fighting began to subside about 2 A.M. as Nureddin ordered the second withdrawal of his troops. It had been a close call for Townshend, and luck surely played a part in it, for the better part of one Turkish division, the Fifty-first, never arrived on the battlefield. Like Hoghton's column earlier, it lost its way in the desert.

"When the morning of 24th November came there was no enemy in sight," Townshend noted. He made his way back to the High Walls to talk to General Nixon, but the commander in chief and his staff had all left for Kut. What Nixon thought now about the qualities of the Turkish soldier is not recorded. But Townshend had come around. "There is *no soldier in Europe*—I underline that statement—to compare with the Turk when on the defensive and entrenched," he wrote. "They dig in as quickly as moles." As it turned out, Johnny Turk hadn't done so badly on the offensive, either.

Townshend knew it was useless to go forward, so he began a withdrawal. The retreat got underway at 2 P.M. on the twenty-sixth, in good order. He was abandoning the battlefield to the enemy, and by his own definition of success or failure, that spelled failure. He was heading south, and the Turks were in pursuit. The fabled Townshend luck had expired amid those ancient ruins.

The army fell back on a village called Llaj, where Townshend said he would pause to eat up his supplies. What supplies? There's no evidence he had any supplies at Llaj. Braddon concluded that Townshend was now a changed man, and had been ever since he returned from sick leave in India. "After Ctesiphon," he wrote, "in his telegrams, communiques, diaries and autobiography, he reveals himself as a man whose mind was governed almost entirely by wishful thinking."

And what made him think he had time to pause? Aerial reconnaissance showed Nureddin was hot on his trail, with as many as twelve thousand infantrymen. Townshend had once talked about regrouping at Al-'Aziziya, gathering his reinforcements, and resuming the attack on Baghdad. Now he talked about falling back on Kut, "a strategical point we are bound to defend."

But on December 1, before they could rest, Townshend's weary warriors had to fight one more battle at another little village, called Umm al-Tubul (the Mother of Tombs). With the help of extraordinarily accurate shooting by the artillery's eighteen-pounders—"What a splendid gun is our 18-pounder field-gun!" burbled Townshend—and the timely arrival of reinforcements, the Fourteenth Hussars and the Second Queen's Own West Kent Regiment, Nureddin was turned back with heavy losses. Muhammad Amin, the Turkish staff officer, said that the shelling "totally disorganized" the entire Thirteenth Army Corps, and that there was a chance the British could have "taken prisoner the whole three Turkish divisions" had they chosen to continue the fight.

Townshend thought about it, briefly, and then ordered his army to continue the retreat. Perhaps he was upset by the loss of *Firefly* and little *Comet* to Turkish gunfire and the capture of a barge loaded with three hundred or more of his wounded soldiers. Perhaps he was disturbed by Nixon's offer to loan him the services of his own chief of staff, Major General Sir George Kemball. "He is only a little junior in rank to me," Townshend wrote. "In what capacity does Kemball come to me?" He decided he didn't need another general also in line for promotion. "Townshend was never one to take second place," wrote Barker.

Why did he want to stop at Kut? He had never thought Kut so important before; that was Nixon's thinking. "He had begun to remember Chitral," Braddon concluded, referring to the fort where Townshend had withstood a siege for forty-six days on the Northwest Frontier. Millar, the other campaign historian, wasn't so sure. Maybe it was a good idea, because by digging in at Kut Townshend "would block the advance of the Turkish army as it was as dependent upon the river for transport supplies as was Townshend." A. J. Barker, Townshend's biographer, who did what he could to be fair to the man, shared Millar's view.

But that's not why Townshend said he was going to hunker down at Kut. He said he had no other choice because his troops were too exhausted to keep marching. Delamain, one of his own commanders, said that was patently untrue; his troops could have resumed marching the day after arriving at Kut. Edward O. Mousley, a young artillery officer, joined Townshend's army a few days after the battle at Ctesiphon, and he wrote in his diary they seemed in pretty good spirits to him, too. "It was only the battered condition of the gun carriages, the gaping wounds in the diminished teams of horses, and that quiet 'balanced up' look in the eyes of every Tommy that told a reality more grim." Otherwise, he said, the troops went to work just as if they were on maneuvers.

The fact is, Townshend *wanted* to endure a siege at Kut. Chitral probably was part of his thinking; after all, his performance there earned him a brief flirtation with fame and glory. He was actually invited to Buckingham Palace. But he may have been thinking even more of another siege—Gordon's at Khartoum. As a young marine, he had been a part of the relief expedition; after it was over, and Gordon was hailed as a martyr, he saw an entire nation fall prostrate at the dead hero's feet. Needless to say, Townshend had no death wish, simply an obsessive ambition to be promoted and to be recognized as the great warrior he thought himself to be. What he wanted, and no one seems to have thought about this, was to be a live Gordon—to endure a heroic siege, be rescued by Nixon (or somebody), and go home to England in triumph. Unfortunately, the Turks had other ideas.

He and his weary Sixth Division marched into Kut the morning of December 3, to find that Nixon had already hightailed it south to Basra. Townshend thought of the words of Lord Bacon—"Honorable retreats are no ways inferior to brave charges . . ."—and then he cabled Nixon he would go no further.

"Reinforcements will be pushed up to you with every possible speed," Nixon replied. But it would be 147 days before the Kut garrison marched out, as frail, sick, hungry prisoners of war.

Kut was an Arab town with a population of about six thousand nestled in the southwest corner of a little peninsula formed by a U-shaped crook in the Tigris River. "Our first impression of Kut was not a pleasing one," wrote Major Charles H. Barber, a medical officer, in his memoirs. "Approaching it from the east, almost the first thing that caught the eye was a gibbet—always a gruesome-looking object. And on the bank around it, backed by an irregular row of squalid-looking, mud-colored houses, lay a heterogenous collection of oil tins, a decrepit native boat, and a wireless station, with a tent or two for operators: a veritable East End."

The town, Major Barber wrote, "consists of an extended river front, perhaps half a mile in length; and back from this and running roughly right angles to the stream lie a series of streets at various intervals, and running more or less parallel to each other. Cross-streets between these are few and far between and very irregular. On the left, as you face the town from the river, is the Turkish 'Serai,' with its roomy barrack square, its headquarters office, and its flagstaff. Just behind it stands the mosque and the lofty minaret, famous for its graceful proportions and topped by its turquoise dome. To the right of the Serai lie the bazaars, the lower and lesser one parallel to the river, the main one at right angles to this. Both are covered in by matting spread over wooden rafters. . . . Farther to the right, houses and khans stretch away to the garden at the eastern end, whilst between the houses and the river lies a strip of bare, uneven bank that serves all the purposes of a wharf."

On the north end of town was the dump, "covered with the village refuse, rubbish heaps, dead dogs, and scores of living ones." Kut smelled, good days and bad.

The British position also included a small redoubt on the right side of the Tigris, on the site of what the British called a wool press. In fact, it was an old licorice factory. They held it for the whole length of the siege.

Townshend's own field report showed he had 10,398 fighting men at Kut, including 1,555 cavalrymen. They wouldn't be of much help in a siege—and their horses would require all that fodder—so he built a rickety bridge across to the right bank of the Tigris and sent the cavalry force south to Ali Gharbi, where the advance units of the relief force already were gathering. Townshend wanted to expel at least some of the Arabs from the village, but Sir Percy Cox, the chief political officer, insisted that they be allowed to remain. Women and children dying in the desert wouldn't do much for the British image, he argued. Once again, Townshend caved in, without serious protest. The airplanes were the next to go; they didn't have a proper runway at Kut.

There was still time to march out of Kut, for the Turkish circle hadn't been closed. But Townshend had made up his mind; he would dig in, and when he destroyed the last bridge across the Tigris his fate was pretty much sealed.

The Turkish guns opened fire on December 9, and Townshend noted that they had an obvious advantage: "The fire from our guns went from the centre to the circumference [and] so was divergent and disseminated, while that of the enemy was directed from the circumference to the centre and this converged and concentrated." Kut, in fact, now completely surrounded, had become a stationary bull's-eye for almost every Turkish gun in Mesopotamia. More than thirty of them were powerful new field guns, most of them made by Krupp, but one of them was an ancient brass mortar, which fired a brass-cased projectile that took ten or more seconds to explode after it hit the ground. The troops called the ancient weapon "Farting Fanny" (the officers called it "Flatulent Fanny") and made souvenirs from its brass fragments.

Townshend's old friend, General Aylmer, arrived in Basra the next day, December 10, to take command of the relief force. He cabled Townshend that he had the "utmost confidence in defender of Chitral and his gallant troops to keep flag flying till we can relieve them."

Later that same day, the Turkish infantry rose out of their trenches and began an assault on an old fort anchoring the northeastern corner of the British position. (The British position at Kut was surrounded by water on three sides and exposed to frontal assault at one end, a line running roughly northeast to southwest.) The Turks were cut down by machine gun fire, but managed to come far enough forward to dig another line closer to the British guns. They attacked again on Christmas Day, and almost broke through. They actually entered a corner of the fort before they were thrown back. Townshend called it "regular bludgeon work, with men throwing bombs at each other at ten yards' distance."

This was the last major assault on Kut, with the Turks settling down to a starve-them-into-submission campaign they had every intention of winning. That decision may have had something to do with the fact that the great Field Marshal von der Goltz had arrived. One day, a British artillery lieutenant actually spotted the portly old German inspecting some Turkish trenches no more than seven hundred yards away. He lined up his fieldpiece and let fly, the shell exploding close enough to give von der Goltz a scare. When Townshend heard about what had happened, he was furious, and the offending artillery officer was "severely reprimanded." Braddon argued that Townshend wanted to keep von der Goltz alive because the old German would be easier to surrender to than the cruel Turks, when that inevitable time arrived, but Braddon was always harder on Townshend than anyone else.

As Townshend and his men dug in—deeper and deeper—General Nixon continued to bungle the arrangements for relieving him. Nothing was more scandalous than the conditions at Basra, where the fresh troops and all the supplies arrived. Sir George Buchanan, for years chief engineer of the port of Rangoon, had been sent to Mesopotamia to bring some order out of the chaos. "I had never before in my life seen such a hopeless mess and muddle and I wondered whether this was the usual accompaniment of war," he wrote. "It seemed incredible that we should have been in operation of Basra for over a year, so little had been done in the time." As many as fourteen ships were backed up in the Tigris, trying to unload. It took them, on average, six weeks.

"Buchanan was horrified," wrote Millar. What made it even worse was that his son was a subaltern in the Black Watch, part of the newly arrived Seventh Division. But at first General Nixon wouldn't even see him, and when he did consent to a brief discussion he said he couldn't imagine what help Buchanan could provide. Maybe, said Nixon, he could do something about dredging the Tigris.

Nixon, always a stupid man, was now, by all accounts, a sick one, too. He was finally replaced by General Sir Percy Lake, chief of staff to Sir Beauchamp Duff, the Indian Army's commanding officer.

Sieges are always a nasty business; this one was particularly nasty. The first plague was lice, "myriads" of them, according to Major Barber, the medical officer. "Our wretched patients would sit for hours picking them off their blankets and shirts." Next came fleas, "and if not fleas, then mosquitoes; failing mosquitoes, or in addition to, the sand fly is provided." Then, too, said Major Barber, "there is always the snake, the centipede or the scorpion to fall back upon."

By early January, the defenders could hear the guns of the relief column, desperately trying to break through the Turkish lines. Aylmer launched his Seventh Division, the Black Watch on the right, the night of January 12–13. After losing 1,113 killed and wounded, they were forced to withdraw. He tried again on January 18–19, with very much the same results. They lost twice as many men the second time.

Aylmer told General Lake that he was facing the better part of three Turkish divisions, numbering as many as nine thousand infantry, just about what Aylmer had left in his relief column. And the Turks were dug in now, fighting their kind of war.

Perhaps, Aylmer suggested, Townshend could try to break out of the town and link up with the relief force. But Townshend would have none of that, constantly confusing his superiors by giving sharply varying estimates of how much food he had left.

He never ventured very far from his headquarters, a two-story mud house. There, Braddon wrote, "he kept Boggis and his radio operators busy with a torrent of messages to Basra, and to his friends in London—actors and Gaiety Girls." He arose from his truckle bed at 6 A.M., climbed up to the roof to look around, ate his breakfast at eight, and drafted his telegrams, orders, and communiqués until lunchtime. He read military history most of the afternoon. Sometimes he would take Spot for a walk, though the poor fox terrier was deathly afraid of gunfire, and would scurry for home at the first indication of Turkish belligerence.

It is true that he spent most of his time in his headquarters, drafting messages "or gazing out across the Turkish lines from his observation post on the roof," his biographer, Barker, conceded. And it is also true that a critical report of the expedition, published in 1923, suggested "visits by the commander and his staff to the troops would have been even more effective" than his barrage of "communiqués." But, Barker lamely insisted, that's a little unfair. General officers weren't supposed to put themselves at risk during World War I and anyway, he visited the troops in the hospitals. The *British* troops.

Aylmer tried to break through again in March, but with no better results. Aylmer was finished. "Flesh and blood," he said, "cannot do more than the troops have done against the enemy. . . ." He sent a farewell message to Townshend on March 12. "The War Office say that my conduct of operations has been unfortunate, and have ordered my suspension. I need not tell you how deeply I grieve that I have not been able to relieve you. . . . It all looks so easy when you sit in an armchair at the War Office! . . . Goodbye and God bless you all, and may you be more fortunate than myself."

Gorringe was chosen to replace Aylmer, and was promoted to lieutenant general. "But he's junior to me," Townshend allegedly complained to an aide, according to Braddon, and then burst into tears. Townshend sent a message to Lake, Nixon's replacement, saying Gorringe's promotion was "a slight on my record of service." He had the grace to say that he was "deeply concerned to have brought up the question of promotion at so inopportune a time, but my active-service record is an honourable one and like my family before me for the past 300 years, I have served the state well." His men were now subsisting on five ounces of bread and a little mule meat each day, and the officers' starving horses were eating each other's tails. And poor General Hoghton, who had been lost in the desert at Kut, ate some bad grass and died.

Gorringe made a final effort at breaking through on April 22, but even with reinforcements he was no more successful than Aylmer. An attempt was made to prolong the agony by dropping supplies to the Kut garrison from airplanes, but most of the bundles crashed into the desert—the idea of parachutes hadn't yet been realized—and were gobbled up by the Arabs and the Turks.

It came down, finally, to a suicide mission—running the old steamer *Julnar*, loaded with 270 tons of supplies, twenty-five miles up the river past the Turkish guns. But the Turks had an answer to that; they had stretched a rope across the channel, and it fouled *Julnar*'s propellers. She swung ashore, and was captured by waiting Turkish troops. They killed most of her all-volunteer crew.

That night, Lord Kitchener cabled from London that Townshend could commence surrender negotiations. Townshend cabled Basra on the twenty-seventh that he had met with a powerful new Turkish general, Khalil. True to type to the very end, he would complain in his memoirs that he had conducted the whole campaign "with not a word of praise or reward," which of course simply wasn't true.

"Your gallant troops will be our most sincere and precious guests," the slender, suave Turkish general promised Townshend. That was an even bigger lie.

Before the British abandoned Kut, where they had lost 1,746 men in the 147-day siege, they blew up all their guns and dumped everything else in the river. Shortly before 1 P.M. on April 29, Lieutenant Green tapped out a last message on his wireless— a simple good-bye—and then blew it up with a guncotton charge.

By late afternoon, Turkish troops were swarming through Kut, most of them quietly looting the possessions of the British garrison. "Their uniforms were ragged and patched in all directions," wrote Major Barber. "Their boots were worn beyond hope of repair, and they were generally [the] most disreputable-looking specimens of a modern army. But they were good-natured fellows—broad, strong as oxen, with plenty of bone, ruddy complexions, and in many cases blue eyes and ginger whiskers. They looked what they were, I suppose—just easy-going, illiterate Anatolian peasantry." One of them stole Major Barber's revolver.

Four days later, Townshend, with a handful of aides and Boggis, was packed upriver in a motor launch. (Arrangements were made for Spot, the fox terrier, to be sent back to England, and he actually made the trip safely.) Eventually, the officers were separated from the rank and file and taken by boat upriver to Baghdad.

T. E. Lawrence—the Lawrence of Arabia—had quite magically appeared to take part in the surrender negotiations, and he was able to offer a million pounds if the Turks would ransom the garrison. They declined, and the offer was doubled. They still refused. Then they ordered the British troops, minus all their officers, to march nine miles north to Shamran. They were given a few biscuits, which were as hard as bricks, at the end of the day.

"The following morning," Braddon wrote, "they began to die. Frothing at the mouth, their bowels and stomachs disintegrating into a greenish slime, dehydrated and moaning, they died one after the other." The doctors said it was something called enteritis. The next morning, Townshend motored by in his Turkish launch, and the men who could stand lined the bank and cheered him. All but one of the officers sailed away, leaving their men behind, and hardly anyone complained. The one officer who refused to abandon his men was a Gurkha.

Whipped by their Kurdish guards, Kut's rank and file "dragged one foot past the other, one foot past the other, one foot past the other, interminably." Many of them simply sat down and died. They marched on and on, some of them to remote corners of Turkey, where they were forced to build a railway line. More than a third of them died.

Townshend, meanwhile, was taken to Baghdad, where he was supposed to have been the guest of von der Goltz. But the old general had died a few days earlier of typhoid, and so a disappointed Townshend was put up somewhere else. He remained in Baghdad for a week, attending a dinner party as Khalil's guest one evening, "and discussed strategy with his erstwhile opponent."

Townshend's biographer, Barker, admitted that nothing did more to damage Townshend's reputation than "his behavior as a prisoner-of-war."

He was greeted in Constantinople by a formal guard of honor and, "in an open landau, with mounted armed guards, driven through the city to be acclaimed by the mob." He was eventually put up on the island of Prinkipo (now Büyükada) in a seaside house, the Villa Hampson, that "resembled an English country vicarage," free to go where he pleased. He even connived, unsuccessfully, to get his wife, Alice, to come join him. Old photographs show him standing in front of the comfortable cottage, Boggis at his side. It was a pleasant interval, except for the shocking news from home that the marchioness, the wife of Townshend's first cousin, had produced a son after twelve years of trying. That meant Townshend would never inherit either the title or the estate.

Turkey pulled out of the war in October 1918, and Townshend offered his help to the Turkish high command in arranging the terms of surrender. He actually did play a minor role in setting some of the conditions. Typically, he took all the credit.

He finally arrived home in England in November 1918 to join Alice, his daughter Audrey, and, of course, Spot. But his reception was cool. "Only his personal friends made any fuss," Barker wrote. He lobbied, once again, for a new assignment and a promotion. But the army and the government had had enough of him. He was elected from a safe seat to the House of Commons, but he didn't like that much.

He retired to his estate, Vere Lodge, in Norfolk, "and arranged the goods and chattels he had collected over the years, and made the place comfortable." Spot died in July 1922, a terrible blow to the old general. Townshend followed on May 18, 1924. It rained on the funeral, at the end of which the "last post" was played by a bugler from the Norfolks.

✦

An Anglo-Indian army, four times the size of Townshend's, resumed the offensive in Mesopotamia late in 1916, recaptured Kut, and entered Baghdad on March 11, 1917.

The victors in the war created Iraq during the peace negotiations, and Britain put Faisal I on the Iraqi throne in 1921. Independence wasn't gained finally until 1932. A British army returned during World War II for the same reason as in World War I—to guard the precious oil supply. The monarchy was overthrown in a coup in 1958, in which a young army officer named Saddam Hussein took a key role. He eventually emerged as the country's dictator in the 1970s. He invaded Kuwait in the summer of 1990, prompting intervention by an American-led army in January 1991.

Hussein's forces were easily defeated, but the dictator retired with his elite units to Baghdad, where he remained in power in 1995, a constant source of irritation for the nations who thought they had brought his cruel reign to an end on the desert battlefields.

ELEVEN

Major General Manuel Fernandez Silvestre and the Riffian Rebellion in Morocco (1921–1926)

"How difficult to understand the Spaniards exactly," the Duke of Wellington once remarked. Spain, he reckoned, "is the only country where two and two don't make four."

In 1898 (see chapter 9), Spain had lost almost all of her colonial empire—Cuba, Puerto Rico, the Philippines—to the rambunctious Americans, allowing herself to be seen by the rest of the world as a fading, incompetent power. And yet, starting in 1904, she agreed to "sublet" from the French the northern part of Morocco, including the mountainous Rif, unexplored by Europeans and home to some of the most dangerous fighting men in the world. The result would be a catastrophic colonial disaster, in which Spain lost an entire army—Morocco, one observer said, became "a vast military cemetery"—and eventually slipped into a chilling civil war that gave rise to the cruel Franco dictatorship. The duke was right: difficult to understand.

France and Spain, with England's good wishes, simply split up Morocco, an independent nation, into separate spheres of influence without consulting the ruler—the sultan—or any of his people. They drew boundary lines on maps, carving up territory none of them had even seen and without any regard to the tribal populations involved. "This system," an observer reported, "is not one that can be recommended."

Spain had maintained presidios, or small outposts, at Ceuta, just across from Gibraltar, and at Melilla, more than 130 miles to the east, for more than four hundred years. Now it was given control of an area stretching from the Atlantic Ocean in the west to a point near the Algerian border to the east, and from the Mediterranean Sea in the north to a point in the desert near the Wergha River in the south. Tangier, the great powers agreed, would continue its independent ways, as an international enclave.

As late as 1912, when these new conditions became effective, northern Morocco was unknown territory. Only "one or two [Europeans] had been able to visit the cedar forests that lie to the south of Fez [Fés]," Walter Harris, for many years the Moroccan correspondent for the *Times* of London, reported. "A few had traveled in the southern Atlas [Mountains] and pushed on into the Sus . . . and that was almost all."

The difficulty, Harris said, was that these white, sometimes redheaded Berber tribesmen "were often as inhospitable to the Arab as they were to the foreigner." They realized, Harris believed—and he knew them better than any other European—"that once their resistance to exterior influences was broken down, their independence would be lost."

The Riffian tribesmen lived in the mountains—passengers on ships making their way back and forth in luxurious comfort in the Mediterranean could see the peaks—and they were not interested in being colonized, and surely not by Spain. This was spectacular country. Vincent Sheean, the American correspondent, was rhapsodic when he first saw it. "Crimson mountains," he said, "flung against a sky of hieratic blue, gorges magnificent and terrifying, peaceful green valleys between protecting precipices." It reminded him a little of Colorado.

Harris estimated the Berber population of the Rif was a quarter of a million in a country of about four million. Technically, these Berber tribesmen were Muslims, but in fact most of them were pagans, worshiping holy springs and groves of trees. Children bitten by a mad dog were told to swallow a hair from its tail in a glass of water drawn from a sacred spring; sick children were suspended from branches of mystic trees.

And they fought, year in and year out, generation following generation, all the time. Riffians made the Hatfields and the McCoys look like Quaker spinsters. A celebrated feud began when members of one family killed a dog belonging to another family, and then refused to pay the required blood money. "Twelve men were killed in combat the first day," reported David Hart, a student of Riffian tribal customs. "Each side collected allies," he said, and soon the feud involved hundreds of tribesmen who had no idea why it had begun. "In the following years, 40 men died on one side, 62 on the other."

"I have known whole familes treacherously massacred at a feast of 'reconciliation,'" the *Times*'s Harris pointed out. "The sheikh Duas of Anjera murdered his rival Deylan and his four sons while seated partaking of his hospitality in his own guest-room. A volley was fired by his retainers from without the door and windows and the deed was accomplished."

The "blood feud," Harris said, "is universal." Making it even deadlier was a system of family and even tribal alliances, called *liffs*, in which one family, or one tribe, called on another for help. Typically, if one group was in trouble, it would parade a bull to the mosque of another group, and then kill the prized animal, blood flowing down the steps. No Riffian community could then honorably refuse to participate in the other group's blood feud.

This was hardly the kind of place to send the ragamuffin Spanish army, led by some of the world's most corrupt, ignorant, and incompetent officers, but that, at the urging of King Alfonso XIII, was just what Spain set out to do.

What was the point? National honor, of course. The armies defeated by the Americans had come home in disgrace, and the campaign veterans had told lurid tales of incompetence and corruption. The officers, though still mostly ignorant and corrupt, sought redemption; besides, there was no chance of promotion while serving time in garrisons at home. They argued, too, that if the Moroccan coast was occupied by an unfriendly great power—Germany was always a threat—ports in the south of Spain would be put at risk. And so a Spanish occupation of the Moroccan coast was essential in the interests of Spanish national security.

The church was still a major force in Spanish affairs, and many priests remembered Moorish domination of their country and the will of Isabella I, written in 1504. She instructed her heirs to be "very obedient to the Holy Mother Church, . . . and that they shall not desist from the conquest of Africa, or from fighting for the Faith against the infidels." Priests, many of them corrupt, came to Spanish Morocco as missionaries.

While there might not have been much gold in those Riffian hills, surely there was a lot of iron and probably other metals as well. Businessmen in Spain wanted to develop those assets.

The king was part of the problem, too. Though not without some sensitivity and intelligence, Alfonso liked to play various roles, and chief among them was the role of the warrior. He had been tutored by army officers and he liked to dress up in army uniforms. He played favorites among his top generals, often with disastrous results, raising fears among the rest of the officer corps of a royal clique. He was clearly on the side of the *africanistas*, the imperialists who hoped to restore Spain's glory in Africa.

In attempting to pacify their new colony, the Spaniards faced two remarkable men: the ruffian Ahmad ibn Muhammad Raisuli, a world-class
scoundrel from the Jibal, in western Morocco; and the great soldier-states-
man, Abd el-Krim, the portly, bearded leader of the most warlike of the
tribes in the Rif, the Beni Urriaguel. The treacherous Raisuli, "the scourge
of the northwest," was the son of a sherif and a descendant of the Prophet
himself. For all that, he was a brigand and, as a young man, spent four years
in chains in the pasha of Tangier's dungeons. He emerged, marked for life,
a different man—living only, according to one observer, for "lust of war and
lust of gold."

Raisuli routinely took prisoners and held them for hostage. One of those
prisoners, Ion Perdicaris, said he was an American citizen, and his plight
became the dramatic highlight of the 1904 Republican convention, when
Theodore Roosevelt ordered the message, "I want Perdicaris alive or
Raisuli dead," cabled to the American consul in Tangier. And, to prove he
meant it, he sent seven warships to Tangier.

The whole business was ludicrous—Perdicaris might not even have
been an American citizen, and if he was, he certainly had been a draft evad-
er during the Civil War. While Roosevelt blustered, Perdicaris and Raisuli,
old friends, caroused. Raisuli eventually collected $70,000 in ransom from
the sultan and sent the fraudulent Perdicaris on his way. Roosevelt won
the election.

Abd el-Krim was a different sort altogether. His father was a judge, and
he sent both of his sons to Spanish schools. The names are confusing: the
famous Abd el-Krim's full name was Mohamed ben Abd el-Krim; his
younger brother, who would one day be the commanding general of the
Riffian army, was Mhamed ben Abd el-Krim. For simplicity, Abd el-Krim
hereafter will mean the older son, the man who would soon capture the
world's attention.

In 1907, Abd el-Krim (though not himself an Arab) was named Arab secretary of the Bureau of Native Affairs in Melilla. In 1912, he took another
job, as an assessor, learning all about mining claims and ore deposits in his
Riffian homeland. His rise, encouraged by the Spaniards, was very rapid.
In 1914, he was named chief judge for the Melilla district. The next year,
he was editing the Arabic pages of *El Telegrama del Rif*. His father, at the
same time, was back in the family village, Ajdir, smuggling arms, and his
brother was in Spain learning to be a mining engineer.

In his editorials in the Melilla newspaper, Abd el-Krim harshly attacked
the French, annoying their colonial administrators across the border. The

French apparently complained to the Spanish in Melilla, and Abd el-Krim was arrested and thrown in jail. He emerged from prison a different man, too. Now he lived only to defeat Spain. He went back to work for the newspaper, keeping his thoughts to himself. Then, in January 1919, he took what was supposed to be a twenty-day leave. He disappeared into the hills to prepare for war.

With his father and his brother, called home from Spain, Abd el-Krim began recruiting a small following. They met for the first time on April 11, 1920, at Ajdir, which is not far from Alhucemas Bay, with its great Spanish island fortress, to form a *harka*, an army to begin the fight against the Spaniards. A Spanish gunboat, the *Lauria*, having been told about the meeting, lobbed a few shells from its anchored position in the bay in the general direction of the rebels. The Riffians fired a few meaningless shots in return.

"There is nothing on earth," the Duke of Wellington also said, "so stupid as a gallant officer." He had in mind someone very much like thirty-seven-year-old Major General Manuel Fernandez Silvestre, a tall, handsome man with a huge bushy handlebar mustache. Silvestre had served with gallantry in Cuba, where he was wounded either sixteen times or sixty, depending on the source. (Sixteen is more likely; to be wounded 60 times in one campaign borders on carelessness.) He had been in and out of Morocco since 1904, and during his time in Spain he had formed a friendship with the king. The ladies loved him and so did members of his personal staff: they called him by his nickname, Manolo. "Silvestre was a real-life character as flamboyant as any to be found in the pages of a romantic novel," David Woolman, the historian, wrote.

In their fight against Spain, the Riffians were going to benefit from a piece of good luck, for Silvestre was also a truly terrible general.

Though Silvestre would be the one to lead the Spanish army to destruction, he was actually Spain's number two general in Morocco. The senior officer was General Dámaso Berenguer, another of the king's favorites. He and Silvestre had been classmates at the military academy, but Silvestre held seniority on the officers' list and, in fact, had once been Berenguer's commanding officer. Berenguer was now high commissioner of Morocco, operating from his headquarters at Tétouan, south of Ceuta in western Spanish Morocco, where he was trying to deal with Raisuli and pacify the various tribes in the Jibala. Silvestre was in command at Melilla, 130 miles away, in eastern Spanish Morocco, facing Abd el-Krim. No roads connected the two Spanish bases, and communication was possible only by sea.

Berenguer was an intelligent and conservative officer and a good administrator. He had visited the legendary French commander, Marshal Hubert Lyautey, in Rabat, and studied his extraordinary success in pacifying French Morocco. Caution, taking one step at a time, he learned, was the secret. Berenguer's greatest fault—and it was a key to the Spanish disaster—was his unwillingness to force that strategy on Silvestre. He apparently feared that while he was a favorite of the king, Silvestre was an even greater favorite, and that it would therefore be in his best interests to allow his fire-breathing deputy to plan his own war.

In his area of operations, Berenguer carefully followed Marshal Lyautey's advice, moving slowly and cautiously to pacify his part of the new colony. Late in 1920, his forces captured Chechaouèn, deep in enemy territory in the Jibala, far to the south of Tétouan. Three days later, though, Spanish whores arrived, tin-roofed cantinas opened, and Spanish soldiers hooted at Muslims on their way to the mosque. That was not Marshal Lyautey's way. Berenguer's campaign against Raisuli was going more slowly, but even there he had managed to isolate the old ruffian in the hills of his loyal Beni Aros tribesmen.

The two Spanish generals met aboard the *Princesa de Asturias*, an 1896 cruiser that somehow had escaped destruction in the Spanish-American War, in Alhucemas Bay in March 1921 to talk about Silvestre's plans. Silvestre reassured his worried commanding officer and said that he had all the troops and equipment he needed. He insisted that he didn't expect much opposition from the Moors. More and more, Silvestre and his staff had come to believe the Riffians wouldn't be a problem. "The only way to succeed in Morocco is to cut off the heads of all the Moors," one of his officers said. It was, of course, not Lyautey's way (when he was attacked by Abd el-Krim, most of the tribesmen in French Morocco remained at his side, because he had dealt with them honestly and fairly).

Berenguer, seemingly, was impressed. He told Vizconde Eza, the war minister in Madrid, that Silvestre was well on his way to taking Alhucemas Bay, in the heart of the Rif domain, and winning an easy victory. Eza was impressed too. Silvestre, he was convinced, finally had learned to discipline his reckless nature.

Silvestre commanded twenty-five thousand men—twenty thousand Spanish regulars and five thousand native troops, called Regulares—from his headquarters in Melilla. But half of his Spanish regulars were illiterate recruits who had been rushed into service with almost no training. The equipment waiting for them was no better: an earlier inspection had indicated that as many as three-quarters of the rifles in the Melilla arsenal were in poor, or even useless, condition. The barracks were disreputable; no one seemed to be in charge of sanitation. Hospitals—the few that existed— were just as bad, and sickness was a problem everywhere.

Soldiers and their wives, investigators discovered after the disaster had occurred, routinely sold rifles and cartridges in the marketplaces for fresh vegetables. The ordinary infantrymen couldn't read; most of the officers couldn't read maps, relying on *cojones*, their gut instincts (or, more precisely, their testicles) instead. The result was that units were constantly becoming lost. The officers pilfered everything from their storage warehouses, just as they had done in Cuba, and some of them became improbably rich. Funds to build roads and railways were diverted to the benefit of the commanding officers. The officers spent most of their time in Melilla gambling and whoring, sometimes molesting the native Moorish women; they spent almost as much time at home on leave.

Spanish infantrymen were scattered in small outposts called *blocaos*. "Many of these lacked any sort of toilet," the American historian Stanley Payne wrote, "and the soldier who ventured out of the filthy bunker risked exposure to the fire of lurking tribesmen."

Morale among these troops was understandably awful. They ate tobacco juice to give themselves a yellow, jaundice-like pallor, hoping to escape active duty. They scratched themselves with nettles and burned themselves with hot coins. They debauched with the whores, hoping to come down with venereal disease.

They were paid thirty-four cents a day, living on coffee and a little bread for breakfast, and beans and rice, and maybe a little meat, the rest of the day. The fact they were willing to fight at all is a tribute to their peasant endurance. Silvestre and Berenguer knew this, and so did the authorities in Madrid. They simply didn't believe they needed to do very much about it.

"Ill-fed, ill-clothed, ill-treated, the youth of Spain, courageous and patient, had been systematically deprived of almost everything to which they had a right," the *Times*'s Harris reported.

Silvestre had taken this unhappy army and strung it out in those awful blocaos and larger forts—144 of them in all—from Sidi Dris on the Mediterranean south across the mountains to Anual and Tizi Azza, and from there eastward to Dar Drius, Batel, Monte Aruit, and, finally, Melilla itself. The smallest blocao was manned by maybe a dozen men; the larger forts—Anual as an example—contained garrisons of as many as eight hundred men.

With this line, Silvestre was already deep into the Rif, but he insisted on going even farther. Abd el-Krim, watching patiently, warned the Spaniards that if Silvestre crossed the Amekran River, running south to north and and emptying into the Mediterranean at Sidi Dris, more tribes would rise against him. "This man Abd el-Krim is crazy," Silvestre replied. "I'm not going to take seriously the threats of a little Berber caid [judge] whom I had at my mercy a short time ago. His insolence merits a new punishment."

Silvestre was a fool, and big trouble was heading his way. In late May, isolated groups of armed Berbers began attacking his supply columns. That was serious business, for Silvestre was stretched very thin and had done almost nothing to stock his outposts—most of them located hundreds of yards from the nearest water—with provisions. On May 29, in his first indication that this might involve more than just "a kick in the pants" to the Moors, he wrote Berenguer that he might need reinforcements after all and said that further advances would have to be given careful consideration before they were undertaken.

Yet, on June 1, 1921, this stupid man crossed the Amekran—his and his army's Rubicon—and sent a detachment of two hundred men to occupy a village called Abaran. Many of the troops were native Regulares, and they promptly mutinied, killing the Spaniards and most of their officers, including the unit's commander, a Captain Salafranca. The survivors—most of them Spanish artillerymen—escaped, fleeing to the other side of the Amekran. The mutineers joined the native Temasamani tribesmen in the rebellion that was now sweeping across the Rif.

Berenguer was not pleased. He rushed by warship to visit Silvestre off Sidi Dris on June 5 and suggested—suggested!—that Silvestre might be well advised to suspend his offensive until Berenguer could clean up his own operations and begin a supporting attack on the Rif from the west. Silvestre was adamant; he didn't need help and he wanted to continue his advance. Some sources said the discussion became so heated that Silvestre tried to wring his commanding general's neck, and had to be restrained by his own officers. In any event, neck wringing or not, it is clear that Berenguer indicated to his second in command that he should do nothing rash. He followed up that line of thought in telegrams for the next forty-eight hours.

Yet, on June 8, three days later, Silvestre sent another detachment deeper into Rif territory to build a new base at a village called Igueriben, three miles south of Anual. Abd el-Krim sensed the climax was approaching, and distributed a proclamation to the tribesmen. "The Spaniards have already lost the game," he said. "Look at Abaran! They have left their dead mutilated and unburied, their souls vaguely wandering, tragically denied the delights of Paradise."

The Riffians closed in on the new Spanish base, and mounted captured Spanish guns on the peaks of nearby mountains. Silvestre cabled Berenguer that the situation was becoming "somewhat delicate" and that maybe some reinforcements would be helpful right now. He may, finally, have had some intimation of impending disaster, for he began having trouble sleeping and digesting his food. Perhaps he took some comfort in a personal message from his king: "Hurrah for real men!" Alfonso said. The real men were in the garrison at Igueriben, commanded by Major Julio Benitez, and it was a desperate situation. Benitez was surrounded, and he couldn't reach his only water supply at Anual, the big Spanish base, only three miles away. The two posts were in touch by heliograph, a system of reflecting mirrors with shutters mounted on the hills that relayed messages by Morse code. "Heroes of Igueriben, who honor the name of Spain, resist," Melilla urged. "Your heliographs have been received with *vivas* for Spain," Benitez replied. "The garrison swears to its general that it will surrender only to death."

Without water, Woolman wrote, they began drinking the juice from pimiento and tomato cans, and then sweetened vinegar and ink, and, finally, their own urine.

Anual sent one relief column through the narrow gorge separating the base from Igueriben on June 19. But, with the Riffians controlling the heights, the column was cut to pieces, returning to Anual with 152 dead. Silvestre had missed most of this because he had been inspecting another of his posts. He returned, by motorcar, to Anual on the twenty-first, and sent a second column—3,000 men, all he could collect—in another effort to lift the siege at Igueriben. He watched from the parapet as the column set out, and he watched as the survivors came stumbling back. Silvestre, increasingly distraught, sent a heliograph message ordering Benitez to surrender the garrison. Benitez replied he would rather die. Silvestre sent a final message: abandon the post and fall back on Anual. The brave defenders streamed out of their fort and tried to fight their way through the Riffian hordes. Benitez, along with most of the garrison, was hacked to death. Only 11 men managed to reach Anual, and 9 of those died in the next few hours from heat prostration and exhaustion.

Silvestre now—at last—knew the worst. Overwhelmed with grief, he began chewing his own mustache and swearing to himself. Abd el-Krim's men had begun investing Anual within hours of the fall of Igueriben and now they swarmed outside its walls. Silvestre called a council of war late at night on the twenty-first, and he and all his officers agreed the situation was untenable—he insisted ammunition for both rifles and guns was running short, though that probably was untrue —and that the only way out was a general retreat. He sent his final message at 4:55 A.M. on the twenty-second, announcing the retreat would begin within hours.

Silvestre still had four thousand men under his direct command, along with modern weapons, including machine guns and artillery. Thousands more men were stretched out behind him in blocaos and small forts. Ships from the Spanish navy cruised the coastline, waiting to give support. Airplanes and armored cars had begun to arrive, and some of them might have been called into service. Ranged against him were no more than three thousand tribesmen, the pick of the Rif. Most of them were members of Abd el-Krim's own fierce Beni Urriaguel tribe.

An orderly retreat should have been possible, but Silvestre failed to organize one. The orders, such as they were, were whispered to the officers, and they were told to keep quiet about it. The troops, totally ignorant of what was happening, began leaving Anual about 10 A.M. on the twenty-second, and they were hardly outside the walls when they began to panic. "Units broke up and became incoherent," Vice Admiral Cecil V. Usborne, the British historian, wrote. Soldiers threw their rifles away and ran off in every direction through "the terrible heat and dust of the Moroccan summer."

Silvestre and a few of his top-ranking officers remained behind on the Anual parapets. As he watched his army break up, Silvestre is alleged to have shouted: "Run, run, the bogeyman is coming!" The tribesmen crashed through the gates of the fort and attacked the few defenders inside. Silvestre was killed and his body probably was hacked to pieces. A Spanish survivor said Silvestre's head was cut off and paraded through the Rif in triumph. Another story suggested Abd el-Krim captured the general's red sash and wore it for weeks thereafter (another account said he wore a yellow sash). This is even more improbable: photographs of Silvestre show him in a khaki field uniform wearing a Spanish version of the Sam Browne belt, and no sign of a red (or yellow) sash.

The panicked soldiers, running helter-skelter toward the mountains, were easy prey. Some were stabbed to death; others were "shot down like rabbits," including Silvestre's own teenage son. The entire garrison, with the exception of a cavalry unit, the Cazadores de Alcántara, was destroyed.

Abd el-Krim's men, almost out of ammunition themselves, picked up the Mausers where they had been thrown, along with thousands of cartridges, plus all the abandoned Spanish guns.

Yet, awful as it was, Anual was just the beginning. With its fall, the *Times*'s Harris said, "began the great disaster." The problem was, there was no safe place for the Spaniards to go. The blocaos were indefensible, even more so now that Abd el-Krim had his own artillery, and no one had thought to stock the larger outposts with food or other provisions. The Spaniards never believed anything like this was even remotely possible. One by one, the Spaniards abandoned their posts, the Regulares deserted to the enemy, and the whole line collapsed in a retreat that Harris said may have been "unparalleled in its horrors."

Surrendering did no good; the Spanish commander at Dar Quebdana tried that, and his entire command was killed at knife point. The five hundred men in the Sidi Dris garrison attempted to fight their way to the beach, and rescue by two Spanish warships, but fewer than a dozen succeeded. Farther south, the Spanish garrison at Zoco el Telata der Metalsa pulled up stakes and headed for the border, and the comforting arms of the French army. Only a third of them made it.

General Navarro, Silvestre's second in command, managed to bring some order out of the chaos; he pulled three thousand survivors together and marched them to the fortified village of Monte Arruit, only eighteen miles south of Melilla and connected to that city by railway, on the twenty-ninth. But his troops were exhausted, and there were no medical supplies of any kind in the town; hundreds died of heat prostration and gangrene. Once again, water was a problem; again and again, the Spaniards built their bases without any thought of getting to a supply of water. At Monte Arruit, water was almost a mile away.

Airplanes from Melilla tried to drop supplies to the besieged garrison, including large blocks of ice, but the pilots were no more accurate in dropping provisions than they were in dropping bombs. Most of the supplies landed outside the town, and were eagerly scooped up by delighted Riffians.

Navarro's only fighting troops were cavalrymen commanded by Lieutenant Colonel Fernando Primo de Rivera (a cousin of the future dictator). He was badly wounded in the left arm and ordered his troopers to amputate it with a razor (and without anesthetics). Gangrene set in, and he died.

Berenguer arrived in Melilla by warship on July 23, followed the next day by reinforcements from Ceuta that included a detachment of the Tercio, the Spanish foreign legion, led by a young officer named Francisco Franco. Even with the reinforcements, Berenguer felt powerless to relieve Monte Arruit. The biggest problem was that there were hardly any soldiers in the Melilla garrison. Berenguer could only find eighteen hundred, and some of them were clerks or malnourished and untrained recruits. Lots of troops who were supposed to be in Melilla were in Spain on leave, or didn't exist anywhere except on fraudulent rosters.

Yet, it is hard to accept that Berenguer couldn't have made some move to relieve his besieged outposts. While Monte Arruit was eighteen miles away, Zeluan was only twelve miles distant, and Nador was actually a suburb of Melilla. That no relief was attempted "must stand to Spain's discredit," Harris said. "Her dead . . . were the victims of incompetence and disorganization, and—I am only quoting the speeches of Spanish deputies in the Cortes a month or two later—of corruption."

Navarro surrendered on August 9, and watched in despair as most of his command was massacred by triumphant tribesmen; only six hundred men were marched off to captivity, including Navarro, and not very many of them survived.

Abd el-Krim and his mountain tribesmen now ruled the Rif. They had destroyed—utterly wiped out—a professional European army of twenty thousand men, capturing one hundred thirty cannon, twenty thousand rifles, and four hundred machine guns, and all the Spanish stores. Melilla, swarming with terrified refugees, now lay open to them. "Twelve years' work and sacrifice were wiped out—and the Rifs were bombarding the town of Melilla with artillery captured from the Spaniards," the *Times*'s Harris wrote.

Melilla was divided into two sections—the old town, a fortified bastion on a rocky hill jutting out into the sea, and the lower, modern city, connected to the old town by a narrow isthmus. Normally, forty thousand people lived in the new town; many of them had taken refuge in the old fortified part of the city; others had escaped by boat. Spanish soldiers were hard to find, and some of their officers, terrified of the Berber tribesmen, were hiding in cellars. Food was running low, and water had to be brought in by boat from Málaga, on the other side of the Mediterranean.

"All is lost, including honor," Berenguer said.

Now was Abd el-Krim's great opportunity—and he did . . . nothing.

He said later he feared if he attacked the town it would result in "international repercussions," but he already was creating repercussions around the world, much of it sympathetic to his cause. The real reason, it was said, was that the Spanish fortress was too strong, and that his cannon weren't mobile enough to knock the walls down. More likely, his tribes-men—they now numbered twenty thousand or more—had had enough. They were tired of killing—they had cut enough Spanish throats—and they wanted to go home to harvest their crops. And so Abd el-Krim's vic-torious army simply melted away into the Rif.

The reprieved Spaniards slowly, tentatively, emerged from their fortress. Everywhere they looked they saw the rotting bodies of their comrades. "The ruins of the fortifications at Monte Arruit resembled an abattoir, covered as they were with dried blood and littered with rotting, mutilated corpses—the remains of the prisoners slaughtered after their surrender by the Berbers," Payne wrote. "Everywhere were ruins and un-buried corpses. Before Zeluan and Monte Arruit could be occupied whole days were spent in getting rid of the dead and purifying the wells," Harris said.

King Alfonso must have been appalled; after all, he was closely tied to the Spanish army. But his only comment, after hearing of the disaster, was reported to be: "Chicken meat is cheap."

Others were horrified. It was one thing to be defeated by the upstart Americans; it was quite another to be routed by fewer than five thousand mountain tribesmen (the number who had actually done the fighting). "If we continue like this," said a deputy in the Cortes, "we shall soon find that we have no Morocco, no army, and no Spain." The old government fell, and the new prime minister, Antonio Maura, told the Cortes: "Every-where, there is the same misgovernment and the same laxity."

Military observers were stunned by Abd el-Krim's military exploits in routing a European army, and insisted he must be employing European officers to make it all possible. The fact that his personal bodyguard goose-stepped with German precision and that his troops generally saluted in ap-proved Teutonic style suggested the answer. But the only German serving with Abd el-Krim was the mysterious Joseph Klemms, originally from Düsseldorf and a runaway from his prosperous family at an early age. He joined the Berbers after escaping from the French Foreign Legion, where he had been caught cooking the company books. He converted to the Muslim religion, married several young Berber women, and from time to time led dashing raids against the Spaniards, leaving a kind of mark of Zorro—in this case the mark of the "German Hadj"—on the bodies of his victims. His career, popularized in the yellow press, may have impressed Sigmund Romberg, for his *Desert Song* allegedly was based on some of Klemms's exploits.

But Klemms was never a serious adviser to Abd el-Krim. This Berber army was built by Berbers, most of them members of the chieftain's own tribe. Abd el-Krim's soldiers collected their guns from the battlefield—thousands of Mausers, Remingtons, and St. Étiennes. Woolman, the campaign historian, said they learned to strip Spanish bombs to make hand grenades. They were equipped with as many as two hundred cannon, most of them Schneiders, and more than two hundred machine guns. The ammunition was stored in strategically placed caves. Abd el-Krim even bought three old airplanes, hopelessly out of date, and installed a rough-and-ready telephone system.

"The Riffian warriors," Woolman wrote, "were generally tough, valiant, resourceful fighters, and superb shots, whose endurance gave them an amazing mobility. They could walk as much as 30 miles a night over mountain trails and yet be perfectly fit to attack at daybreak. Each man carried a gun, a long, straight dagger, cartridges, bread, and fruit. He slept wherever he happened to be, pulling the hood of his *jellaba* over his face.... These men firmly believed one Riffian was the equal of six Spaniards...."

The new Spanish general in the east was Ricardo Burguete, in command of thirty thousand men supported by armored cars, airplanes, warships (including a small aircraft carrier), and even a navy dirigible. He was instructed to negotiate with Raisuli—a foolish idea, for Raisuli didn't believe in negotiation—to pacify the Rif by peeling tribes away from Abd el-Krim, and to get the Spanish prisoners of war back.

Foolishly, though, he continued to advance into the Rif, moving on Tizi Azza, southeast of Anual, and setting up an outpost on a mountaintop; supplies could be brought forward only through another of those deadly narrow gorges. On November 1 and 2, 1922, the Riffians attacked in strength; though the Spaniards clung to their position, they lost more than two thousand men. Spaniards, at home, were aghast; they had come to believe the army had put a stop to these terrible engagements. In response, Madrid told Burguete to suspend offensive operations.

Burguete's major achievement was securing the release of the Spanish prisoners, upon payment of more than $400,000 to Abd El-Krim in ransom. Of the 600 prisoners taken in 1921, only 325 survived. "The survivors arrived in a pitiable state, . . . bearing the marks of the chains they had been forced to wear during captivity," Woolman said.

The year 1923 began as a standoff. The Spaniards controlled much of the territory they had lost earlier, but Abd el-Krim ruled supreme inside the Rif itself. Now—at the peak of his power among his own people—Abd el-Krim established a new nation, a republic with himself as president and a kind of rudimentary central assembly. But no one doubted who was in charge: Abd el-Krim's word was law.

Spain was torn. The *africanistas* still believed victory was possible in Morocco, and they were outraged that their government had paid ransom to win freedom for the captured soldiers. The other side, the *abandonistas*, simply wanted to get out of this mess. Army units en route to Morocco mutinied in August, and others refused to board troopships at Málaga. Left-wing mobs in Barcelona cheered for the new nation in Morocco and jeered the Spanish flag.

This was a situation ripe for a coup, and it took place on November 13, 1923, when the aristocratic General Miguel Primo de Rivera, the second marquis of Estella, seized power, and, with the support of the increasingly unpopular king, established a military dictatorship. The fifty-three-year-old Primo de Rivera was really too nice, many thought, to be a dictator. "A bottle, some cards, and a beautiful dame / mark the coat of arms of our Primo's name," went a popular piece of doggerel.

Primo de Rivera was that odd creature—a moderate dictator. He had seized power not to win glory for Spain in North Africa; he wanted, instead, to make a withdrawal. He visited Morocco in July of 1924, and inspected all of the major Spanish posts. One of these posts, at Ben Tieb, near Tizi Azza, was manned by Tercio legionnaires. They served him nothing but eggs, dish after dish. In Spain, eggs, in a rude metaphor, represent testicles, or guts; and the officers were telling their dictator that they didn't believe he had enough. One of the officers, Lieutenant Colonel Franco, the future dictator, gave a toast in which he said the hearts of the soldiers of the legion were filled with "distrust."

When Primo de Rivera rose to speak, he was greeted with boos and catcalls. He ignored the demonstration and proceeded to tell the best officers in his army about his plans to withdraw. And when he was finished, he said, very quietly, "And on the day when your orders are given to you, you will have no choice but to obey them, whatever they may be."

Franco, fearful he had gone too far in his speech, offered his resignation, but Primo de Rivera refused to accept it. Two months later, Franco was still unhappy and spoke to several key officers about capturing Primo de Rivera and putting him in a military prison. The other officers said it wouldn't work, and talked him out of it.

Franco's foreign legion was Spain's toughest fighting force. Officially, it was the *Tercio de Extranjeros*, founded in 1920 and named for invincible soldiers who had served Spain in the sixteenth century. The founder was an extraordinary man named Major José Millan Astray y Terreros. He had served with some distinction in the Philippines and taught at the military college. He had also visited French Foreign Legion posts in Algeria in 1919 and studied how that organization worked. He was a fanatic with a morbid interest in death. He wrote the new legion's creed, which included the motto *Viva la muerte!* (Long live death!) and the anthem *"El novio de la muerte"* (The betrothed of death).

By the time he had finished fighting in the Rif, Millan Astray had lost an arm, an eye, one of his legs, and most of the fingers on his remaining hand. He had become a living testament to the accuracy of Riffian gunfire. Spain remembers him as "the glorious mutilated one."

The Tercio, along with reorganized Regulare units, would form an elite corps in the new Spanish army, and provide imperialists back home some evidence that military honor, after all, wasn't entirely lost.

The key to Primo de Rivera's withdrawal strategy was the Spanish base at Chechaouèn, a holy Muslim city, with its garrison of ten thousand men, forty miles south of Tétouan in the western part of the colony. With Primo de Rivera personally taking command, the relief force entered Chechaouèn, largely unopposed, on September 30. Troops were sent out to bring in the garrisons of nearby smaller posts; some of them ran into heavy sniper fire, frequently losing as many men as they were supposed to be saving. Then the rain began to fàll, turning the dusty roads into quagmires of mud.

Abd el-Krim, seeing what Primo de Rivera was attempting to do, rapidly moved some of his forces, commanded by his brother, Mhamed, to join Jibali tribesmen led by Ahmed Heriro in meeting the challenge. The two commanders agreed that the best strategy would be to wait until the Spaniards, with their sick and wounded and all their stores, began their march to Tétouan.

Primo de Rivera sensed morale among his own men was drooping, and issued an unusual order on November 3. "It is regrettable," he said, "that the troops should give way at this moment to pessimism which is destroying the morale of the army. In order to remedy this disgraceful weakness I order all commanding officers, officers, and soldiers to refrain from all criticism or discussion of these questions, and to put immediately under arrest any military subordinate, or civilian, who may disobey me."

Webb Miller, an American correspondent, was along to watch the Span-

ish operation, and in fact was riding in style in Primo de Rivera's own His-
pano-Suiza limousine. "Repeatedly," he wrote, "the car became bogged
down in mudholes; we had to get out to push, or tear branches from bushes and carry stones to give the rear wheels traction." Miller asked his driver why they didn't use chains. Never heard of them, he was told. Why,
then, he asked, didn't they build turnout places on the one-lane road, "and
establish signallers on the hills and let the traffic run one way for a while,
then upon signals from the outpost release the traffic in the other direction?" Not possible, he was told. "The Riffi would shoot the signallers."

Vincent Sheean, the American correspondent, didn't actually see the
fighting, but he got an inkling of what it must have been like when he traveled along the road between Chechaouèn and Tétouan three months after the evacuation took place. "At Dar Koba," he said, "we came upon the
first valley of death, where the black birds flew low over the bodies of
[General Castro] Girona's soldiers." Sheean's guide "wrapped his turban
tightly across the lower half of his face so the smells were excluded; he mo-
tioned me to do likewise, and to breathe only through the folds of gauze.
In this manner we escaped some of the nausea of an old battle field; but
our poor horses reared and plunged in terror at the smell of their own kind
lying half-devoured along the hillsides."

They moved on to the next village, Cheruta, and found it "was still a
more terrible spectacle than Dar Koba. At Cheruta, surely, the incompetence of the Spanish generals was incontestable. The post was built so low
that it could never have been easy to defend, even against the merest
handful of enemies; and to evacuate it was virtually impossible. Here the
bodies lay sometimes five and six deep, blackened and half devoured, or
sometimes isolated and picked clean, with bones whitening in the brilliant
African sunlight. I tried counting them as we took our way down the hill-
side to regain the Chaouen-Tetuan road. . . . There were 600 bodies, or
more, in that space no larger than the stately courtyard of the Ministry of
War in Madrid."

Thousands of Spaniards died, but this time, at least, there was no widespread panic. This time, too, there were individual instances of extraordinary heroism. One of them occurred at a place called Wad Nakla, where
Sheean saw what he described as "the battered monument of a deed of
Spanish heroism almost Roman in its quality." The monument, he said,
consisted of three wrecked Spanish armored cars. They had been placed
there in the middle of the Chechaouèn-Tétouan road, near a riverbank, to
cover the army's retreat. "Long after the army had disappeared the 14

Spanish soldiers inside the three [disabled] cars continued to fire their machine guns and rifles at the Riffi. The main body of Riffi pursuers went on after the Spanish army, and a detachment remained to capture the armored cars and make their defenders prisoners. The 14 Spaniards remained in those cars, without food or drink, for three days, firing every time the Riffi tried to capture them. . . . On the third day the Riffi dragged mountain cannon to the top of a hill overlooking the river bank, and sent their shots plowing through the tops of the cars. Out of the 14 men, eight were killed and two severely wounded. Four begrimed and exhausted Spanish soldiers, too weak to walk, surrendered to the Riffi.

"By order of the Riffi captain the company which captured the cars stood at salute when the four survivors were brought out," Sheean said. "When . . . Abd El-Krim heard the story of their exploit, he ordered them to be put first on the list of prisoners to be exchanged or ransomed to the Spanish."

The bedraggled Spanish army, what was left of it anyway, stumbled into Tétouan on December 13. "Never had I seen soldiers in such a state of exhaustion, dejection, and filth," wrote Webb Miller, the American journalist, who was there. "Several were barefooted, the soles of their shoes worn off."

"You are entering Tetuan in triumph," Primo de Rivera told his soldiers. "Bravo!" But he knew better. "Abd el-Krim has defeated us," he confided to Miller. "He has the immense advantages of the terrain and a fanatical following. Our troops are sick of the war and have been for years. They don't see why they should fight and die for this strip of worthless territory."

For fear it would be too shocking, Spain never released casualty figures for the operation. But, in abandoning four hundred posts and blockhouses and the big base at Chechaouèn, losses amounted to almost 20,000, including 1 general, 6 lieutenant colonels, 8 majors, 175 other officers and about 18,000 or 19,000 men. The retreat had been just as disastrous as the one from Anual in 1921.

Through his chief of staff, Ignacio Despujol, Primo de Rivera issued another of his amazingly candid statements: "I am every day more convinced that the surprise attacks on the part of the enemy are much less due to his competence than to our own incapacity and negligence. Often the soldiers march in close order, half asleep, their ears covered by the collars of their cloaks and with their rifles unprepared." In the future, he said, officers would be held accountable for properly training their soldiers.

One of the big losers in the Spanish retreat from the Jibala was the scoundrel Raisuli. Cut off, he was now at the mercy of his nemesis, Abd el-Krim. First, though, Abd el-Krim tried reason. He sent messengers asking Raisuli to join the war against Spain. The old villain cut the ears off one messenger and shaved the hair off the head of the next, a vile insult to a Muslim. Ahmed Heriro, with some Riffian regulars and Jibali volunteers, surrounded Raisuli's palace in the hills at Tazrut on January 24, 1925, and demanded his surrender. When he refused, Heriro wheeled up his artillery and began firing at the palace. The walls crumbled and Heriro's troops stormed the palace.

Sheean witnessed the surrender. "First came a detachment of 20 Riffi regulars," he wrote, "with their orange and green felt turbans and their uniform short jebellas. . . . After them came the contrivance which carried Raisuli. It was a huge square box of wood, with a pole extending from each of its four corners. Each pole rested on the shoulders of four men, so that 16 men in all bore the weight of the box. Inside, on a pile of rugs and cushions, lay the sherif himself.

"He was lying on his haunches, half turned to the right, with his elbows supporting the upper part of his body. He was bloated beyond human semblance, from the dropsy which had victimized him these four years past. His face was hidden under the folds of his turban, drawn tightly across; only his furious beady little eyes, darting angrily from side to side, gave hint of life under the white mass of his robes."

Sheean tried to interview him, but the old man would have none of it. "Why do you come to me?" he asked. "I have said I wished to see nobody. I want nothing but to die. I do not want to be the prisoner of dogs and the sons of dogs." He died several weeks later, and Abd el-Krim stood alone.

That was not exactly an ideal situation for the French in their Moroccan colony, where they controlled twenty times as much territory as the Spanish, and with only sixty thousand troops, half of them natives. "Although there is no immediate danger," Marshal Hubert Lyautey wrote Paris early in 1924, "nothing could be so bad for our regime as the installation so near Fez [Fès] of an independent Mussulman state, modernized and supported by the most warlike tribes, with a morale exalted by success against the Spaniards, making Krim the center of attraction, not only to our dissidents, but to all those Moroccan elements, particulary the young, for whom recent events . . . have broadened their horizon and raised xenophobic aspirations."

Why the French had not come to the aid of the embattled Spaniards earlier is something of a mystery. Possibly it had something to do with the fact that Lyautey, an extraordinary man and a great colonizer, didn't seek war. Perhaps it had something to do with national jealousies. The French held the Spanish army in such utter contempt that they didn't think Abd el-Krim's successes were really that impressive. "You have seen the great Abd el-Krim," a French official in Paris told American correspondent Paul Scott Mowrer. "These native chiefs . . . we know them well. They are really simple fellows. Properly handled, they respond to kindness. There is, of course, not the slightest chance that this one will ever attack us."

"This one"—meaning Abd el-Krim—launched his attack against the French on April 12, 1925.

The French had built a series of forts and blockhouses south of the 1912 border with Spanish Morocco on both sides of the Wergha River, and felt— the Maginot Line comes to mind—that their position was impregnable. Abd el-Krim believed the river was the correct dividing line, and objected to French inroads on the north bank, home to the Beni Zerwal tribe. He felt he and these tribesmen were united by a liff, and that he couldn't allow their homeland to become a part of French Morocco. He wrote several letters to the *Times*'s Harris, pointing out that he had been no part of the 1912 treaty that split Morocco into French and Spanish spheres. In crossing the Wergha, he told Harris, the French had broken their word, undoing all the good work he had achieved.

His attack was sudden, well-organized, and overwhelming.

French posts fell, one by one, just like the Spanish posts had fallen. "Anarchy spread over the whole region," Harris wrote. "Jibala tribesmen and the Riffis were miles behind the French posts, and Fez [Fès] was in danger." Fès was the historic capital, a sacred city, filled with holy men and scholars. Nothing Abd el-Krim had ever done could possibly rival its capture; the deed would echo throughout the Muslim world.

Some of the sixty-six French posts on the Wergha River line were manned by just a sergeant and a maybe only a dozen men. One of these little posts, built on a barren ridge at a place called Beni Derkul, was commanded by Sub-Lieutenant Pol Lapeyre, a recent graduate of the military academy at Saint-Cyr, with a garrison of thirty-nine men, including one French and two native sergeants. They had one 75 mm cannon and two machine guns. The spring was three hundred yards away, but the young lieutenant had been wise enough to fill dozens of empty petrol cans with water and bring them into the little fort.

The Berber tribesmen began to surround his post on April 15. "We are for it now," he wrote in his diary, which was recovered years after the battle by Rupert Furneaux, an Abd el-Krim biographer.

The defenders began dying on May 2: "Two of the night watch nicked, a Frenchman killed instantly."

Messages arrived by heliograph and airplane, and Lapeyre could reply by heliograph. "Have no fear," he said in a message on May 4, "the Riffians will never take us alive."

The Riffians attacked the night of May 18: "We received grenades and even shells. These caused me some great losses; three killed and one wounded. This time they threw themselves on the [barbed] wire and in one place they succeeded in getting past by throwing large bundles of raffia [palm leaves] on to it. But the attack was suppressed. . . . It is all one. I, who wished to see the combat, am worn out. I am very tired and overworked and would be overjoyed to see the relief come."

The next morning, a squadron of French airplanes "scraped over my roofs" and dropped huge bars of ice. Some of them actually landed inside the fort. A note was attached: "To our friends up there from the mechanics of the 4th. Courage! We are thinking of you."

By May 30, Lapeyre wrote that he noticed "weakening in many people. The pemmican and biscuit barely go around. Our destiny is sealed on the 6th if nobody comes. . . . The thirst is fearful. Are they thinking of us in France?"

The nearest fort, Bibane, fell to the Riffians on June 6, and Lapeyre said that during the night the enemy put dead French soldiers on spikes, upside down, outside his fort. "A fire was flickering its last at the foot of one of the stakes." Someone serving with the Riffi shouted, in German, "and asked how many of us Europeans were left in the post." One of the French soldiers shouted back, "Balls to the lot of you."

"I fear we are goners," the young lieutenant wrote on June 11. Using cannon shells, he constructed a huge mine, and prepared to blow up the fort and everyone in it. "At dusk, placed fifteen cannon shells in the mine. . . . Seven of us remain alive [out of 40] including the badly wounded one. Fortunately the magazine hasn't been hit."

At 11 P.M., the garrison still holding out at Ain Kebir heard the explosion and saw flames shoot up from Beni Derkul. When the post was recaptured, the diary was found stuffed in a wall, along with a letter Lapeyre had written to his commanding officer, Captain Petrie. *Au revoir, Capitaine*," Lapeyre concluded. When the fighting was over, a statue was dedicated to the young lieutenant's memory, and stands at Saint-Cyr today.

Abd el-Krim surely expected stout resistance from the French, but he was surprised by the way these small posts held out, week after week. It slowed down his advance and allowed the French to pull themselves together.

Marshal Henri Philippe Pétain, the hero of Verdun, was dispatched to Morocco in July to inspect the front. "The brutal fact," he concluded, "is that we are unexpectedly attacked by the most powerful and the best armed enemy that we have ever met with in our colonial campaigns."

But reinforcements, including tanks, were now arriving, and the French, with Lyautey himself making all the decisions, despite his advancing years and poor health, began to fight their way back. Still it wasn't easy. Suddenly, these proud French determined it might well be in their interest to plan a coordinated campaign against Abd el-Krim with the Spaniards. The two powers would put it into motion with 360,000 soldiers—200,000 with the Spaniards, 160,000 with the French.

The Spanish contribution was an amphibious landing at Alhucemas Bay, in the heart of Rif territory and only a mile or two from Abd el-Krim's headquarters at Ajdir. With a flotilla of one hundred ships (including a few French warships, to show solidarity), the Spanish army began disembarking at Cabadilla beach, just west of the bay, on the other side of a headland, on September 8, 1925.

The old Spanish army, Silvestre's panic-stricken army at Anual, was no longer recognizable. This was Primo de Rivera's army and it came equipped with a dirigible, eighty-eight land-based aircraft and twelve seaplanes, thirty-six warships, and dozens of landing craft, some of them last used by the British at Gallipoli. The eight thousand Spanish troops, led by the legionnaires of the Tercio, were well-equipped, and there was plenty of food and water.

Abd el-Krim had expected the Spaniards to land on the beaches of the horseshoe crescent that was Alhucemas Bay. He was surprised—and he hadn't been surprised very often until now—by the landing on the other side of the headland. He counterattacked the next two nights, but the Spaniards kept coming ashore. It was Abd el-Krim's last great battle, and he and his Riffians fought tenaciously. It took the Spaniards fifteen days to cover two miles.

On October 2, the Spaniards overran Ajdir itself. A month later, Primo de Rivera turned over the command of the army to his deputy, General José Sanjurjo, and returned to Spain. The war dragged on, and some of it turned very nasty. Poison gas was used for the first time, and a squadron of

Spanish aircraft, piloted by American volunteers, dropped gasoline bombs on women and children.

The last battle of the war was fought in early May of 1926, southeast of Ajdir. The Spaniards lost another thousand men but they finally destroyed Abd el-Krim's fierce Beni Urriaguels, the heart and soul of his army.

It was over.

◆

On May 22, 1926, General Sanjurjo and members of his staff traveled by motorcar to Anual, where they stood bareheaded in the dust and rubble, remembering their fallen comrades. Five days later, Abd el-Krim and his family surrendered to the French (there was never a thought of turning themselves in to the Spanish). On September 2, this remarkable man and his party of 150 were put aboard a French warship and exiled to Réunion, an island in the Indian Ocean.

Franco launched his attack on the Spanish Republic from Morocco in 1936, accompanied by hundreds of Moroccan volunteers. His army, hardened by its fighting in the Rif, eventually triumphed in a war that set the scene for the greatest war of all, World War II. Franco ruled Spain until his death in 1975.

France didn't withdraw from Morocco until 1956, and Spain reluctantly pulled out soon after, though maintaining its ancient presidios at Ceuta and Melilla. They were still in Spanish hands as late as 1995, a bone of contention to King Hassan and the Royal Moroccan Army.

The Riffians, tough as ever, still come down from the mountains to join the Moroccan army, where they remain the best fighting men in North Africa.

Conclusion: American Mini-disaster in Somalia (1993)

Captain Thomas Waggener and his Virginia rangers accompanied the British general, Edward Braddock, in his disastrous expedition against the French and Indians at Fort Duquesne in 1755. Waggener, a colonial officer, told Braddock he couldn't beat the Indians in the woods with European tactics. Braddock, an arrogant man, wouldn't listen: How much could an American ranger know about going to war?

Quite a lot, it turned out. By 1993, the Rangers were an elite corps in the American army, the most powerful military force in the world, while the British army was in sharp decline, barely able to defeat Argentina in the Battle of the Falkland Islands. The American Rangers, the arrogant ones now, specialized in secret, high-tech, fast-moving counterterrorism operations. They had taken part in the invasions of Grenada and Panama, and had sent commandos behind enemy lines during the war in the Persian Gulf in 1991 looking for but not finding, those clumsy Scud missiles being launched by Iraq against Israel.

These Rangers were superbly conditioned, highly trained, powerfully motivated professional soldiers. In the summer of 1993, 238 years after the battle on the Monongahela, they found themselves in dusty Mogadishu, the capital of what had been the nation of Somalia, the one-time Italian colony on the Red Sea. Somalia in 1993 much resembled Haiti two hundred years earlier, in 1793—a country "in a hideous state of anarchy."

The government had collapsed, the army had broken up, and all semblance of the rule of law had vanished as Somali warlords, with their own militia armies, fought each other for supremacy. As a result of the chaos, the economy was a shambles and people were starving. The United Nations, with American support, resolved to intervene and bring some order out of the chaos so food could be delivered to the population.

United Nations expeditions are generally well-intended. No longer lusty grabs for land, trade, power, and world standing, these are peace-keeping operations, in which multinational forces under the blue-and-white UN banner are sent here and there around the world to separate squabbling forces.

That's what happened in Somalia; it began as a well-intended, multi-national expedition to stabilize a chaotic situation in which thousands of innocent people were dying every week. But it quickly deteriorated into a campaign to wipe out the uncooperative warlords, among whom the most uncooperative and most warlike was Mohamed Farah Aidid (sometimes spelled Aideed). And, for dismayed Americans, it ended with a haunting television picture—the body of Master Sergeant Gary Gordon being dragged triumphantly through the streets of Mogadishu by a Somali mob.

War is a nasty, brutish business, and noble thoughts and a UN flag don't change that basic fact for the soldier being required to take a part. Mis-takes happen in "good" expeditions just as often as they happened in "bad" ones, and mistakes happened all the time in Somalia. What went wrong in Somalia—arrogance, contempt for the enemy, bad intelligence, overreliance on advanced equipment, incompetent political leadership—are very much the same things that went wrong in earlier military disasters chronicled in this book. Some things simply never change.

The most reliable account of the October 3 and 4, 1993, American dis-aster in Somalia, in which eighteen American soldiers were killed and eighty-four wounded, was written by reporter Rick Atkinson and appeared as a two-part series in the *Washington Post* on January 1 and 2, 1994. Addi-tional details appeared in a review of the disaster written for the Senate Armed Services Committee by two of its members, Republican senator John Warner of Virginia and Democratic senator Carl Levin of Michigan. A quirky book, *Mogadishu!*, by Kent DeLong and Steven Tuckey, pub-lished in December 1994, gives more information.

Serious trouble began on June 5, 1993, when twenty-four Pakistani peacekeeping soldiers were killed in a Mogadishu ambush. The UN Se-curity Council voted the next day to punish the people responsible. The leading suspect was the warlord Aidid. United Nations' commanders put a $25,000 price on his head and ordered him to be arrested. He promptly went into hiding, and the specially trained soldiers from the United States were called in to track him down.

The original idea, Atkinson wrote, was to send fifty commandos from a secret special unit called Delta Force to do the job, code-named Caustic Brimstone. But that soon expanded to a larger concept, called Gothic Serpent, which added a Ranger company and sixteen helicopters from Task Force 160, a special operations aviation unit, to the original Delta Force.

The detachment, now numbering 440 men, began arriving in Somalia in August. It was commanded by Major Generals William F. Garrison and Thomas M. Montgomery, but it was Montgomery who planned the raid. "I agreed with the mission to get Aidid," he told Senate investigators later. "I would have placed a $1 million price on his head. The Somalis are in it for greed and riches."

Most of these special troops had trained with rapid-firing C-130 gunships, but these awesome gun platforms didn't accompany them to Mogadishu, where they might have been helpful. When things began to get sticky, General Montgomery requested tanks and fighting vehicles, but his request was turned down in Washington. The heavy armor would have been helpful in the rescue effort that followed the raid.

Phase One, wrote Atkinson in the *Post*, would last just four days, during which the 440-man detachment, now named Task Force Ranger, would set up operations and familiarize itself with the terrain. Phase Two would put the detachment to work, with all its secret, high-tech gear and macho training, to find Aidid. But if he couldn't be found (and, of course, he never was), Task Force Ranger would turn to Phase Three, capturing his key aides.

Humint—human intelligence, meaning about twenty spies employed by the Central Intelligence Agency—was supposed to pinpoint the warlord's whereabouts. Humint, though, wasn't always up to the job. Atkinson reported that the CIA's chief spy, a Somali, shot himself in the head playing Russian roulette. And when American troops attacked a house they had been told was a hideout for Aidid, they snared eight prisoners who turned out to be employees of the UN Development Program.

Americans distrusted the Italian peacekeepers in Somalia, thinking they were sympathetic to the warlords. And so when five Rangers saw a suspicious Land Rover in the Italian embassy parking lot, they put the vehicle under observation. When the driver saw that he was being observed, he roared away. A U.S. reconnaissance helicopter gave chase, and American soldiers finally ran the Land Rover down. Rangers had been boasting the driver was Aidid himself. In fact, he was another UN employee.

At about the same time, Atkinson wrote, some of the Delta Force commandos became convinced that the wily Aidid was working in the airfield mess hall.

Commanders in Aidid's Somali National Alliance had been watching the performance of Task Force Ranger with more than just idle curiosity. Aidid himself had been trained by the French army. Senators Warner and Levin had interviewed him during their trip to Somalia. "He is no stranger to military tactics," they concluded. "He is, and was, no fool." One of his chief commanders, Colonel Sharif Hassan Giumale, had attended a Russian military academy and served in the old Somali army, and he developed his own plan for fighting the Americans. "Giumale's concept was simple," Atkinson wrote. "Task Force Ranger stressed speed, so the militia had to react more quickly. The Americans' greatest technical advantage—helicopters—had to be neutralized with barrage fire using rocket-propelled grenades"—and the militia had a lot of them.

Giumale acknowledged that Task Force Ranger was an elite force, but he believed the Americans seriously underrated the militia's fighting skills. That, he thought, gave him an advantage.

The two forces met in battle on October 3 and 4, and Giumale won.

It started when Task Force Ranger commanders were told by one of their spies that some of Aidid's top aides were planning to hold a meeting in a house near the Olympic Hotel in a part of town called Bosnia, even by the militiamen. At 3:40 P.M., Atkinson wrote, four MH-6 "Little Bird" helicopters filled with Delta Force troopers landed in the streets near the house where the meeting supposedly was taking place. They were followed by Black Hawk helicopters carrying Rangers, but the Black Hawks were too big to land in the narrow streets, so the Rangers had to slide down ropes to get to the ground. One of them, Private First Class Todd Blackburn, was badly injured when he lost his grip and fell forty feet to the ground.

Delta Force troopers stormed the house and captured twenty-four prisoners, including two "Tier One" aides to Aidid, Omar Salad Elmi and Mohamed Hassan Awale. "I think we've got the guys you sent us in for," one of the Delta Force officers radioed his headquarters. "We're ready to get out of Dodge."

The easiest way to get out would have been by helicopter. But the Black Hawks couldn't land, and so Task Force Ranger set up a twelve-vehicle convoy to do the job. It was then, about 4 P.M., that the trouble began. The pilot of one of the Black Hawks, still hovering overhead, radioed in distress: "Six-One's going down, Six-One's going down."

Helicopter 6-1 had been hit by a simple rocket-propelled grenade, the weapon Colonel Giumale knew all along would tend to even the odds. The helicopter, out of control, slammed into an alley near Freedom Road, about three hundred yards east of the house where the prisoners had been captured. The two pilots were killed in the crash; five other men—four Delta Force snipers and a crew chief—were injured.

The American commanders were surprised, and appalled, by the ability of the Somalis to down sophisticated helicopters with simple rocket-propelled grenades. But, said the report to the Senate Armed Services Committee, "they had mastered the use of [these weapons], and cleverly massed them in critical locations." Once the first helicopter went down, General Garrison told the senators, "we lost the initiative."

Garrison and his commanders, back at headquarters, quickly put in motion several rescue missions. A Little Bird helicopter was the first to arrive at the crash scene, rescuing two of the wounded Americans. A search-and-rescue Black Hawk, number 6-4, arrived a few minutes later, and fifteen soldiers dropped down ropes to reinforce the men at the crash scene. While hovering overhead, the rescue helicopter was hit by another rocket-propelled grenade, all but severing its main rotor blades, Atkinson wrote in the *Post*. It broke up more slowly, but it finally slammed into the ground, too, knocking down several shacks.

Two Ranger platoons, riding in Humvees, were also on their way, racing to the scene of the original Black Hawk crash. They brought the number of American soldiers at, or near, the scene of the first crash to ninety, no match for the hundreds of militiamen, some of them transported by rickety old buses, who were now swarming all around them, firing their AK-47 rifles and rocket launchers. Freedom Road, Atkinson wrote, was becoming a killing ground for the Americans.

The Americans tried desperately to pull the dead pilots from the wreckage of Black Hawk 6-1, but they wouldn't budge. DeLong and Tuckey report in their book that one of the pilots—a grisly detail—had to be pulled out in pieces.

The convoy returning the prisoners to the airfield was told to turn back, and reinforce the beleaguered Americans at the crash scene. But the streets of Mogadishu are as narrow and confusing as those of Kabul, in Afghanistan, and the convoy got lost. Finally, it rounded a corner to see the Olympic Hotel. By now, the commanders back at headquarters were beginning to sense disaster, so they told the convoy to come back to the airfield. That way, at least, the Americans would still have the twenty-four prisoners.

American commanders now began to deal with the situation piecemeal, sending out units much too undermanned and underpowered to do any good. A small Ranger relief column had barely left the airfield before it was attacked; it was forced to turn back. Another small unit from the Tenth Mountain Division's Quick Reaction Force was ambushed by militiamen and escaped only after firing off an astonishing sixty thousand rounds of rifle ammunition and hundreds of grenades in a running fight that lasted thirty minutes.

The four crewmen from the second helicopter that crashed apparently were all still alive, and there was no one there yet to protect them. Another Black Hawk, this one designated number 6-2, was sent to help, carrying two Delta Force snipers, Sergeant First Class Randall D. Shughart and Master Sergeant Gary I. Gordon. They were both extraordinarily brave and resourceful men, but just what two men were supposed to do against hundreds of well-armed militiamen was never made clear. The Black Hawk, piloted by Warrant Officer Michael Goffena, delivered the two snipers to the crash scene, and then was hit by still another rocket-propelled grenade as it pulled away. Goffena, with three wounded crewmen, kept the helicopter in the air until it reached the safe confines of the city's New Port.

The two snipers managed to pull the wounded copilot from the helicopter's cockpit, but they never saw any sign of the pilot himself. Michael Durant, the copilot, somehow survived, but the two brave snipers were killed. Later, it was poor Gordon's body that was dragged by a mob through the streets of Mogadishu, and captured by the television cameras.

Back on Freedom Road, meanwhile, the Americans had taken cover inside four houses. Colonel Giumale, Atkinson reported, wanted to blast the Americans out of those four houses with a mortar barrage. But, Atkinson said, he was talked out of it by Somalis who pleaded for the lives of the Somali civilians who were also inside the house.

Americans were rapidly learning their lessons. The report to the Senate committee put it nicely: "One of the weaknesses of a unit like Task Force Ranger, whose combat capabilities were unparalleled, is the belief by the unit members and its commanders that they can accomplish any mission." Because of this "supreme confidence," they concluded, "command must provide more oversight to this type of unit than to conventional forces."

Americans were also learning, once again, that helicopters are vulnerable, and in this kind of street fighting it would be a lot more helpful to have some tanks. But the Americans didn't have any tanks, of course, and so they were forced to ask Pakistani and Malaysian commanders if they could borrow theirs.

Four Pakistani tanks and twenty-eight Malaysian armored personnel carriers joined the Tenth Mountain Division's Quick Reaction Force in the first large-scale effort to relieve the American position on Freedom Road. It was 11:15 P.M., and dark, and the streets were still swarming with Somali militiamen. Two of the Malaysian vehicles, carrying Mountain Division soldiers, turned the wrong direction on National Street and were ambushed by militiamen. Both vehicles were destroyed by those ubiquitous rocket-propelled grenades, and one of the Malaysian drivers was killed.

The rest of the convoy got through, finally reaching the besieged Americans at 2 A.M. on October 4. By 7 A.M., Atkinson said, "after a ragged, exhausting retreat, all survivors had reached safety." They took refuge in a crumbling old sports stadium on 21 October Road, where the wounded were given medical attention.

It was all for nothing. The prisoners taken by the Americans on October 3, 1993, were released in January 1994, and the whole business of taking Aidid prisoner was abandoned. American troops headed home, wondering why they had been sent to Mogadishu in the first place.

But eighteen Americans had died on October 3 and 4—additional proof, if any was still needed, that all military expeditions, good ones and bad ones, have consequences.

Dead soldiers have names. These are the names of the eighteen Americans who died in Mogadishu during those two days in October 1993:

Chief Warrant Officer Donovan L. Briley, North Little Rock, Ark.
Corporal James M. Cavaco, Forestdale, Mass.
Specialist Dominick M. Pilla, Vineland, N.J.
Sergeant Lorenzo M. Ruiz, El Paso, Tex.
Specialist James E. Smith, Long Valley, N.J.
Master Sergeant Timothy L. Martin, Aurora, Ind.
Sergeant First Class Earl R. Fillmore Jr., Blairsville, Pa.
Staff Sergeant Daniel D. Busch, Portage, Wisc.
Sergeant James C. Joyce, Denton, Tex.
Private First Class Richard W. Kowalewski Jr., Crucible, Pa.
Private First Class James H. Martin Jr., Collinsville, Ill.
Chief Warrant Officer Clifton B. Wolcott, Cuba, N.Y.
Sergeant Cornell L. Houston, Compton, Calif.
Sergeant Thomas J. Field, Lisbon, Maine
Master Sergeant Gary I. Gordon, Lincoln, Maine
Chief Warrant Officer Raymond A. Frank, Monrovia, Calif.
Sergeant First Class Randall D. Shughart, Newville, Pa.
Staff Sergeant William D. Cleveland Jr., Peoria, Ariz.

Annotated Bibliography

1. General Edward Braddock and the French and Indian War
(1754–1763)

Lee McCardell's *Ill-Starred General: Braddock of the Coldstream Guards* was still in print in 1995, and remains a reliable popular history of the campaign. The best standard work is an old one, Winthrop Sargent's *History of an Expedition Against Fort DuQuesne in 1755*. Ebenezer Denny's military journal is indispensable.

Denny, Ebenezer. *Military Journal of Ebenezer Denny*. Philadelphia: n.p., 1859.

Franklin, Benjamin. *Autobiography*. New York: Henry Holt & Co., 1912.

Freeman, Douglas Southall. *George Washington*. Vol. 2. New York: Charles Scribner's Sons, 1948.

Hamilton, Charles. *Braddock's Defeat, The Journal of Captain Robert Cholmley's Batman, The Journal of a British Officer, Halkett's Orderly Book*. Norman, Okla.: University of Oklahoma Press, 1959.

Lowdermilk, Will H. *Major-General Edward Braddock's Orderly Books from February 26 to June 15, 1755*. Cumberland, Md.: J. Anglim, 1880.

McCardell, Lee. *Ill-Starred General: Braddock of the Coldstream Guards*. Pittsburgh: University of Pittsburgh, 1958.

Munson, James D. *Colonel John Carlyle, Gent*. Alexandria, Va.: Northern Virginia Regional Park Authority, 1986.

Netherton, Ross. *Braddock's Campaign and the Potomac Route to the West*. Falls Church, Va.: 1989.

Pargellis, Stanley. *Military Affairs in North America 1748–1765*. New York: D. Appleton-Century Co., 1936.

Sargent, Winthrop. *The History of an Expedition Against Fort DuQuesne in 1755*. Philadelphia: Historical Society of Pennsylvania, 1855.

Spendelow, Lt. Charles. *General Braddock's Expedition*. Dartford, England: I. A. Ritchie, 1963.

2. Brigadier General Josiah Harmar and Major General Arthur St. Clair and the Indian Wars on the Northwest Frontier (1790–1791)

Wiley Sword's *President Washington's Indian War* is a treasure-house of useful information about these two disastrous expeditions. Alan Eckert's Tecumseh biography is helpful, too, but it contains far too many reconstructed conversations. Arthur St. Clair's book is an apologia, but indispensable all the same.

Eckert, Alan W. *A Sorrow in Our Heart: The Life of Tecumseh.* New York: Bantam, 1992.

Flexner, James Thomas. *George Washington and the New Nation, 1783–1793.* Boston: Little, Brown, 1970.

Freeman, Douglas Southall. *George Washington.* Vol. 6. New York: Scribner, 1949.

Guthman, William H. *March to Massacre: A History of the First Seven Years of the United States Army, 1784–1791.* New York: McGraw-Hill, 1975.

Lossing, Benson J. *The Pictorial Field Book of the War of 1812.* New York: Harper & Brothers, 1868.

Prucha, Francis Paul. *The Sword of the Republic: The United States Army on the Frontier, 1783–1846.* New York: Macmillan, 1969.

St. Clair, Arthur. *A Narrative of the Manner in Which the Campaign Against the Indians Was Conducted, Under the Command of Major General St. Clair.* Philadelphia: Jane Aitken, 1812.

Sargent, Winthrop. "Winthrop Sargent's Diary While with General Arthur St. Clair's Expedition Against the Indians." *Ohio Archaeological and Historical Quarterly* 33 (1924).

Sword, Wiley. *President Washington's Indian War: The Struggle for the Old Northwest, 1790–1795.* Norman: University of Oklahoma Press, 1985.

3. British and French Generals and Their Disastrous Efforts to Restore Slavery to Haiti (1791–1804)

Books about the slave rebellion come in all shapes and sizes, and not one of them comes even close to putting what happened in context. C. L. R. James tried hardest in *The Black Jacobins,* but the prose is murky and the Marxist twist disconcerting. Michael Duffy and David Geggus are valuable on the English expedition, and Sir John Fortescue is both overpowering in his knowledge of his subject and a delight to read.

Cole, Hubert. *Christophe, King of Haiti.* New York: Viking Press, 1967.

Duffy, Michael. *Soldiers, Sugar, and Seapower: The British Expeditions to the West Indies and the War Against Revolutionary France.* Oxford, England: Oxford University Press, 1987.

Ehrman, John. *The Younger Pitt: The Reluctant Transition.* Stanford, Calif.: Stanford University Press, 1983.

Fortescue, Sir John W. *A History of the British Army.* Vol. 4, pt. 1. London: Macmillan & Co., 1906.

Fregosi, Paul. *Dreams of Empire: Napoleon and the First World War, 1792–1815.* London: Hutchinson, 1989.

Geggus, David Patrick. *Slavery, War, and Revolution: The British Occupation of Saint Domingue, 1783–1798.* Oxford, England: Oxford University Press, 1982.

James, C. L. R. *The Black Jacobins: Toussaint Louverture and the San Domingo Revolution.* New York: Vintage Books, 1963.

Korngold, Ralph. *Citizen Toussaint.* New York: Hill and Wang, 1965.

Leyburn, James G. *The Haitian People.* New Haven, Conn.: Yale University Press, 1966.

Ott, Thomas O. *The Haitian Revolution, 1789–1804.* Knoxville: University of Tennessee Press, 1973.

Pachonski, Paul, and Reuel K. Wilson. *Poland's Caribbean Tragedy: A Study of Polish Legions in the Haitian War of Independence, 1802–1803.* Boulder: East European Monographs, 1986.

Palmer, Michael A. *Stoddert's War: Naval Operations During the Quasi-War with France, 1798–1801.* Columbia, S.C.: University of South Carolina Press, 1987.

Ros, Martin. *Night of Fire: The Black Napoleon and the Battle for Haiti.* New York: Sarpedon, 1994.

4. General Charles MacCarthy and the First Ashanti War (1824)

Of all the campaigns described in this book, this one remains the most obscure. T. Edward Bowdich's *Mission from Cape Coast Castle to Ashantee* is a great travel book. W. Walton Claridge's *History of the Gold Coast and Ashanti* is a classic.

Bowdich, T. Edward. *Mission from Cape Coast Castle to Ashantee.* London: Cass, 1966.

Claridge, W. Walton. *A History of the Gold Coast and Ashanti.* London: J. Murray, 1915.

Dupuis, Joseph. *Journal of a Residence in Ashantee.* London: H. Colburn, 1824.

Edgerton, Robert B. *The Fall of the Asante Empire.* New York: Free Press, 1995.

Ellis, Alfred B. *A History of the Gold Coast of West Africa.* London: Chapman and Hall, 1893 (reprinted 1969).

Lloyd, Alan. *The Drums of Kumasi.* London: Longmans, 1964.

Metcalfe, George E. *Great Britain and Ghana.* University of Ghana. London: T. Nelson, 1964.

Reindorf, Rev. Carl Christian. *History of the Gold Coast and Asante.* Basel, Switzerland: [the author,] 1895.

Ricketts, Major H. I. *Narrative of the Ashantee War.* London: Simpkin & Marshall, 1831.

5. Major General William George Keith Elphinstone and the First Afghan War (1839–1842)

Sir John Kaye's *History of the War in Afghanistan* is the standard history of the First Afghan War, though Sir John's continuing belief that only God could really explain what happened is sometimes maddening. Patrick Macrory's *The Fierce Pawns* is a wonderful book. The three diaries—by Sir Vincent Eyre, Henry Havelock and, most of all, Lady Sale—are immensely revealing.

Dupree, Louis. *Afghanistan.* Princeton, N.J.: Princeton University Press, 1980.

Eyre, Sir Vincent. *The Kabul Insurrection of 1841–42.* London: W. H. Allen & Co., 1879.

Havelock, Henry. *Narrative of the War in Afghanistan*. London: H. Colburn, 1840.
Heathcote, T. A. *The Afghan Wars*. London: Osprey, 1980.
Kaye, John William. *History of the War in Afghanistan*. London: R. Bentley, 1851.
Macrory, Patrick A. *The Fierce Pawns*. Philadelphia: Lippincott, 1966.
Morris, Mowbray. *The First Afghan War*. London: S. Low, Marston, Searle & Rivington, 1878.
Norris, James A. *The First Afghan War, 1838–1842*. Cambridge, England: Cambridge University Press, 1967.
Ram, Sita. *From Sepoy to Subedar*. London: Routledge & K. Paul, 1970.
Sale, Lady Florentia. *The First Afghan War*. London: Harlow, Longmans, 1969.

6. Major General Sir George Pomeroy-Colley and the First Boer War (1880–1881)

The Second Boer War, the big one, has gotten much more attention but some fine books were written about the opening round. Joseph Lehmann's *The First Boer War* is a first-class account. Thomas Fortescue Carter was an obscure Natal journalist, but he wrote a splendid firsthand account of what he saw in *A Narrative of the Boer War*.

Austen, G. F. *The Diary of G. F. Austen*. Roodesport, England: Cum Books, 1981.
Barnett, Correlli. *Britain and Her Army, 1509–1970*. New York: William Morrow, 1970.
Bellairs, Lady Blanche. *The Transvaal War*. Cape Town: C. Struik, 1972.
Bowle, John. *The Imperial Achievement: The Rise and Transformation of the British Empire*. New York: Little, Brown, 1974.
Carter, Thomas Fortescue. *A Narrative of the Boer War*. London: J. Macqueen, 1900.
Doyle, Arthur Conan. *The Great Boer War*. Cape Town: C. Struik, 1976.
Duxbury, George R. *David and Goliath*. Johannesburg: South African National Museum of Military History, 1981.
Emery, Frank. *Marching over Africa*. London: Hodder and Stoughton, 1986.
Farwell, Byron. *Mr. Kipling's Army*. New York: W. W. Norton, 1981.
Haggard, H. Rider. *The Last Boer War*. London: K. Paul, Trench, Trubner & Co., 1900.
Lehmann, Joseph. *The First Boer War*. London: Cape, 1972.
Norris-Newman, Charles L. *With the Boers in the Transvaal*. Johannesburg: Africana Book Society, 1976.
Ransford, Oliver. *The Battle of Majuba Hill*. New York: Crowell, 1967.

7. Major General Charles "Chinese" Gordon and the Fall of Khartoum (1884–1885)

There has never been a shortage of material about Chinese Gordon's stand at Khartoum, but the best work is still Gordon's own remarkable journal. Count Edward Gleichen's book, *With the Camel Corps up the Nile*, gives a vivid picture of the rescue mission.

Allen, Bernard M. *Gordon and the Sudan*. London: Macmillan & Co., 1931.
Bermann, Richard A. *The Mahdi of Allah*. New York: Macmillan & Co., 1932.
Buchan, John. *Gordon at Khartoum*. London: P. Davies, 1934.

Churchill, Winston. *The River War*. New York: Longman, Green, 1899.

Farwell, Byron. *Queen Victoria's Little Wars*. New York: Harper & Row, 1972.

Gleichen, Count Edward. *With the Camel Corps up the Nile*. London: Chapman & Hall, 1888.

Gordon, Charles G. *The Journals of Major General C. G. Gordon*. New York: Negro Universities Press, 1969.

Moorehead, Alan. *The White Nile*. New York: Harper, 1960.

Nutting, Anthony. *Gordon: Martyr and Misfit*. London: Constable, 1966.

Steevens, G. W. *With Kitchener to Khartoum*. New York: Dodd, Mead & Co., 1915.

Symons, Julian. *England's Pride*. London: H. Hamilton, 1965.

Waller, John H. *Gordon of Khartoum: The Saga of a Victorian Hero*. New York: Atheneum, 1988.

Wilson, Sir Charles. *From Korti to Khartum*. Edinburgh: W. Blackwood & Sons, 1886.

Wortham, H. E. *Chinese Gordon*. Boston: Little Brown, 1933.

8. General Oreste Baratieri and the First Ethiopian War (1895–1896)

One book puts all the others in the shade here—George Fitz-Hardinge Berkeley's *The Campaign of Adowa and the Rise of Menelik*. Gerald Portal's *My Mission to Abyssinia* is another splendid travel book.

Barker, A. J. *The Civilizing Mission*. New York: Dial Press, 1968.

Berkeley, George Fitz-Hardinge. *The Campaign of Adowa and the Rise of Menelik*. London: Constable & Co., 1935.

Hollis, Christopher. *Italy in Africa*. London: H. Hamilton, 1941.

Marcus, Harold G. *A History of Ethiopia*. Berkeley: University of California Press, 1994.

Portal, Gerald H. *My Mission to Abyssinia*. New York: Negro Universities Press, 1969.

Wylde, Augustus. *Modern Abyssinia*. London: Methuen & Co., 1901.

9. Major General William R. Shafter and the Spanish-American War (1898)

Theodore Roosevelt overshadows everyone else in the Santiago campaign, and so it is useless to start anywhere else than with his own book, *The Rough Riders*. Richard Harding Davis really was a pretty good journalist, and his book, *The Cuban and Porto Rican Campaigns*, contains some nice touches. David Trask's campaign history, *The War with Spain in 1898*, is a good, solid account.

Carlson, Paul H. *Pecos Bill*. College Station, Tex.: Texas A&M University Press, 1989.

Cosmas, Graham A. *An Army for Empire*. Columbia, Mo.: University of Missouri Press, 1971.

Davis, Richard Harding. *The Cuban and Porto Rican Campaigns*. Freeport, N.Y.: Books for Libraries Press, 1970.

Dierks, Jack Cameron. *A Leap to Arms*. Philadelphia: Lippincott, 1970.

Keller, Allan. *The Spanish-American War*. New York: Hawthorn Books, 1969.

Miley, John D. *In Cuba with Shafter*. New York: C. Scribner's Sons, 1899.

Morris, Edmund. *The Rise of Theodore Roosevelt*. New York: Coward McCann & Geoghegan, 1979.

O'Toole, G. J. A. *The Spanish War*. New York: W. W. Norton, 1984.

Post, Charles Johnson. *The Little War of Private Post*. Boston: Little, Brown, 1960.

Roosevelt, Theodore. *The Rough Riders*. New York: C. Scribner's Sons, 1899.

Trask, David F. *The War with Spain in 1898*. New York: Macmillan, 1981.

Wheeler, Major General Joseph. *The Santiago Campaign, 1898*. Freeport, N.Y.: Books for Libraries Press, 1970.

10. Major General Charles Vere Ferrers Townshend and the Mesopotamian Campaign in World War I (1915–1916)

Russell Braddon's *The Siege* is one of the best books ever written about military disasters. Charles Vere Ferrers Townshend was an awful human being and a reckless general, but it's hard to know what happened here without reading his own explanation, *My Campaign in Mesopotamia*.

Barber, Charles H. *Besieged in Kut and After*. Edinburgh: W. Blackwood & Sons, 1917.

Barker, A. J. *Townshend of Kut*. London: Cassell, 1967.

Braddon, Russell. *The Siege*. New York: Viking Press, 1969.

Millar, Ronald. *Death of an Army*. Boston: Houghton Mifflin, 1970.

Mousley, Edward O. *The Secrets of a Kuttite*. London: John Lang, 1921.

Townshend, Charles Vere Ferrers. *My Campaign in Mesopotamia*. London: T. Butterworth, 1920.

11. Major General Manuel Fernandez Silvestre and the Riffian Rebellion in Morocco (1921–1926)

David Woolman's book, *Rebels in the Rif*, is the best standard history of Abd el-Krim's war against Spain and France. Walter B. Harris was there, and his book, *France, Spain, and the Rif*, is invaluable. The American journalist Vincent Sheean wrote two interesting books dealing with the Rif.

Furneaux, Rupert. *Abdel Krim*. London: Secker & Warburg, 1967.

Harris, Walter B. *France, Spain, and the Rif*. New York: Longmans, Green & Co., 1927.

Morel, E. D. *Morocco in Diplomacy*. London: Smith, Elder & Co., 1912.

Payne, Stanley G. *Politics and the Military in Modern Spain*. Stanford, Calif.: Stanford University Press, 1967.

Petrie, Sir Charles. *The Spanish Royal House*. London: G. Bles, 1958.

Regan, Geoffrey. *Great Military Disasters*. New York: M. Evans, 1987.

Sheean, Vincent. *Personal History*. New York: Doubleday & Co., 1935.

————. *An American Among the Riffi*. New York: Century Co., 1926.

Usborne, Vice Admiral Cecil V. *The Conquest of Morocco*. London: S. Paul & Co., 1936.

Woolman, David S. *Rebels in the Rif*. Stanford, Calif.: Stanford University Press, 1968.

Index